THE MACMILLAN
Bible Atlas

THE MACMILLAN

Bible Atlas

REVISED EDITION

by

YOHANAN AHARONI

Professor of Archaeology
Chairman of Department of Archaeology, and Institute of Archaeology
Tel Aviv University

and

MICHAEL AVI-YONAH

Professor of Archaeology and History of Art
The Hebrew University of Jerusalem

Prepared by

CARTA, LTD.

MACMILLAN PUBLISHING CO., INC.
NEW YORK
COLLIER MACMILLAN PUBLISHERS
LONDON

Macmillan Publishing Co., Inc.
866 Third Avenue, New York, N.Y. 10022
Collier Macmillan Canada, Inc.

Portions of this volume have been previously published as follows:
CARTA'S ATLAS OF THE BIBLE by Yohanan Aharoni, Ph. D. The Hebrew University of Jerusalem, copyright © 1964 by Carta, Jerusalem. All rights reserved.
CARTA'S ATLAS OF THE PERIOD OF THE SECOND TEMPLE,
THE MISHNAH AND THE TALMUD by Michael Avi-Yonah,
Professor of Archaeology and History of Art, The Hebrew University of Jerusalem. Assisted by Shmuel Safrai, Senior Lecturer in Jewish History, The Hebrew University of Jerusalem.
Copyright © 1966 by Carta, Jerusalem. All Rights Reserved.

Library of Congress Cataloging in Publication Data

Aharoni, Yohanan, 1919–1976.
  The Macmillan Bible atlas.

  1. Bible—Geography—Maps.   I. Avi-Yonah, Michael,
1904–1975, joint author.   II. Carta
III. Title.
G2230.A2 1977   912'.56   77–4313
ISBN 0–02–500590–1

15   14   13   12   11   10   9   8

Printed in the United States of America

PREFACE

This Atlas is the product of cooperation between two Hebrew University scholars and Carta, Jerusalem, cartographers. Professor Y. Aharoni edited the Old Testament section (maps 1–171), while Professor M. Avi-Yonah edited the section dealing with the later periods (maps 172–264); the cartographic and technical preparation was directed by Emanuel Hausman. The two sections were originally prepared, drawn, and published in slightly different form in separate Hebrew volumes by Carta, Jerusalem.

The purpose of the Atlas is to show, as far as possible through maps of each event, the changes and historical processes in the lands of the Bible. In the first part of the Atlas, the Jewish people were located mainly in the small area of the Holy Land; by the time of the Bar Kokhba Revolt, however, a large part of the people was scattered among the nations. We were guided by the most recent knowledge in Bible, historical, and archaeological research, and new concepts in educational instruction. In the light of these, we have attempted to provide a balanced viewpoint. In many instances, of course, we have had to choose between conflicting views in matters where only additional discoveries and further research may be decisive.

The focal point of the Atlas is the Holy Land, and one of our aims was to place it within its proper relation to the surrounding lands, most of which played an important part in its history. There are, therefore, many maps showing the Holy Land as a part of the Ancient East or the Greco-Roman world as a whole. We have tried to include within these maps every place and event in neighboring lands touching upon the Bible and the history of the Land of the Bible, even if not specifically mentioned in the Scriptures. It should be noted, however, that this is not an atlas of the Ancient East or of the Hellenistic and Roman Empires, nor have we attempted to be conclusive in regard to surrounding lands.

In general, if there is any doubt as to the identification of a site, this has been indicated in the index of place names, not in the maps. As for borders we often possess only information of a general nature. We often have details on border settlements, but data as to exact bordercourses is mostly lacking. In writing texts this raises little difficulty, for it normally suffices to state that "the border runs from A in the east to B on the coast," and so forth. On maps, however, one must be definitive, for a line once drawn lends itself to only one interpretation. Many of the routes of campaigns and journeys, especially those of the New Testament, are also conjectural. Indeed, in the light of modern scholarship it is extremely difficult to accept the geographical details of the Evangelists and of the first part of Acts at face value. In many cases the starting point of a route is known, as well as the

destination and often also a number of stations along the way. Details of each particular route or border were arrived at on the basis of topical and topographical logic, for in an historical atlas, conjecture must complement fact.

The impetus for this Atlas came from the late Amnon Soferman, C.E., co-founder of Carta, Jerusalem, who conceived it in its basic form and devoted to it the last months of his life.

Mr. Israel Eph'al, Instructor at the Tel Aviv University, and Dr. Shmuel Safrai, Senior Lecturer at the Hebrew University, Jerusalem, assisted in the preparation of the Old Testament and later sections, respectively. Thanks and appreciation are due to Professor William D. Davies, George Washington Ivey Professor of Advanced Studies and Research in Christian Origins, Duke University, for his valuable advice and assistance throughout the preparation of this Atlas. Clement Alexandre and Peter Nevraumont, both of the Macmillan Company, New York, read the manuscript and offered many valuable suggestions.

The physical preparation of the Atlas was devotedly carried out by the staff of Carta, Jerusalem especially M. Sofer and A. Nur, cartographers, Mrs. S. Zioni and N. Karp, graphic artists, and R. Grafman, who adapted the text and maps for this English edition.

PREFACE TO THE SECOND EDITION

The first edition of this atlas enjoyed eight printings in as many years. But eight years of research and excavations have enriched our knowledge of Biblical times immensely, making a second edition imperative. Freshly discovered sites have been ascertained as fitting Biblical descriptions. This, in turn, called for revision of theories, which brought in its wake changes of boundaries, routes and other features.

Certain significant revisions appertain to ancient Jerusalem. Extensive digs have been made for the past nine years on and around the site of ancient Jerusalem. The wealth of finds has allowed us to present a more accurate picture of Jerusalem at its various stages of development in this second edition.

TABLE OF CONTENTS

LIST OF SYMBOLS

★   City mentioned in sources to map

•   City not mentioned in sources to map

⊛   Capital mentioned in sources to map

◉   Capital not mentioned in sources to map

❋   District capital mentioned in sources to map

⊙   District capital not mentioned in sources to map

⊡   Fortress mentioned in sources to map

☐   Fortress not mentioned in sources to map

⊠   Camp

⚑   Revolt

⚔   Battlefield

⊶   Attack, siege of city

⊷   Conquest of city

←   Campaign, attack, or journey

⟩⟩⟩   Flight

———   Road

••••••••   Border of kingdom, state, or tribe

••••••••••   District border

○   Spring

Other symbols appear in the legends to the individual maps.

A NOTE ON SOURCES

Geographical names and quotations from the Bible are from the Revised Standard Version. Those from the Apocrypha are from the American Bible Society edition. If the spellings in the Versions are not consistent, preference has been given to that spelling closest to the Hebrew form. Geographical names and quotations from external sources are based, in the main, on *Ancient Near Eastern Texts Relating to the Old Testament*, edited by J. Pritchard, Princeton University Press, and the Loeb edition of Josephus' works, but certain modifications have been made. In the spelling of classical placenames, Latinized forms have generally been used ; the "a" in "ae," however, has been eliminated in most cases, except in such names as Caesar and Aegina, where accepted usage dictates otherwise. The variant spellings "tel" and "tell" represent the Hebrew and the Arabic, respectively.

A NOTE ON THE CHRONOLOGY

The chronology of the kingdoms of Assyria, Neo-Babylonia, and Persia is accurate to within two years.

The chronology of Israel to the end of the Solomonic period is conjectural; from the time of Rehoboam to Manasseh, accuracy is to within plus or minus ten years. From Josiah to the end of the period, dates are accurate to within two years.

The chronology of Egypt in the New Kingdom is based on the "low" chronology (of Albright and others), differing from the "high" chronology (of Breasted and others) by fourteen years. In the older periods, conjecture is much more manifest; here also we have generally preferred the "lower" chronology.

The chronology of the Hellenistic and Roman periods is fairly well established and presents no special problems. The dates of events mentioned in the New Testament have been fitted, as far as possible, within the general chronology framework.

LEGEND OF GEOGRAPHICAL NAMES

	Biblical	Contemporary Non-Biblical	Noncontemporary
Major City	**Jerusalem**	*Sepphoris*	
City or Village	Caesarea	Philadelphia	(Nagada)
Country, Kingdom, State, or Tribe	J U D A H		
Mountain, River, or Region	*Jordan Valley*		

Names in parentheses are non-contemporary or modern; where appended to another name, however, they may be contemporary variants.

Names within ⬚ frames are of places as yet unidentified, though their general location is known from the sources.

THE MACMILLAN
Bible Atlas

This shall be your land with
its boundaries all round.

(Numbers 34:12)

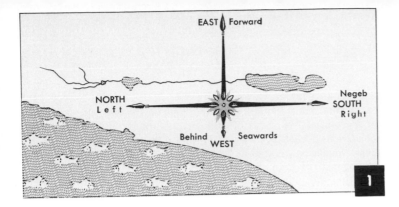

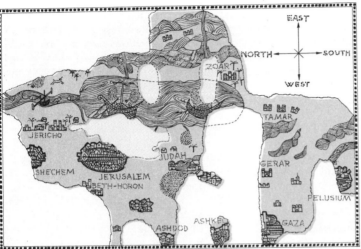

Section of the Medeba Map (place names translated from the Greek)

THE LORD said to Abram... Lift up your eyes, and look from the place where you are, northward and southward and eastward and westward; for all the land which you see I will give to you and to your descendants for ever.

(Genesis 13:14–15)

THE FOUR WINDS OF THE HEAVENS AND THEIR NAMES

To THE NORTH the winterbound, snow-covered mountains of the Lebanon; to the south the semiarid Negeb; to the east the wide desert; to the west the Great Sea—these are the natural borders of Palestine. Within their confines was enacted the history of Israel from the days of the Patriarchs on. A look at the landscape, its roads and ancient settlements, and the countries surrounding it are a prerequisite for a proper understanding of this history.

We possess no ancient map depicting the Holy Land in the biblical period. If such did exist, we can assume that it would face eastward, for in the Hebrew Bible the word "forward" also means east, "behind" means west, "right" means south, and "left" means north. Benjamin ("son of the right") is the southernmost tribe of the Rachelite tribes; the Dead Sea is also referred to in the Hebrew as the "forward [eastern] sea"; the Great Sea, the Mediterranean of today, is also called the "latter [western] sea."

One of the oldest maps extant is the Medeba map. This is a mosaic floor dating from the sixth century A.D. in a church at Medeba, to the east of the Dead Sea. This map was intended to show the Holy Land of the Bible and faces eastward. At the center appears the Dead Sea, on which sail two boats. It was prepared more than one thousand years after the Destruction of the First Temple, and thus is of limited value for the identification of ancient sites.

I WILL send them out that they may set out and go up and down the land, writing a description of it with a view to their inheritances. . .

(Joshua 18:4)

THE WAY TO SHILOH

THE BIBLE does not, as a rule, give many descriptions of settlements, their location and character—these matters were taken for granted then. Only a few verses diverge from this rule, the outstanding case being the description of the site of Shiloh in the story of the abduction of wives for the Benjaminites: "So they said, 'Behold, there is the yearly feast of the Lord at Shiloh, which is north of Bethel, on the east of the highway that goes up from Bethel to Shechem, and south of Lebonah'" (Judg. 21:19). Nothing could be more accurate. Why did the biblical writer give such detail to the location of a site as famous in ancient times as Shiloh? Probably because Shiloh had been destroyed by the Philistines, and early in the period of the Monarchy, when the story was written down, it lay in ruins.

Unlike Shiloh, most locations are merely described in vague terms in the Bible. Thus, in reconstructing the ancient map of the Holy Land in the various periods, we must lean heavily on four factors:

1. analysis of the history, character, and general topography of the individual site in the light of available sources;

2. identifications in later sources;

3. the preservation of the ancient name, with possible modifications during transfer from Hebrew to Aramaic and Arabic; and

4. archaeological examination of the site under consideration in the light of the above data.

JUDG. 21:19

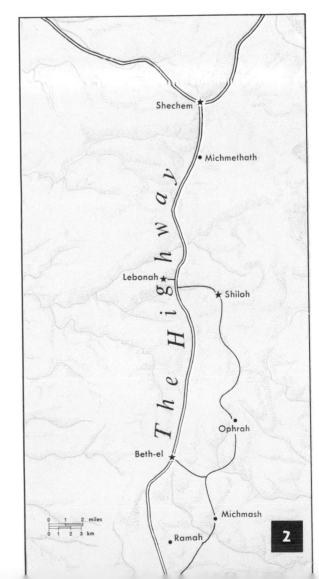

ARCHAEOLOGICAL research has made great strides in our times, and many details of the map of the ancient Holy Land are now agreed upon.

The decisive geographical factor in the history of Palestine is its outermost position at the southwest end of the settled, fertile lands of the Near East. These lands stretch crescent-like from the Persian Gulf to the Sinai Peninsula: the so-called Fertile Crescent. On the west, this crescent touches the Mediterranean Sea. On the north and the east it is surrounded by high, nearly impassable mountains, the Amanus, Taurus, Ararat, and Zagros ranges. Within the hollow of the Fertile Crescent lies the extensive Syrian-Arabian Desert, extending on the west into the wilderness of Paran (the Sinai Peninsula). This latter separates the Holy Land from Egypt.

Today the Fertile Crescent is divided between Iraq, Syria, Lebanon, Jordan, and Israel; its fertility stems from two factors—flat lands and an abundance of water. This is especially true of the area known by the Greek name Mesopotamia—"between the two rivers." This is the richest part of the Fertile Crescent, whose broad plains are watered and fertilized by the flow of the two large rivers, the Tigris and the Euphrates. "The river" of the Bible is the Euphrates. Syria and Palestine are less fortunate, for they represent the narrow and lean parts of the Fertile Crescent and of the two Palestine is the smaller and the poorer; rivers are small and do not allow passage of boats; the riverbeds are deep and in ancient times there was little possibility of utilizing their waters for irrigation. Land is uneven and ridges leave only limited plains. Rains fall mostly in one season and their amount diminishes progressively as one goes farther south.

In spite of its being the smallest and the poorest section, at the edge of the Fertile Crescent, Palestine held an important geopolitical position as a bridge between the lands of the Fertile Crescent and Egypt, the land of the Nile. Mesopotamia on the one side, and Egypt on the other, were lands of large rivers, and in both of them, the foundations of civilization were laid toward the end of the fourth millennium. Similar geographical and economic features assisted in the development of both these lands: there are extensive plains, whose fertility is dependent upon large, long rivers passing through them. A river is the primary joining and uniting factor within each of the two countries. It provides convenient arteries of communication and irrigates the land. This, of course, was dependent upon there being a governmental apparatus capable of instilling order, peace, and security, and of mobilizing manpower for the construction of dams and canals on a wide scale. Under such conditions rose the first mighty kingdoms with the power to impose organization and unity on their individual settlements, and even rule over areas beyond their own borders. In the Fertile Crescent this was the historical stage on which appeared in succession Sumer and Accad, Mitanni and the Hittites, and later the Arameans, the latter having given their name to the northern part of Mesopotamia—Aram Naharaim. In contrast, Egypt was closely confined and homogeneous in development, only the various dynasties succeeding one another over the years, from the time of the Early Kingdom down through the Middle and into the Late Kingdoms. Communications between Egypt and the kingdoms of the Fertile Crescent passed of necessity through Palestine, thus establishing its destiny as a land-bridge. Military campaigns swept in succession through Palestine, which in many periods was held by one or the other of the great powers; yet no major cultural development came about in either civilization without Palestine having some part in it.

THE ANCIENT NEAR EAST— PHYSICAL

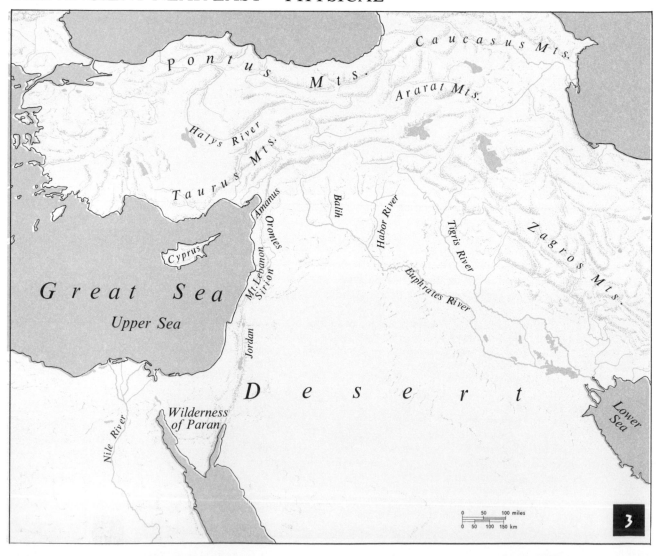

3

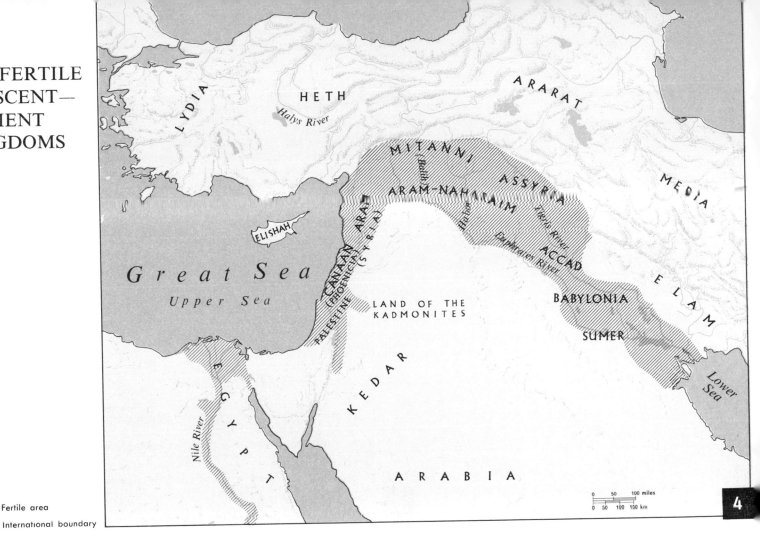

THE FERTILE CRESCENT— ANCIENT KINGDOMS

LYDIA

HETH

Halys River

ARARAT

MITANNI

MEDIA

ARAM-NAHARAIM

ASSYRIA

Balih

Habor

Tigris River

ACCAD

Euphrates River

ELISHAH

ARAM (SYRIA)

Great Sea

Upper Sea

BABYLONIA

CANAAN (PHOENICIA SYRIA)

PALESTINE

SUMER

ELAM

LAND OF THE KADMONITES

Lower Sea

KEDAR

Nile River

EGYPT

ARABIA

░░ Fertile area

–·–·– International boundary

| 0 | 50 | 100 miles |
| 0 | 50 | 100 | 150 km |

4

THE FERTILE CRESCENT— MODERN STATES

Black Sea

U.S.S.R.

Caspian Sea

TURKEY

Anatolian Plateau

KURDISTAN

IRAN (PERSIA)

CYPRUS

Mesopotamia

SYRIA

Mediterranean Sea

LEBANON

Syrian Desert

Tigris River

IRAQ

ISRAEL

JORDAN

Euphrates River

EGYPT

KUWAIT

Persian Gulf

Western Desert

Sinai

Nafud Desert

NEUTRAL TERRITORY

Nile River

Red Sea

SAUDI ARABIA

| 0 | 50 | 100 miles |
| 0 | 50 | 100 | 150 km |

5

Raising water from river to canal
(relief from palace of
Sennacherib at Nineveh)

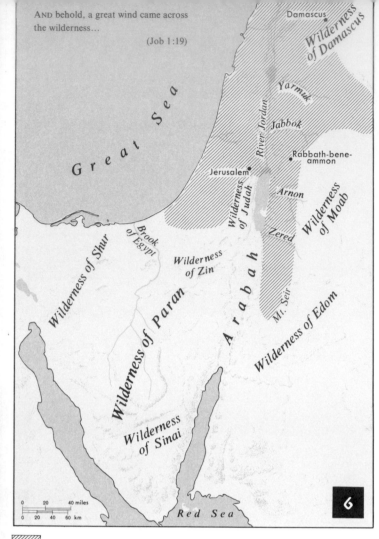

AND behold, a great wind came across the wilderness...

(Job 1:19)

Area of settlement

THE DESERTS SURROUNDING PALESTINE

THE HOLY LAND lies between the sea and the desert, and both influence its nature. The westerly wind brings life-giving rains, whereas the easterly brings only the dryness of the desert. The higher a place, or the closer to the sea, the more wet the climate.

The southern part of Palestine lies within an arid zone that runs around the globe; the extensive desert regions enclose the Holy Land on the south and east, with lofty Mount Seir jutting like a finger toward the heart of the wilderness.

There is no natural border separating the settled area from the desert regions, and the hungry nomads of the desert have beaten on the doors of the Holy Land since time immemorial. The influence of the desert is extreme in the history of the Holy Land, and an awareness of this wilderness is echoed throughout the pages of the Bible.

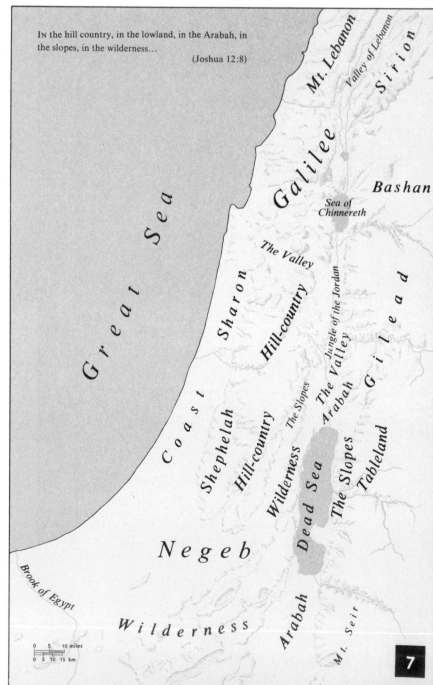

IN the hill country, in the lowland, in the Arabah, in the slopes, in the wilderness...

(Joshua 12:8)

THE GEOGRAPHICAL REGIONS OF PALESTINE

THE FACE of the Holy Land is most varied, mainly because of sharp climatic differences from region to region. The major feature of the relief of the Holy Land and Syria is the deep rift stretching from northern Syria through the valley of Lebanon, the Jordan valley, the Arabah and the Gulf of Elath, down to the southeastern coast of Africa. This cleft divides Palestine into its western part and the eastern "Transjordan"; there are great differences in altitude within short distances. The distance between Hebron and the mountains of Moab as the crow flies is no more than 36 miles, though in traversing this, a descent from + 3,000 feet down to − 1,300 feet below sea-level (the lowest spot on the face of the earth) is made, followed again by an ascent to more than + 3,000 feet. These contrasts form the dry Arabah at the edge of the Judean Desert, with its rugged scarps, and opposite are the fertile and watered plateaus of Transjordan. These variations of land and climate brought about extremely different patterns of settlement within Palestine, which resulted in corresponding political divisions in most periods.

In several instances, the major distinct regions of the Holy Land are clearly defined and listed in the Bible according to topography and climate (Deut. 1:7; Josh. 10:40; 11:16; Judg. 1:9; and so forth).

Even such a list as the geographical administrative classification of cities of Judah is divided into four major regions: the Negeb (south), the Shephelah (lowlands), the hill-country, and the wilderness (Josh. 15:21, 33, 48, 61).

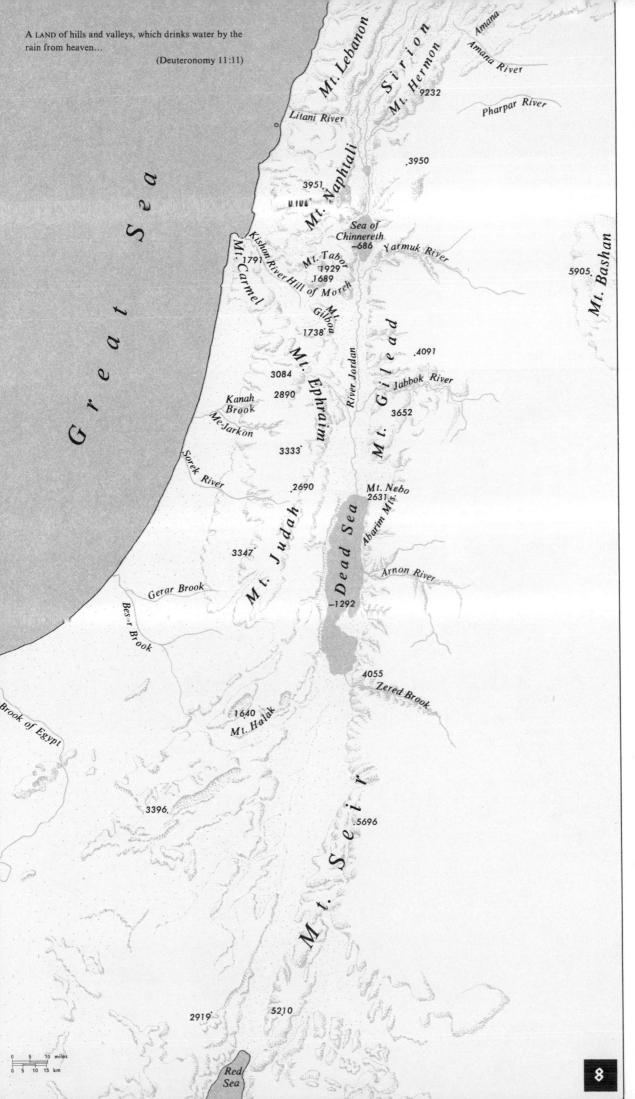

A LAND of hills and valleys, which drinks water by the
rain from heaven...

(Deuteronomy 11:11)

THE MOUNTAINS
AND STREAMS
OF PALESTINE

Great Sea

Mt. Lebanon

Sirion

Mt. Hermon
9232

Amana

Amana River

Litani River

Pharpar River

.3950

Mt. Naphtali

3951.

Sea of Chinnereth
-686

Yarmuk River

Mt. Bashan

5905.

Kishon River

Mt. Carmel
1791

Mt. Tabor
1929

Hill of Moreh
1689

Mt. Gilboa
1738

.4091

River Jordan

Mt. Gilead

Jabbok River

3084

3652

2890

Kanah Brook

Me-Jarkon

Mt. Ephraim

3333

Sorek River

.2690

Mt. Nebo
2631

Abarim Mts.

Dead Sea

Mt. Judah

3347

Gerar Brook

Arnon River

Besor Brook

-1292

4055

Zered Brook

Brook of Egypt

1640
Mt. Halak

3396.

.5696

Mt. Seir

2919.

5210

Red Sea

0 5   10 miles
0 5 10 15 km

1640 = Altitude in feet

8

THE INTERNATIONAL ROUTES
IN THE ANCIENT EAST

THE main highways played a most important part in the history of the Holy Land. The settlements of Palestine are located at the crossroads of the Ancient East. The most important route was the highway from Mesopotamia to Egypt, and on it were founded the important political centers. From earliest times commercial caravans plied the major highways carrying their products, precious objects, and luxuries; and providing for the needs of the caravans, and their security, became a constant source of income. These ways, however, were not open for trade and commerce alone: military campaigns and conquests also trod them throughout history, leaving in their wake destruction and desolation. In most periods the Holy Land was dominated by major foreign powers, northern or southern, who mainly strove to secure a hold on these routes.

The mountainous nature of Palestine dictates the locations of the routes. The major international route was the "way of the sea"—

Is. 8:23 (later called the "Via Maris"), leading north from Egypt along the coast, through the Jezreel Valley to Hazor and Damascus. On the southern coastal plain it split into two branches, uniting again in the Sharon plain, to pass close along the foot of the hills. The main route from the Sharon passes through Wadi Ara—the Aruna pass—opening out at the keypoint of the Jezreel Valley, Megiddo.

The second international route was the King's Highway (Num. 21:22), which passes through the hill-country of Transjordan, close to the desert. This is the secondary route from Damascus to Egypt, its importance lying in the fact that the roads to Arabia branch off from it. There existed various other secondary, local roads, which were used largely by local traffic, and in time of need they also served as alternatives for international trade caravans. The maps show only the more important routes, especially those mentioned by name in the Bible.

WE WILL go up by the highway; and if we drink of your water, I and my cattle, then I will pay for it...
(Numbers 20:19)

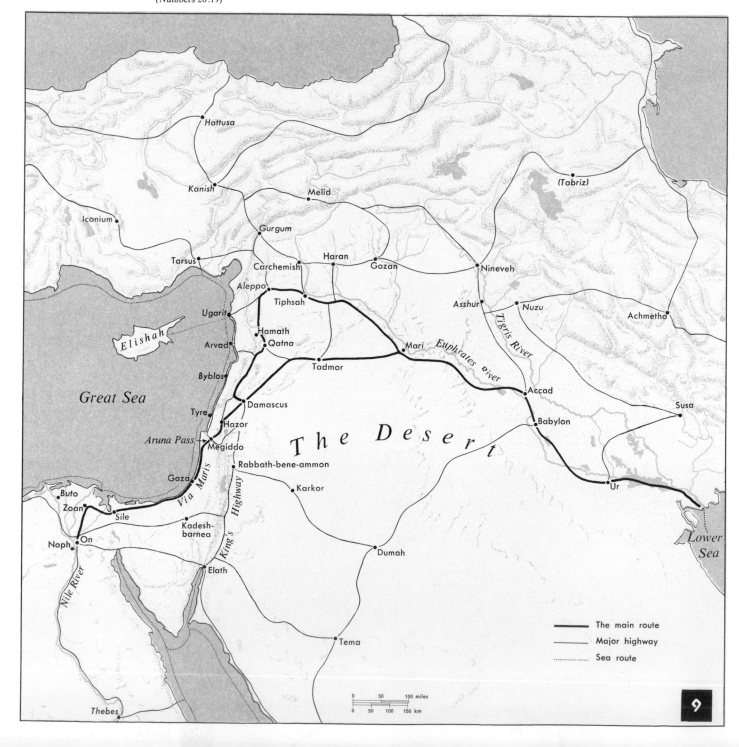

BUILD UP, build up the highway, clear it of stones...

(Isaiah 62:10)

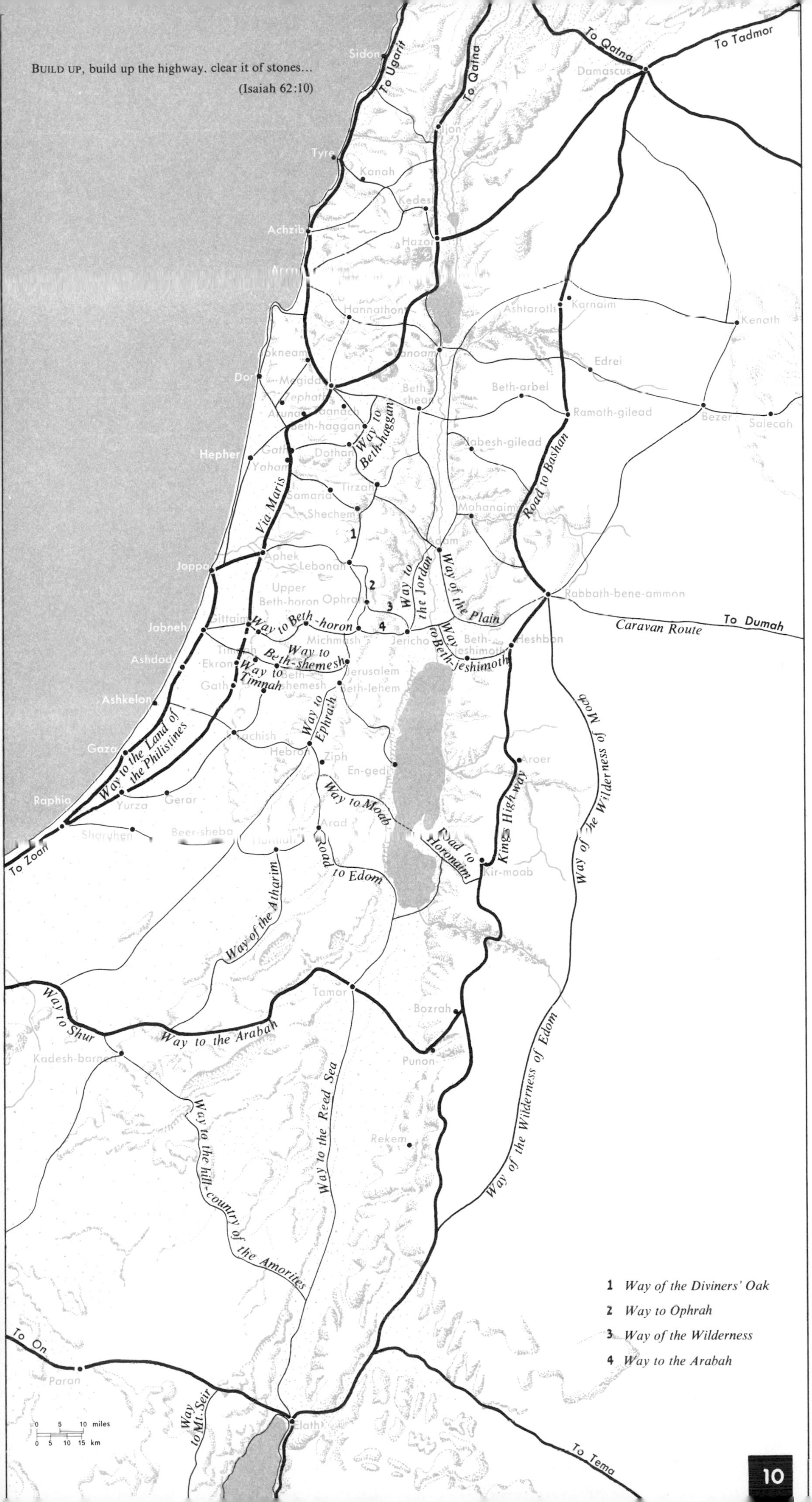

To Ugarit

To Qatna

To Qatna

To Qatna

To Tadmor

Damascus

Sidon

Tyre

Kanah

Kedesh

Achzib

Hazor

Arm...

Hannathon

Ashtaroth

Karnaim

Kenath

Jokneam

Janoam

Beth-arbel

Edrei

Dor

Megiddo

Beth-shean

Way to Beth-haggan

Taanach

Beth-haggan

Gath

Dothan

Jabesh-gilead

Ramoth-gilead

Bezer

Salecah

Hepher

Yoham

Tirzah

Via Maris

Samaria

Shechem

Mahanaim

Road to Bashan

1

Aphek

Lebonah

Way to the Jordan

Adam

Way of the Plain

Joppa

2

Upper

Beth-horon

Ophrah

3

Rabbath-bene-ammon

Caravan Route

To Dumah

Jabneh

Gittaim

Way to Beth-horon

4

Michmash

Jericho

Way to Beth-jeshimoth

Heshbon

Ashdod

Ekron

Way to Beth-shemesh

Beth-shemesh

Jerusalem

Beth-lehem

Gath

Way to Timnah

Timnah

Ashkelon

Lachish

Way to Ephrah

Hebron

Ziph

En-gedi

Aroer

Way of the Wilderness of Moab

Gaza

Way to the Land of the Philistines

Raphia

Yurza

Gerar

Arad

Way to Moab

Road to Horonaim

Kir-moab

King's Highway

Sharuhen

Beer-sheba

Hormah

Road to Edom

Way to the Reed Sea

Way of the Athariim

Way of the Wilderness of Edom

To Zoan

Tamar

Way to Shur

Way to the Arabah

Bozrah

Kadesh-barnea

Punon

Rekem

Way to the hill-country of the Amorites

To On

Paran

1 *Way of the Diviners' Oak*

2 *Way to Ophrah*

3 *Way of the Wilderness*

4 *Way to the Arabah*

——— Major highway

——— Local road

0 5 10 miles

0 5 10 15 km

Way to Mt. Seir

Elath

To Tema

10

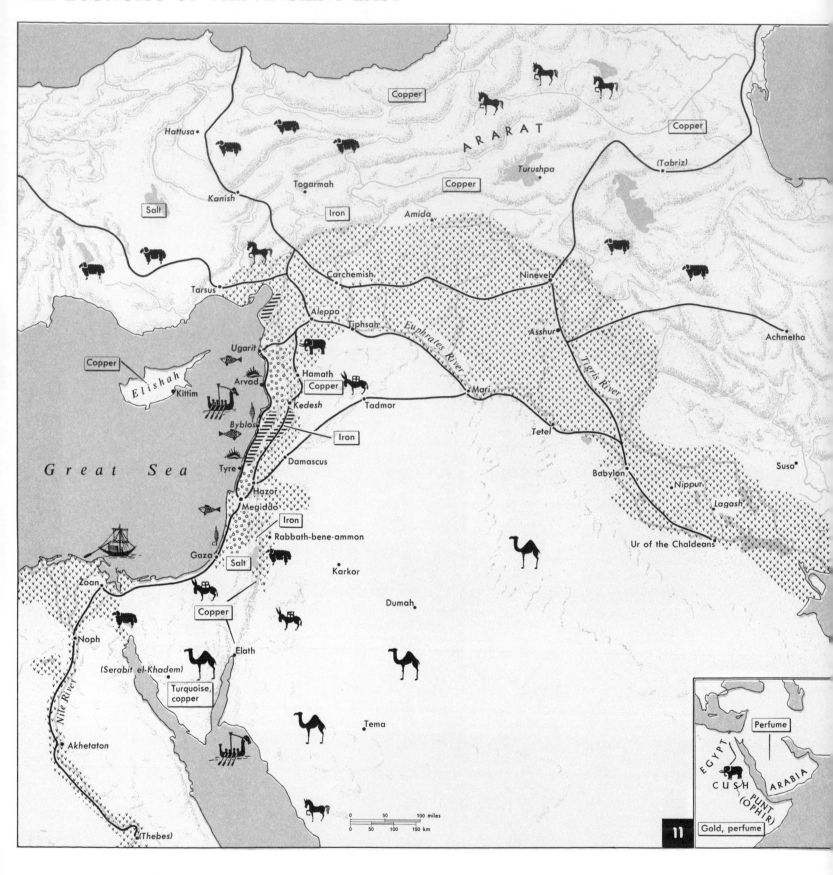

He who tills his land will have plenty of bread...

(Proverbs 12:11)

THE ECONOMY OF THE ANCIENT EAST

Copper

ARARAT

Hattusa

Copper

(Tabriz)

Togarmah

Turushpa

Copper

Kanish

Salt

Iron

Amida

Carchemish

Nineveh

Tarsus

Aleppo

Tiphsah

Euphrates River

Asshur

Achmetha

Ugarit

Hamath

Copper

Mari

Tigris River

Arvad

Kittim

Kedesh

Tadmor

Elishah

Copper

Byblos

Tetel

Iron

Susa

Damascus

Babylon

Great Sea

Tyre

Nippur

Hazor

Lagash

Megiddo

Iron

Rabbath-bene-ammon

Ur of the Chaldeans

Gaza

Salt

Karkor

Zoan

Copper

Dumah

Noph

Elath

(Serabit el-Khadem)

Turquoise, copper

Tema

Nile River

Akhetaton

0   50   100 miles
0 50 100 150 km

11

Perfume

EGYPT

CUSH

ARABIA

PUNT
(OPHIR)

Gold, perfume

(Thebes)

Field produce
Construction timber
Fruit trees
Forests

 Dates
 Sycamores
 Cedars
 Wheat
 Barley
 Sheep
 Cattle
 Camels
 Horses
 Fishing
 Perfume

A LAND of wheat and barley, of vines and fig trees and pomegranates, a land of olive trees and honey...a land whose stones are iron, and out of whose hills you can dig copper.

(Deuteronomy 8:8–9)

FOOD PRODUCTION was the basis of ancient economy. Diet was monotonous and much simpler than that of today; each area relied mainly upon its local produce. Although there were places where grain and other foodstuffs were marketed, the scope of such commerce was limited.

In the Ancient East grain production took place in the river countries. In the outlying, marginal regions, in the deserts and northern plains, sheep-raising was common, as was cattle- and horse-breeding in certain areas. Camel-breeding on a large scale, mainly in the Arabian Desert, did not start until the end of the second millennium. The donkey was the chief beast of burden. In Palestine, too, grain was produced, though animal-husbandry and horticulture were more important.

Another major branch of economy in the Ancient East was the smelting and working of metals. An important source of gold lay in the Land of Punt, to the south of Egypt; this may have been the biblical Ophir to which Solomon's ships sailed (1 Kings 10:11, and so forth). The two most common metals, used in weapons and tools, were copper and iron, which were mainly produced in Asia Minor and the Caucasus, as well as in Cyprus. According to the Bible, iron and copper were mined in the mountains of the Holy Land (Deut. 8:9); evidently reference is made here to the few mines in the marginal areas: the Valley of Lebanon, southern Gilead, and especially the copper mines on either side of the Arabah.

In the mountains of Lebanon and in the Anti-Lebanon (Sirion) stood forests of cedar and other woods, an important source of construction timber not only for Palestine and Syria, but also for Egypt and Mesopotamia. The forests of the Hauran and Mount Seir (Edom) probably served only local needs.

The coastal cities became centers of the textile industry, partly because they were close to the source of the Murex shells used in making "Tyrian purple," a dye reserved for precious textiles. The Hellenistic name for Canaan, Phoenicia is connected with the Greek word for reddish-purple—*phoenix* (this meaning may also have been attached to the name Canaan). In documents of the fourteenth century B.C. found at Ugarit—the port city on the north Syrian coast—mention is made of textiles imported from Acco, Ashdod, and Ashkelon. In both Ugaritic documents and later Accadian sources, Ashdod and possibly also Ashkelon are mentioned as centers of fish exports. Thus, we may assume that a fish-preserving industry existed in the southern coastal cities. It seems that in various periods salt was obtained from the Dead Sea and from Mount Sodom, as witnessed by the name "Ir-hammelah" the city of salt—at the northwestern end of the Dead Sea. The cultivation of various types of aromatic gums for perfumes in the Dead Sea region was also of some importance, the region having the proper climate for such. The main centers of perfume production, however, lay in southern Arabia.

The various crafts remained the trade secrets of family and tribal associations within particular areas. A speciality in the Jordan Valley, near Succoth, was the casting of metal utensils (1 Kings 7:46), as confirmed by archaeological excavations at Succoth proper. At Tell Beit Mirsim (Ashan) on the border of the Shephelah, a quarter originally settled by textile dyers was uncovered.

A well-developed art in Canaan was ivory carving, the luxury product being used by the wealthy and royalty in architectural and furniture ornamentation. Tusks were imported from Kush (Nubia) and the land of Ni in northern Syria. The centers of this industry in the Canaanite period were located along the coast and, in the Israelite period, primarily at Damascus, Hamath, and perhaps Samaria.

Commerce thus generally occupied an important position in the economy of Palestine, especially in those areas along the main trade routes.

THE ECONOMY OF PALESTINE

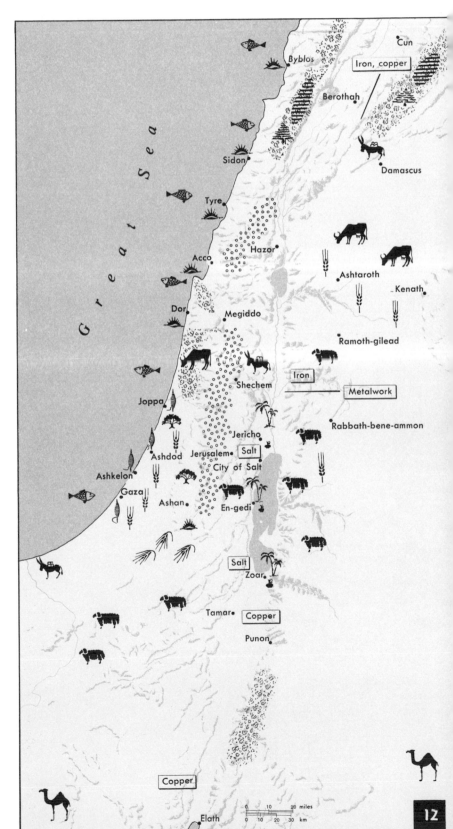

an ple   Textiles   Ivory   Caravans   Phoenician   Egyptian

C o m m e r c e

COMPARATIVE CHRONOLOGY OF EARLY CIVILIZATIONS

Period	Date	Mesopotamia	Syria-Palestine	Egypt
Neolithic (Late Stone Age)	5000	Jarmo Hassuna, Nineveh I Samarra, Nineveh II	Jericho IX Byblos A Ras Shamra V (Ugarit) Amuq	El-Fayum A
Chalcolithic (Stone-Copper Age)	4000 3500	Tell Halaf Tell el-Ubeid Erech	Megiddo XX, Hamath L Yarmuk (Shaar Ha-Golan) Jericho VIII Teleilat Ghassul, Beer-sheba	Deir Tasa El-Badari El-Amrah, Nagada I
Early Bronze Age I	3150 2850	Jemdet Nasr	Early Canaanite Period I	El-Gerzeh, Nagada II

THE EARLY CULTURES IN THE MIDDLE EAST

THE BUDS of human civilization are recognized in the development of food production (agriculture) and in the founding of towns and organized settlements. Traces of such are found already in the Middle Stone age (Mesolithic), some 10,000 years ago. According to our present knowledge, Jericho is the oldest city in the world, for in the seventh millennium it was already surrounded by a massive stone wall. Jarmo, in northern Mesopotamia, is more or less contemporary, though it appears to have been no more than a village. Only future research will prove whether Jericho was truly the first city and unique at that time, and whether to the Jordan Valley, the smallest of the river valleys of the Fertile Crescent, belongs the designation "the cradle of civilization."

During the fifth millennium (the Late Stone age—Neolithic), and the fourth millennium (the Chalcolithic), the progress of man is in evidence throughout the Fertile Crescent. In this period, Mesopotamia takes to the fore, but in Egypt, too, parallel developments are taking place, as also in the countries between—Palestine and Syria. These early cultures are today named after the sites where they were first discovered; in the comparative table the major cultures are listed chronologically.

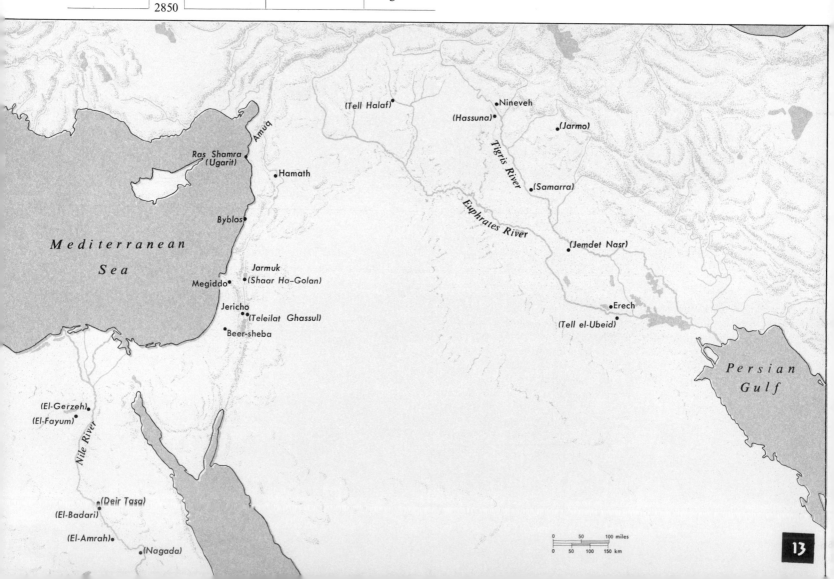

Tigris River

Euphrates River

Nile River

C U S H

Pishon River

Gihon River

HAVILAH

0 50 100 150 miles
0 100 200 km

14

GEN. 2: 10–14

japheth—Cretan (wall painting at Cnossus)

Ham—Ti, Queen of Egypt
(beginning of fourteenth century B.C.)

GEN. 10; CHRON. 1: 4–23

Shem—Assyrian
(relief from palace of Sargon at Khorsabad)

A RIVER flowed out of Eden to water the garden, and there it divided and became four rivers.

(Genesis 2:10)

THE RIVERS OF THE GARDEN OF EDEN

WHERE are the ancient centers of civilization according to the Bible? The answer to this is hinted at in the description of the four rivers emerging from the Garden of Eden. It is natural that the ancients should believe the rivers of Eden to be those flowing through the lands most abundant in water, the foremost being the Tigris and the Euphrates in Mesopotamia. The Pishon and the Gihon have not been identified and may have merely been symbolic. But since Havilah is one of the regions of Cush (Gen. 10:7), it would seem that the two major branches of the Nile (the Blue and the White) are intended.

FROM THESE the coastland peoples spread. . .in their lands, each with his own language, by their families, in their nations.

(Genesis 10:5)

THE FAMILIES OF THE NATIONS IN THEIR LANDS (TABLE OF NATIONS)

IN THE BIBLE there has been preserved a unique list of the nations of the world, within the scope of the people of Israel, the list of the family of man ("the generations of the sons of Noah"). The lands of the world and the peoples are divided into three main lines: the sons of Shem in Mesopotamia and Arabia, the sons of Ham in Egypt and within its sphere of influence, and the sons of Japheth in the northern and western lands. Included in the list are also royal cities and important centers within the Fertile Crescent: in the land of Shinar (southern Mesopotamia) and the land of Canaan. Even if not all the identifications are certain—and some of the names have not been identified at all—the general division is quite clear: three spheres of peoples and lands, which meet in the region of the Holy Land.

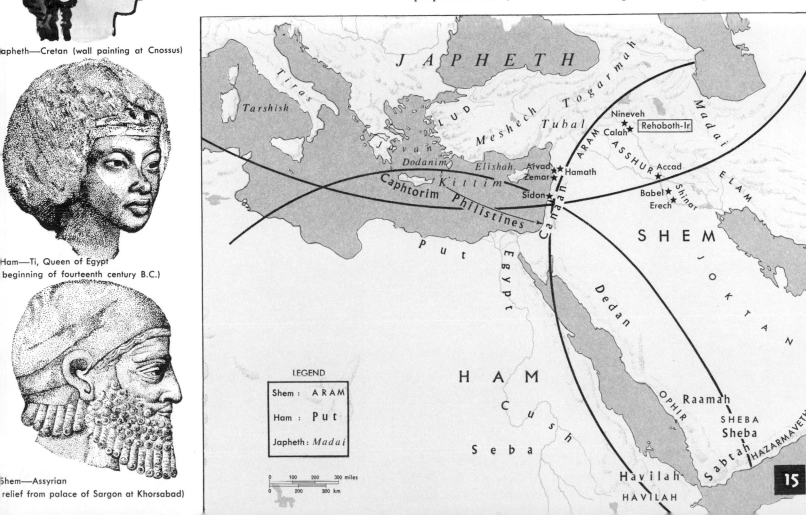

J A P H E T H

Tiras

Tarshish

Lud

Meshech *Tubal* *Togarmah*

Nineveh ★

Rehoboth-Ir

Madai

Javan

ARAM

Calah ★

ASSHUR

Elam

Dodanim

Elishah

Arvad ★ ★ Hamath

Accad ★

Zemar ★

Kittim

Babel ★

Sidon ★

★ Shinar

Caphtorim *Philistines*

Erech ★

Canaan

S H E M

Put

Egypt

J O K T A N

Dedan

H A M

Cush

OPHIR

Raamah

Seba

SHEBA

Sheba

Sabtah

HAZARMAVETH

Havilah

HAVILAH

LEGEND

Shem : A R A M

Ham : Put

Japheth: *Madai*

0 100 200 300 miles
0 200 300 km

15

Archaeological Excavations in Palestine

IN the present century—mainly in the last fifty years—large-scale excavations have taken place at many tels containing the remains of successive cities, one raised over the other. The word "tel" in Hebrew, and in closely related Semitic languages, signifies the almost flat-topped, artificial settlement mounds so conspicuous in the plain-regions of the Middle East. During the Canaanite and Israelite periods, the central cities remained in the same locations, being built over and over again on the sites; initial settlement was usually located on easily defensible hillocks with convenient sources of water, access to fields and control over the nearby roads. As a city was destroyed, buildings disintegrated, adding yet another layer of rubble to the height of the tel.

In modern excavations, research is devoted mainly to these layers or strata (thus: stratigraphy). Even the smallest object found is ascribed to its individual layer. The meticulous differentiation of strata is based largely upon pottery fragments found within each. Pottery is ideally suited to this task for two reasons: when a pottery vessel is broken it becomes worthless and is discarded and forgotten; but pottery stands up well to the ravages of time. Thus, there is an abundance of pottery sherds in each layer. The dating of the different strata has become progressively more accurate with additional comparisons of the stratigraphies of various sites, on the basis of a methodical study of the various types of vessels (thus: typology), further refined by finds of inscriptions and documents within the strata.

The earliest cultures in the history of the Holy Land are known to us only from archaeological research. Most recent discoveries in the Jordan Valley prove that man appeared in Palestine in the Lower Pleistocene Age, estimated to be at least half a million years ago. This early man lived in Palestine before the final depression of the Jordan Valley to its present depth. In several caves in Mount Carmel and in Galilee, skeletons of Paleolithic man have been uncovered. These are of the more advanced type of Neanderthal man discovered in Europe. The scientific name of this type is *Palaeanthropus Palaestinensis*—"Early Palestinian Man." The last phase of the cave dwellers, in the Mesolithic Age (about 10,000 to 8,000 B.C.), parallels the end of the last Ice Age in Europe. At this time began the first true settlement in Palestine; no major climatic changes have taken place since then. The earliest culture has been termed Natufian, after caves in Wadi en-Natuf on the western slopes of the central hill-country. This was a transitional phase of man, from hunting and gathering of food to crude agriculture and animal husbandry.

The revolutionary transition of man in Palestine, from cave dweller to founder of villages and towns, is best seen at Jericho, the one city of this period known to show such extensive accomplishments in construction and technology. This is in contrast to the usual open sites scattered here and there near readily arable land.

The progress of early civilizations was not always smooth and peaceful. Declines and retrogressions followed peaks of achievement. New conquering people dislodged inhabitants from their settlements, or settled in their midst. In the Chalcolithic period (the fourth millennium B.C.) many settlements were founded, mainly in the fertile valleys and on the edge of the desert. It was at this time that copper first came into use alongside stone implements. The later phase of this age is called the Ghassulian culture, after a group of small mounds

THE CHALCOLITHIC PERIOD
FOURTH MILLENNIUM B.C.

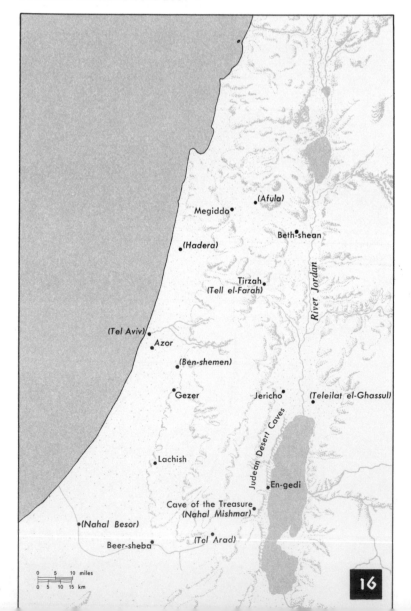

THE CANAANITE PERIOD
(THE BRONZE AGE)
3150 TO 1200 B.C.

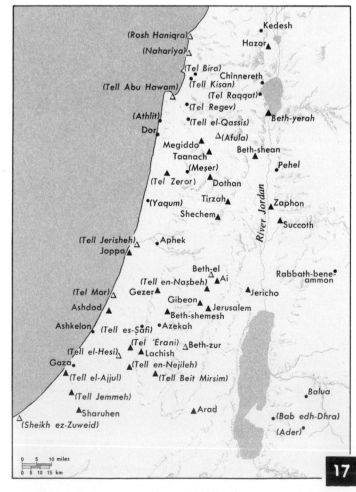

THE ISRAELITE PERIOD (THE IRON AGE)

1200 TO 587 B.C.

Kedesh
Achzib △
Hazor ▲
(Tel Harashim)
(Tel Bira) △
Chinnereth
(Tell Abu Hawam) •
(Tell Kisan)
Karnaim •
Shikmona △ △
(Tel Regev) △
(En-gev) •
(Tell el-Amr)
Dor •
(Afula) △
Megiddo ▲
Beth-shean ▲
Taanach ▲
Ramoth-gilead △
(Tel Zeror) △ Dothan ▲
Pehel •
Tirzah △
Samaria ▲ Zaphon ▲
Shechem ▲ Succoth ▲
(Makmish) △
(Meṣad Hayarqon) △ (Tell Qasile) △
Shiloh △
Joppa △ (Tell Jerisheh) △
Beth-el △ △ Ai
Rabbath-bene-ammon △
(Meṣad Hashavyahu) △
(Tell en-Nasbeh) △
Jericho △
(Tel Mor) △ Gezer ▲ Gibeon ▲ Gibeah of Saul ▲
Heshbon △
Ashdod ▲ Beth-shemesh ▲ ▲ Jerusalem
(Khirbet Qumran) △
(Ramat Rahel) △
Ashkelon • (Tell es-Ṣafi) △ • Azekah
(Tel Ṣippor) △ • (Tell el-Judeidah)
(Tel 'Erani) △ Lachish △ Beth-zur △
(Tell el-Hesi) △ Mareshah △
Dibon △
• Gaza (Tell en-Nejileh) △
Aroer •
En-gedi ▲
Balua •
(Tell el-Ajjul) • (Tell Beit Mirsim) •
(Tell Jemmeh) •
▲ Sharuhen Arad △
△ (Sheikh ez-Zuweid) Beer-sheba ▲ (Tell Malhatha) △
(Tell Esdar) •
(Meṣad Gozal) •
(Khirbet Rithma) • • (Athar Haroeh)
(Timna) •
(Ramat Matred) •
Ezion-geber ▲
0   5   10 miles
0   10   15 km
Kadesh-barnea •

18

• Trial excavation or minor remains   △ Excavation   ▲ Major excavation

in the southeastern part of the Jordan Valley, where the culture was first discovered (Teleilat Ghassul); it later became well known from several sites near Beer-sheba. These settlements spread over wide areas and were not fortified; the inhabitants were engaged in agriculture, herding, and household industries, including copper working. Their technical and artistic achievements are quite remarkable. A cache of copper utensils found in the "Cave of the Treasure" in the Judean Desert surpasses in both quality and beauty all other such objects known from the East from the same period. Among the lands of the early civilizations, Palestine held a respectable position till the end of the fourth millennium B.C.

THE PERSIAN, HELLENISTIC, AND ROMAN PERIODS

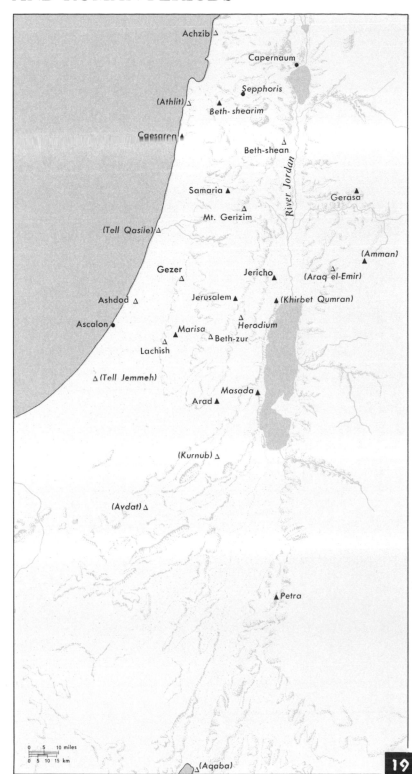

Achzib △
Capernaum •
Sepphoris •
(Athlit) △ Beth-shearim ▲
Caesarea ▲
Beth-shean △
Samaria ▲
Gerasa △
Mt. Gerizim △
(Tell Qasiie) △
Amman (△)
Gezer △
Jericho ▲
(Araq el-Emir) △
Ashdod △
Jerusalem ▲ ▲ (Khirbet Qumran)
Ascalon •
Herodium △
Marisa ▲
Lachish △ △ Beth-zur
(Tell Jemmeh) △
Masada ▲
Arad ▲
(Kurnub) △
(Avdat) △
Petra ▲
0   5   10 miles
0   5   10   15 km
(Aqaba) △

19

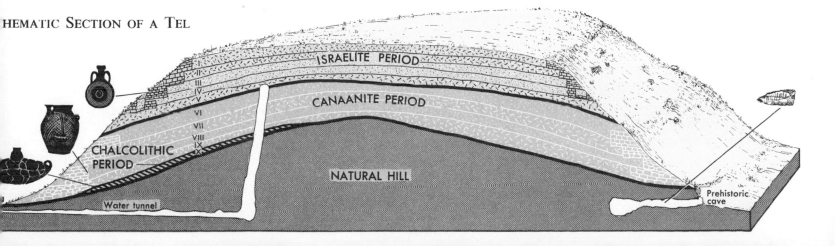

ISRAELITE PERIOD
CANAANITE PERIOD
CHALCOLITHIC PERIOD
NATURAL HILL
Water tunnel
Prehistoric cave
I II III IV V VI VII VIII IX X

THE BEGINNING of his kingdom was Babel, Erech, and
Accad, all of them in the land of Shinar.

(Genesis 10:10)

THE first large empires of the Ancient East arose early in the third
millennium B.C. In southern Mesopotamia, powerful city-
kingdoms were centered at Kish, Larak, Lagash, Umma, Erech,
and Ur. This land, later referred to in the Bible as the land of Shinar,
was then called Sumer. Sumerian culture laid the foundations of
civilization in the Middle East, its influence extended over the "land
of the west" (Syria and Palestine) as far as Egypt.

Egypt at about this time was united by its earliest kings, those of the
first dynasty. From that time on, Egypt represented one of the
mightiest powers, and even in the earlier periods its influence reached
countries far to the north: Na'armer, evidently the first king able to
unite all Egypt, at about the middle of the twenty-ninth century B.C.,
possibly penetrated into Palestine, as may be evident from a decorated
cosmetic palette found in Egypt and on the basis of his name on a sherd
of Egyptian pottery found in excavations at Tel 'Erani near modern
Kiriat-Gat. The gigantic pyramids built under the kings of the second
to fifth dynasties are imposing monuments to the organizational
power and capability of Egypt in those early days.

The political center of Mesopotamia in the twenty-fourth century
B.C. moved from Sumer in the south to Semitic Accad in the north,
the exact location of which has not yet been ascertained. Sargon I
of Accad founded this empire and enforced his authority not only over
Sumer and Dilmun (Bahrein) in the south, but also conquered the
area of Subartu, north of Asshur, reaching even the Amanus mountains and the "Upper Sea," the Mediterranean.

Mesopotamia and Egypt in the third millennium are known to us
from many written documents, while Palestine in the same period was
still in its "proto-history," since as yet no documents from this time have
been discovered here. Some day inscriptions may come to light, for
excavations have revealed that during this same third millennium—the
Early Bronze Age—there were rich and powerful city-kingdoms
with well-advanced cultures in Palestine. There were cities which
covered an area of 25 to 50 acres, enclosed within strong fortifications
up to 25 to 30 feet thick, like those at Megiddo and Beth-yerah. (Map
21 shows only the major centers.) Although the history of this period
is still obscure, there can be little doubt that both Palestine and Syria
took an active part in its cultural development.

THE ANCIENT EAST
IN THE THIRD MILLENNIUM

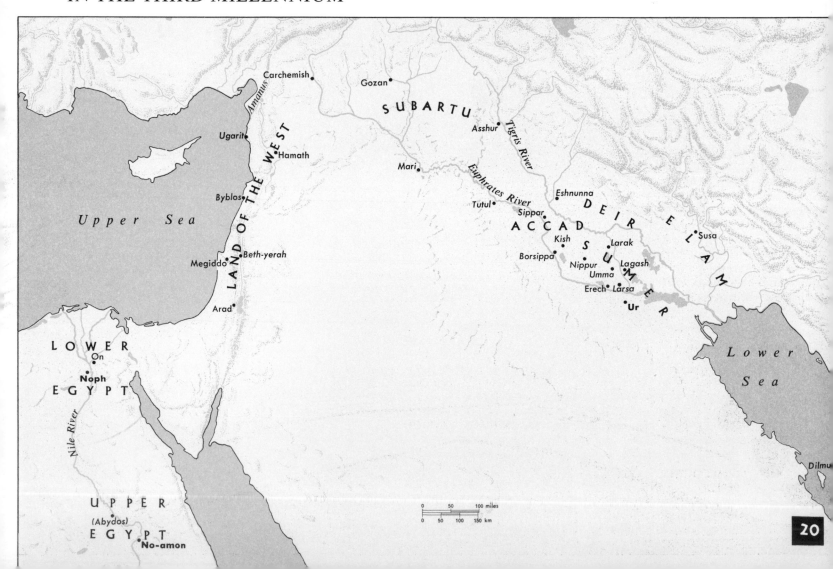

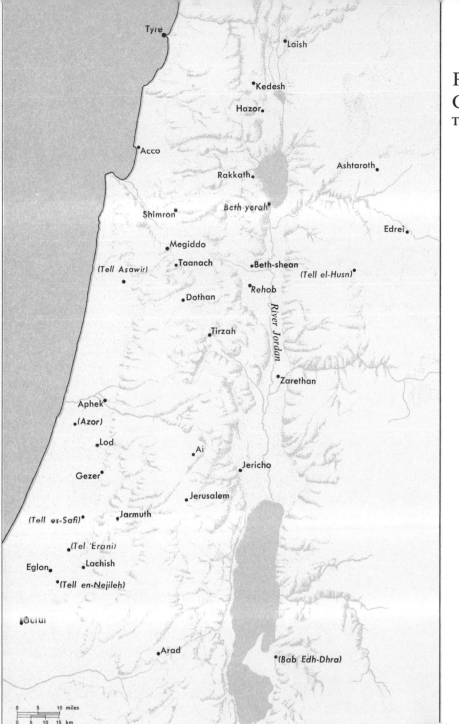

PALESTINE IN THE EARLY CANAANITE PERIOD
THIRD MILLENNIUM B.C.

Prostrated enemies and plan of fortress
(on cosmetic palette of Na'armer)

21

THE CAMPAIGN OF PEPI I
CA. 2350 B.C.

THE sole historical information on Palestine from the Early Bronze Age is an Egyptian inscription telling of five military campaigns in the time of Pepi I (middle of the twenty-fourth century B.C.) to the "land of the Sand-Dwellers," the ancient Egyptian name for the lands to the east of Egypt. One campaign is described in detail —the Egyptian army set out in two columns, one by land and one by sea; the sea group arrived earlier and landed behind a prominent ridge, the "Nose of the Antelope's Head," probably the Carmel. The conquered land was evidently the plain of Acco and a part of the Jezreel Valley, where the Egyptians destroyed fortresses, sacked settlements, uprooted fig trees and vines, and took booty. A picture of the settlements flourishing at the time, especially in the coastal plains, is conjured up by this vivid description.

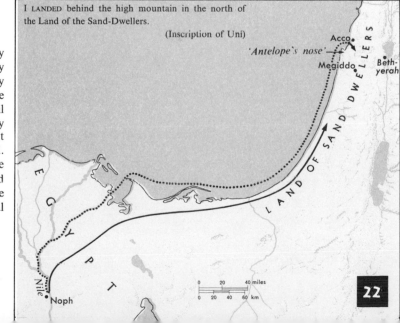

I LANDED behind the high mountain in the north of the Land of the Sand-Dwellers.

(Inscription of Uni)

——— Land route
········ Sea route

22

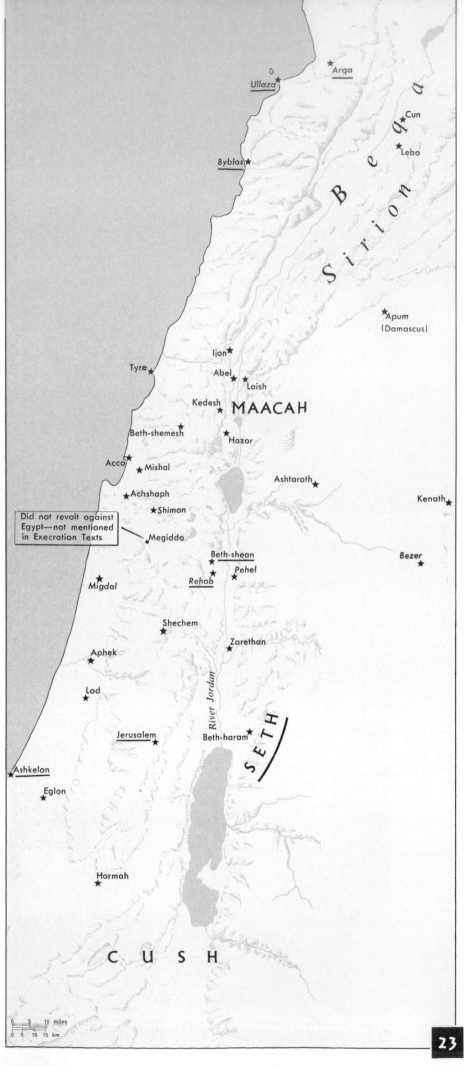

PALESTINE IN THE EXECRATION TEXTS

20TH TO 19TH CENTURIES B.C.

IN the closing centuries of the third millennium, a wave of noma[ds] speaking a West Semitic tongue, swept over all the centers of [the Fertile] Crescent. In Accadian documents they are called the "People [of] Amurru (=the west)," and in the Bible the Amorites. No kingd[om] withstood them, and in the first centuries of the second millenni[um] new kingdoms arose under Amorite dominance. These were in t[urn] absorbed by Hammurabi, the greatest king of the first Babylon[ian] dynasty, about the middle of the eighteenth century B.C.

In Palestine a similar picture is presented: every political cente[r of] the Early Canaanite period was destroyed, and throughout the l[and] there are traces of the nomads coming from the north, bringing v[ith] them new traditions of pottery and copper. This was the earliest ph[ase] of the Middle Canaanite period. Remains of nomad dwellings [and] burials have been found at most tels, but are most common in [the] highlands of Transjordan and in the Negeb — both regions having [not] been inhabited till this period. The origin of and direction taken [by] this nomadic wave is still disputed, but it seems to have disappea[red] by the 20th century B.C. and its place usurped by an Amorite popu[la]tion speaking a West Semitic dialect. From then on, settlement [was] continuous at most of them, until the Israelite conquest.

Egypt was ruled by the twelfth dynasty in the twentieth a[nd] nineteenth centuries B.C. In this period the kingdom expanded a[nd] reached a pinnacle in its development and power; its rule extended o[ver] part of Palestine and the Phoenician coast. The first documents tr[uly] dealing with Palestine are from this period: the most important [are] the "Execration Texts," inscribed sherds or clay figurines in the fo[rm] of captives, bearing the names of rebels and enemies of Egypt, acco[m]panied by curses and maledictions. Mention is made of cities a[nd] tribes within the Egyptian sphere of influence and rule. Two gro[ups] of these texts have been found; the earlier group is from the mid[dle] of the twentieth century, the later from the end of the ninetee[nth] century B.C. In the first group only a few, mostly unidentified na[mes] are mentioned, beside Jerusalem and Ashkelon. The names of th[ree] or four local rulers are mentioned in connection with each local[ity]. In the second group there are sixty-four city-names, most of wh[ich] have been identified through later sources; these are precee[ded] generally by the name of only one ruler. This difference indicate[s a] change in the structure of settlement and social order in Palest[ine] during the twentieth and nineteenth centuries B.C. This is the per[iod] of transition from nomadic to settled life, from patriarchal and tr[ibal] rule to city-kingdom, among the Amorites.

The names of the rulers are definitely West Semitic in charac[ter] compounded with such theophoric elements as -am, -ab, -ah, [and] -hadad, and so forth. These names, quite common at the time, [are] similar to the Patriarchal names of the Bible.

EXECRATION TEXTS—THEBES, SAKKARA, EGY[PT]

★   City mentioned in later Execration Texts

Byblos   City also mentioned in earlier Execration Texts

LIST OF LATER EXECRATION TEXTS

Place	Ruler	Place	Ruler
1 Hormah*	Atamar-ab	22 *Shrmry*	Ammu-tile
2 Ashkelon*†	*Mry*	23 Southern *Mrshky*	Y. . .kir
3 Ashan*† (Beth-shean)	Niqmepa	24 Northern *Mrzhky*	Ranna (?)
4 (Beth) Haram*	Yittin-hadad	25 Ash[ta]roth*	Ya. . .l
5 Migdol*	Abi-rah	26 *Ahmut*†	*Kar*
6 Shechem*	Ibish-hadad	27 Bezer*	*Ymr*
7 Cun?*	Asaph-hadad	28	*Apr-rny*
8 Pehel*	*Apr-anu*	29 *Msh*	*Sqr* (?)
9 Aphek*	*Yanka*	30 Sirion*	*Apr-y. . .mut*
10 Any (ayin)	*Atalim*	31 Lebo*	*Apr-. . .*
11 Achsaph*	*Yaprn*	32 Kana*	*Apr-b. . .*
12 Asaph	*Apr-asaph*	33 Southern Apum*	. . .
13 Mishal*	*Yrl*	34 Northern Apum*	Ahu-Kabkabu
14 Rehob*†	Yakmis-am	35 Tyre*	. . .*ru*
15 Hazor*	*Gs*	36 *Yanqa*†	. . .*a*
16 (Kede)sh* (?)	Zabilu-hadad	37 *Mky** (Maacah)	Shemesh-. . .
17 *Sapm*	Hauron-ab(um)	38 . . .*ryn*	. . .
18 Ijon*	Ki-shahar-ab	39 Southern *Qrhm*†	*Hmy*
19 Zr(m) (Ziri-bashan)	Yanzum-hadad	40 Northern *Qrhm*†	Yasar-kuna
20 Biqa*	Samar-har	41 Zarethan*	Ammu-lubu
21 Ara	Lavi-la-hadad	42 Ophr. .a	Ammu-. . .
		43 *Ybly*	Shemesh-*apilim*
		44 Lod*	. . .*pa*. . .
		45 Jerusalem*†	. . .
		46 . . .*ry*	. . .-hadad
		47 Abel*	. . .
		48 *Asnas*	*Thrs*
		49 Acco*	Tar-am
		50 Tribes of Cush*	. . .*ay*
		51 Tribes of Cush*	. . .*y*
		52 Upper Shutu*†	Shumu-ab
		53 Lower Shutu*†	*Yk. . .m*
		54 Arqa(ta)*†	Ammu-hr. . .
		55 Shimon*	Abrahan
		56 *Qrqrm*	*Abu*. . .
		57 Shusu	Yakmis-am
		58 Eglon* (?)	Yarpa-el
		59 Laish*	Hauron-*ab*. . .
		60 Beth-she(mesh)*(?)*Ytpr*	
		61 Tribe of Arqa(ta)*†	—
		62 Chiefs of *Mky**	(Maacah?)
		63 Tribes of Byblos*†	—
		64 All rulers of *Yanqa*†	
		Ullaza*† (in another list)	

*Identified in map
†Mentioned also in older Execration Texts

ation Text on clay
ne from Sakkara

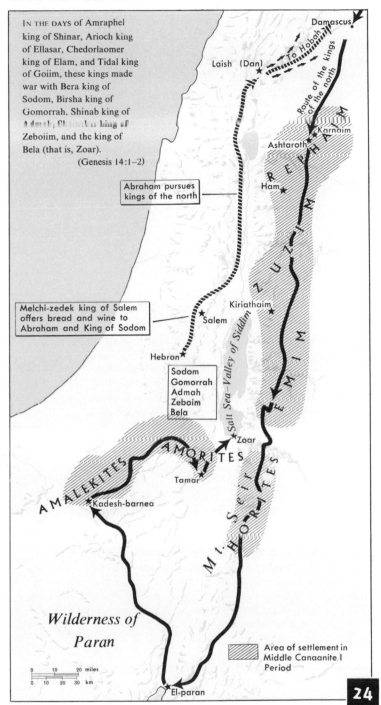

THE CAMPAIGNS OF THE KINGS OF THE NORTH
20TH CENTURY B.C.

IN THE DAYS of Amraphel king of Shinar, Arioch king of Ellasar, Chedorlaomer king of Elam, and Tidal king of Goiim, these kings made war with Bera king of Sodom, Birsha king of Gomorrah, Shinab king of Admah, Shemeber king of Zeboiim, and the king of Bela (that is, Zoar).

(Genesis 14:1–2)

Abraham pursues kings of the north

Melchi-zedek king of Salem offers bread and wine to Abraham and King of Sodom

Sodom
Gomorrah
Admah
Zeboim
Bela

Wilderness of Paran

Area of settlement in Middle Canaanite I Period

0 10 20 miles
0 10 20 30 km

24

THE earliest historical event in the Bible is the war of the four kings of the north against the kings of the valley of the Dead Sea. This is undoubtedly a very old tradition, for many of the place names involved were no longer recognized in the period of the Israelite Monarchy, when the story probably crystallized. It was then found necessary to expound by appending later names, as with "the Valley of Siddim (that is, the Salt Sea)." "Bela (that is, Zoar)," and similarly, "Shaveh(-Kiriathaim)," "Hazazon(-Tamar)," and so forth. Archaeological research has revealed that settlement ceased in the region traversed by these kings in their campaigns—Transjordan and the Negeb—at the end of the twentieth century at the latest. The names of the kings of the Dead Sea valley are Amorite and belong to the corpus of names of the Patriarchs and of the Execration Texts. Not one of the kings figuring in the story has been identified and, historically, the episode remains obscure. Nor is it clear where the cities of this valley were located. The narrator of the story, in a later period, placed them at the southern end of the Dead Sea, and thus was Bela identified with Zoar.

GEN. 14

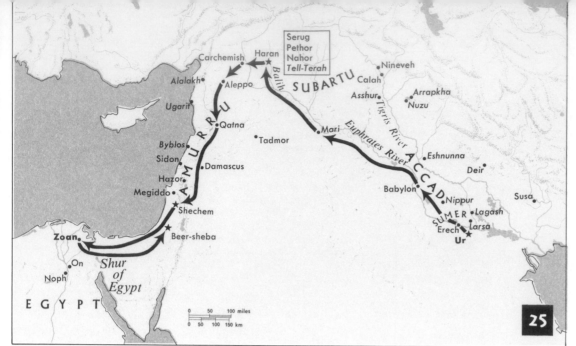

Go from your country and your kindred and your father's house to the land that I will show you.

(Genesis 12:1)

THE TRADITION OF ABRAHAM'S WANDERIN[G]
EARLY SECOND MILLENNIUM B.C.

25

GEN. 11:31– 13:1

T HE narrative of the wanderings of the Patriarchs fits well the reality of the first half of the second millennium B.C., during which the Amorite tribes spread over the lands of the Fertile Crescent. Palestine and Syria are described in documents of the Second millennium as one geographical entity, Amurru (the "west"), that is, the land to the west of the Euphrates river (the land of the Amorites, in the Bible). Thus is the land described in the stories of the Patriarchs: "from the river of Egypt ... to the great river, the river Euphrates, from the wilderness and from the Reed Sea to the Great Sea" (Gen. 15:18; Ex. 23:31; Deut. 1:7; 11:24; Josh. 1:4).

Abraham's origins are linked to Ur (the form "Ur of the Chaldees" is an anachronism, for the Chaldeans arrived there only in the eleventh century B.C.). Ur is well known as an important center in the land of Sumer; it reached its zenith under the kings of the third dynasty of Ur, who around 2060– 1950 B.C. revived for the last time the ancient cultural traditions of the Sumerians. The names of several of Abraham's relatives are also the names of known cities: Abraham's father, *Terah* the son of *Nahor* the son of *Serug,* moved to *Haran* in northern Mesopotamia and from thence Abraham set out to the Promised Land; Rebekah the wife of Isaac came from the city *Nahor,* and Laban the *Aramean,* Jacob's father-in-law, was from the city *Haran* in Padan-*aram.* All these are places around the river Balih in northern Mesopotamia. Haran and Nahor are often mentioned in the Mari documents of the eighteenth century B.C., and cities named Tell-terah and Serug are known from later Assyrian sources.

GEN. 12: 6 — 35 : 29

ABRAHAM AND ISAAC IN THE LAND OF CANAAN
EARLY SECOND MILLENNIUM B.C.

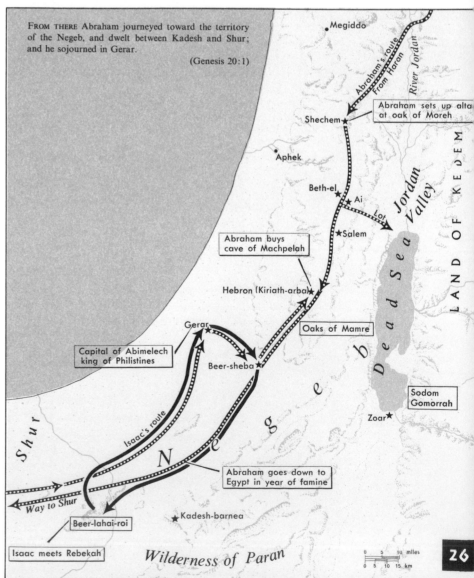

FROM THERE Abraham journeyed toward the territory of the Negeb, and dwelt between Kadesh and Shur; and he sojourned in Gerar.

(Genesis 20:1)

26

Map labels

Tyre

Laish

Kedesh

Hazor ◉

Acco Rehob

Shemesh-edom

Achshaph

Yanuam

Edrei

From Haran

Megiddo

Beth-arbel

Taanach

Ramoth-gilead

Rehob

Jacob

Gath

Dothan

Jabbok River

Tirzah

Simeon and Levi
destroy Shechem

Shechem ★ Succoth ★ Penuel ★ ★
Mahanaim

Jacob comes
to be called Israel

Aphek

Gath-rimmon

River Jordan

Beth-el ★

Gezer

Beth-shemesh

Jerusalem

Ephrath
(Beth lehem) ★

Burial of Rachel

Ashkelon

Beth-zur

(Tell en-Nejileh)

Lachish

Hebron ★

Beth-eglaim

(Tell Beit Mirsim)

Gerar

Esau

Sharuhen

Hormah Arad

5   10 miles
10   15 km

Mt. Seir

GEN. 31—35

Inset map

Jabbok River

Jabbok Ford Penuel ★

Mahanaim ★

0   0.5   1 miles
0   0.5   1 km

Text

THE SAME night he arose and took his two
wives, his two maids, and his eleven
children, and crossed the ford of the
Jabbok.

(Genesis 32:22)

JACOB'S TRAVELS
IN THE LAND OF CANAAN
MID-SECOND MILLENNIUM B.C.

The places in Palestine attached to the Patriarchal
tradition are situated along the central mountain
route from Shechem to Hebron, and in the Negeb;
the stories of Jacob relate to the central part of Gilead
as well. These regions were sparsely settled in those
days, thus providing extensive pasturage among the
forests and in the outlying, semiarid regions. There
were early urban centers in these areas, such as Shechem
and Jerusalem, known from the time of the Execration Texts; there is a tradition concerning Hebron
that it was founded somewhat before Zoan (Tanis),
the capital of Egypt under the Hyksos (Ex. 13:22).
The Patriarchs generally dwelt in peace near these
cities, which were used to camps of nomads on their
fringes.

The important centers of settlement in Palestine
are not mentioned in the Patriarchal accounts; most
of them were located in the north and in the valleys, far from the Patriarchal habitat. In the twentieth
to eighteenth centuries B.C., many city-kingdoms
were founded here, mostly on older tels; they
quickly developed and reached new achievements in
the material culture of Palestine. Under the thirteenth
dynasty, there was a rapid decline of Egyptian
power; Egypt itself finally being conquered about
1720 B.C. by kings of the north from centers in
Palestine and Syria. The next 150 years—the Hyksos
period—were remembered with abhorrence in Egypt.
The name Hyksos in Egyptian means "foreign rulers"
(that is, barbarians).

27

Parade of celebrants (on "Peace Panel," Standard of Ur)

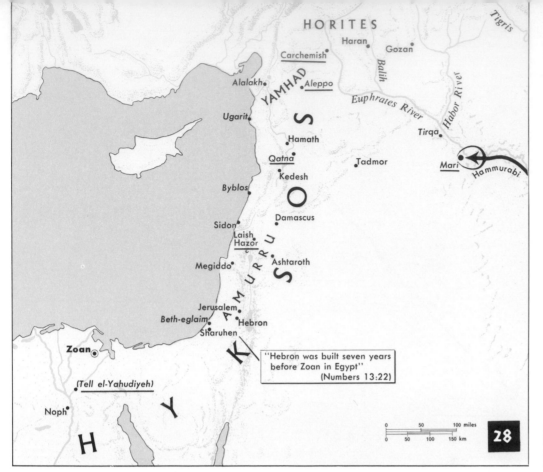

AND there came, after a surprising manner, men of ignoble birth out of the eastern parts, and had boldness enough to make an expedition into our country, and with ease subdued it by force.

(Manetho, quoted by Josephus, Against Apion I, 14)

THE HYKSOS KINGDOM
CA. 1720 TO 1570 B.C.

Mari   Central city

INSCRIPTION, TOMB OF AHMOSE, SON OF EBEN, COMMANDER, ARMY OF AHMOSE—EL-KAB, UPPER EGYPT

WE have few details on the Hyksos period or its kings. Their capital in Egypt was at Zoan (Tanis) in the northeastern Nile delta, and their rule, in one form or another, extended over Palestine and Syria to the region of the Euphrates. The first Hyksos chieftains bore Semitic names, though with time Hurrian elements became evident among their rulers. In the history of Egypt, this period was regarded as one of decline and depression, though in the region as a whole it was a time of development and abundance; the many luxury wares found in excavations bear witness to extensive commercial activity. The might of the Hyksos stemmed from a new weapon, the war chariot, which quickly became the principal striking force of the powerful armies of the Ancient East. The major Hyksos cities were surrounded by massive embankments and glacis (sloped ramparts) built of beaten earth, rising out of a fosse (moats) on the outside. This method of fortification was probably first used in protecting large fortified areas for horses and chariots. Such an enclosure was appended to the city of Hazor, its area there reaching more than 175 acres, in contrast to the 15–18 acres of the city proper built on the tel. In time, buildings were constructed within the enclosure. Similar massive enclosures have been found at Tell el-Yahudiyeh in Egypt, at Qatna in the Valley of Lebanon and at Carchemish on the Euphrates. These enormous cities were undoubtedly centers of Hyksos rule, and Hazor in this period became the capital of Palestine (Amurru). It,

together with Laish, is the only city in Palestine referred to in the Mari archives (Mari was an important political center on the Euphrates conquered in the eighteenth century B.C. by Hammurabi), and Hazor is mentioned as lying on the international trade route passing through Aleppo (the "Land of Yamhad") and Qatna. The biblical notation that "Hazor formerly was the head of all those kingdoms" (Josh. 11:10) may refer to this period.

The Hyksos rulers were expelled from Egypt by Ahmose I, the founder of the eighteenth dynasty, around 1570 B.C. The only document telling of this event relates that, after having conquered Zoan, the Egyptians pursued the Hyksos forces into Palestine and after a siege of three years occupied Sharuhen.

The New Kingdom in Egypt was ushered in with the rise of the eighteenth dynasty, the period of Egyptian imperialism, during which the Egyptian kings strove to attain the boundaries of the former Hyksos empire in Palestine and Syria. This region was then called Retenu, and Hurru (the Land of the Hurrians, the latter having become an important element among the ruling classes of the Palestinian cities). Egypt's major rival in the north during this period was the kingdom of Mitanni, also called Naharin (=Naharaim). Inhabited by Hurrians, its center was located between the Habur River and the northern Euphrates; the capital may have been at Haran. It enforced its rule over Asshur and put great pressure on Syria and Palestine.

ZOAN was destroyed. . . Sharuhen was put to siege for three years.

(Inscription in tomb of Ahmose, son of Eben)

THE EXPULSION OF THE HYKSOS
CA. 1570 B.C.

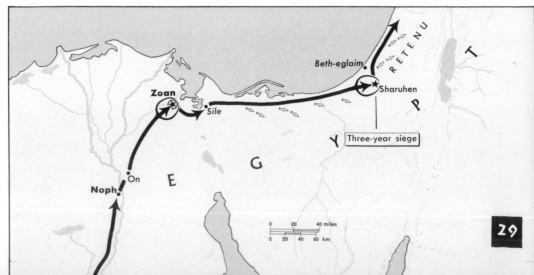

Three-year siege

← Egyptian force

⇠ Retreating Hyksos

Hattusa

H I T T I T E S

(Kurkh)

Carchemish   Haran   Gozan   Washshukanni   Nineveh

Alalakh   M I T A N N I   Asshur

Aleppo   (N A H A R I N A)   Nuzu

Ugarit   Balih   Habor

ELISHAH   Hamath   Tirqa

Arvad   Qatna   Tadmor

Sumur   Kedesh

Ullaza

Byblos

Upper Sea

Sidon   Damascus

Tyre

Hazor   Ashtaroth

Megiddo

Joppa   Jerusalem

Gaza   Sharuhen

Eshnunna

Tutul   B A B Y L O N I A   Tigris River

Sippar   Susa

Babylon

Euphrates River   Ur

M E D I A

E L A M

Noph   On

(Sakkara)

E
G
Y
P
T

(El-Hiba)

(Beni Hasan)

Nile River

(Medinet Habu)   No-amon

(Armant)   (Karnak, Luxor)

0	50	100 miles
0	50	100 150 km

THE MIDDLE EAST IN
THE MID-SECOND MILLENNIUM B.C.

Canaanite chariot (on gold bowl from Ugarit)

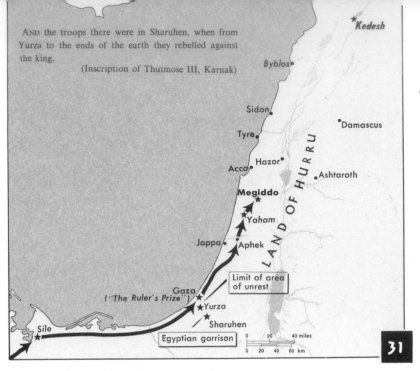

AND the troops there were in Sharuhen, when from Yurza to the ends of the earth they rebelled against the king.

(Inscription of Thutmose III, Karnak)

INSCRIPTIONS, THUTMOSE III—KARNAK, GEBEL BARKAL, ARMANT, EGYPT

THE DEPLOYMENT OF FORCES FOR THE BATTLE OF MEGIDDO

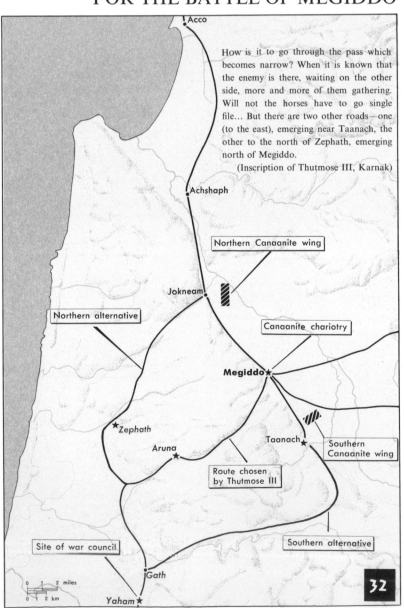

How is it to go through the pass which becomes narrow? When it is known that the enemy is there, waiting on the other side, more and more of them gathering. Will not the horses have to go single file... But there are two other roads—one (to the east), emerging near Taanach, the other to the north of Zephath, emerging north of Megiddo.

(Inscription of Thutmose III, Karnak)

1468 B.C.

THE CAMPAIGN OF THUTMOSE III

THUTMOSE III, king of Egypt, stabilized Egyptian rule in the Land of Retenu with a number of military campaigns. During his first campaign he secured a decisive victory over a league of Canaanite kings in a battle near Megiddo. This battle is the first in history to be recorded in such detail.

At the head of the league of rebel cities stood the kings of Kedesh (on the Orontes) and Megiddo; the Egyptian army marched in ten days from Sile, the important border fortress in Shur (=the wall) of Egypt, to Gaza, the main Egyptian base in Canaan known at this time as "The Ruler's Prize." Eleven days later, the Egyptians reached Yaham in the Sharon plain; there Thutmose conferred with his officers on how to advance on Megiddo. Three alternative routes lay before them from the Sharon plain to Megiddo: by way of Aruna. the shortest but most dangerous, because of its narrow defile; and two, more convenient but longer roads, that of Taanach in the south, and that of Zephath in the north. The officers, having received false information that the Canaanites were blocking the Aruna route, advised the king to proceed along one of the other routes. Rejecting their counsel, the king set out at the head of his troops along the Aruna pass and reached the Qina Valley to the south of Megiddo without meeting any Canaanite resistance. It then transpired that the southern wing of the Canaanite infantry was waiting near Taanach, while their northern wing was north of Megiddo, probably near Jokneam.

Why did the Canaanites split their forces, thus losing the advantage of Megiddo's natural position, blocking exit from the dangerous Aruna defile? It would seem that the reason lay in the normal Canaanite tactics. Not relying on their infantry, they put emphasis on surprise attack by concealing their chariots. Had the Egyptians come by way of Taanach or Jokneam, the Canaanite infantry would have feigned a retreat, allowing their chariotry, probably hidden near Megiddo, to sweep suddenly over the enemy advancing across the open plain.

The battle proper took place on the morning of the Egyptian arrival on the Megiddo plain. The Canaanite chariotry now sped toward the Egyptians who were drawn up in three wings. The Canaanites were repulsed, the battle turning into their complete and utter rout. The pursuing Egyptians were so close on the heels of the fleeing Canaanites that the people of Megiddo feared to open the gates of the city, instead hauled their comrades up the walls by ropes. Had the Egyptians not tarried over loot in the Canaanite field-camp outside the city, as related in Egyptian records, they would have conquered Megiddo then and there. But the booty taken in the field included 924 chariots.

Megiddo itself fell after a siege of seven months. Only eight years later Kedesh on the Orontes was taken, in Thutmose III's sixth campaign. In his later campaigns, he reached Mitanni (Naharin), thus restoring all of Palestine and Syria to Egyptian control.

After a victorious campaign, Egyptian kings would carve "topographical lists" of conquered cities on their temple walls, showing rows of vanquished city kings being brought before the pharaoh as captives, each with the name of his city written below. The list of Thutmose III is the oldest, comprising a most important source on the cities of Palestine. It includes 119 names, 65 of which have been reasonably identified; these latter are indicated in the map. The list possibly includes the names of several regions rather than the names of their central cities, as in the case of Negeb (Gerar?), "The Valley" (Rehob?), and Galilee (Kedesh?). The order of the list is evidently in accord with the Egyptian administrative division of the Land of Canaan, organized around three centers: Gaza, Sumur, and Kumidi.

INSCRIPTION, THUTMOSE III—KARNAK, EGYPT

THE BATTLE OF MEGIDDO

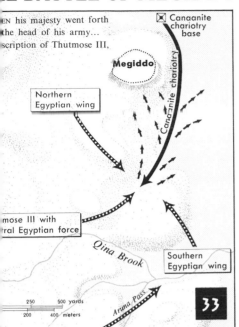

...EN his majesty went forth
...the head of his army...
...scription of Thutmose III,

Canaanite chariotry base ⊠

Megiddo

Northern Egyptian wing

Canaanite chariotry

...mose III with ...ral Egyptian force

Qina Brook

Southern Egyptian wing

Aruna Pass

250 500 yards
200 400 meters

33

...CRIPTIONS, THUTMOSE III—KARNAK,
...EL BARKAL, EGYPT

...of list of cities conquered by Thutmose III
...ef in temple of Ammon at Karnak)

THE CITY-LISTS
OF THUTMOSE III

CITY LISTS, THUTMOSE III—KARNAK, EGYPT

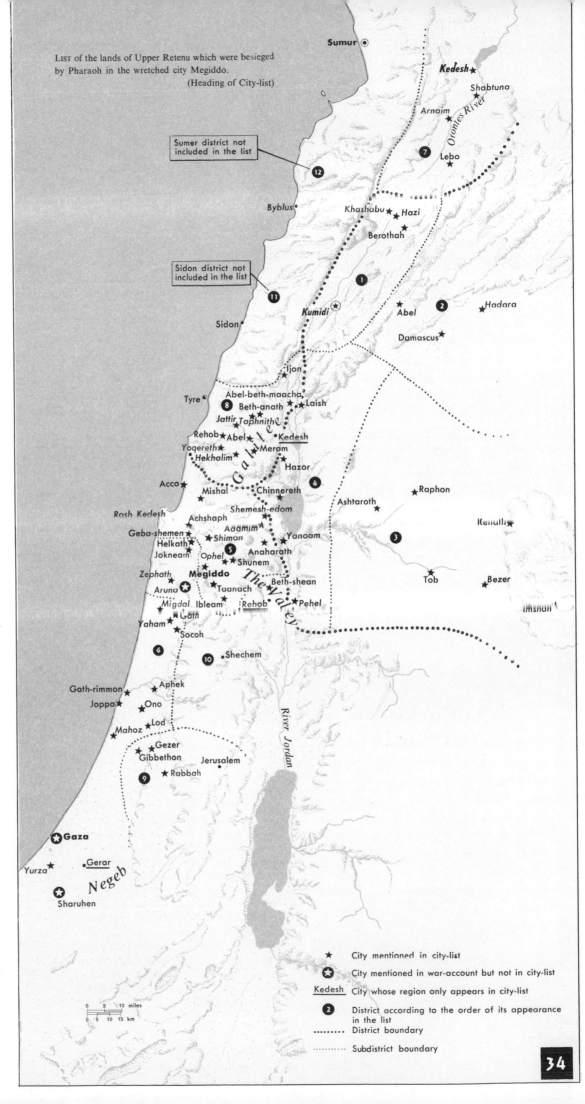

LIST of the lands of Upper Retenu which were besieged
by Pharaoh in the wretched city Megiddo.
(Heading of City-list)

Sumur ◉

Kedesh ★

Shabtuna ★

Arnaim ★   Lebo ★   Orontes River

7

Sumer district not included in the list

12

Khashabu ★   Hazi ★

Byblus •

Berothah ★

Sidon district not included in the list

1

11

Kumidi ★

Abel ★   **2**   Hadara ★

Damascus ★

Sidon •

Ijon ★

Abel-beth-maacha ★

Tyre ★   **8**   Beth-anath ★   Laish ★

Jattir ★ Taphnith ★

Rehob ★   Abel ★   Kedesh ★

Yogereth ★   Merom ★

Hekhalim ★   _Galilee_

Hazor ★

Acco ★   **4**

Misha! ★   Chinnereth ★   Ashtaroth ★   Raphon ★

Shemesh-edom ★   Kenath ★

Rosh Kedesh ★   Achshaph ★   Adamim ★

Geba-shemen ★   Shimon ★   Yanoam ★   **3**

Helkath ★   **5**   Anaharath ★

Jokneam ★   Ophel ★   Shunem ★   Bezer ★

Zephath ★   Megiddo ✪   _The Valley_   Beth-shean ★   Tob ★

Aruna ✪   Taanach ★   Rehob ★   Pehel ★   Imshah

Migdal Ibleam ★

Gath ★

Yaham ★   Socoh ★

6

10   Shechem ★

Gath-rimmon ★   Aphek ★

Joppa ★   Ono ★

Mahoz ★   Lod ★

Gezer ★   River Jordan

Gibbethon ★   Jerusalem ★

9   Rabbah ★

Gaza ✪

Yurza ★   • Gerar

Negeb

✪

Sharuhen

★ City mentioned in city-list

✪ City mentioned in war-account but not in city-list

Kedesh City whose region only appears in city-list

2 District according to the order of its appearance in the list

······ District boundary

- - - Subdistrict boundary

0 5 10 miles
0 5 10 15 km

34

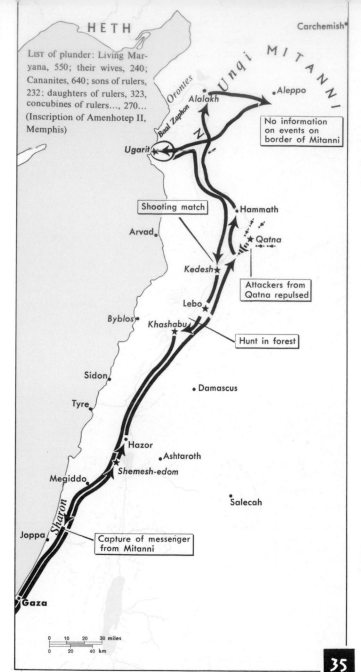

No information on events on border of Mitanni

Shooting match

Attackers from Qatna repulsed

Hunt in forest

Capture of messenger from Mitanni

THE FIRST CAMPAIGN OF AMENHOTEP II
1431 B.C.

FOR three centuries after the victory of Thutmose III, Egyptian rule in Palestine was consolidated. In addition to Gaza, Sumur and Kumidi, cities such as Joppa, Beth-shean and Ullaza became Egyptian bases. The Egyptians did not interfere with the running of the other Canaanite city-kingdom, as long as they accepted Egyptian authority, paid tribute, secured the roads passing through their territories and supplied chariots, auxiliary troops, food, and other provisions for the Egyptian army. This form of rule was effective as long as Egypt was powerful. The minute Egypt was troubled internally the system began to collapse. Canaanite unrest was fomented by Mitanni and—in the Amarna period and later—by the Hittites, Egypt's greatest rivals in Syria.

Already in the days of Amenhotep II, the son of Thutmose III, cracks began to appear in the structure of the Egyptian empire. To subdue revolts in Canaan, the king was forced to set out on two successive campaigns. Amenhotep—more than any other pharaoh—set up monuments to glorify his personal valor, passing over, however, some of the major but less complementary events of his campaigns, especially his defeats. These must be gleaned from between the lines. During his first campaign, the revolt reached Shemesh-edom (later Adamah of Naphtali) in Lower Galilee. From here Amenhotep unsuccessfully attempted an invasion of Mitanni, as is hinted by the passage: "His majesty, going *south*, reached Ni (in the northern Orontes Valley)." The northernmost city conquered by Amenhotep II was Ugarit. On his return through the valley of Lebanon he subdued Kedesh, hunted in the forest of Lebo, and conquered Khashabu. When he was passing through the Sharon plain, a messenger of the king of Mitanni (the "Prince of Naharin") fell into Amenhotep's hands; this messenger carried a letter, in the form of a clay tablet tied and slung around his neck; it undoubtedly dealt with matters concerning the Mitanni-inspired rebellion.

MONUMENTS, AMENHOTEP II—KARNAK, MEMPHIS, AMADA, ELEPHANTINE, EGYPT

35

THE SECOND CAMPAIGN OF AMENHOTEP II
1429 B.C.

THE FAILURE of the first campaign may be inferred by Amenhotep II's setting out two years later on a second campaign in order to put down revolts in the Sharon and in the Jezreel Valley. A fragment of an Egyptian monument of about this period, mentioning a victory over foreigners from Mitanni, was found at Kinnereth. This may relate to Amenhotep II's second campaign and may indicate the southern extent of the Mitannian upheaval within the Egyptian province.

The lists of booty of the two campaigns of Amenhotep reflect the make-up of the population of the Holy Land in this period. The local inhabitants are called Horites (Hurru). They were led by city rulers, noble families, and a chariot-warrior class called *maryanu*. The Apiru-Habiru (=Hebrews; see map 39), seminomads, and Shasu marauders (Bedouin) constituted a large part of the population. The term Canaanite in this period refers only to the merchant class which ruled in the coastal cities. The term was later (from the fourteenth century B.C. on) applied to the province as a whole forcing the older names Retenu and Hurru into obscurity.

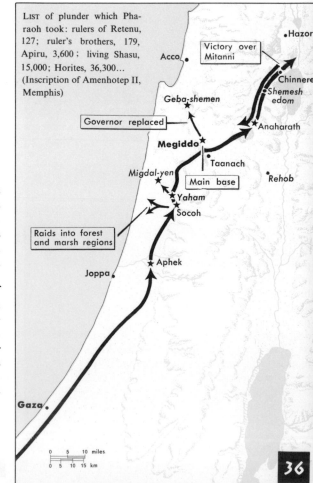

Victory over Mitanni

Governor replaced

Main base

Raids into forest and marsh regions

MONUMENTS, AMENHOTEP II—KARNAK, MEMPHIS, EGYPT

36

EGYPT IN THE AMARNA AGE

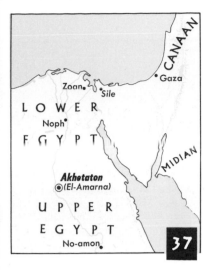

37

An El-Amarna Letter

THE KINGS OF CANAAN IN THE AMARNA AGE

CA. 1400 TO 1350 B.C.

THE El-Amarna Letters are a most informative source on the Land of Canaan. These were part of the royal archives of the Egyptian kings Amenhotep III and his son Amenhotep IV (Ikhnaton), found at El-Amarna, the capital of Egypt under the latter king. They comprise 350 clay tablets written in Accadian, the *lingua franca* of that period; about one-half of them are letters to these kings from Canaanite rulers.

At this period there was peace between Egypt and Mitanni. Mitanni was occupied with struggles to the north, and Ikhnaton with his religious reformations in Egypt proper. There was no need for Egyptian punitive expeditions; so long as Egyptian rule in the province remained secure, the Egyptian king cared little for affairs in Canaan. The letters of the Canaanite kings are full of mutual accusations; they reveal a picture of cities ruling over small areas, each endeavoring to extend its dominion at the expense of its neighbors. Egyptian rule was challenged only in middle Syria, under Hittite pressure, the latter power having meanwhile succeeded Mitanni as the major contestant for power in this area. A kingdom arose in the mountains of Lebanon, under the older name Amurru, extending its rule over the cities of the Canaanite coast, from Sumur to Byblos. Amurru with time became a Hittite vassal.

EL-AMARNA LETTERS

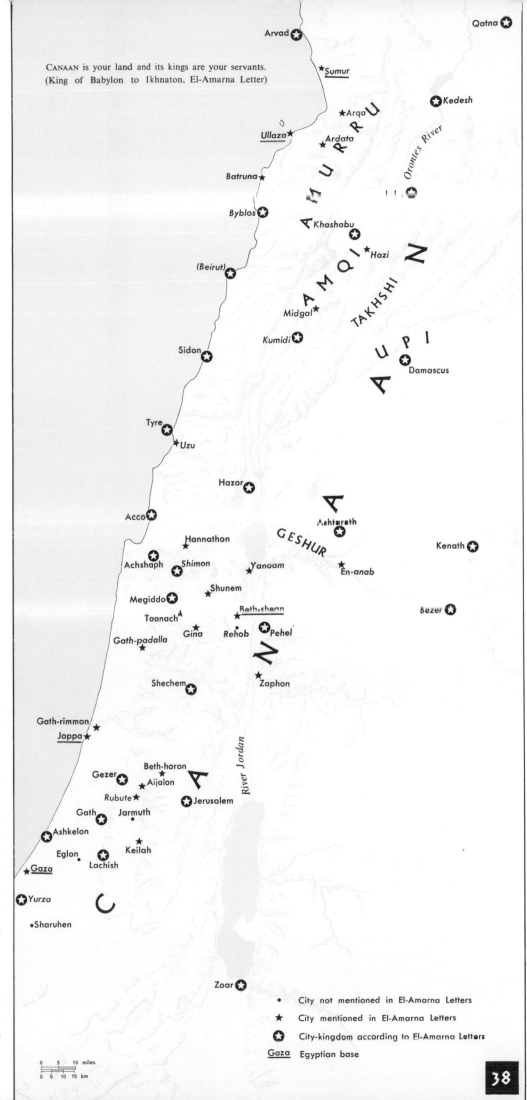

CANAAN is your land and its kings are your servants.
(King of Babylon to Ikhnaton, El-Amarna Letter)

- City not mentioned in El-Amarna Letters
★ City mentioned in El-Amarna Letters
✪ City-kingdom according to El-Amarna Letters
Gaza Egyptian base

0   5   10 miles
0 5 10 15 km

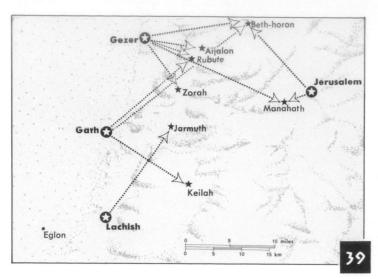

JERUSALEM AND THE CITIES OF THE SHEPHELAH IN THE AMARNA LETTERS
CA. 1400 TO 1350 B.C.

C ITY-KINGDOMS extending over relatively large areas thrived especially in the hill-region, where settlement was sparse. In their conflicts they sought the aid of seminomadic tribes, the Apiru-Habiru who menaced the security of Palestine. The southern hill-country was dominated by the kingdom of Jerusalem; its main rivals in the Shephelah were Gezer, Gath, and Lachish. In one of his letters, Abdu-heba king of Jerusalem accuses Milkilu king of Gezer and Shuwardata king of Gath of conquering Rubute (Beth-shemesh?) and threatening Bet-ninib, a city in the Land of Jerusalem, probably Beth-horon.

EL-AMARNA LETTERS

★ City-kingdom according to El-Amarna Letters

◁⋯⋯⋯⋯ Intercity connection according to El-Amarna Letters

THE KINGDOM OF SHECHEM AND ITS NEIGHBORS IN THE AMARNA LETTERS
CA. 1400 TO 1350 B.C.

T HE rule of Labayu, king of Shechem, extended over the whole of Mount Ephraim and encroached upon the territories of Jerusalem and Gezer, as well as the Sharon and the Jezreel. One letter states that Labayu destroyed Shunem. The Egyptian authorities put an end to his activities and ordered that he be brought to Egypt. While being transfered from Megiddo to Acco for deportation by ship, he escaped at Hannathon, but was killed during flight by the people of Gina. This most likely occurred at the "ascent of Gur which is by Ibleam," on the way to Beth-haggan, where Jehu slew Ahaziah, king of Judah, more than five hundred years later (2 Kings 9:27).

Shunem was not rebuilt, but the Egyptians took care to plough its fields to assure their treasury of continued income. The agricultural work was carried out by the King of Megiddo through a corvée from Japha-Japhia at the southern edge of Lower Galilee. In the days of the Israelite settlement, Shunem was included among the cities of Issachar, and Japhia is found on its border (Josh. 19:12, 18). How this tribe settled under the tutelage of the Canaanite cities in the Jezreel Valley is intimated in the Blessing of Jacob: "Issachar is a strong ass, crouching between the sheepfolds; he saw that a resting place was good, and that the land was pleasant; so he bowed his shoulder to bear, and became a slave at forced labor" (Gen. 49:14–15).

EL-AMARNA LETTERS

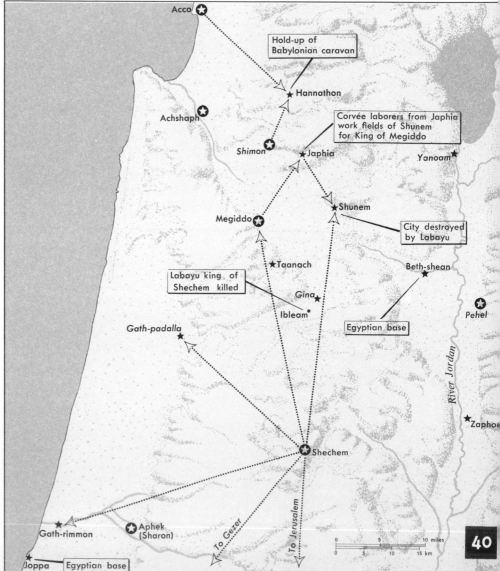

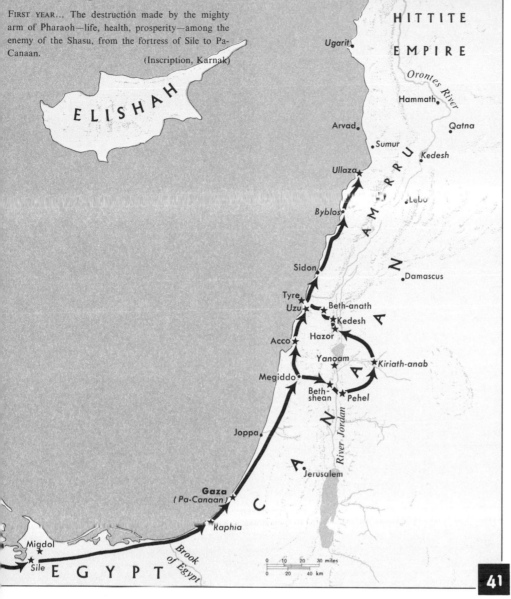

First year... The destruction made by the mighty arm of Pharaoh—life, health, prosperity—among the enemy of the Shasu, from the fortress of Sile to Pa-Canaan.

(Inscription, Karnak)

HITTITE EMPIRE

Ugarit

Orontes River

Hammath

ELISHAH

Arvad
Sumur
Qatna

Kedesh

Ullaza

Lebo

Byblos

Sidon
Damascus

Tyre
Uzu
Beth-anath
Kedesh

Acco
Hazor

Yanoam
Kiriath-anab

Megiddo

Beth-shean
Pehel

River Jordan

Joppa

Jerusalem

Gaza
(Pa-Canaan)

Raphia

Migdol

Sile   E G Y P T   *Brook of Egypt*

41

₣ EXPEDITION OF SETI I
THE LAND OF CANAAN
3 B.C.

▬ Egyptian force

◂◂◂ Canaanite force

MONUMENT, SETI I—BETH-SHEAN; RELIEFS—KARNAK; VARIOUS CITY LISTS—EGYPT

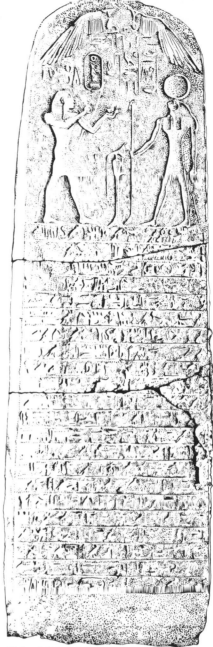

Stele of Seti I from Beth-shean

ON this day Pharaoh was told: The wretched enemy in the city of Hamath... holds the city of Beth-shean by treaty with Elah of Pehel. He does not allow the ruler of Rehob to leave his city.

(Beth-shean stele of Seti I)

A PART OF THE CAMPAIGN OF SETI I
IN THE REGION OF BETH-SHEAN
1303 B.C.

GREAT EFFORTS to secure Egyptian domination over the Land of Canaan were made in the thirteenth century by Seti I, Rameses II, and Merneptah, pharaohs of the nineteenth dynasty. In the first year of his reign, Seti had reached as far north as Ullaza, an important port city on the Lebanese coast. A victory stele found at Beth-shean describes part of this campaign, in the region of the Egyptian base there. Another monument, also from Beth-shean, tells of the victory of Seti I over Apiru at Mount Yarmuta (biblical Jarmuth or Remeth), which was within the tribal area of Issachar (Josh. 19:21; 21:29). Apiru tribes were to be found throughout the hill regions during the late fourteenth century B.C.

The temple reliefs of Seti depict cities in the Land of Canaan, showing topographical details which aid us in their identification; thus, Yanoam is shown surrounded by a river, evidently the Jordan.

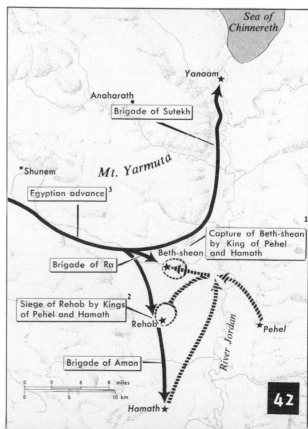

Sea of Chinnereth

Yanoam

Anaharath
Brigade of Sutekh

Shunem
Mt. Yarmuta

Egyptian advance [3]

Capture of Beth-shean by King of Pehel and Hamath

Brigade of Ra
Beth-shean [1]

Siege of Rehob by Kings of Pehel and Hamath
Rehob [2]
Pehel

Brigade of Amon
River Jordan

Hamath

42

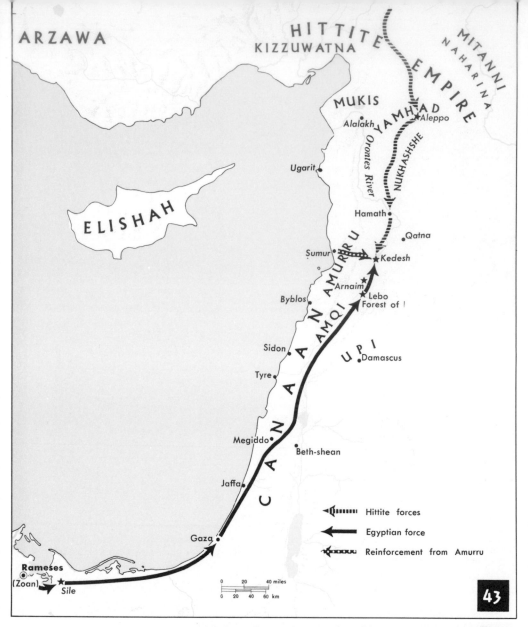

ARZAWA

HITTITE EMPIRE
KIZZUWATNA

MITANNI
NAHARINA

MUKIS

YAMHAD

Alalakh • Aleppo

Ugarit •

NUKHASHSHE

ELISHAH

Orontes River

Hamath

• Qatna

Sumur •   ★ Kedesh

A M U R R U

Arnaim ★
      ★ Lebo
Forest of

Byblos •

A M Q I

U P I

Sidon •

• Damascus

C A N A A N

Tyre •

Megiddo •
      • Beth-shean

Jaffa •

Gaza •

Rameses
(Zoan)
      ★ Sile

◄▐▐▐▐▐ Hittite forces

◄━━━━ Egyptian force

◄▌▌▌▌▌ Reinforcement from Amurru

0   20   40 miles
0 20 40 60 km

43

AND NOW the wretched enemy from Heth, together with many foreign lands, lay concealed and prepared for battle north-east of Kedesh.

(Kedesh Victory Poem)

THE EXPEDITION OF RAMESES II TO KEDESH
1286 B.C.

THE decisive war between the Hittites and Egypt over the rule of Syria took place in the fifth year of the reign of Rameses II. The Hittite army was concealed behind the tel of Kedesh on the Orontes, but Rameses believed false information, obtained from two Bedouin, that the Hittites were to be found far to the north in the region of Aleppo. After setting up his camp, along with one of his divisions, the Hittite chariotry burst forth into a second Egyptian division marching on the road. The remaining two divisions were at that time on the other side of the river. The Hittites immediately began to loot the Egyptian camp; Pharaoh and his personal guard put up a stout defense with their backs to the river. Just when the battle seemed lost, an unexpected reinforcement, in the form of an Egyptian "commando" unit from Amurru, arrived and surprised the Hittites engrossed in their looting; they were forced from the camp, Rameses thus being given the opportunity to reorganize his army. Finally the Hittites found themselves between two Egyptian divisions and beat a hasty retreat to Kedesh. These details are given by Rameses who regarded the battle as a brilliant Egyptian victory. This account, however, is at variance with the actual events. He in fact incurred heavy losses and was quite fortunate in being able to extricate himself, with the greater part of his army intact. The Hittites remained in control of Kedesh; and they also held sway over the kingdom of Amurru to the west.

RELIEFS—THEBES, LUXOR, ABU SIMBEL; INSCRIPTIONS—THEBES

THE BATTLE OF KEDESH
1286 B.C.

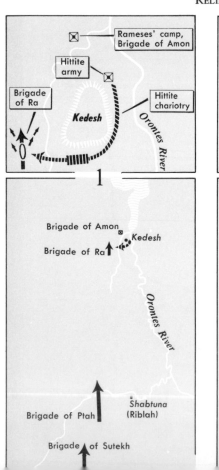

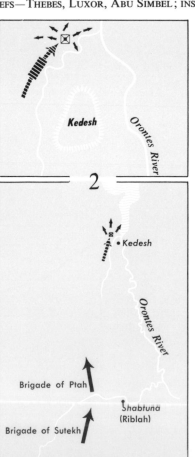

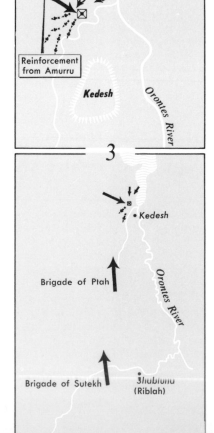

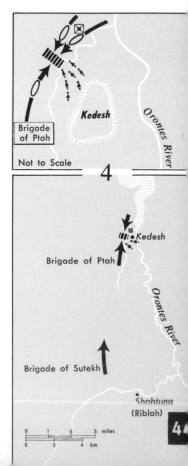

I HAVE describe for you the nature of a *mahir*. I have outlined for you the roads of the foreign lands. I have listed for you the foreign lands and the cities in their proper order.

(Papyrus Anastasi I)

THE LAND OF CANAAN IN THE DAYS OF RAMESES II

BEFORE 1270 B.C.

LATER WARS weakened both powers, and in Rameses' twenty-first year (about 1270 B.C.) a peace treaty was signed defining the border between them in middle Syria, south of Kedesh. This is reflected in the biblical borders of the Land of Canaan (Lev. 34:1–12) (see map 50)

A satirical document preserved from the days of Rameses II (Papyrus Anastasi I) describing the trials and tribulations of an unsuccessful scribe on the roads of Canaan provides us with an instructive picture of the major cities and highways in this period. One interesting passage has a description of the narrow pass of Aruna, relating the hazards posed by Bedouin hostility. In this passage, mention is made of the "Chief" of Asher. Although this locality is not specifically defined, it is hardly incidental that the name of this Israelite tribe appears in connection with a pass through the hill-region.

In the inscriptions of Rameses II, Dibon and another town in Moab together with various tribes in Meir are first mentioned, evidence of the settlement of Moab and Edom. Excavations at Timna, moreover, have revealed the existence of Egyptian copper-mines employing local labour, including Midianites.

Gaza   Egyptian base

★   City mentioned in Papyrus Anastasi I

—   Major highway

◀—   Route described in Papyrus Anastasi I

45

CANAAN is plagued by every evil. Ashkelon is carried off, Gezer taken, Yanoam is like that which is not, Israel is desolate, its seed is nought.

(Merneptah Stele)

RUS ANASTASI I—EGYPT

THE CAMPAIGN OF MERNEPTAH

1220 B.C.

WE possess no additional information on Palestine during the reign of Rameses II, though his son Merneptah again set out on a campaign to the Land of Canaan; in a victory poem, the name Israel appears for the first and only time on Egyptian monuments. This inscription, called the "Israel stele," is definite evidence of the presence of Israelites in the Land of Canaan at about 1220 B.C.

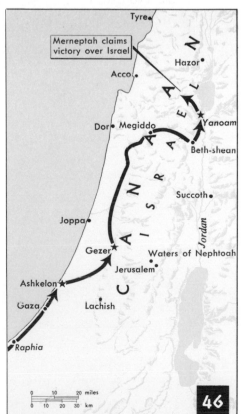

Merneptah claims victory over Israel

46

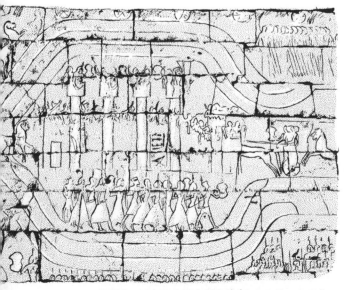

Kedesh-on-the-Orontes (relief of Rameses II at Luxor)

VICTORY STELE OF MERNEPTAH —THEBES, EGYPT

THE SALE OF JOSEPH
14TH CENTURY B.C.

A CARAVAN of Ishmaelites coming from Gilead, with their camels bearing gum, balm, and myrrh, on their way to carry it down to Egypt.

(Genesis 37:25)

Ishmaelite caravan to Egypt

Megiddo

Dothan

Joseph sold into slavery

Shechem

Joppa

Beth-el

Jerusalem

Gilead

Sons of Jacob with flocks

To Egypt

Gaza

Hebron

Dead Sea

Beer-sheba

0 5 10 miles
0 5 10 15 km

47   GEN. 37

they did not come as conquerors. The circumstances of their journey and settling in the Land of Goshen are more suited to the El-Amarna period, or thereabouts.

The passage "Now there arose a new king over Egypt, who did not know Joseph" (Ex. 1:8) evidently relates to Rameses II, during whose rule the people of Israel left Egypt. Rameses II is the outstanding king of the nineteenth dynasty, which ruled Egypt at the start of the thirteenth century B.C. His new capital, named "Rameses," was built in place of the older Zoan (Tanis), using forced labor in its construction. The Israelites may have taken advantage of Rameses' weakness after his defeat at Kedesh, though we do not have sufficient information to ascertain this definitely.

The Israelites did not pass along the short section of the Via Maris from Egypt, called in the Bible the "way of [to] the Land of the Philistines" (the name is of a later period); they avoided it because of the many Egyptian stations and fortresses along the way. Migdol and Baal-zephon, mentioned at the start of the Exodus (Ex. 14:2; Num. 33:7), are known from Egyptian sources as fortresses at the northeastern edge of the Delta, and it is thus clear that the Exodus started in the north, and that it is in this region that Yam Suph (the Reed Sea) is located (in later periods the name denoted the gulf of Elath—1 Kings 9:26; and so forth).

None of the many desert encampments (Num. 33:8–34) has been located definitely, and the locations of those shown in the map are conjectural. Only that of Kadesh-barnea, the region rich in springs at the southern edge of the Land of Canaan, is positive. This oasis was the center of Israelite settlement in the desert, and around it the tribes first rallied as one nation having a common spiritual vision. The many stages in the desert are evidently scattered throughout the Sinai Peninsula, which in biblical times was called the wilderness of Paran. According to tradition, Mount Sinai is one of the granite mountains in the south of the peninsula, the region where the ancient Egyptians mined turquoise and copper.

T WO major events at the dawn of Israelite history are the Exodus from Egypt and the encampment at Mount Sinai.

The story of Joseph serves to explain the journey of the people of Israel to Egypt. Journeys of nomadic tribes during years of drought to find pasturage for their flocks were common. From Egyptian documents we know of such movements through border fortresses, collectively referred to in the Bible as Shur (= the wall) of Egypt. Scholars are divided in opinion as to when the Israelites journeyed to Egypt; some place the event in the Hyksos period, as did Josephus. It is, however, difficult to believe that their stay in Egypt lasted such a long time; and it should be remembered that, according to the story,

EXODUS AND THE ROUTE OF THE WANDERING
EARLY 13TH CENTURY B.C.

GOD did not lead them by way of the land of the Philistines, although that was near; for God said, "Lest the people repent when they see war, and return to Egypt.

(Exodus 13:17)

He rebuked the Red Sea and it became dry . . .

(Psalms 106:9)

Gaza

Baal-zephon

Reed Sea

Migdol

Way to the Land of the Philistines

Rameses (Zoan)

Etham

Way of the Atharim

Arad

Shur of Egypt

Wilderness of Shur

GOSHEN

Pithom

Succoth

Way to Shur

Kadesh-barnea

Way to the Arabah

Wilderness of Zin

Wilderness of Paran

Way to the Reed Sea

On

Noph

Way to the Hill-country of the Amorites

Way to Mt. Seir

Timna

Abronah

Jotbathah

Elath (Ezion-geber)

Nile River

(Serabit el-Khadem)

Dophkah

Hazeroth

Paran

Rephidim

Wilderness of Sinai

Mt. Sinai

Di-zahab

Reed Sea

MIDIAN

0 10 20 30 miles
0 20 40 km

48

KADESH-BARNEA
EARLY 13TH CENTURY B.C.

So YOU remained at Kadesh many days...

(Deuteronomy 1:46)

Main spring

Azmon

Karka

Kadesh

En-mishpat

Kadesh-barnea

Hazar-addar

49

0 2 4 miles
0 2 4 6 km

NUM. 20:13; DEUT. 1:19-46

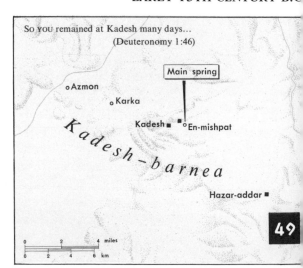

⊛ Capital

■ Border fortress

✪ City and border fortress

—— Major highway

Ex. 12:37—19:1;
Num. 10:11—12; 33:1–36

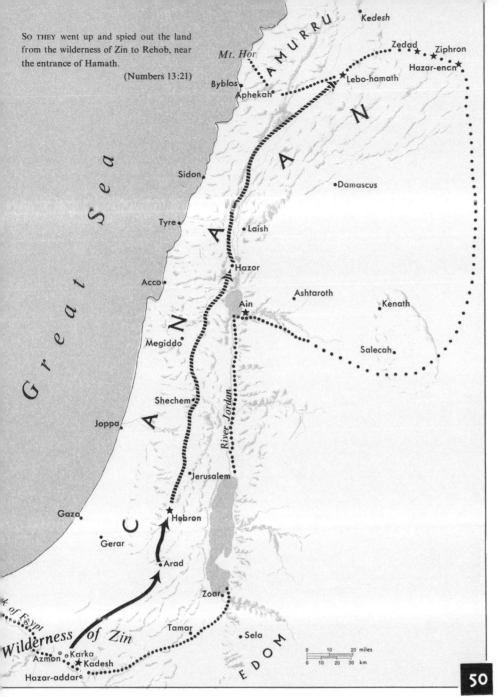

So THEY went up and spied out the land from the wilderness of Zin to Rehob, near the entrance of Hamath.

(Numbers 13:21)

THE TRAVELS OF THE SPIES AND THE LIMITS OF THE LAND OF CANAAN

EARLY 13TH CENTURY B.C.

ALL attempts to penetrate into the Land of Canaan began from Kadesh-barnea. It was from here that Moses sent out the spies. The story of the spies relates mainly to Hebron and Caleb, who had settled nearby, though the final Israelite objective is mentioned as being Lebo-hamath (the "entrance of Hamath"), at the northern extremity of Canaan. The borders of the Land of Canaan, coveted by the tribes, are described in detail in Ex. 34:1–12. The description of the borders begins at the southeastern shore of the Dead Sea and continues through Kadesh-barnea to the Brook of Egypt. In the north is Lebo-hamath, ancient Lebo, later included in the neo-Hittite kingdom of Hamath (thus "Lebo-hamath"). From thence it passed on to desert posts far to the northeast of Damascus, then descended south and west to the Sea of Chinnereth, returning to the Dead Sea through the Jordan Valley. This list of borders does not coincide with Israelite settlement in any period, but rather reflects the Egyptian province of Canaan, as defined in the Egyptian-Hittite treaty signed following the battle of Kedesh. These, then, were the borders of the Land of Canaan which the Israelite tribes found upon their arrival.

```
••••••••••    Border
• • • • •      Conjectured border
⟵             Spies' route
-◁▭▭▭▭    Continuation of route to border of Land of Canaan
```

50

NUM. 13; 34:1–12
JOSH. 13:4
EZEK. 47:19

WHEN the Canaanite, the king of Arad, who dwelt in the Negeb, heard that Israel was coming by the way of Atharim, he fought against Israel...

(Numbers 21:1)

THE BATTLE OF ARAD

EARLY 13TH CENTURY B.C.

THE ISRAELITES first attempted to penetrate from the south; this failed because of the strong resistance offered by the inhabitants of the Negeb, the Canaanites and the Amalekites who blocked their way northward through the eastern Negeb to the Judean hills. According to the Bible, the area was dominated by the king of Arad; the place-name Hormah (Hebrew *herem*, destruction) is associated with the Israelite defeat.

NUM. 14:44–45; 21:1–3; 33:40; DEUT. 1:41–44

Brickmaking (tomb painting at Thebes, fifteenth century B.C.)

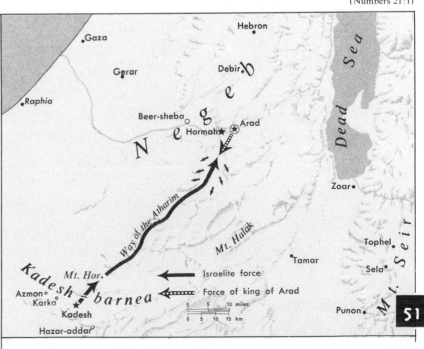

⟵   Israelite force
-◁▭▭   Force of king of Arad

51

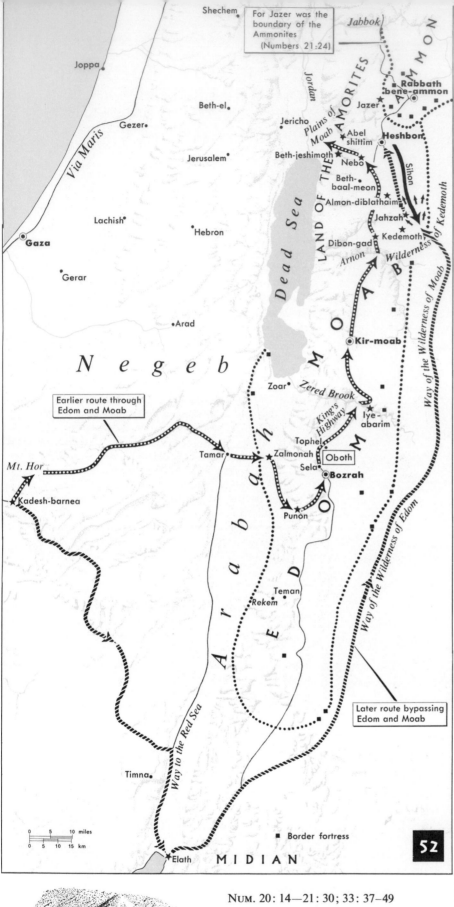

For Jazer was the boundary of the Ammonites (Numbers 21:24)

Earlier route through Edom and Moab

Later route bypassing Edom and Moab

■ Border fortress

52

Num. 20: 14—21: 30; 33: 37—49

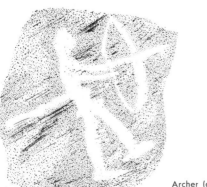

Archer (graffito in Negeb)

Come to Heshbon, let it be built, let the city of Sihon be established.

(Numbers 21:27)

THE PENETRATION INTO TRANSJORDAN

THE Israelite conquest began in eastern Transjordan, beyond the borders of the Land of Canaan. In this sparsely settled region, there were extensive lands for pasturage (Ex. 32:1–4). Peoples related to the Israelites had already settled in the southern parts of Transjordan, soon forming organized kingdoms—Edom, Moab, and Ammon. The Amorite kingdom of Heshbon was located between Moab and Ammon; its ruler, Shion, warred against Moab's first king and conquered the entire plateau of Moab to the Arnon River (Ex. 21:26). Moses exploited this political situation by asking the Kings of Moab and Edom to grant the Israelites passage through their lands on the King's Highway, to reach the territory of Sihon (Ex. 20:14–21; Judg. 11:17); when refused this permission, Moses turned southward to Elath, avoiding Edom and Moab, and then penetrated Sihon's kingdom from the eastern desert (the wilderness of Kedemoth). Since that time, the Arnon has been considered the traditional border between the Israelite tribes and Moab, even though Moab never accepted the fact and took every opportunity to regain control over "the plain," north of the Arnon.

In contrast, the picture revealed by the list of desert stations shows a direct route, passing through the heart of Edom and Moab to "the plains of Moab" opposite Jericho (Ex. 33:37–49). Many scholars are of the opinion that this list reflects a tradition of an older wave of immigration by several tribes, prior to the setting up of the Transjordanian kingdoms. The biblical traditions concerning the camp at Abel Shittim and the fierce war against the Midianites are connected with this movement, which probably took place in the fourteenth century B.C.

THE VIEW FROM MOUNT NEBO

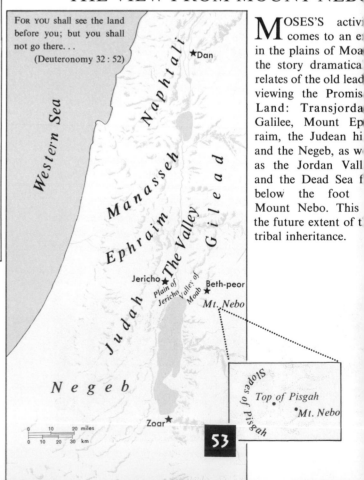

For you shall see the land before you; but you shall not go there...

(Deuteronomy 32:52)

MOSES'S activi[ty] comes to an e[nd] in the plains of Moa[b]; the story dramatica[lly] relates of the old lead[er] viewing the Promis[ed] Land: Transjorda[n], Galilee, Mount Ep[h]raim, the Judean hi[lls] and the Negeb, as w[ell] as the Jordan Vall[ey] and the Dead Sea f[ar] below the foot [of] Mount Nebo. This [is] the future extent of t[he] tribal inheritance.

53

Deut. 34: 1–3

So JOSHUA burned Ai, and made it for ever a heap of ruins, as it is to this day.

(Joshua 8:28)

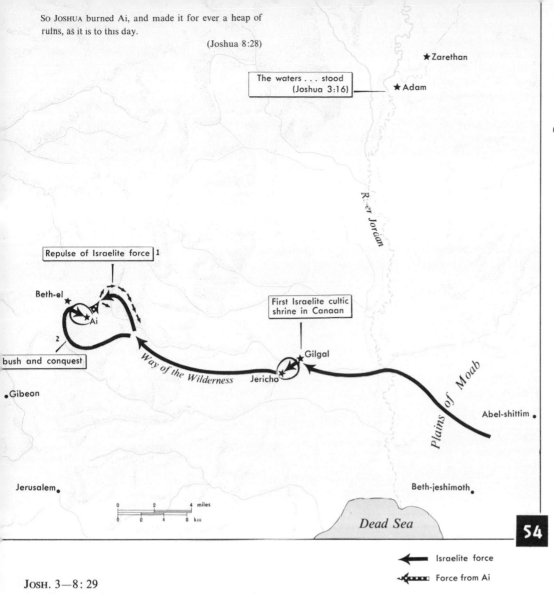

The waters . . . stood
(Joshua 3:16)

★ Zarethan

★ Adam

R. er Jordan

Repulse of Israelite force │1

Beth-el ★

★ Ai

2

bush and conquest

Way of the Wilderness

First Israelite cultic shrine in Canaan

Gilgal

Jericho

Plains of Moab

Gibeon ●

Jerusalem ●

Abel-shittim ●

Beth-jeshimoth ●

0   2   4 miles
0   4   6 km

Dead Sea

54

JOSH. 3—8:29

⟵ Israelite force

⟸ Force from Ai

THE NARRATIVE OF THE CONQUEST OF THE LAND OF CANAAN

THE conquest of the Land of Canaan begins with the crossing of the river Jordan; the first spot reached by the tribes was Gilgal, east of Jericho (Josh. 4:19). Gilgal was evidently the first place sanctified in the Land of Canaan, serving for a time as the center of the Israelite tribes; it was not by chance that Saul, the first Israelite king, was crowned there (1 Sam. 11:15).

Related to Gilgal are the stories of the conquests of Jericho and Ai. These stories contain many legendary shadings and historically they are enveloped in obscurity. The conquest of Jericho and Ai in this period has received no archaeological confirmation. At Ai this question is especially difficult, for the city seems to have been utterly destroyed a thousand years before the time of Joshua. Some scholars are of the opinion that, in the biblical narrative, Ai was substituted for nearby Beth-el; others assume that the source of the story of the conquest of Ai is a popular legend, surrounding the sanctuary at Gilgal, and was intended to explain the ruined cities dotting the landscape in this area. On the other hand, the conquest of Beth-el, described in I Judges: 22–26, has been substantiated by archaeological excavations.

THE REGION OF SHECHEM

THE continuation of the story of the conquest relates the building of the altar on Mount Ebal. This seems to reflect the tradition that, upon the conquest of the hill-country, the Israelite sanctuary at the oaks of Moreh, near Shechem, became the center for the Israelite tribes. Shechem had always been the capital of Mount Ephraim; even in the El-Amarna period, there were Hebrew tribes nearby; thus Shechem's central role at the start of the period of settlement.

DEUT. 11: 26–32; 27; JOSH. 8: 30–35

YOU SHALL set the blessing on Mount Gerizim and the curse on Mount Ebal.

(Deuteronomy 11:29)

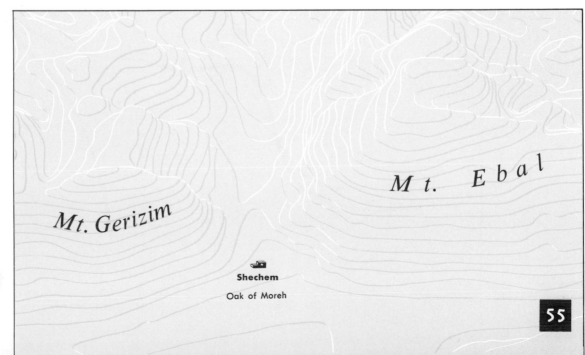

Mt. Gerizim

Mt. Ebal

Shechem

Oak of Moreh

55

IN reconstructing the Israelite conquest, it must be remembered that the Bible describes only select events; undoubtedly there were many more battles, not specifically mentioned, only echoes of which remain in the narrative. On the other hand, there is a tendency to ascribe to all of Israel events relating to single tribes. Thus Joshua is credited with many of the victories even though the family of Beriah, to which he belonged, lived in the hills of Beth-el between Naaran and Beth-Horon (Chron. 7:23–8), and his military activity was probably limited to the battle of Gibeon. This tendency is quite obvious in the stories on Hebron and Debir, whose conquest is ascribed first to Caleb and Kenaz (Josh. 15:13–19; Judg. 1:12–15), then to Judah (Judg. 1:10–11), and finally to Joshua and the entire people of Israel (Josh. 10:36–39). The events ascribed to Joshua are presented in the Book of Joshua, whereas the deeds attributed to the various tribes were collected in the Book of Judges; thus, not always is it possible to ascertain the proper chronological order of events. Bits of information on the various tribal conquests are found in the first chapter of Judges; just because they seem not to fit into the general picture is no reason to doubt their historical validity.

The most accurate archaeological evidence related to the narrative of the conquest has been found at Lachish. In the stratum revealing the destruction of the Canaanite city, there was found a bowl bearing an Egyptian inscription dated to the fourth year of a pharaoh, the name not being given. The earliest pharaoh to whom this could refer is Merneptah (ruled 1224–1214 B.C.), and thus it may be safely assumed that Lachish did not fall to the Israelites before 1220 B.C. The excavations at Eglon (Tell el-Hesi) and Ashan (Tell Beit Mirsim), near

Lachish, also revealed Canaanite cities destroyed toward the end of the thirteenth century. Therefore, three phases can be discerned in the conquest of this southern part of the Land of Canaan:

1. *The battle of Gibeon.* Here the Israelites rallied around Joshua to come to the aid of the four Gibeonite cities, which had been attacked by a league of five southern Canaanite cities led by Jerusalem. The flight of the Canaanites down the steep descent of Beth-horon became an utter rout; this is retold in a victory poem, only a short part of which has been preserved in the Bible.

2. *The invasion of the southern tribes* in consequence of the foregoing victory. Judah apparently approached from the north and, after a victory near Bezek, conquered Jerusalem; the tribe did not occupy the city, but rather proceeded southward to the Judean hills and the Shephelah. Later, the Jebusites became firmly entrenched in Jerusalem; from whence they came and how they conquered the city remains unknown. The clans of Caleb and Kenaz probably came from the south, conquering the region of Hebron and Debir; Kenite clans settled the region of Arad, coming through the "city of palms" (not Jericho, but Zoar or Tamar). The tribe of Simeon, who came—probably with Judah—from the north, settled in the vicinity of Beersheba, from thence proceeding to conquer Hormah.

3. *The conquest of the cities of the southern Shephelah,* with Lachish at their center, was the last phase in the settlement of the southern tribes. Even the aid of the King of Gezer could not save Lachish from the Israelite onslaught. Makedah, an unidentified city in the Lachish region, was also conquered at this time. This conquest began upon the decline of the nineteenth Egyptian dynasty, at the end of Merneptah's reign, at a time when the Canaanites were deprived of a major protecting power.

THE BATTLE OF GIBEON
MID-13TH CENTURY B.C.

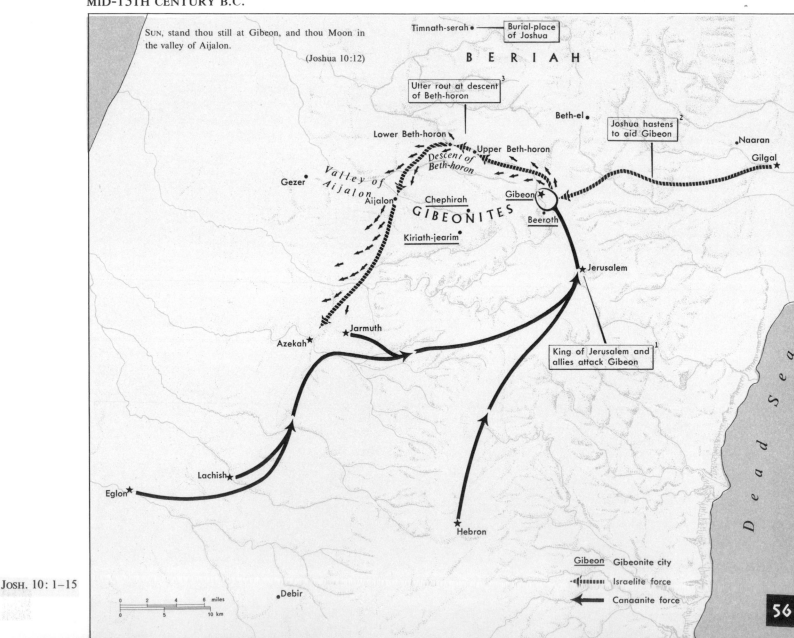

SUN, stand thou still at Gibeon, and thou Moon in the valley of Aijalon.

(Joshua 10:12)

Gibeon Gibeonite city

Israelite force

Canaanite force

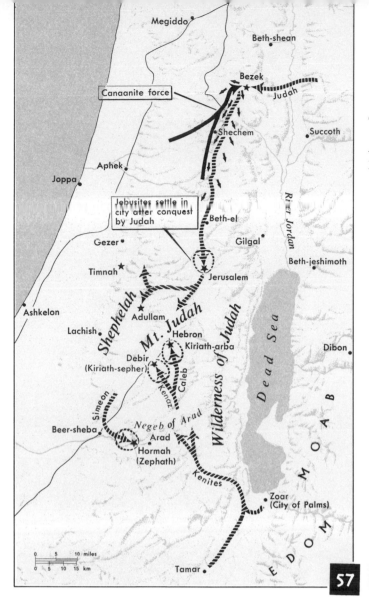

Megiddo

Beth-shean

Bezek

Canaanite force

Judah

Shechem

Succoth

Aphek

Joppa

Beth-el

Jebusites settle in
city after conquest
by Judah

Gezer

Gilgal

Beth-jeshimoth

River Jordan

Timnah

Jerusalem

Ashkelon

Shephelah

Adullam

Mt. Judah

Lachish

Hebron

Kiriath-arba

Debir
(Kiriath-sepher)

Caleb

Kenaz

Wilderness of Judah

Dead Sea

Dibon

Simeon

Negeb of Arad

Beer-sheba

Arad

Hormah
(Zephath)

Kenites

M O A B

Zoar
(City of Palms)

E D O M

0   5   10 miles
0   5   10   15 km

Tamar

THEN JUDAH went up and the LORD gave the Canaanites
and the Perizzites into their hand; and they defeated...
them at Bezek.

(Judges 1:4)

THE RISE OF JUDAH
AND THE SOUTHERN TRIBES
LATE 13TH CENTURY B.C.

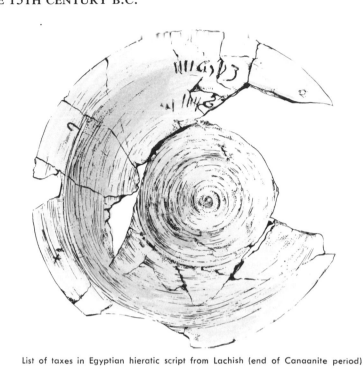

List of taxes in Egyptian hieratic script from Lachish (end of Canaanite period)

57 JOSH. 10: 36–39; JUDG. 1: 1–20;
GEN. 38; 1 CHRON. 2; 4

THE CONQUEST OF
THE CITIES OF
THE SHEPHELAH
END OF 13TH CENTURY B.C.

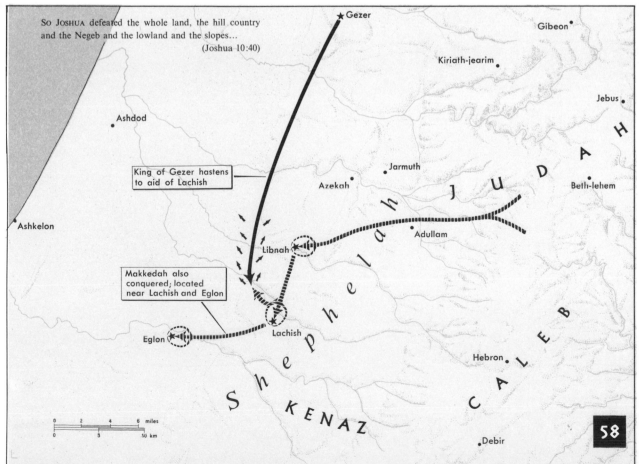

So JOSHUA defeated the whole land, the hill country
and the Negeb and the lowland and the slopes...

(Joshua 10:40)

Gezer

Gibeon

Kiriath-jearim

Jebus

Ashdod

King of Gezer hastens
to aid of Lachish

Jarmuth

Beth-lehem

Azekah

J U D A H

Ashkelon

Makkedah also
conquered; located
near Lachish and Eglon

Shephelah

Libnah

Adullam

Eglon

Lachish

Hebron

Shephelah

C A L E B

K E N A Z

Debir

◄◼▥▥▥▥ Israelite force

◄━━━ Canaanite force

JOSH. 10: 28–35

0   2   4   6 miles
0   5   10 km

58

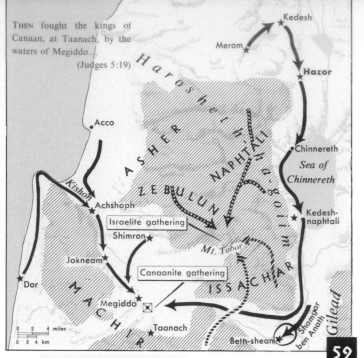

THEN fought the kings of Canaan, at Taanach, by the waters of Megiddo.

(Judges 5:19)

JOSH. 12: 19–23; JUDG. 4–5

THE WAR OF DEBORAH— THE DEPLOYMENT OF FORCES

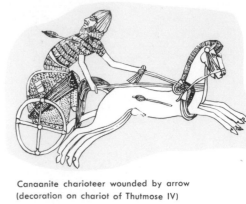

Canaanite charioteer wounded by arrow (decoration on chariot of Thutmose IV)

◄•••••••••	Israelite force
◄──────	Canaanite force
◄--------	Israelite volunteers
⊠	Canaanite chariot camp
▨	Area of continuous Israelite settlement

THE WAR OF DEBORAH— THE BATTLE

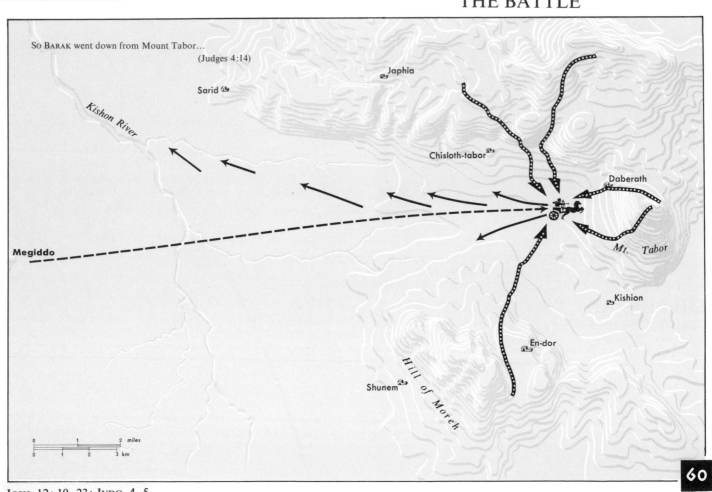

So BARAK went down from Mount Tabor...

(Judges 4:14)

JOSH. 12: 19–23; JUDG. 4–5

THE DEATH OF SISERA

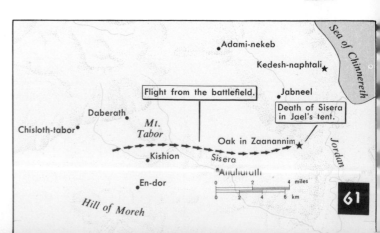

Flight from the battlefield.

Death of Sisera in Jael's tent.

JUDG. 4: 17–22; 5: 24–30

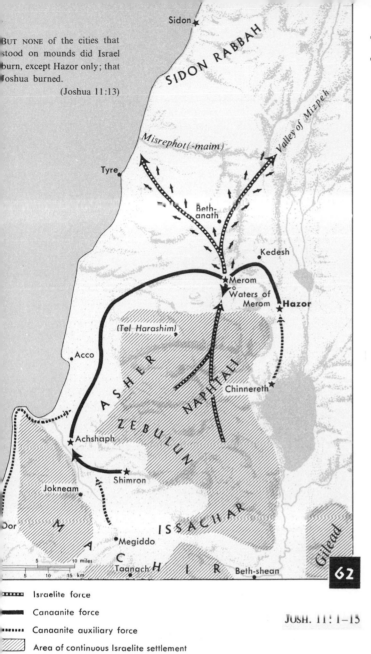

BUT NONE of the cities that stood on mounds did Israel burn, except Hazor only; that Joshua burned.

(Joshua 11:13)

62

JOSH. 11:1–15

▰▰▰▰ Israelite force

▬▬▬ Canaanite force

▪▪▪▪▪ Canaanite auxiliary force

▨▨▨ Area of continuous Israelite settlement

THE BATTLE OF
THE WATERS OF MEROM

—prose and poetry—which complement one another. The battle was preceded by the acts of Shamgar the son of Anath who, inspired by Jael, the wife of Heber the Kenite, smote the Philistines (Judg. 3:31). We may assume that he razed the Egyptian fortress at Beth-shean, where mercenary Philistine occupational forces were stationed (see figure on page 64). Consequently the Canaanites and the Israelites in the north remained without an overlord, leading to a decline in security along the roads (Judg. 5:6); after a period of Canaanite oppression, the Israelite tribes revolted, gathering on Mount Tabor for the decisive battle. This mountain was a holy site marking the borders of the tribes of Naphtali, Zebulun, and Issachar (Deut. 33:18–19). Most of the Israelite forces were from Naphtali and Zebulun, the Galilean tribes which suffered greatly at the hands of Sisera; volunteers also came from Issachar and the three tribes of Mount Ephraim. At this time, Machir still dwelt to the south of Jezreel, later moving to Transjordan where his clan was considered a part of Manasseh (see map 65). This, too, points to the early date of the battle. Kedesh in Naphtali, the birthplace of Barak, the son of Abinoam, is not the Canaanite Kedesh in Upper Galilee, but rather Khirbet Qedish, an extensive Israelite site overlooking the Sea of Chinnereth, only a few hours' walk from Mount Tabor.

The names of the individual Canaanite kings involved are not enumerated in Judges. (Most of them are probably given at the end of the list of vanquished kings in Joshua 12 in the section dealing with Galilee and the northern valleys.) Sisera gathered the Canaanite chariotry "at Taanach, by the waters of Megiddo" (Judg. 5:19), and after crossing the upper reaches of the Kishon River, proceeded toward Mount Tabor. The Canaanites were fully confident in the surprise element and striking power of their chariotry, a weapon entirely lacking in the Israelite camp. The chariots, however, could not negotiate Mount Tabor and the forested hills of the Galilee, and the initiative remained with Barak. The Israelites attacked on a rainy day: the defeat of the Canaanite chariotry turned into a rout, the Kishon, swollen by the downpour, preventing escape.

Sisera himself abandoned his chariot, which had become stuck in the mire, and fled on foot through the hills of Lower Galilee toward the Jordan Valley; he met his death in the tent of Jael, the wife of Heber the Kenite. The family of Heber was descended from Hobab, the father-in-law of Moses; its encampment located at Elon (=oak of) Zaanannim, on the border between Naphtali and Issachar (Josh. 19:33), was evidently a holy site, as its name would indicate (compare Elon [=oak of] Moreh, "the oak of the pillar at Shechem"). This assumption is supported by the discovery of an Israelite sanctuary at Arad, where the clan of Hobab also dwelt in the days of the conquest of the Holy Land (Judg. 1:16). Thus it is likely that Jael was a revered priestess, familiar to both Canaanites and Israelites. Sisera evidently sought refuge in her sanctuary.

In the battle of the waters of Merom the names of only four Canaanite cities are mentioned. Instead of Madon, which is unknown, we should read Merom, following the Greek of the Septuagint version. Merom (and the nearby waters of Merom) was where the Canaanites had gathered. We are not given details of the actual battle, which took place not far from Hazor; this conflict seems to have been the last Canaanite attempt to defend Upper Galilee. Farther south there were many Israelite settlements (such as Tel-harashim near Pekiin) founded at the start of the Israelite period; these undoubtedly put great pressure on the Canaanite regions, the situation coming to a head in the battle of the waters of Merom.

The excavations at Hazor prove that this city was utterly destroyed about the end of the thirteenth century B.C. On its ruins there settled squatters from these same Israelite villages in Galilee, as is indicated by the pottery found on the site. The destruction of Hazor also provides archaeological proof that the wars in the north occurred at the time of the decline of the nineteenth Egyptian dynasty, when Egyptian rule in Canaan was extremely weak, opening the way for the decisive wars between Israel and Canaan.

THE BIBLE describes two wars in which the Israelites vanquished the Canaanites in the north of the Holy Land: the battle of the waters of Merom and the war of Deborah. In both, Jabin, king of Hazor, led the league of Canaanite kings. Thus tradition relates the two conflicts to about the same period. Deborah's victory brought about the decline in power of Jabin, king of Canaan (Judg. 4:24), but the destruction of Hazor is connected with the battle of the waters of Merom (Josh. 11:10–11). Thus some scholars hold that Deborah's victory preceeded that of the waters of Merom, which latter appears in the Book of Joshua only because it was ascribed to Joshua later. Others consider that Sisera of Harosheth-hagoiim stood at the head of the Canaanites at the start of the war of Deborah, and that the tradition that Sisera was "the commander of ... Hazor" is secondary. No city, however, named Harosheth-hagoiim is known, either from the external sources or from the Bible; the various identifications of this "city" are entirely unfounded. There is much cause for caution here, as the other major cities, such as Hazor, Megiddo, Shimron, are well known from several sources. It is difficult to believe that an unknown city should suddenly appear at the head of all these older centers and then revert to obscurity. It would seem more reasonable to assume that the names Harosheth-hagoiim and Galil-hagoiim are synonymous and refer to the wooded hills (Hebrew: harosheth) inhabited by various nations and tribes, over which the Canaanites strove to rule, under the leadership of Hazor.

The war of Deborah is one of the few mentioned in the Bible which can be reconstructed in most of its details, thanks to the two accounts

AND THESE are the kings of the land whom Joshua and the people of Israel defeated on the west side of the Jordan...

(Joshua 12:7)

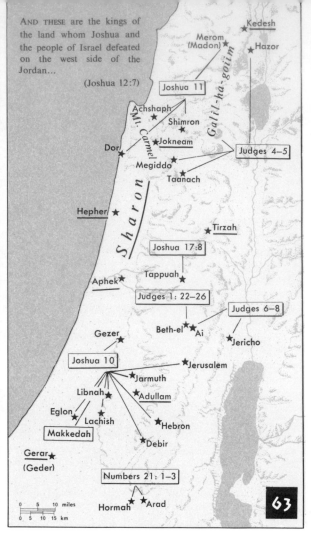

Kedesh — City or district not mentioned in account of conquest

JOSH. 12: 7–24

THE LIST OF KINGS OF CANAAN
12TH CENTURY B.C.

THE LIST of vanquished Canaanite kings is a summary of the stories of the conquest contained in the Books of Joshua and Judges. Its major importance lies in recording city names not mentioned in the actual accounts, and thus fills in some gaps in the picture of the wars of the conquest. Besides the kings of the north, the list contains several cities in Mount Ephraim and in the Sharon, Adullam in the Shephelah, and "the king of Goiim in Gilgal," or according to the Septuagint, "the king of Goiim in Galilee," that is, probably, Galil-hagoiim.

AND six hundred men of the tribe of Dan, armed w weapons of war, set forth from Zorah and Eshtac
(Judges 18

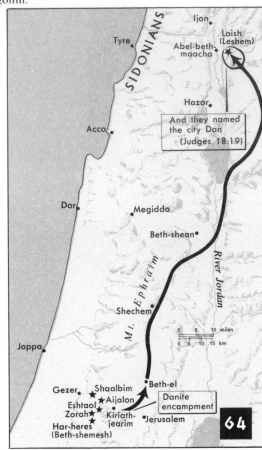

And they named the city Dan
(Judges 18:19)

Danite encampment

THE MIGRATION OF THE TRIBE OF DAN
EARLY 12TH CENTURY B.C.

NOT ALL the tribes succeeded in taking possession of their given inheritances during the early period of the settlement. An outstanding example is the movement of the tribe of Dan from the Shephelah (Judg. 1:34–35; note that the Philistines are not yet mentioned!), to the Canaanite city of Laish in the north. Although within the sphere of influence of Sidon (Judg. 18:7), Laish received no aid from its protector at the time of its greatest peril (Judg. 18:28). The Danites passed through Mount Ephraim within Israelite territory, foraging and looting on their way. After the conquest of the Canaanite city, they settled there, calling it Dan after their patronymic.

JUDG. 17—18; JOSH. 19:47

MACHIR THE SON OF MANASSEH
12TH CENTURY B.C.

OTHER movements of tribes and clans from one region to another are hinted at in passing, identical clan and place names occurring in different tribal contexts. Thus, the wanderings of Machir to northern Gilead are clearly reflected in the genealogical list of Manasseh. In the days of Deborah, Machir still dwelt in northern Mount Ephraim (Judg. 5:14), later becoming the "father" of Gilead, that is, the inhabitant of Gilead, while Manasseh inherited his place west of the Jordan. This explains the strange phenomenon that clans settled in northern Mount Ephraim, and still to be found there in the period of the Israelite Monarchy (see map 137), were included in the genealogical list as sons of Transjordanian Machir and Gilead.

NUM. 32: 39–40;
JOSH. 17: 1–6; 1 CHRON. 7: 14–19

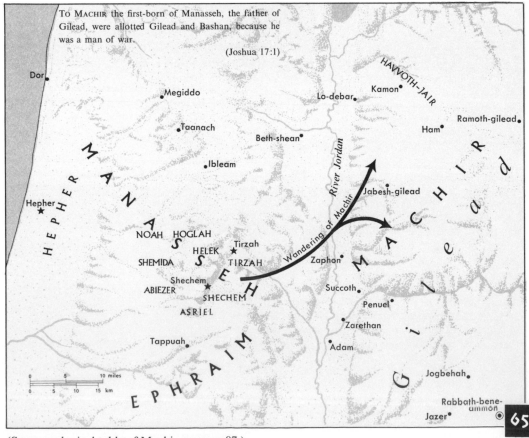

To MACHIR the first-born of Manasseh, the father of Gilead, were allotted Gilead and Bashan, because he was a man of war.

(Joshua 17:1)

(See genealogical table of Machir on page 87.)

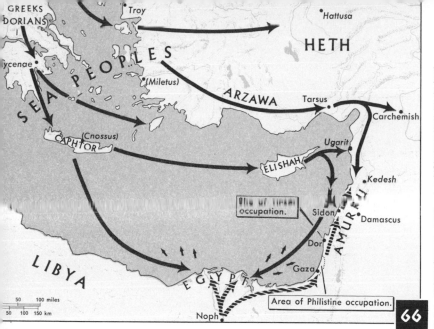

THE RISE OF THE SEA PEOPLES
1168 B.C.

RELIEFS, INSCRIPTIONS—MEDINET HABU;
PAPYRUS HARRIS I—EGYPT

ıımıı Egyptian force

▬▬ Sea Peoples

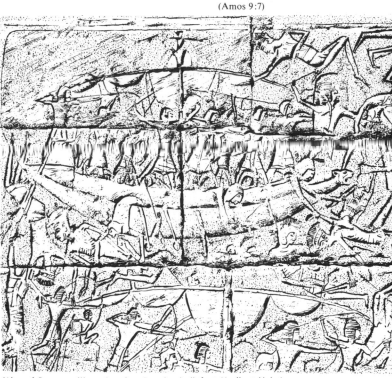

DID I not bring up Israel from the land of Egypt,
and the Philistines from Caphtor and the Syrians from
Kir?

(Amos 9:7)

War of Rameses III against Sea Peoples (relief at Medinet Habu)

THE TRAVELS OF WEN-AMON
EARLY 11TH CENTURY B.C.

DURING the twelfth century two decisive developments, related to each other, took place in the history of the Holy Land: the arrival of the Sea Peoples and the cessation of Egyptian rule. The Sea Peoples were Indo-Europeans from the Aegean Islands and Asia Minor. They set out eastward under pressure of the Dorian Greeks. Their pressure was felt already in the thirteenth century B.C., though the main invasion, which toppled the kingdoms of the Ancient East, climaxed in the eighth year of Rameses III (about 1168 B.C.), the second pharaoh of the twentieth dynasty. This ruler restored order in Egypt and tried to renew Egyptian suzerainty over Palestine. In his words, " . . . The foreign lands conspired in their islands. . . . No land could stand up to their might, from Hatti, Kode (?), Carchemish, Arzawa, and Alashiya on, being defeated one by one. A camp was set up somewhere in Amurru. They slaughtered its people, and the land was as if it had never been. They came toward Egypt, fire preceeding them. Their league comprised the Philistines, Tjeker, Shekelesh, Denyen, and Weshesh. . ."

Rameses boasts that he succeeded in repulsing this invasion; according to his reliefs, he fought not only on land but also at sea. However, Rameses' "victory" did not prevent the Philistines from ultimately settling in the southern coastal plain of Palestine and gaining control over Gaza, the administrative capital of the Egyptian province of Canaan. Egyptian domination in Palestine had seemingly come to an end.

This situation is reflected in an Egyptian tale from approximately 1100 B.C. Wen-amon, a priest of the temple of Amon at Karnak, sailed to Byblos to purchase lumber for the sacred bark of Amon. The account of this adventurous journey contains many indications of the lack of Egyptian influence along the coasts of Palestine and Phoenicia. From the section relating to his stay at Dor, we know that this area was inhabited by one of the Sea Peoples, the Tjeker. Also revealed in this story is the farflung maritime commerce of the Sea Peoples in this period.

JOURNEY OF WEN-AMON; PAPYRUS—EL-HIBA, EGYPT

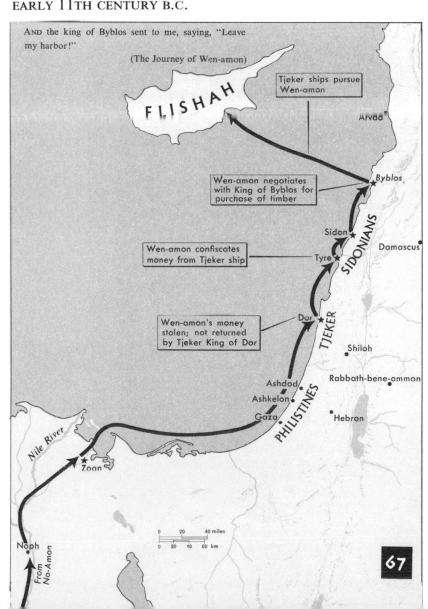

AND the king of Byblos sent to me, saying, "Leave my harbor!"

(The Journey of Wen-amon)

THE LIMITS OF ISRAELITE CONTROL

IN the twelfth century the principal rival peoples in Palestine were well established in their respective areas: the Israelites in the hill-country, the Canaanites in the northern valleys and plains, and the Philistines in the southern coastal plain. The latter was thus known as Philistia, a name which, much later, was conferred on the entire country in the form of Palestine.

Several passages in the Bible confirm that the Israelites were not able to overcome the strongly fortified Canaanite cities in the plains, for "they have chariots of iron, and ... are strong" (Josh. 17:18). In the descriptions of several tribal inheritances, the Canaanite cities not conquered are enumerated (Josh. 15:63; 17:11–13); a combined list is given in Judg. 1:21–35. These cities were in the north, in Jezreel and along the Phoenician coast, except Jebus-Jerusalem, Gezer, and the nearby Amorite cities. Even though unconquered, these cities were considered as belonging to the various tribal territories. Some of them were later put to forced labor by the Israelites (Judg. 1:28, 30, 33, 35). Some dwelt in the midst of Israel (Judg. 1:29), just as it is written that Asher dwelt in the midst of the Canaanites (Judg. 1:32), in the plain of Acco and along the Phoenician coast, where the Canaanites held sway.

In time there were also changes in the tribal claims of rule over Canaanite regions. The Amorite cities which had pressured Dan were included within the territory of the house of Joseph (Judg. 1:35). It is stated that "in Issachar and in Asher" Manasseh possessed Dor and the cities of Jezreel (Josh. 17:11), that is, they were first included in the tribal territories of Issachar and Asher, but later Manasseh prevailed. Only six Israelite tribes appear in the description of the tribal territories in Judges 1 (Benjamin, Manasseh, Ephraim, Zebulun, Asher, and Naphtali) and, these as will be seen later (map 71), were united in the league of the northern tribes, centered on Shiloh.

JOSH. 15:63; 16:10; 17:11–18;
JUDG. 1:21–35

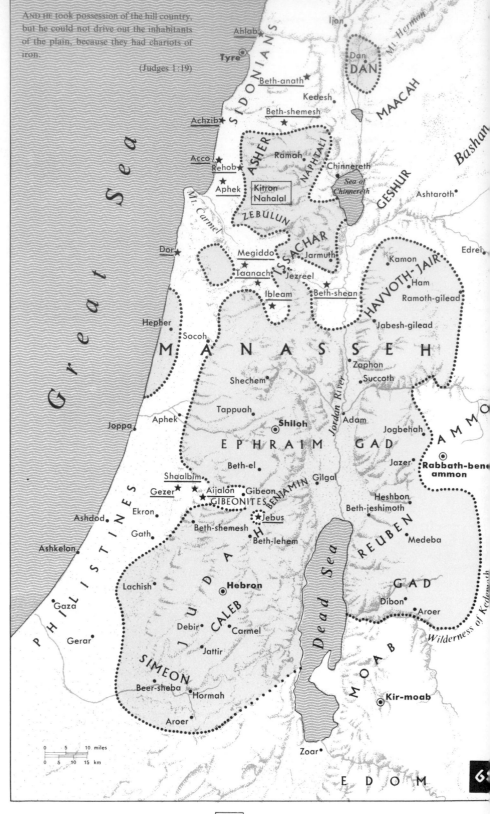

AND HE took possession of the hill country, but he could not drive out the inhabitants of the plain, because they had chariots of iron.

(Judges 1:19)

Area of Israelite control

Gezer   Canaanite city not conquered (according to Judg. 1)

Beth-anath (relief of Rameses II at Thebes)

THE LAND THAT
YET REMAINS

Siege of city in Land of Amurru
(relief of Rameses III at Medinet Habu)

This is the land that yet remains...
(Joshua 13:2)

☐ "The land that yet remains"

Aphek Canaanite city not conquered (according to Judg. 1)

••••••• Border of Land of Canaan

Josh. 13:1–6; Judg. 3:1–3

BESIDES the Canaanite regions included within the tribal territories, we find in the Bible the term "the land that yet remains" (Josh. 13:1–6; Judg. 3:1–3). This term included Philistia in the south, and the Phoenician-Sidonian coast up to Byblos, the Lebanon to Aphek on the Amorite border, and the Valley of Lebanon from Baal-gad beneath Mount Hermon to Lebo-hamath, in the north. It included parts of the Land of Canaan (compare Ex. 34:1–12; map 50), into which the Israelite tribes had never penetrated. These regions were beyond the area of Israelite settlement even in later periods, though in the expansionist periods of the kingdom of Israel some of them came under Israelite rule. The "boundary of the Amorites" in this connection was the border of the Amorite-Amurru kingdom in the Lebanon, well-known to us from Egyptian New Kingdom sources.

The Israelite areas of settlement were thus limited in the main to the hill regions and to Transjordan. The pressure of the indigenous population spurred on large-scale Israelite settlement activity, including deforestation and founding of settlements in sparsely populated areas. Traces of this activity in the hill region have been discovered in archaeological surveys in Transjordan, Judah, Mount Ephraim, and Galilee. This trend brought about the most important changes in the settlement pattern of Palestine in any historical period. Uninhabited areas were for the first time populated, the number of inhabitants doubled and new centers established in the interior. The Israelite settlement radically changed the face of the map, and continuity of settlement, one of the prerequisites for the internal unification of the Holy Land into a single kingdom, was first achieved during the Israelite Monarchy.

THE TRIBES
12TH CENTURY B.C.

JOSH. 13—19

AND THESE are the inherit-
ances which the people of
Israel received in the land of
Canaan...

(Joshua 14:1)

AND JOSHUA charged those who went to write the
description of the land, saying, "Go up and down and
write a description of the land, and come again to me;
and I will cast lots for you here before the LORD in
Shiloh."

(Joshua 18:8)

Mesopotamian border marker
(ca. twelfth century B.C.)

THE BORDERS
OF THE TRIBAL
TERRITORIES
12TH TO 11TH CENTURY B.C.

.... Tribal border

●●●●●● Political border in days of David

JOSH. 15—16

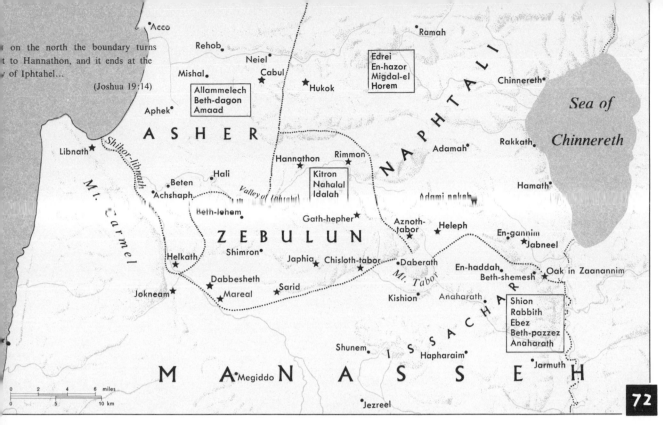

on the north the boundary turns
to Hannathon, and it ends at the
y of Iphtahel...

(Joshua 19:14)

Allammelech
Beth-dagon
Amaad

Edrei
En-hazor
Migdal-el
Horem

Kitron
Nahalal
Idalah

Shion
Rabbith
Ebez
Beth-pazzez
Anaharath

Acco
Rehob
Neiel
Cabul
Mishal
Hukok
Ramah
Chinnereth

Aphek
Libnath
Hali
Beten
Achshaph
Beth-lehem
Hannathon
Rimmon
Adamah
Rakkath

ASHER
NAPHTALI
Sea of
Chinnereth

Gath-hepher
Aznoth-tabor
Heleph
Hamath
Adami-nekeb

ZEBULUN
Helkath
Shimron
Japhia
Chisloth-tabor
Daberath
En-gannim
Jabneel

Joknem
Dabbesheth
Mareal
Sarid
Kishion
Mt. Tabor
Anaharath
En-haddah
Beth-shemesh
Oak in Zaanannim

Shunem
Hapharaim
Jarmuth

MANASSEH
Megiddo
ISSACHAR
Jezreel

Mt. Carmel
Shihor-libnath
Valley of Iphtahel

0 2 4 6 miles
0 5 10 km

72 JOSH. 19:10–39

T HE DESCRIPTION of the tribal territories in Josh. 13–19, is compiled from two different sources: a description of the borders of the tribes, and a list of their cities. Most scholars believe that the city list reflects the situation in a later period, at which time the kingdom was already divided into administrative districts. This is quite evident in the list of the cities of Judah, where they are divided according to clear-cut geographical groupings (see map 130). On the other hand, the description of the borders probably originates in the period of the Judges, at which time the definition of the boundaries between the tribes was of vital importance. Border after border is defined by border points listed in geographical order. Outstanding features in the landscape, such as mountains or their slopes, springs, brooks, and so forth, were used as markers. The list of border points is drastically abridged and, in its present form, the original detailed description remains only in places of special interest, such as near Jerusalem.

In the descriptions, however, of Issachar, Dan, Simeon and the Transjordanian tribes, only lists of cities and general topographical designations are given. The description, moreover, of the border of Judah is actually missing: its southern boundary, as given, is that of the Land of Canaan (see map 50) and most of its northern boundary

is identical with the southern border of Benjamin. Only two border sections are at variance with the territory of the Israelite settlement in the period of the Judges—the northwestern parts of the borders of Judah and Asher. These were the limits of the kingdom under David, bordering Philistia and Tyre (compare 2 Sam. 24:5–7; map 106), and they were used evidently to complement the other border descriptions.

Thus there are only six tribes whose border descriptions have been preserved in the Bible; these are the tribes (of Galilee and Mount Ephraim) included in the list of unconquered Canaanite cities (map 68). This must be the league of northern Israelite tribes centered around Shiloh, which adopted the name Israel, in its more limited sense, in contrast to Judah. During the period of the Judges, the bond between the tribes of the north and those of the south became rather loose and the two groups did not cooperate in any common war venture (compare the war of Deborah, or Gideon's war). It may be assumed that the tribes of the south were organized into a similar league, centered on Hebron. This would have included Judah, Simeon, Caleb, Kenaz, Jerahmeel, and the Kenites. In time, the contrast between Israel and Judah became greater until, at the end of the period of the Judges, they appear as two separate units, which even the United Monarchy under David and Solomon failed to integrate.

THE BORDERS OF THE TRIBE
OF BENJAMIN AND ITS NEIGHBORS

15—18

THEN THE boundary goes up by the valley of the son of Hinnom at the southern shoulder of the Jebusite (that is, Jerusalem); and the boundary goes up to the top of the mountain that lies over against the valley of Hinnom, on the west, at the northern end of the valley of Rephaim...

(Joshua 15:8)

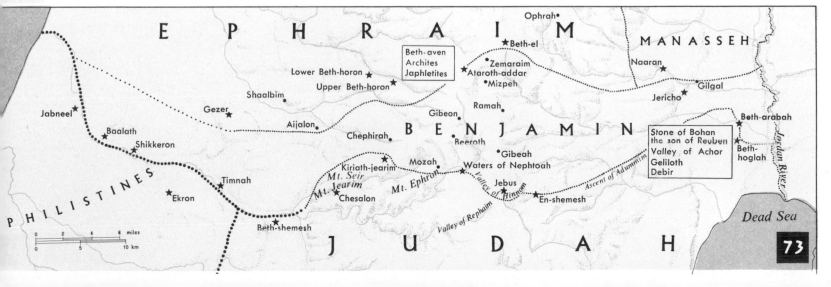

Ophrah
Beth-el
EPHRAIM
MANASSEH

Beth-aven
Archites
Japhletites

Lower Beth-horon
Upper Beth-horon
Zemaraim
Ataroth-addar
Mizpeh
Naaran
Gilgal

Shaalbim
Gezer
Jericho

Jabneel
Aijalon
Gibeon
Ramah
Beth-arabah

Baalath
Shikkeron
Chephirah
Beeroth
BENJAMIN

Stone of Bohan
the son of Reuben
Valley of Achor
Geliloth
Debir

Kiriath-jearim
Mozah
Gibeah
Waters of Nephtoah
Beth-hoglah

Timnah
Mt. Seir
Mt. Jearim
Chesalon
Jebus
En-shemesh
Jordan River

Ekron
Mt. Ephron
Valley of Hinnom

PHILISTINES
Beth-shemesh
Valley of Rephaim

JUDAH
Dead Sea

0 2 4 6 miles
0 5 10 km

73

AND the people of Israel served Eglon the
king of Moab eighteen years.

(Judges 3:14)

THE WAR OF EHUD
12TH TO 11TH CENTURY B.C.

JUDG. 3: 12–30

EPHRAIM

Beth-el

To Seirah

Ehud flees, warns Israel
after killing King of Moab

Ehud returns alone
from Gilgal to Jericho

River Jordan

Beth-nimrah

Mizpeh

Naaran

Michmash

Gilgal

Seizing of fords
across the Jordan

Gibeon   Geba

Jericho

Beth-arabah

Abel-shittim

Beeroth   Gibeah

Ehud and bearers
of gifts go down
to Jericho to meet
the King of Moab

Beth-hoglah

Plains of Moab

Beth-haram

Jebus

0   2   4 miles
0 2 4 6 km

Beth-jeshimoth

74

BENJAMIN

◄▌▌▌▌ Israelite force

◄ ◄ ◄ Moabites

FOR WHENEVER the Israelites put in seed the Midianites
and the Amalekites and the people of the East would
come up…

(Judges 6:3)

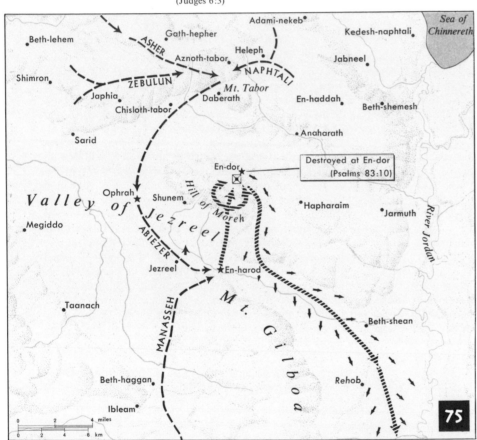

Beth-lehem

ASHER

Gath-hepher

Adami-nekeb

Kedesh-naphtali

Sea of
Chinnereth

Aznoth-tabor

Heleph

NAPHTALI

Jabneel

Shimron

ZEBULUN

Mt. Tabor

Japhia

Daberath

En-haddah

Beth-shemesh

Chisloth-tabor

Sarid

Anaharath

En-dor

Destroyed at En-dor
(Psalms 83:10)

Valley of

Ophrah

Shunem

Hill of Moreh

Hapharaim

Jarmuth

River Jordan

Jezreel

Megiddo

ABIEZER

Jezreel

En-harod

MANASSEH

Mt. Gilboa

Beth-shean

Taanach

Beth-haggan

Rehob

Ibleam

0   2   4 miles
0 2 4 6 km

75

THE WAR OF GIDEON
12TH CENTURY B.C.

JUDG. 6—8; PS. 83: 10–11

◄▌▌▌▌ Israelite force

☒ Midianite camp

◄ ─ ─ Gathering of Israelite warriors

◄─ ─ ─ Flight of Midianites

Arabian warriors mounted on camels
(relief from palace of Asshurbanipal at Nineveh

THE LORD is with you, you
mighty man of valor.

(Judges 6:12)

Mt.
Tabor

En-dor

Ophrah

Hill of Moreh

Megiddo

En-harod

Beth-shean

Ibleam

Tabbath

Jabesh-gilead

Abel-meholah

Tirzah

Gideon punishes
Succoth and Penuel

Shechem

Succoth

Penuel

Ephraimites seize
fords of the Jordan

Zarethan

Shiloh

Adam

Jogbehah

Became dung for
the ground
(Psalms 83:10)

Rabbath-bene-
ammon

Beth-el

River Jordan

Gilgal

Caravan Route

To Karkor

Jebus

0   5   10 miles

THE PURSUIT AFTER
THE MIDIANITES
12TH CENTURY B.C.

JUDG. 7—8

76

THE KINGDOM OF ABIMELECH
12TH CENTURY B.C.

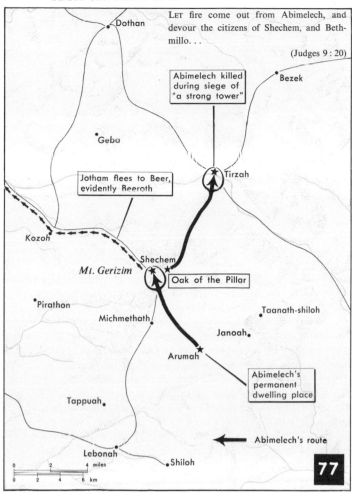

LET fire come out from Abimelech, and devour the citizens of Shechem, and Beth-millo...

(Judges 9:20)

Abimelech killed during siege of "a strong tower"

Jotham flees to Beer, evidently Beeroth

Oak of the Pillar

Abimelech's permanent dwelling place

← Abimelech's route

0   2   4 miles
0   2 4   6 km

77

JUDG. 8:30—9:57

THE ESTABLISHMENT of the tribes in their various territories continued during the twelfth century. The bonds between the tribes loosened under the relatively calm conditions. No strong enemies threatened the security and holdings of the Israelite peasants. Here lies the disadvantage of a historical atlas: it is easier to sketch a map of a short military episode than to show generations of peaceful toil which build the foundations for a healthy life of a nation in its land.

The wars described in the Bible are mostly against neighbors and invaders coming from the desert, taking every opportunity to loot and destroy. In times of danger, leaders rose to the call of the tribes—the divinely inspired Judges. They generally held leadership even after their wars of deliverance. The number of warriors mustered around them was small and they were summoned only from among their own and neighboring tribes. Groups of a few hundred men under audacious leadership could by surprise overcome their enemies, who were also small, unorganized bands.

Only one of the Judges, Othniel the son of Kenaz, came from a southern tribe. The historical and geographical circumstances of his war are unknown. Ehud was of the tribe of Benjamin and acted with the assistance of the people of southern Mount Ephraim. His daring personal deed is described; the circumstances under which the King of Moab was able to penetrate to Jericho, the "city of palms," with the aid of the Ammonites and the Amalekites, are, however, unknown. Gideon was of the tribe of Manasseh, and his family, that of Abiezer, dwelt at Ophrah. The location of Ophrah is doubtful, though as Gideon was active in Jezreel and, since his brothers were killed at Tabor (Judg. 8:18–19), it is probably in this area. It may be identical to Afula, where there is a tel with suitable remains, and was perhaps called Aper in the city list of Thutmose III (map 34). The family of Abiezer was probably one of the clans of Manasseh which penetrated into the territory of Issachar (Josh. 17:11); it should be noted that Issachar is not mentioned in the story of Gideon's war, even though the battle took place within its territory. The enemy whom Gideon fought were highly mobile Bedouin marauders mounted on camels; they infiltrated from the desert and filled the valleys with their flocks

and tents, harassing the Israelite populace scattered in open settlements. Gideon was not content with a mere attack on the enemy camp, but chased the raiders far into the desert. Jephtah was a Gileadite; he freed the Israelite settlements in Transjordan from Ammonite pressure. His outstanding ability as a leader is related in the account of his campaigns. Also noticeable is the extreme contrast between the tribes which dwelt on either side of the Jordan. This latter found expression even in the different dialects of Hebrew used by each group (Judg. 12:6).

The reign of Abimelech, the son of Gideon, which lasted for three years, represents a peculiar episode in the period of the Judges—an attempt to pass leadership on through inheritance, to establish a kingship. In his venture, Abimelech was aided by the older Canaanite population of Shechem, which considered him one of their own because of his maternal lineage. They provided him with "silver out of the house of Baal-berith" (Judg. 9:4). The remains of this Canaanite temple, also called Beth-millo, were uncovered during excavations at Shechem. Abimelech refused, however, to commit himself to the rulers of Shechem and made Arumah, between Shechem and Shiloh, his capital. Soon after, relations deteriorated completely, since the Canaanites of Shechem were not prepared to accept him as an Israelite king (Judg. 9:28). Abimelech razed Shechem to its foundations and, moreover, tried to extend his domination over the other Canaanite cities which remained in the midst of Manasseh in Mount Ephraim. He met his death at the siege of the fortress (tower) of Thebez, and thus ended his short "reign." The location of Thebez is unknown. The identification with Tubas is highly doubtful. Thebez may be a corruption of the name Tirzah, an important Canaanite city near Shechem (Josh. 12:24).

THE WAR OF JEPHTAH
END OF 12TH CENTURY B.C.   JUDG. 11—12:7

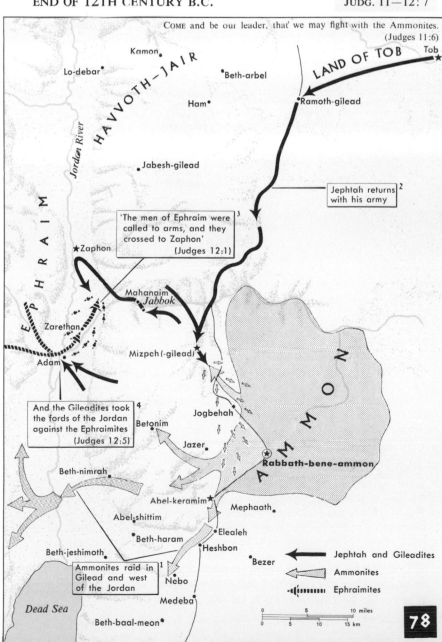

COME and be our leader, that we may fight with the Ammonites.

(Judges 11:6)

LAND OF TOB

Jephtah returns with his army [2]

'The men of Ephraim were called to arms, and they crossed to Zaphon' (Judges 12:1) [3]

And the Gileadites took the fords of the Jordan against the Ephraimites (Judges 12:5) [4]

Ammonites raid in Gilead and west of the Jordan [1]

← Jephtah and Gileadites

⇐ Ammonites

⋘ Ephraimites

0   5   10 miles
0   5   10   15 km

78

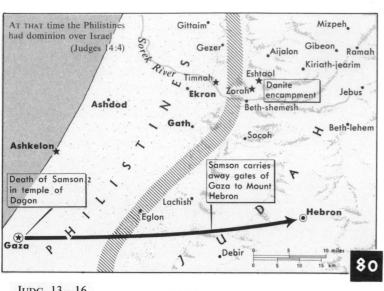

JUDG. 13—16

Border area between Judah and Philistia

80

Decorated Philistine bowl

JUDAH AND PHILISTIA
IN THE DAYS OF SAMSON

T HE STRUGGLE with the Philistines, the strongest of Israel's enemies, forms the background to the Samson stories.

The Philistines came to the Land of Canaan in the twelfth century, several generations after the arrival of the Israelites (map 66). They settled along the southern coast, north to the Me-jarkon region. They were centered on three main cities: Gaza, Ashkelon, and Ashdod, important coastal cities well known from the Canaanite period. Two centers farther inland, Gath and Ekron, developed in the area of Philistine settlement in the Shephelah. Gath was an important city already in the Canaanite period, but Ekron was evidently founded by the Philistines. At the start of the eleventh century five Philistine cities were organized into a confederation based on military cooperation; their territory spread over the southern coastal plain. The Philistine warrior was heavily armed, as for instance was Goliath the Gittite (map 91). The Philistines probably brought with them the art of iron-working and they preserved an absolute monopoly in this field down to the time of Saul (1 Sam. 13:19–22). Remains of their settlements can be detected on the basis of pottery types peculiar to them, painted in red and black, the patterns stemming from Mycenean motifs.

The border area between Judah and Philistia ran along the middle of the Shephelah; it was here that the two peoples met, in war and in peace. In the stories of Samson, we have a description of life in the northern Shephelah in the region of the valley of Sorek. The events took place between Israelite Zorah and Philistine Timnah, one of Ekron's daughter cities; the former is high on a ridge, the latter down in the valley. The tribe of Dan had previously attempted to settle in this territory. Samson was related to one of the Danite families which had remained there. In the days of Samson the Philistines had already gained the upper hand, ruling various parts of Judah (Judg. 15:11). The stories of the mighty hero who took vengeance on the tyrant Philistines were undoubtedly quite popular in the Israelite villages. Even so, the neighborly ties between the Israelite settlements and those of the Philistines in the outlying districts are quite apparent. These relations are clearly reflected at Israelite Beth-shemesh, for among its ruins an abundance of Philistine pottery vessels was found.

FROM DAN to Beer-sheba, including the land of Gilead, and the congregation assembled as one man to the LORD at Mizpah.
(Judges 20:1)

THE STORY
OF THE CONCUBINE IN GIBEAH
12TH CENTURY B.C.

T HE BOOK OF JUDGES ends with the story of the fraternal war between Benjamin and the other Israelite tribes, following the ravishing of the concubine of a Levite at the hands of the people of Gibeah in Benjamin. This story reflects the general situation during the period of the Judges: "In those days there was no king in Israel; every man did what was right in his own eyes" (Judg. 21:25, etc.). Although there was no central political rule in Israel in this period, there was evidently a confederation of tribes formed around a central sanctuary (similar to the Greek amphictyony). If one tribe violated the laws of the league, the council would meet to confer punishment. The historical circumstances, however, of the Israelite war against Benjamin remain obscure. It may have occurred at an earlier period, for at the end of the period of the Judges, Benjamin was a strong, well-established tribe, and Gibeah in Benjamin became the first capital of Israel, under Saul. An earlier settlement at Gibeah was apparently destroyed before the middle of the twelfth century, and at the same period a number of settlements in the region were abandoned.

JUDG. 19—20

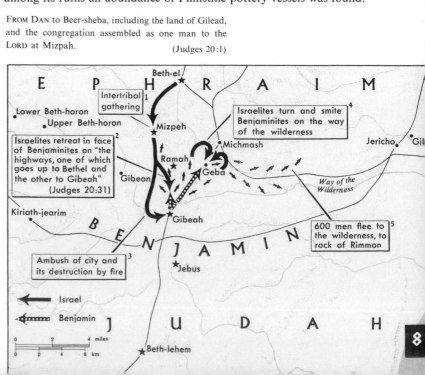

8

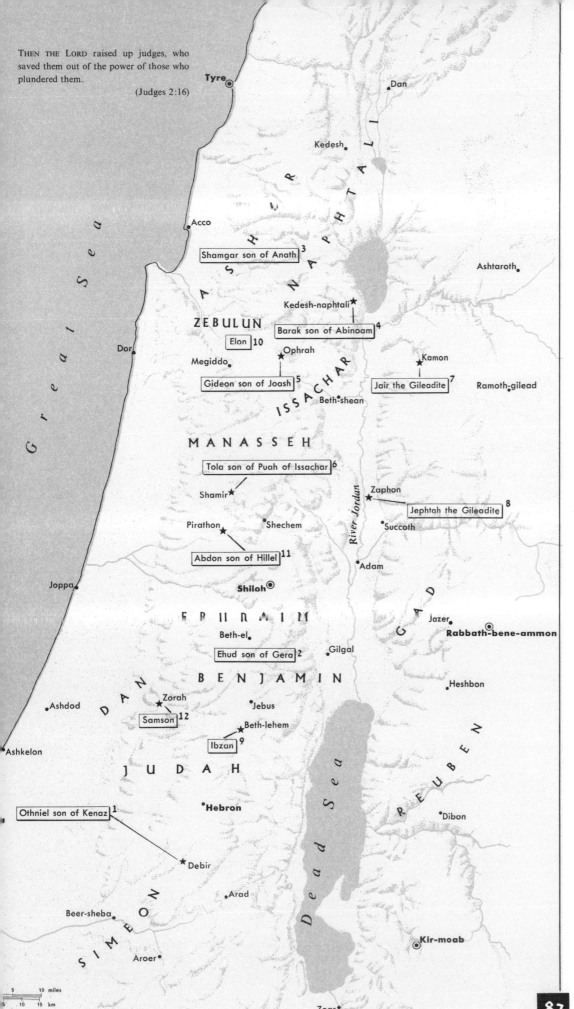

THEN THE LORD raised up judges, who saved them out of the power of those who plundered them.

(Judges 2:16)

Tyre

Dan

Kedesh

A S H E R

N A P H T A L I

Acco

Shamgar son of Anath ³

Ashtaroth

Kedesh-naphtali ★

ZEBULUN

Barak son of Abinoam ⁴

Dor

Elon 10

Ophrah ★

Megiddo

Kamon ★

Gideon son of Joash ⁵

I S S A C H A R

Jair the Gileadite ⁷

Ramoth-gilead

Beth-shean

M A N A S S E H

Tola son of Puah of Issachar ⁶

Zaphon ★

Shamir ★

Jephtah the Gileadite ⁸

Pirathon ★

Shechem

Succoth

Abdon son of Hillel ¹¹

Adam

Joppa

Shiloh ◎

E P H R A I M

Jazer

G A D

Beth-el

Rabbath-bene-ammon ◎

Ehud son of Gera ²

Gilgal

B E N J A M I N

Heshbon

Zorah ★

Jebus

Ashdod

Samson 12

Beth-lehem ★

Ashkelon

Ibzan 9

J U D A H

R E U B E N

Othniel son of Kenaz ¹

Hebron

Dibon

★ Debir

Dead Sea

Arad

S I M E O N

Beer-sheba

Kir-moab ◎

Aroer

Great Sea

River Jordan

5 10 miles
5 10 15 km

Decorated Philistine jug

BESIDES the great Judges of deliverance, the Book of Judges also mentions several "minor Judges" (Judg. 10:1–5; 12:8–15), who judged the people from their native cities. Their wealth is usually emphasized in the Scriptures, and no tradition concerning wars under their leadership has come down to us. The tribal league (or possibly two leagues) may have been led by Judges, the position passing from tribe to tribe in rotation. In times of peace, their authority was quite limited. Five "minor Judges" are given and it may be more than incidental that the total number of Judges mentioned in the Book of Judges is twelve, a Judge for each tribe. It is doubtful whether these were the only "minor Judges"; their names may have been chosen on the basis of their tribal affiliations, in order to provide each tribe with a Judge, even if not a deliverer.

THE BATTLE OF EBEN-EZER
CA. 1050 B.C.

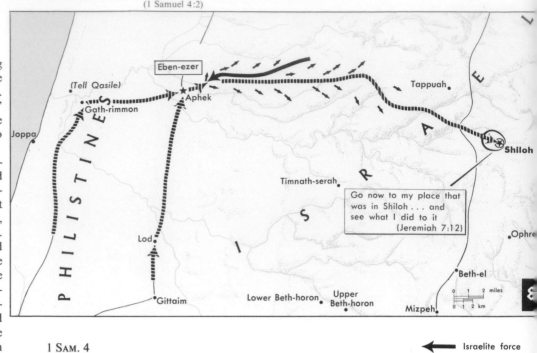

IN the mid-eleventh century events were leading toward a decisive battle between Israel and the Philistines for supremacy in the Land of Canaan. This conflict gave birth to the "Philistine empire," which lasted for a short time only, and later to the Israelite kingdom, which was founded in reaction to Philistine pressure.

Our information on the dramatic struggle is fragmentary, and only a shadow of the events is revealed by the folk stories preserved. The major battle occurred between Aphek and Eben-ezer. Ancient Aphek, located at the source of the Jarkon River, became a border city at the northern edge of Philistia. The exact location of Eben-ezer is unknown, and we can only surmise that the battle took place to the east of Aphek. It resulted in the absolute defeat of the Israelite tribal league, and Shiloh itself was destroyed, as indicated by excavations there. This explains the fact that Shiloh is never again mentioned as an Israelite center, that the descendants of the priests of Shiloh were settled at Nob near Jerusalem at the time of Saul (1 Sam. 21:2 ff.), and the later hints as to the fate of the city (Jer. 7:12, 14; 26:6, 9; Ps. 78:60).

Go now to my place that was in Shiloh ... and see what I did to it (Jeremiah 7:12)

1 SAM. 4

← Israelite force
◀▥▥▥ Philistine force

Carts of Sea People drawn by oxen (relief of Rameses III at Medinat Habu)

THE ARK of the Covenant, which had been brought from Shiloh to the battlefield, fell into Philistine hands. The wonderful story of its wanderings and return gives us a glimpse into the life of the central cities of northern Philistia and their border areas. From Philistine Ekron, the Ark was removed to Beth-shemesh in Judah, where the people were harvesting wheat in the valley; this was the vale of Sorek, near Timnah, in whose fields Samson had loosened his foxes (1 Sam. 15:1–5). The people of Beth-shemesh passed the Ark on to the "hill of" Kiriath-jearim (1 Sam. 7:1; 2 Sam. 6:3–4; and see Josh. 18:28), the early Hivite-Gibeonite city on the southern border of Benjamin, which is also the southernmost border of the northern Israelite tribes there. The Ark remained there until David recovered and transferred it to Jerusalem, for lack of a ritual center to take the place of Shiloh. Consequently Samuel, the spiritual leader of Israel in these days of extreme crisis, each year made a circuit of the tribal and ritual centers on the borders of Benjamin and Ephraim.

The Bible contains another tradition of a war in the days of Samuel, in which the Israelites defeated the Philistines, again in connection with Eben-ezer (1 Sam. 7:7–14). According to this account, conquered cities from Ekron to Gath returned to Israel and, following the victory, a peace treaty was signed between Israel and the cities of the Amorites which had in the past harassed the tribe of Dan (Judg. 1:34–35). This is confirmed by the archaeological excavations at Tel Qasile, a Philistine port city on the banks of the Jarkon River, opposite Gath-rimmon, which was destroyed in the middle of the eleventh century

(stratum XI). This destruction may have been connected with the Israelite victory in the time of Samuel. From the continuation of the account, however, in the Book of Samuel it would seem that the Philistine harassment of Israel did not cease, but rather increased, and that a Philistine governor was appointed over Geba, a city of Benjamin near the border of Ephraim, also called Gibeathelohim (1 Sam. 10:5; 13:3).

Thus it appears that Israelite-Philistine relations were a continuous chain of hostile actions and reactions. The surprising Israelite victory in the days of Samuel may have brought about, in turn, more intensified efforts on the part of the Philistines. They now penetrated to the heart of the Israelite settlement in the hill-country and secured their rule in the conquered regions by installing permanent occupation forces.

The Israelite tribal leagues fell apart in the second half of the eleventh century B.C., and the time was ripe for rule by kingship. Saul, the first of the Israelite kings, arose in the midst of the Philistine oppression. He came from Gibeah of Benjamin, close to Jebusite Jerusalem. This city became Saul's stronghold and the first capital of the kingdom of Israel; henceforth it was known as Gibeah of Saul. Its site, a prominent hill on a central highway near the borders of Israel and Judah, has been revealed in excavations. The biblical account of the route taken by Saul as he found a kingdom while searching for his lost asses in the central Mount Ephraim, is a fine example of the instructive topographical data included in this type of folk tale.

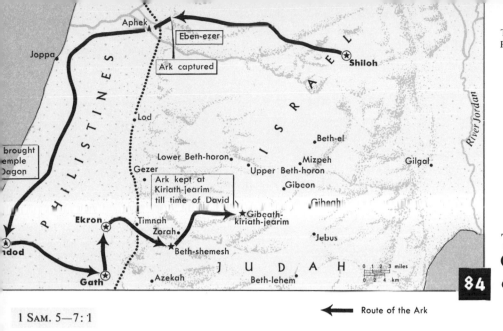

THE ARK of the LORD was in the country of the Philistines seven months.

(1 Samuel 6:1)

THE WANDERINGS
OF THE ARK OF THE COVENANT

84 CA. 1050 B.C.

← Route of the Ark

1 SAM. 5—7:1

AND HE went on a circuit year by year to Bethel, Gilgal, and Mizpah... Then he would come back to Ramah...
(1 Samuel 7:16-17)

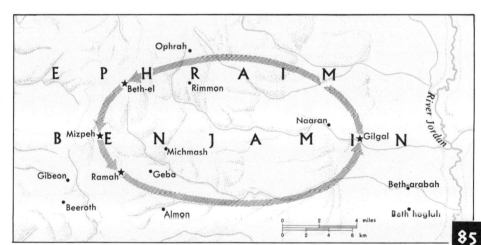

THE CITIES OF SAMUEL
CA. 1030 B.C.

1 SAM. 7: 16–17

---

w the asses of Kish, Saul's father, were

(1 Samuel 9:3)

SAUL SEARCHES FOR HIS ASSES
CA. 1025 B.C.

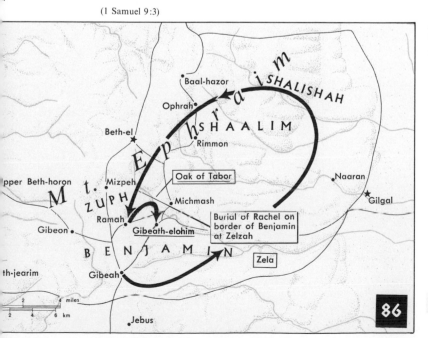

Gibeath-elohim   Seat of Philistine governor

←   Saul's route

1 SAM. 9—10: 16

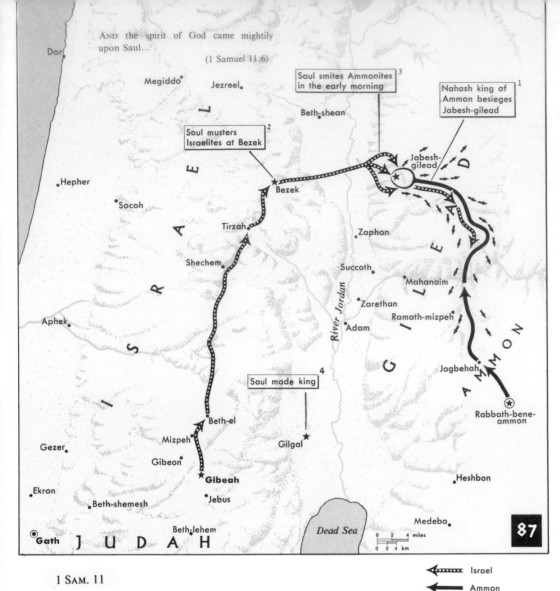

AND the spirit of God came mightily upon Saul...

(1 Samuel 11:6)

Saul smites Ammonites in the early morning ³

Nahash king of Ammon besieges Jabesh-gilead ¹

Saul musters Israelites at Bezek ²

Saul made king ⁴

THE SALVATION OF JABESH-GILEAD

SAUL'S ASCENT to kingship resembles the ri[se] of the deliverer Judges. Jabesh-gilead had bee[n] oppressed by Nahash king of Ammon; Saul salli[ed] forth from Bezek and by a surprise attack on t[he] Ammonites relieved the Israelite city. After th[e] victory Saul did not disperse the forces gather[ed] around him; he was anointed king before God [by] Samuel at Gilgal. It is hardly by chance that the kin[g]dom was founded on the very spot of the first Is[?]raelite center in the Land of Canaan.

The establishment of the kingdom meant op[en] rebellion against Philistine rule. Saul, with 2,000 me[n] went up to Michmash and the southern part of Mou[nt] Ephraim. His son, Jonathan, rallied 1,000 men [at] Gibeah in Benjamin and proceeded to seize Geba a[nd] slay the Philistine governor there. The Philistin[es] reacted immediately, sending considerable forc[es] Saul retreated to Gilgal; later he and the remna[nt] of his army joined forces with Jonathan at Ge[ba] opposite Michmash, the deep Wadi Suweinit separat[?]ing the two hostile camps. Israelite victory w[as] achieved through the overconfidence of the Philistin[es] who were sure of easy victory, having sent punit[ive] troops to the several Israelite regions instead of c[on]centrating their might for a decisive battle. T[he] courage displayed by Jonathan when surprising [the] Philistine forces, passing through the narrow wa[?] also played an important part. Sudden confusi[on] turned into crushing defeat as Saul's forces pursu[ed] the Philistines to the region of the vale of Aijalon.

87

← Israel
← Ammon

1 SAM. 11

THE REBELLION OF SAUL AGAINST THE PHILISTINES

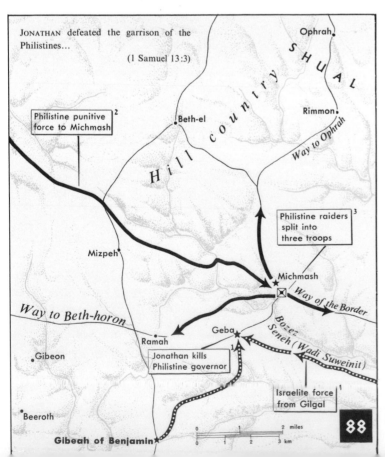

JONATHAN defeated the garrison of the Philistines...

(1 Samuel 13:3)

Philistine punitive force to Michmash ²

Philistine raiders split into three troops ³

Jonathan kills Philistine governor ¹

Israelite force from Gilgal ¹

88

← Israel
← Philistines

1 SAM. 13: 1–18

THE BATTLE OF MICHMASH

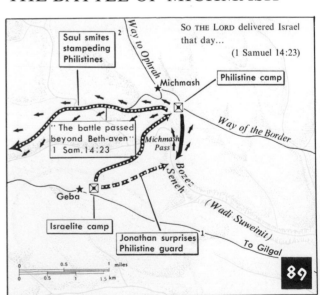

Saul smites stampeding Philistines ²

So THE LORD delivered Israel that day...

(1 Samuel 14:23)

Philistine camp

"The battle passed beyond Beth-aven" 1 Sam. 14:23

Jonathan surprises Philistine guard ¹

Israelite camp

89

1 SAM. 14: 1–46

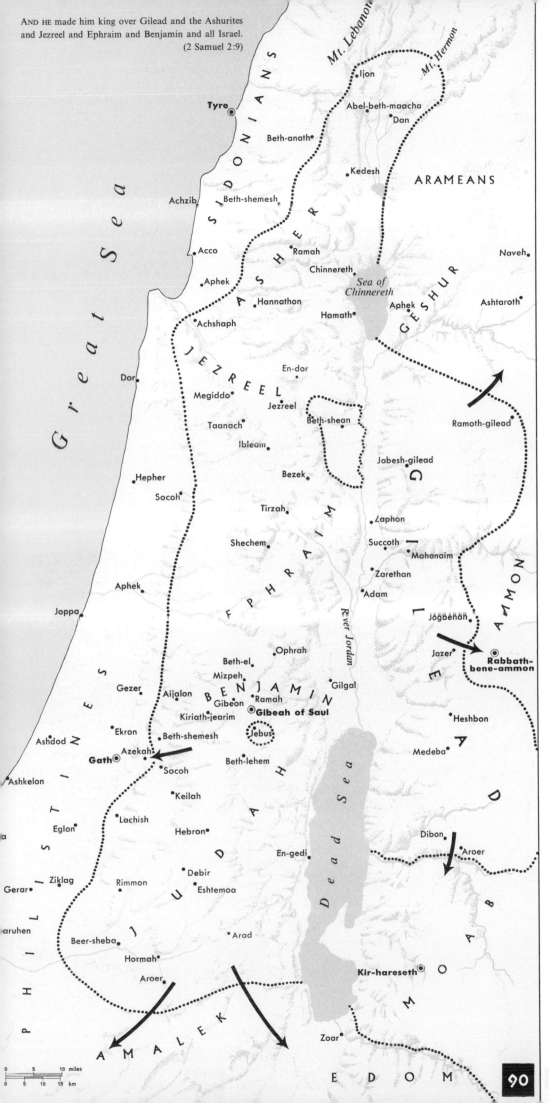

AND HE made him king over Gilead and the Ashurites and Jezreel and Ephraim and Benjamin and all Israel.

(2 Samuel 2:9)

THE KINGDOM OF SAUL
CA. 1025 TO 1006 B.C.

SAUL was the last of the Judges and the first of Israel's kings. Saul not only delivered Israel from the Philistine yoke, but also warred upon all the other surrounding enemies, and he "delivered Israel out of the hands of those who plundered them" (1 Sam. 14:48). In the account of the reign of Saul's son Eshbaal (Ishbosheth—2 Sam. 2:9) the regions of his kingdom are listed as the five areas of "all Israel." These are the regions of dense Israelite settlement: Gilead in Trans-jordan, Asher (incorrectly transmitted as "Ashurites") in Galilee, the plain of Jezreel (named after the major city of Issachar), Ephraim in the central hill-country, and Benjamin. To these must be added Judah, over which Saul had also extended his rule, but which fell to David "in the days of Eshbaal."

The inclusion of Jezreel in this list shows that the Valley of Jezreel lay within the borders of the kingdom. This fact is confirmed by the excavations at Megiddo and Taanach which have demonstrated that these cities fell to Israel in the second half of the twelfth century.

The borders of the kingdom of Israel in the days of Saul were those of the Israelite settlement (1 Sam. 13:19). He made no attempt to impose his rule over the various Canaanite enclaves; even pagan Jebus, very close to his capital, was never conquered by him. The task of uniting the entire Holy Land under a single Israelite king was left to his successor, David.

Philistine sword

← Saul's wars according to 1 Sam. 14:47-48

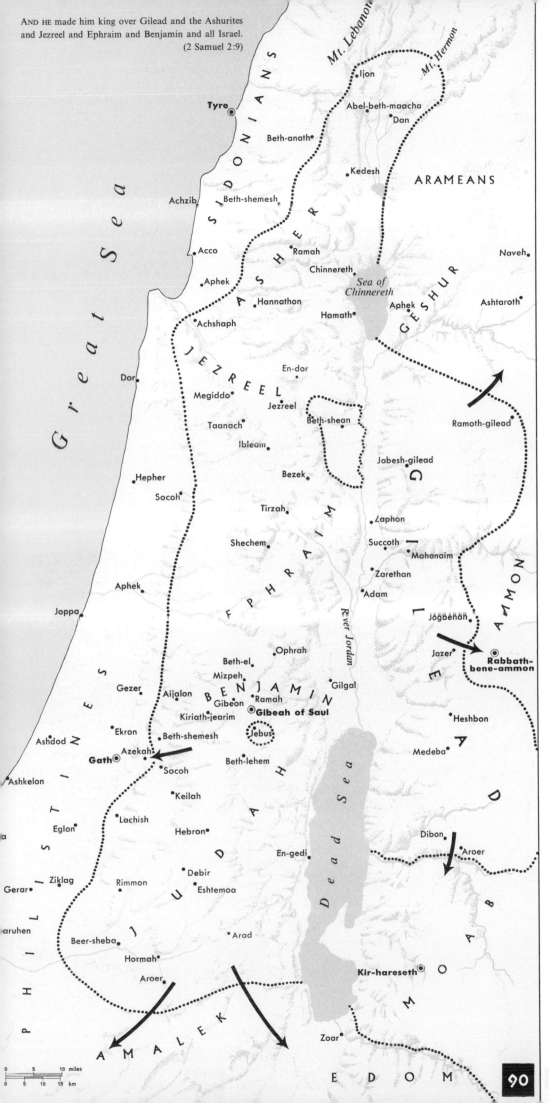Map labels: Great Sea, SIDONIANS, Mt. Lebanon, Mt. Hermon, Ijon, Abel-beth-maacha, Dan, Tyre, Beth-anath, Kedesh, ARAMEANS, Achzib, Beth-shemesh, Acco, Ramah, Chinnereth, Aphek, Sea of Chinnereth, Naveh, GESHUR, Hannathon, Aphek, Hamath, Ashtaroth, Achshaph, ASHER, JEZREEL, En-dor, Dor, Megiddo, Jezreel, Beth-shean, Ramoth-gilead, Taanach, Ibleam, Jabesh-gilead, Hepher, Bezek, GILEAD, Socoh, Tirzah, Zaphon, Shechem, Succoth, Mahanaim, Aphek, Zarethan, Adam, EPHRAIM, Joppa, River Jordan, AMMON, Jogbehah, Jazer, Rabbath-bene-ammon, Ophrah, Beth-el, Mizpeh, Gilgal, Gezer, Aijalon, BENJAMIN, Ramah, Gibeon, Gibeah of Saul, Heshbon, Kiriath-jearim, Jebus, Ekron, Beth-shemesh, Ashdod, Azekah, Gath, Socoh, Beth-lehem, Medeba, Keilah, JUDAH, Dead Sea, PHILISTINES, Eglon, Lachish, Hebron, Dibon, Aroer, Debir, En-gedi, Ziklag, Rimmon, Eshtemoa, Gerar, Beer-sheba, Arad, MOAB, Hormah, Aroer, AMALEK, Zoar, Kir-haresheth, EDOM, Kedesh, 90

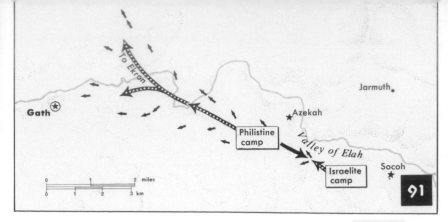

THE BATTLE OF DAVID AND GOLIATH

CA. 1010 B.C.

DAVID came from Beth-lehem in Judah, the most important city in the heart of Judah. His strong mind and body enabled him to rise quickly at Saul's court, to become a "commander of a thousand" (1 Sam. 18:13) and the king's son-in-law (1 Sam. 18:17–30). Saul may have sought firmer ties with Judah through this marriage.

David's battle with Goliath was part of the long conflict with the Philistines lasting throughout Saul's reign. Goliath the Gittite, heavily armed, was the typical Sea People warrior. David faced him armed only with courage, agility, and a sling. The struggle between Israel and Philistia spread throughout the outlying settlements of the Shephelah. The Philistines, who already held Azekah, strove to conquer Socoh on the opposite side of the vale of Elah.

1 SAM. 17

THE NARRATIVE OF DAVID'S WANDERINGS

CA. 1008 B.C.

WITHIN a short time relations between Saul and David became strained, and the two strong personalities often clashed. David fled, first to the Judean Desert where he took refuge in caves and strongpoints among its precipices. Here he gathered a band of malcontents, with whose aid he terrorized the Judean settlements on the desert's edge. Saul pursued him even into this desolate region. The intense patriotism of the two great rivals is quite evident in the tales of this chase: Saul, in spite of his deep hatred for David, sped to battle against the Philistines the moment he heard of an attack, thus giving David the opportunity to escape (1 Sam. 23:27–28); David, on his part, did not take advantage of various opportunities to harm Saul, out of respect to the Lord's anointed (1 Sam. 24:26). In the end Saul prevailed and David saw no recourse but to seek protection under Achish, king of Gath, a leader of his people's enemies.

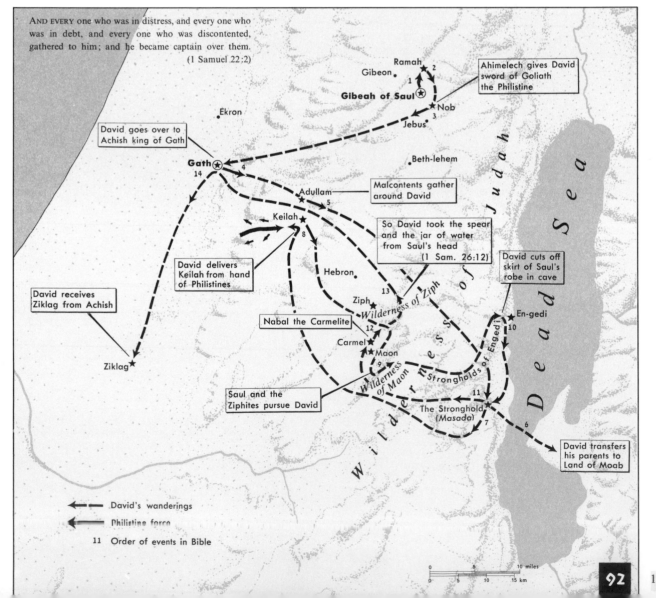

AND EVERY one who was in distress, and every one who was in debt, and every one who was discontented, gathered to him; and he became captain over them.
(1 Samuel 22:2)

Ahimelech gives David sword of Goliath the Philistine

David goes over to Achish king of Gath

Malcontents gather around David

So David took the spear and the jar of water from Saul's head
(1 Sam. 26:12)

David cuts off skirt of Saul's robe in cave

David delivers Keilah from hand of Philistines

David receives Ziklag from Achish

Nabal the Carmelite

Saul and the Ziphites pursue David

David transfers his parents to Land of Moab

David's wanderings

Philistine force

11 Order of events in Bible

Philistine noble
(faience plaque of time of Rameses III, Medinet Habu)

1 SAM. 19:18—27:6

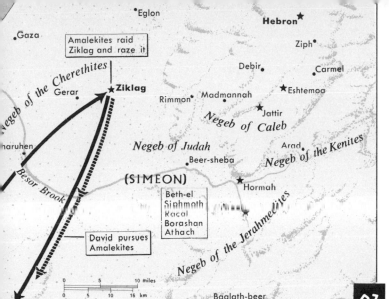

1 SAM. 27: 6–12; 30

93

DAVID AT ZIKLAG
CA. 1007 B.C.

ACHISH not only welcomed David, but put him in charge of Ziklag, one of the cities on the border of Simeon in the Negeb. From subsequent events, it appears that Achish did this not out of love for David, but rather out of animosity for Saul, hoping with the aid of David to incite Judah and the southern tribes to rebel against Saul.

The stories on Ziklag describe the outlying regions and the Negeb, areas under constant pressure from desert marauders, the Amalekites. The Cherethite Negeb is in southern Philistia; more to the east lies the Calebite, Jerahmeelite, Kenite, and Simeonite Negeb. The latter was called the "Negeb of Judah" in this period. David and his band swept over the desert far south. By these conquests and through generous divisions of booty taken from the Amalekites, he won over the southern tribes (1 Sam. 30:26–31).

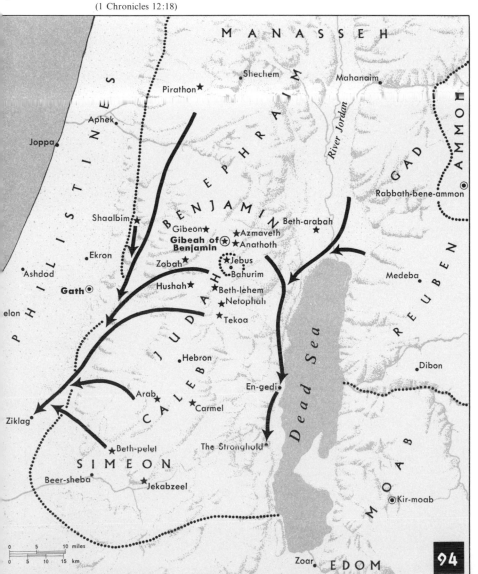

Water flask (eleventh century B.C.)

THE ORIGINS
OF DAVID'S MEN OF VALOR
CA. 1008 TO 1007 B.C.

DAVID'S MEN of valor gathered around him, some still while he was in the desert stronghold (1 Chron. 12:8) and others at Ziklag. They served as the nucleus of his army and were unquestioningly loyal and always ready for daring exploits. Most were from Judah and Benjamin, though some came from more distant tribes, from Mount Ephraim and beyond the Jordan. The unit of "thirty chief men" became a permanent military institution during the reign of David, later their number swelling and including also foreigners, such as Zelek the Ammonite, Naharai of Bèeroth, and Uriah the Hittite (2 Sam. 23:37–39; 1 Chron. 11:39, 41).

2 SAM. 23: 8–39; 1 CHRON. 11: 10—12: 22

94

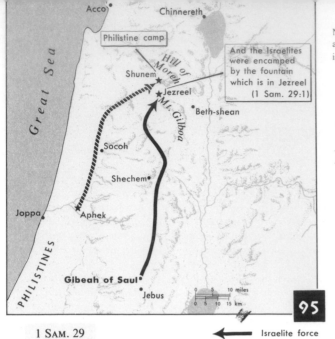

1 SAM. 29

And the Israelites were encamped by the fountain which is in Jezreel (1 Sam. 29:1)

← Israelite force

◄ᴵ ▐▐▐▐▐ Philistine force

Now the Philistines gathered all their forces at Aphek; and the Israelites were encamped by the fountain which is in Jezreel.

(1 Samuel 29:1)

CA. 1006 B.C.

THE DEPLOYMENT FOR THE BATTLE OF GILBOA

THE WARS of the Israelites against the Philistines culminated in Saul's death on Mount Gilboa. Saul fought his last battle on the crossroads of Jezreel. The Philistines attempted to dominate the valley and threatened to cut the tribes of Galilee off from Mount Ephraim.

In order to properly understand the preparations for the battle, and the battle itself, it must be noted that the biblical narrative is not in exact chronological order, but skips from event to event in keeping an account of the activities of Saul and David. In chapter 28 (1 Sam.) there appears the story of Saul's meeting with the medium of En-dor the night before the battle; and in chapter 29 there is an account of the talks between the lords of the Philistines and Achish concerning David, at the start of their campaign. The proper order of events is: the Philistines rallied at Aphek in the Sharon plain, as was their custom when venturing upon campaigns to the north (1 Sam. 29:1); from there the Philistines advanced along the Via Maris to Shunem at the foot of the hill of Moreh, while Saul deployed his army opposite them on Mount Gilboa, favoring the mountainous area as more convenient for his lightly armed Israelite warriors. He encamped at a spring at the foot of Jezreel; it was from here that Saul went to the medium of En-dor in the darkness of night. The next day he died a hero's death on the Gilboa, together with three of his sons. The Philistine victory was absolute and the important cities of Jezreel remained under their control. As a warning, the Philistines fastened the corpses of Saul and his sons to the walls of Beth-shean, and placed their weapons in the temple of Ashtaroth, possibly one of two temples there in this period, the remains of which have been unearthed in archaeological excavations. The men of Jabesh-gilead, remembering Saul's having saved their city from the Ammonites, made a daring move under cover of darkness, and recovered the corpses of Saul and his sons from the walls of Beth-shean, bringing them to Jabesh for decent burial.

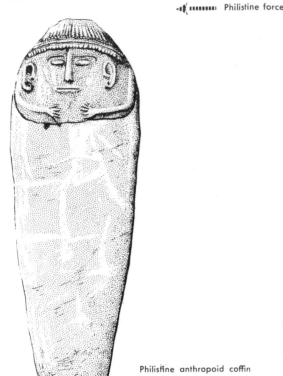

Philistine anthropoid coffin
(Beth-shean, ca. end 12th century B.C.)

1 SAM. 28; 31

THE DEATH OF SAUL

THE men of Israel... fell slain on Mount Gilboa.
(1 Samuel 31:1)

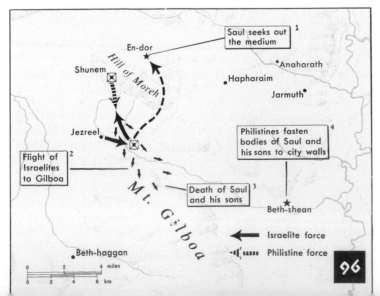

Saul seeks out the medium ¹

Flight of Israelites to Gilboa ²

Death of Saul and his sons ³

Philistines fasten bodies of Saul and his sons to city walls ⁴

← Israelite force

◄ᴵ ▐▐▐▐▐ Philistine force

THE BURIAL OF SAUL

1 SAM. 31: 11–13

THE valiant men arose, and went all night...
(1 Samuel 31:12)

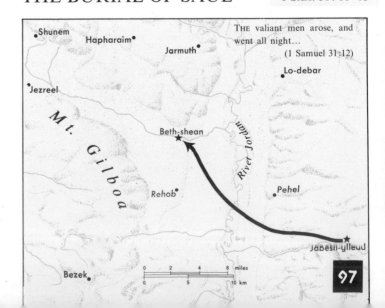

THE KINGDOMS
OF DAVID AND ESHBAAL
CA. 1006 TO 1004 B.C.

2 SAM. 2: 8–11

ABNER the son of Ner, captain of Saul's army, escaped from the
battle of Gilboa with his life. He transferred the capital of Israel
to Mahanaim, across the Jordan, and there crowned Eshbaal, one
of Saul's surviving sons, as king (2 Sam. 2:8; 1 Chron. 8:33). It is
Eshbaal who is also referred to in the Bible, in a derogatory manner,
as Ish-bosheth ("man of disgrace"). Although David, as a vassal of
the King of Gath, had come to the rallying point of the Philistines at
Aphek, he was saved from fighting against his own people, because
the lords of the Philistines were suspicious of him (1 Sam. 29). After
Saul's death, David persuaded the elders of Judah to anoint him in
Hebron as king over Judah; thus, the kingdom was divided. While
David reigned in Judah, Eshbaal reigned in the five remaining
Israelite tribal regions of Saul's kingdom (2 Sam. 2:9–10). It seems that
the Philistines welcomed this split and that Achish continued to regard
David as a loyal vassal, still at his bid.

At first the Philistines seemed to be correct in their assumptions.
The clash at Gibeon was only one of many hostilities which weakened
the forces of the two rival kingdoms. It was as if Israel and Judah had
returned to their former status of local tribal confederations, lacking
strength even to venture beyond their own territories.

THE BATTLE
OF THE POOL OF GIBEON
CA.1005 B.C

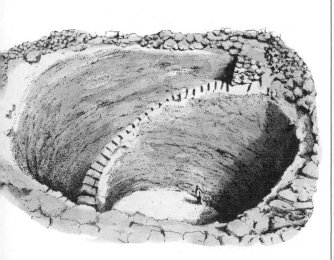

Pool of Gibeon

2 SAM. 2: 12–32

← Abner and his men
⟨⟨⟨⟨ Joab and his men

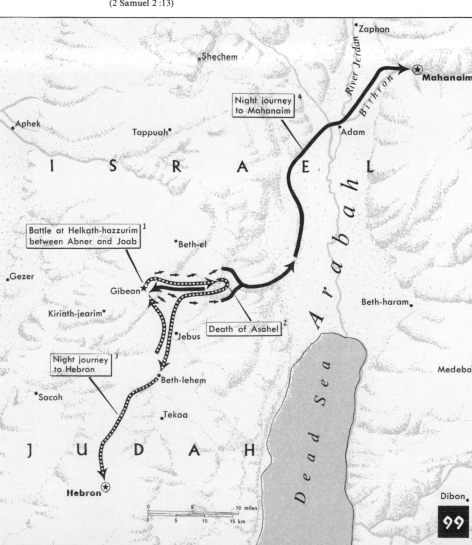

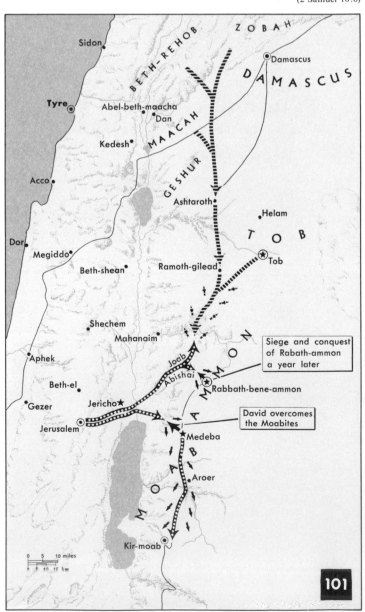

Map 100

- Gittaim
- Lower Beth-horon
- Upper Beth-horon
- Mizpeh
- Gezer
- Aijalon
- Ramah
- Gibeon
- Gibeah
- Kiriath-jearim
- **David again smites and pursues Philistines till Gezer**
- Jebus (Jerusalem)
- Sorek River
- Timnah
- Zorah
- **Baal-perazim**
- Manahath
- Beth-shemesh
- **Philistines go up twice against David**
- Zanoah
- **David smites Philistines at Baal-perazim**
- Valley of Rephaim
- **David conquers Jebus**
- Valley of Elah
- Jarmuth
- Azekah
- Beth-lehem
- **Philistine garrison at Beth-lehem**
- David
- Adullam
- Tekoa
- Keilah
- Hebron

0 2 4 miles
0 2 4 6 km

100

2 Sam. 5; 1 Chron. 11: 4–9; 14: 8–17

← Israelite force
⟵ Philistine force

DAVID took the stronghold of Zion, that is, the city of David.

(2 Samuel 5:7)

THE CONQUEST OF JERUSALEM AND DAVID'S WARS AGAINST THE PHILISTINES
CA. 1000 B.C.

THE QUARREL between Abner and Eshbaal helped David in overcoming both of them and to concentrate in his hands rule over both Judah and Israel. His first action was to conquer Jerusalem, which had been Jebusite, making it his capital. This was one of the most imaginative of David's exploits: he eliminated the foreign wedge between the southern and the northern tribes, and obtained a capital in the neutral area, which became royal property by right of conquest. From this time on, Jerusalem played a central role in the history of Israel. This step ushered in a new policy on the part of David, aimed at conquering the entire Land of Canaan, and to append the foreign enclaves to Israelite territory.

The Philistines now understood—too late—that their vassal had slipped his bonds. They hastened to crush David, and the battles were fought in the Valley of Rephaim, south of Jerusalem (compare Josh. 15:8). The Philistines seemed to have captured Beth-lehem during the conflict (2 Sam. 23:14). David smote them twice, pursuing them through the Shephelah to Gezer.

WHEN THE Ammonites saw... and hired the Syrians of Beth-rehob, and the Syrians of Zobah... and the king of Maacah with a thousand men, and the men of Tob...

(2 Samuel 10:6)

Map 101

- Sidon
- ZOBAH
- BETH-REHOB
- Damascus
- DAMASCUS
- Tyre
- Abel-beth-maacha
- Dan
- MAACAH
- Kedesh
- GESHUR
- Acco
- Ashtaroth
- Helam
- TOB
- Dor
- Megiddo
- Ramoth-gilead
- Tob
- Beth-shean
- Shechem
- Mahanaim
- AMMON
- **Siege and conquest of Rabath-ammon a year later**
- Aphek
- Joab
- Abishai
- Rabbath-bene-ammon
- Beth-el
- Gezer
- Jericho
- Jerusalem
- **David overcomes the Moabites**
- Medeba
- MOAB
- Aroer
- Kir-moab

0 5 10 miles
0 5 10 15 km

101

DAVID'S WARS IN TRANSJORDAN AND AGAINST THE ARAMEANS
CA. 990 B.C.

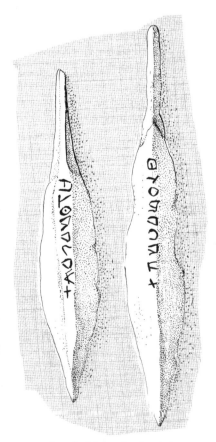

Arrowheads bearing inscription "Arrow of the servant of Lebaoth"

◀⟵ Aramean force
⟵ Israelite force

2 Sam. 8: 2; 10: 6–14; 12: 26–31;
1 Chron. 18: 2; 19: 1—20: 3

AND WHEN the Syrians of Damascus came to help Hadadezer king of Zobah, David slew twenty-two thousand men of the Syrians.

(2 Samuel 8:5)

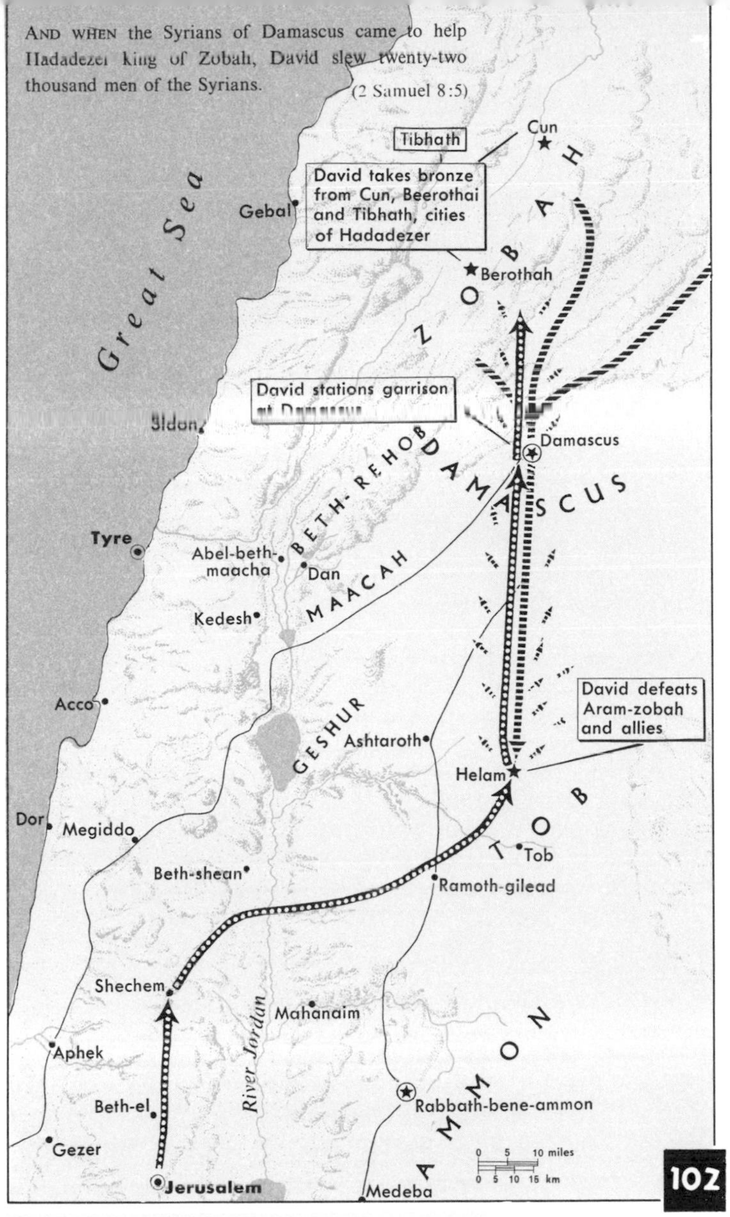

Map labels (map 102):
Great Sea · Tibhath · Cun · ZOBAH · Gebal · David takes bronze from Cun, Beerothai and Tibhath, cities of Hadadezer · ★ Berothah · Sidon · David stations garrison at Damascus · DAMASCUS · Damascus · BETH-REHOB · Tyre · Abel-beth-maacha · Dan · MAACAH · Kedesh · Acco · Ashtaroth · GESHUR · David defeats Aram-zobah and allies · Helam ★ · TOB · Dor · Megiddo · Tob · Beth-shean · Ramoth-gilead · Shechem · River Jordan · Mahanaim · AMMON · Aphek · Beth-el · Gezer · Rabbath-bene-ammon · Jerusalem · Medeba

0 5 10 miles
0 5 10 15 km

102

2 Sam. 8 : 3–10; 10 : 15–19; 1 Chron. 18 : 3–10

THE CONQUEST OF ARAM-ZOBAH AND DAMASCUS

SOON after, David turned to new conquests, and at first he set out against the Arameans in Transjordan to the east. In 1 Chronicles 19:7, it is related that the Arameans camped near Medeba; as this is south of Ammon, we may assume that this relates to David's conquest of Moab. Aramean auxiliaries apparently tried to obstruct David's ambitions from the very beginning. Aram-zobah at this time stood at the head of the Aramean kingdoms in Syria, its center being in the Valley of Lebanon. Its influence reached as far as the region of the Euphrates; Aram-zobah was David's strongest rival for the rule of Transjordan and Syria. His brilliant victories led to the conquest of Damascus and the subjection of Aram-zobah. David became thus ruler of all its vassals. In the region of Lebo-hammath (the "entrance of Hammath"), the traditional northern border point of the Land of Canaan, lay the border between Aram-zobah and the kingdom of Hamath; the gifts sent by Toi king of Hamath to David give evidence of Hamath's recognition of David's supremacy.

The Bible tells only of his gains in Transjordan and Syria, though it is clear that he also broadened the area of his conquests to the west of the Jordan. He vanquished the Philistines, and "took Methegh-ammah out of the hand of the Philistines" (2 Sam. 8:1). The phrase "Methegh-ammah" is unclear, even in the Hebrew; it may mean the "bridle of rule." In any event it is clear that David reduced the Philistine borders to the outskirts of Gath, Ekron, and Ashdod (see map 107) and diminished Philistine military power until it was no longer a serious threat to Israel. The Canaanite cities remaining in the Shephelah, in the Sharon, and in the north of the Holy Land were conquered. A portion of their lands became royal estates, overseen by specially appointed "stewards of king David's property" (1 Chron. 27:25–31).

David's conquest was completed with the campaign against Edom. With the appending of Elath to his kingdom, David was the sole ruler over the two main international trade routes passing through Palestine: the Via Maris and the King's Highway.

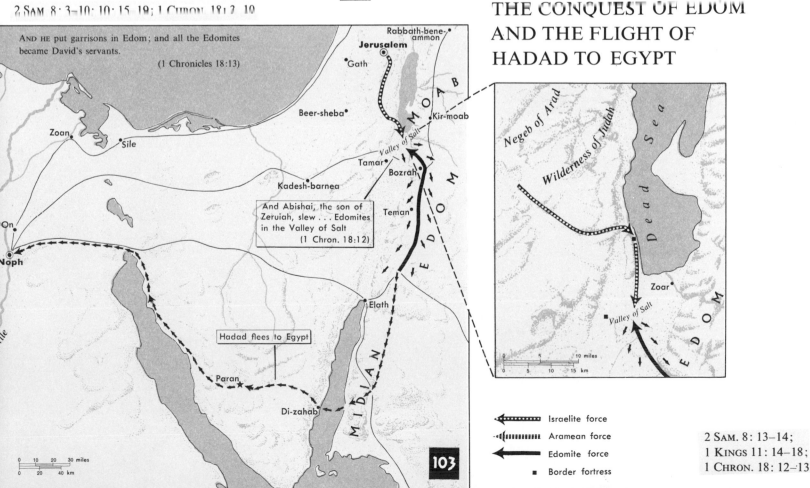

THE CONQUEST OF EDOM AND THE FLIGHT OF HADAD TO EGYPT

AND HE put garrisons in Edom; and all the Edomites became David's servants.

(1 Chronicles 18:13)

Map labels (map 103):
Rabbath-bene-ammon · Jerusalem · Gath · Zoan · Sile · Beer-sheba · MOAB · Kir-moab · Tamar · Valley of Salt · Bozrah · And Abishai, the son of Zeruiah, slew . . . Edomites in the Valley of Salt (1 Chron. 18:12) · Kadesh-barnea · Teman · EDOM · On · Noph · Elath · Hadad flees to Egypt · Paran · MIDIAN · Di-zahab

Inset map labels:
Negeb of Arad · Wilderness of Judah · Dead Sea · EDOM · Zoar · Valley of Salt · EDOM

0 5 10 miles
0 5 10 15 km

0 10 20 30 miles
0 20 40 km

103

Legend:
← Israelite force
← Aramean force
← Edomite force
■ Border fortress

2 Sam. 8 : 13–14;
1 Kings 11 : 14–18;
1 Chron. 18 : 12–13

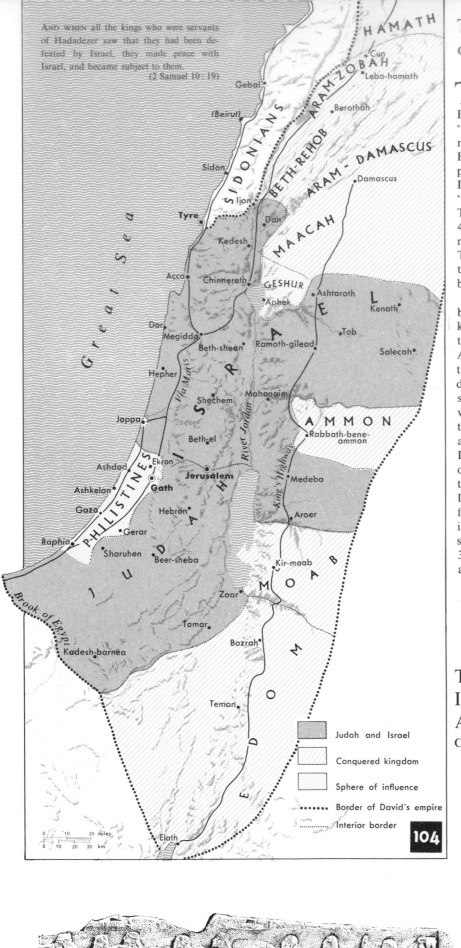

AND WHEN all the kings who were servants of Hadadezer saw that they had been defeated by Israel, they made peace with Israel, and became subject to them.

(2 Samuel 10:19)

Judah and Israel

Conquered kingdom

Sphere of influence

•••••• Border of David's empire

······· Interior border

104

THE KINGDOM OF DAVID
CA. 990 TO 968 B.C.

THE KINGDOM of Israel reached the height of its military an political power under David. The larger kingdoms in the Ancier East were at their nadir, leaving a vacuum in the western part of th "Fertile Crescent." In David, Israel found a brilliant and far-sighte military and political leader, able to exploit the prevailing situatior Following the encounter with Aram-zobah, Israel became the majc power in Syria and Palestine. The extent of the Israelite Empire unde David and Solomon is revealed by the passage concerning Solomon "For he had dominion over all the region west of the Euphrates fror Tiphsah to Gaza, over all the kings west of the Euphrates" (1 King 4:24). In the Hebrew, "west of the Euphrates" is "the other side of th river," the name used by the peoples of Mesopotamia for this area Thus the dominions of David and Solomon spread from Tiphsah o the Great Bend of the Euphrates to Philistine Gaza on the souther border of the Land of Canaan.

This was an administratively complex empire, three main element being discernible within it: the Israelite population; conquere kingdoms; and vassal kings. At the center of the empire stood th tribes of Israel and Judah, to which were appended the Canaanit Amorite regions brought under David's control. Around these la the conquered and tributary kingdoms: Edom, Moab, Ammon, Aram damascus, and Aram-zobah. Israelite governors were appointed ove some of these territories, as in Edom and Damascus (2 Sam. 8:6, 14 while in others members of the local royal house ruled, under th tutelage of the King of Israel. These latter were actually governor as in Ammon. One of the notables of Transjordan, who had come t David's aid during the rebellion of Absalom—Shobi the son of Nahas of Rabbath-bene-ammon (2 Sam. 17:27)—was probably the son c the king of Ammon who died before his kingdom was conquered b David (1 Chron. 19:1). The third element, the vassal kings, had bee forced, in one way or another, to accept David's hegemony; the included Philistia and various kingdoms in northern Transjordar such as Geshur, whose king was the grandfather of Absalom (2 Sam 3:3; 13:37). The relationship with Toi king of Hamath (2 Sam. 8:1C and Hiram king of Tyre was probably of a similar nature (2 Sam. 5:11

FOR he had dominion o
all the region west of
Euphrates from Tiphsah
Gaza, over all the kings w
of the Euphrates...

(1 Kings 4:2

THE ISRAELITE KINGDOM
IN THE DAYS OF DAVID
AND SOLOMON
CA. 990 TO 928 B.C.

—— International highway

Area of sovereignty of king of Israel

Bringing tribute to overlord (relief on obelisk of Asshurnasirpal II from Calah)

⟵ Route of census-takers

106

So the king said to Joab and the commanders of the
army, who were with him, "Go through all the tribes
of Israel from Dan to Beer-sheba, and number the
people…"

(2 Samuel 24:2)

JOAB'S CENSUS

CA. 980 B.C.

THE AREA of Israelite settlement is reflected in the description of
Joab's journey during the census, carried out probably for purposes of taxes and levies. He started from Aroer on the border of
Moab, and reached Sidon and the "fortress of Tyre" (2 Sam. 24:6-7).
The description of the northern part of Joab's journey resembles that
of the northern border of the Tribe of Asher (Joshua 19:28–29). The
"fortified city of Tyre" was undoubtedly the mainland city opposite
the island of Tyre. It is referred to as Ushu in the Egyptian and Accadian
sources, Palaetyrus in the Hellenistic period, and is possibly the biblical
Hosah. Drinking water for Tyre was brought from this city; thus
Tyre's dependence upon David, who controlled its mainland base,
is clearly evident. The description of the census indicates that even
this decidedly Canaanite region, which spread from the plain of
Acco to the Litani River, was included within the Israelite section of
the kingdom.

AND the territory of its inheritance included Zorah,
Eshtaol, Ir-shemesh… with the territory over against
Joppa.

(Joshua 19:41–46)

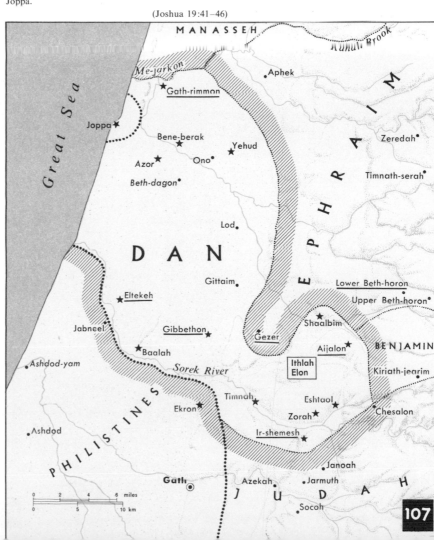

107

THE CITIES OF DAN

A. 980 B.C.

THE LIST of the cities of Dan (Joshua 19:40–46) fits only the time
of David, for prior to this most of the region was outside Israelite
dominion, and later it partly reverted to Philistine control. Thus it is
evident that the border of Philistia in the days of David passed along
the Sorek Valley, on the very border of the city of Ekron. As Ekron
itself was never annexed, its appearance in the list is strange. This
difficulty is resolved by reading in Joshua 19:43: "Timnah of Ekron"
rather than "Timnah and Ekron." Timnah, a common name, was
within the territory of Philistine Ekron, in accord with the tales of
Samson. The port city of Joppa, too, remained unconquered, though
Israel's relations with it were cordial. Most likely, it also accepted
David's dominion, as possibly indicated by the bringing of wood
for the Temple from Lebanon, from Tyre "by sea to Joppa" (2 Chron.
2:16).

Gezer Levitic city

••••• State boundary

------ Tribal boundary

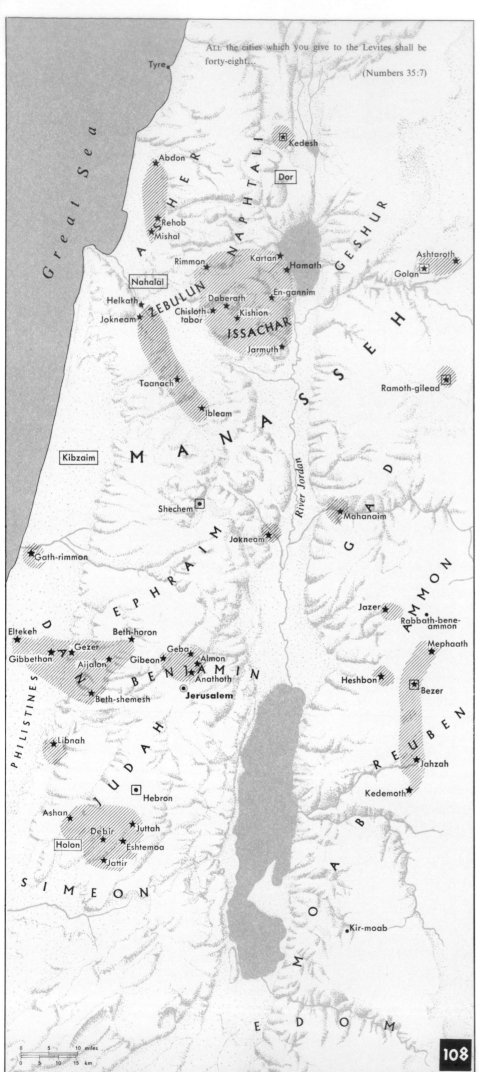

ALL the cities which you give to the Levites shall be forty-eight...

(Numbers 35:7)

Tyre

Kedesh ⊠

Abdon★

Dor

Rehob★
Mishal★

Rimmon★   Kartan★   Hamath★
                                      Ashtaroth★
Nahalal   Daberath★ En-gannim★   Golan★

Helkath★   Chisloth- Kishion★
Jokneam★   tabor★
ZEBULUN   ISSACHAR

                Jarmuth★

Taanach★   Ramoth-gilead ⊠

        Ibleam★

Kibzaim

MANASSEH

Shechem ⊡   Mahanaim★

        Jokneam★

Gath-rimmon★

EPHRAIM   Jazer★
                             Rabbath-bene-
Eltekeh★   ammon
        Gezer★ Beth-horon★
                                  Mephaath★
Gibbethon★ Aijalon★ Gibeon★ Geba★ Almon★
        BENJAMIN   Anathoth★   Heshbon★
Beth-shemesh★   Bezer ⊠
        ⊙ Jerusalem

Libnah★   Jahzah★

JUDAH   Kedemoth★
Ashan★
    Debir★ Juttah★
Holon   Eshtemoa★
        Jattir★
SIMEON

    Hebron ⊡

                              Kir-moab•

Great Sea

ASHER

NAPHTALI

GESHUR

River Jordan

GAD

AMMON

REUBEN

MOAB

EDOM

PHILISTINES

DAN

THE LEVITIC CITIES
CA. 980 B.C.

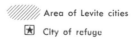

/////// Area of Levite cities

⊠ City of refuge

JOSH. 21; 1 CHRON. 6: 39–6

THE LIST of Levitic cities should also be ascribed to the tim
David, for this is the only period in which all the cities listed
were within the borders of Israel. Most of the Acco plain passed
the hands of Hiram king of Tyre already in the time of Solo
(see maps 113 and 115), and at the end of Jeroboam's reign Gibbet
was again Philistine (1 Kings 15:27).

The forty-eight Levitic cities were spread throughout the tri
four in each tribe. Comparing the two versions of the list (Josh.
1 Chron. 6:39–66), it is possible to reconstruct the original list
much certainty. Hebron and Shechem were most likely added to
list from the list of cities of refuge, as there were four Levitic citie
Judah and in Ephraim even without them.

The populace of these cities was not strictly Levite; the latter ra
dwelt in the cities along side the rest of the people. The cities were
located at the tribal centers, but were on the borders of the tribal a
and in former Canaanite areas. The Canaanite areas were undoubt
extensive and became royal property after the conquest; and it
here that the king could settle the Levites. So it was with the citie
Benjamin in the vicinity of Jerusalem, where all the land which belor
to the house of Saul ultimately passed to the Davidic dynasty. D
settled in these cities Levite families from Judah, loyal to him
his house. They practiced worship and were appointed "for all
work of the Lord and for the service of the king" (1 Chron. 26:30–
It is therefore not surprising that upon the splitting up of the Un
Monarchy Jeroboam expelled the Levites, who returned to Ju
(2 Chron. 11:13–14).

David organized the administration of the kingdom into tw
units over which stood governors. Each unit was named after
Israelite tribe (1 Chron. 27:16–22), though several of the tribes (
as Dan and Simeon) were no longer in existence as such, having
assimilated by their neighbors. This system retained the flavo
tradition, but actually deeply affected the rights of the pre-Mona
tribal leagues, Judah and Israel. Instead of two individual groups
two centers, we now see an overall organization according to
twelve tribes, with Jerusalem at its center, having inherited the pr
inence of both Shiloh and Hebron. The transfer of the Holy Ark f
Kiriath-jearim to Jerusalem signified the concept of a Un
Monarchy (2 Sam. 6).

These developments provided the motives for Absalom's rev
which shook the very foundations of the kingdom. Absalom succe
in gaining the loyalty of the elders of both Judah and Israel, promi
to restore the rights annulled by David. Thus Absalom did not
without consulting these elders, whereas after David's rise to po
we hear nothing of these ancient institutions. Absalom failed,
David, too, was forced to yield: though holding the upper h
David found no recourse but to compromise with the elders of Ju
As a consequence, a new rebellion broke out in all of Israel u
Sheba the son of Bichri, over the matter of David's preferential tr
ment of Judah.

During Absalom's revolt, David sought refuge in Mahanaim
did Eshbaal the son of Saul in his day. It would seem that the Isra
settlement in Transjordan, which lived in constant peril of ra
supported a strong central government which was able to provide
their protection. The location of Mahanaim, in the deep canyo
the Jabbok, serves to explain how Ahimaaz the son of Zadok ou
the Cushite: the Cushite took the more direct, but up-hill-and-do
dale route of the "forest of Ephraim," whereas Ahimaaz ran
longer, though much easier route passing through the Jordan Va
and thus arrived first.

THEN AHIMAAZ ran by the way of the plain, and outran the Cushite.

(2 Samuel 18:23)

THE BATTLE
IN THE FOREST
OF EPHRAIM
CA. 975 B.C.

So ABSALOM stole the hearts of the men of Israel.

(2 Samuel 15:6)

THE REBELLION OF ABSALOM
CA. 978 B.C.

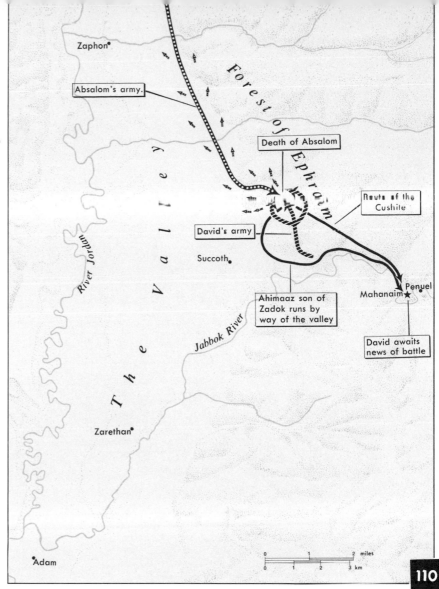

2 SAM. 18

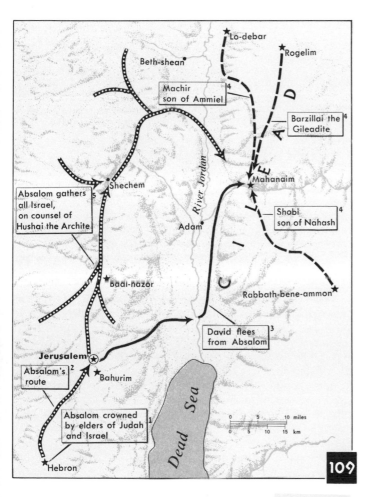

2 SAM. 15—19

WE HAVE no portion in David, and we have no inheritance in the son of Jesse; every man to his tents, O Israel!

(2 Samuel 20:1)

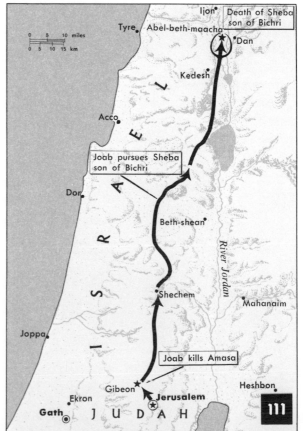

THE REBELLION OF SHEBA
THE SON OF BICHRI
CA. 977 B.C.

2 SAM. 20: 1—22

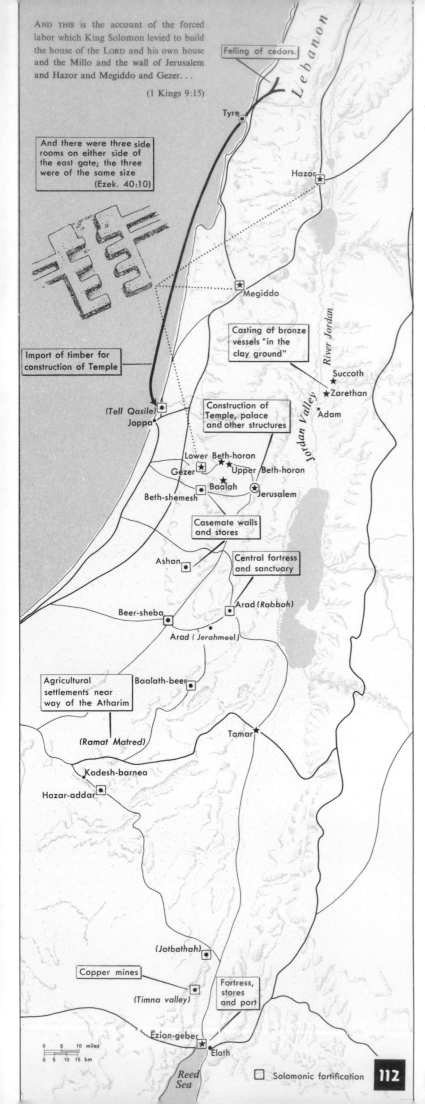

AND THIS is the account of the forced labor which King Solomon levied to build the house of the LORD and his own house and the Millo and the wall of Jerusalem and Hazor and Megiddo and Gezer...

(1 Kings 9:15)

And there were three side rooms on either side of the east gate; the three were of the same size

(Ezek. 40:10)

Import of timber for construction of Temple

Felling of cedars.

Lebanon

Tyre

Hazor

Megiddo

River Jordan

Casting of bronze vessels "in the clay ground"

Succoth

Zarethan

Adam

Jordan valley

(Tell Qasile)

Joppa

Construction of Temple, palace and other structures

Lower Beth-horon

Gezer

Upper Beth-horon

Baalah

Jerusalem

Beth-shemesh

Casemate walls and stores

Ashan

Central fortress and sanctuary

Arad (Rabbah)

Beer-sheba

Arad (Jerahmeel)

Baalath-beer

Agricultural settlements near way of the Atharim

Tamar

(Ramat Matred)

Kadesh-barnea

Hazar-addar

(Jotbathah)

Copper mines

(Timna valley)

Fortress, stores and port

Ezion-geber

Elath

Reed Sea

□ Solomonic fortification

0 5 10 miles
0 5 10 15 km

112

THE BUILDING PROJECTS OF SOLOMON

DAVID transformed Israel from a small state into a power, and Solomon from a poor country of narrow horizons into an international center. At this time a revolution began in the life of the Israelite cities and villages; suddenl they entered the circle of the most advanced cultures of the period. Much wealt flowed into the royal treasuries and Solomon came to be known as one of th great builders in the history of the Holy Land.

Hazor, Megiddo, and Gezer, key points in the kingdom, were built as centra fortress cities; identical gates have been found in all three cities, similar in pla to that of the eastern gate of the temple court, as given in Ezekiel's descriptio (40:10). The remains of fortifications and public buildings from the time o Solomon indicate that not all his works are listed in the Bible. Solomon use construction materials from Phoenicia, transporting them on Phoenician ships Built with perfectly dressed stone and magnificent ornamentation, the Phoeni cian-Israelite capitals ("proto-Aeolian" capitals) bear evidence of the skill o Phoenician construction; these can be seen in various excavations in Palestine where remains from the time of the United Monarchy and later have been found

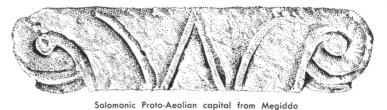

Solomonic Proto-Aeolian capital from Megiddo

THE DISTRICTS UNDER SOLOMON

THESE immense building activities demanded many sources of incom These were supplied by levies on vanquished kingdoms, as well as on th Israelite populace, levy—meaning both forced labor and taxes in kind. I 1 Kings 4 there is a list of the twelve governors of Solomon, among whose duti was to provide provisions for the royal court. The twelve districts of "all Israel did not include Judah, and it is thus obvious that Judah and Israel were regarde as two separate entities by the royal administration. The formerly Canaani cities in the plains were now included in independent districts—Israelite citi in every way; these districts, however, are given according to the names of the principal cities, whereas the other districts are named according to the regul tribal appelations. The city list of the northern tribes in Joshua 19 probab pertains to this administrative division. No similar division of Judah in th period has been preserved, and thus it may be assumed that Solomon exempted from taxes or reduced the levy there.

In spite of the considerable flow into the royal treasury, Solomon's debts creased and he was forced to give to Hiram king of Tyre twenty cities in Gali (1 Kings 9:10–13). From this time on, Cabul was the border between Tyre a Israel. 2 Chronicles 8:2 possibly relates to this; most of the plain of Acco aga became Tyrian territory.

This cession is evidence of growing political weakness, which there are oth indications of as well. Already under Solomon, rumblings of revolt were felt Damascus and Edom (1 Kings 11:14–25), most likely with the encouragemen of Egypt's pharaohs who again coveted Palestine. The Gezer affair too can th be explained: in the Bible we read only that Pharaoh conquered and razed Geze which was a Canaanite city, and gave it as dowry to Solomon, who had marri his daughter (1 Kings 9:16). Nothing is said of what took place prior to the co quest of Gezer and how the Egyptians came to be at this city in northern Ph listia. It appears that the Egyptians had at this time returned and gained contr over Philistia, conquering Gezer as well, even though under David, it was u doubtedly included within Israelite territory, like the other Canaanite citie Solomon, however, still had power to repel the Egyptians from the center of t Holy Land, forcing them to come to peace terms with him. With this treaty, t Egyptians returned to Israel the ruined city of Gezer. Solomon later rebuilt an fortified it; from then on it served as a border fortress against Philistia, which wa under Egyptian rule. The many fortifications constructed at that time be witness to the worsening political situation and the deterioration of security.

////// Border of Solomonic provin

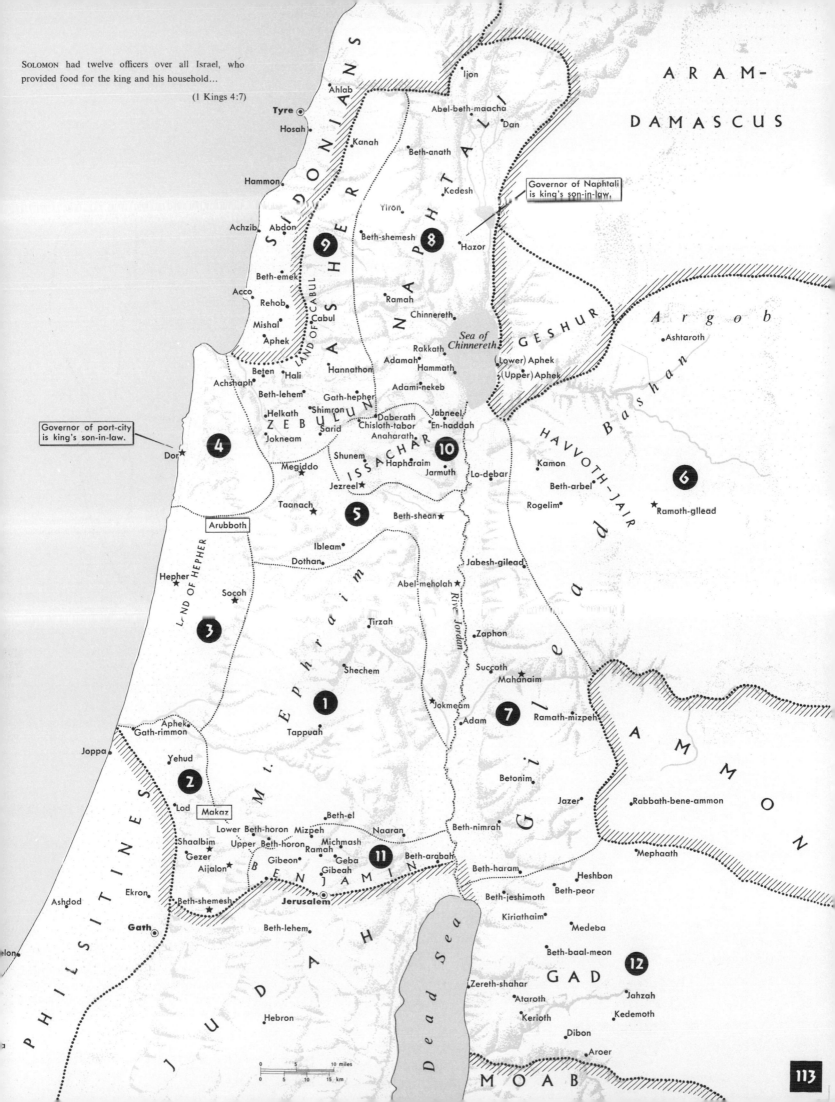

SOLOMON had twelve officers over all Israel, who
provided food for the king and his household...

(1 Kings 4:7)

ARAM-
DAMASCUS

SIDONIANS

Tyre

Hosah
Kanah
Ahlab
Ijon
Abel-beth-maacha
Dan
Beth-anath
Hammon
Kedesh
Yiron
Governor of Naphtali
is king's son-in-law.
Achzib Abdon
Beth-shemesh
9
Hazor
8
Beth-emek
Acco
Rehob
Ramah
Chinnereth
Mishal
Aphek Cabul
ASHER
NAPHTALI
GESHUR
Argob
Ashtaroth
Beten Hali
Hannathon
Sea of
Chinnereth
(Lower) Aphek
(Upper) Aphek
Bashan
Achshaph
Beth-lehem
Rakkath
Adamah Hammath
Governor of port-city
is king's son-in-law.
Helkath Shimron
Gath-hepher
Adami-nekeb
ZEBULUN
Sarid
Daberath
Chisloth-tabor
Jabneel
En-haddah
HAVVOTH-JAIR
4
Jokneam
Anaharath
10
Dor
Shunem
Hapharaim
Kamon
Megiddo
ISSACHAR
Jarmuth
Lo-debar
Beth-arbel
6
Jezreel
Rogelim
Ramoth-gilead
Taanach
5
Beth-shean
Arubboth
Ibleam
Jabesh-gilead
Dothan
Abel-meholah
Hepher
LND OF HEPHER
Socoh
Ephraim
Gilead
River Jordan
Zaphon
3
Tirzah
Succoth
Mahanaim
Shechem
1
Jokmeam
7
Ramath-mizpeh
Tappuah
Adam
Aphek
Gath-rimmon
Joppa
Yehud
AMMON
2
Lod Makaz
Betonim
Beth-el
Naaran
Beth-nimrah
Jazer
Rabbath-bene-ammon
Lower Beth-horon Mizpeh
Shaalbim
Upper Beth-horon Ramah Michmash
Gezer
Gibeon Geba
11
Beth-arabah
Mephaath
Aijalon
Gibeah
Beth-haram
Ekron
BENJAMIN
Beth-shemesh
Jerusalem
Heshbon
Beth-peor
Ashdod
Beth-jeshimoth
Gath
Beth-lehem
Kiriathaim
Medeba
JUDAH
Beth-baal-meon
Hebron
Dead Sea
12
GAD
Zereth-shahar
Jahzah
Ataroth
Kerioth
Kedemoth
Dibon
Aroer
MOAB
PHILISTINES
Mt. Ephraim

0   5   10 miles
0   5   10   15 km

113

THE BUILDING AND EXPANSION OF JERUSALEM

IN the fourth year the foundation of the house of the LORD was laid. . .He was seven years in building it. Solomon was building his own house thirteen years.

(1 Kings 6:37 7:1)

SOLOMON extended the limits of Jerusalem, fortifying and embellishing it as befitting the capital of the large kingdom. The crowning achievement was the building of the Temple in Jerusalem, and though it was intended as the temple of the Davidic dynasty, the temple became the symbol of national unity. Worship in the temple was based on the tradition of the twelve Israelite tribes, a tradition which was never realized in the reality of the royal administration.

A CHARIOT could be imported from Egypt for six hundred shekels of silver, and a horse for a hundred and fifty... they were exported to all the kings of the Hittites and the kings of Syria.

(1 Kings 10:29)

Extention of city in 7th-6th c.

Gate of Ephraim?
Gate of Benjamin?
Fish gate?
MISHNEH
Temple
Palace
MACHTESH?
Walls of Solom[on]
OPHEL
Valley Gate
The Valley
CITY OF DAVID
En-gihon
Hezekiah's tun[nel]
Pool of Siloam
Valley of Hinnom
Kidron Brook
Stairs descending from City of David
Kidron Brook
En-rogel

0 50 100 150 yards
0 50 100 meters

114

2 SAM. 5: 9; 1 KINGS 6—7;
2 KINGS 20: 20; 22: 14; Is. 22: 9–11;
2 CHRON. 2—8; 26: 9; 27: 3; 32: 2–5; 33:

KUE
Samal
Carchemish
Arpad
HITTITE KINGS
Haran
Gozan
Nineveh
Aleppo
BETH — EDEN
Tiphsah
Tribute, corvee
ELISAH
Arvad
Hamath
KINGS OF ARAM
Asshur
Tribute, corvee
Sumur
Tadmor
Anat
Euphrates River
Byblos
Lebo-hamath
Great Sea
Sidon
Horses
Tyre
Damascus
Timber
Joppa
Grain, oil, wine
Gaza Jerusalem
On
Chariots
Noph
The traders and merchants . . . and all the kings of Arabia and the governors of the land brought gold and silver to Solomon (2 Chron. 9:14)
Dumah
Ezion-geber
Tema
From Ophir
Monkeys, parrots, gold, ivory, sandalwood, precious stones
From Sheba
Perfumes, gold, precious stones, spices
Shihor of Egypt
E G Y P T

0 20 40 miles
0 25 50 km

No-amon

KINGS OF ARABIA 115

TRADE UNDER SOLOMON

IN spite of fissures appearing in his large kingdo[m] Solomon continued to hold the important tra[de] routes which passed through Palestine. He control[led] the trade passing along them, and thus greatly [en]riched his coffers. Solomon raised a considerable ar[my] of chariotry, which was based in the "chariot citie[s]" and also became a major broker in the profita[ble] horse and chariot trade (1 Kings 10:28–29). H[is] rule in Edom and on the Gulf of Elath gave him acc[ess] to the lands of southern Arabia and east Africa, fro[m] whence the most precious luxury articles of antiqu[ity] were brought. This rich trade is hinted at in the lege[nd] about the visit of the Queen of Sheba.

1 KINGS 5: 15–32; 9: 26–10: 29;
2 CHRON. 1: 15–17; 2; 8: 17–9: 28

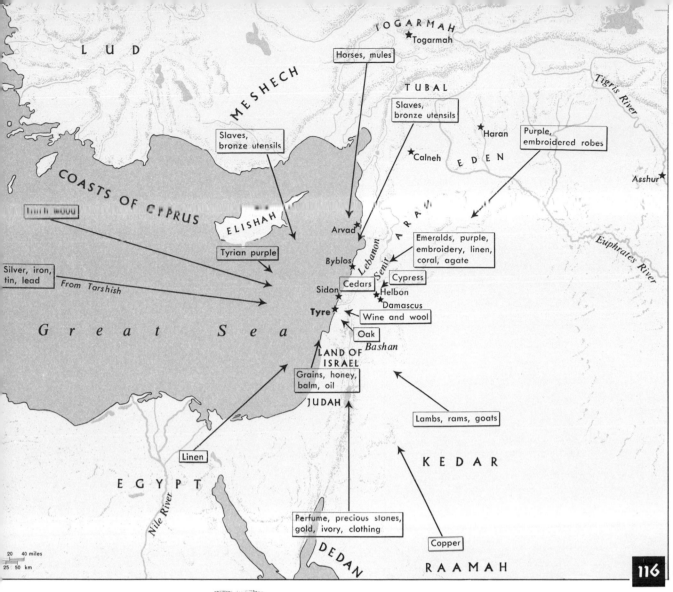

AND say to Tyre, who dwells at the entrance to the sea, merchant of the peoples on many coastlands...

(Ezekiel 27:3)

Map labels:

LUD

TOGARMAH
★ Togarmah

MESHECH

Horses, mules

TUBAL

Slaves, bronze utensils

★ Haran

Purple, embroidered robes

★ Calneh

E D E N

★ Asshur

Tigris River

Euphrates River

COASTS OF CYPRUS

Slaves, bronze utensils

ELISHAH

Thin h wood

Tyrian purple

★ Arvad

Byblos

Lebanon

Senir

A R A M

Emeralds, purple, embroidery, linen, coral, agate

Silver, iron, tin, lead

From Tarshish

Cedars

Cypress

Sidon ★

Helbon

Damascus

Tyre ★

Wine and wool

Oak

Great Sea

Bashan

LAND OF ISRAEL

Grains, honey, balm, oil

JUDAH

Lambs, rams, goats

Linen

K E D A R

E G Y P T

Nile River

Perfume, precious stones, gold, ivory, clothing

Copper

DEDAN

R A A M A H

20 40 miles
25 50 km

116 EZEK. 27

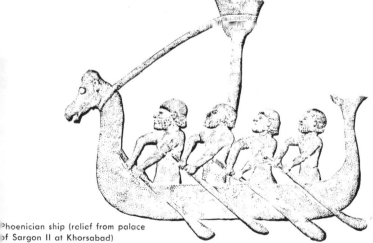

Phoenician ship (relief from palace of Sargon II at Khorsabad)

THE KINGDOM OF ISRAEL lacked the technical knowledge necessary for the development of seafaring commerce on a large scale, and Solomon sought aid from the experienced mariners of Hiram king of Tyre in sending out his "ships of Tarshish." Tarshish, on the Mediterranean (compare Jonah 1:3), was probably Sardinia. The "ships of Tarshish" were a type of large ship suitable for long voyages on the high seas.

Tyre began to develop in his period, to the point where it became the largest maritime power in the Mediterranean. Its merchants founded colonies and ports along the entire Mediterranean littoral, the most famous of these being Carthage. Ezekiel's lamentation (chapter 27) contains a wonderful description of Tyre, "merchant of the peoples on many coastlands." This is probably based on a literary source which predated Ezekiel. So long as the strong treaty between Israel and Tyre remained the two peoples controlled the most important trade routes on land and sea in the Near East.

THE SHIPS of Tarshish traveled for you with your merchandise. "So you were filled and heavily laden in the heart of the seas."

(Ezekiel 27:25)

THE EXPANSION OF THE TYRIANS IN THE MEDITERRANEAN
FROM 9TH CENTURY B.C. ON

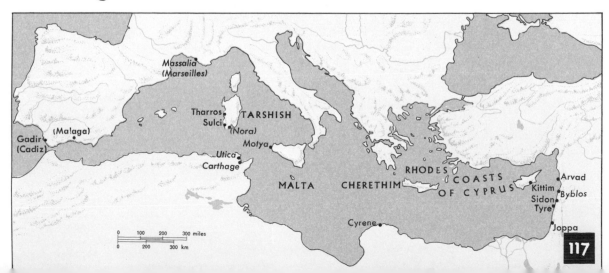

Map labels:

Massalia (Marseilles)

Tharros
Sulci

TARSHISH

(Nora)

Gadir (Cadiz)

(Malaga)

Motya

Utica

Carthage

RHODES

MALTA

CHERETHIM

COASTS OF CYPRUS

Arvad

Kittim

Sidon

Byblos

Tyre

Cyrene

Joppa

0 100 200 300 miles
0 200 300 km

117

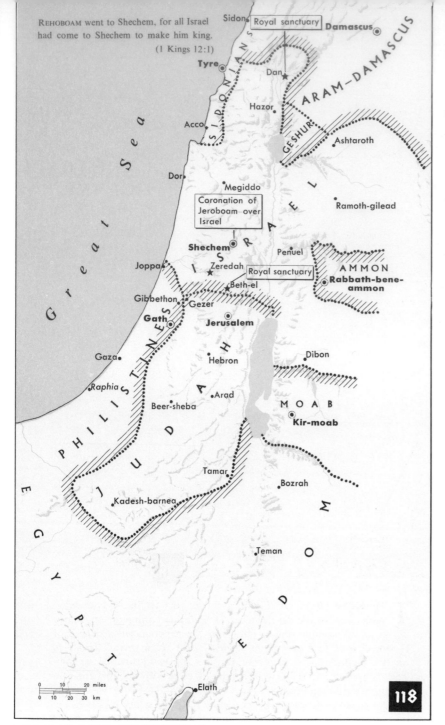

REHOBOAM went to Shechem, for all Israel had come to Shechem to make him king.

(1 Kings 12:1)

Royal sanctuary

Coronation of Jeroboam over Israel

Royal sanctuary

118

1 KINGS 11: 26—12: 33; 2 CHRON. 10

THE DIVISION OF THE KINGDOM
928 B.C.

THE DIFFERENCES between Judah and Israel were never reconciled under David and Solomon, and the northern tribes regarded the rule of the house of David as Judean overlordship. The internal tension, which increased during the reign of Solomon, brought about the division of the kingdom after his death. Rehoboam, Solomon's son, failed to grasp that only by far-reaching concessions to Israel could he preserved the United Monarchy. When revolt broke out among the tribes of the north, Rehoboam was not able to put it down. Only Benjamin—of all the northern Israelite tribes—joined Judah and the House of David, and this was most likely due to its proximity to Jerusalem. The tribes of Transjordan joined the northern kingdom of Israel because of their natural geographic ties. The conquered territories, with the exception of Edom, which was tied to Judah, were also regarded as possessions of Israel. Most of the conquered territories shed the Israelite yoke at the time of the division of the Monarchy. In Damascus and Edom, revolts had already broken out under Solomon, and from data on later periods it appears that Moab and Ammon also gained independence after Solomon's death. The large kingdom founded by David now disintegrated as fast as it had been created. In its place arose two small and mutually hostile states.

THE FORTIFICATIONS OF REHOBOAM
CA. 928 TO 920 B.C.

REHOBOAM dwelt in Jerusalem, and he built cities for defense in Judah.

(2 Chronicles 11:5)

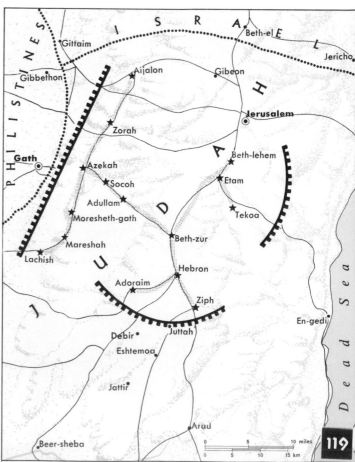

IT IS not known whether the list of fortified cities of Rehoboam in Judah pertains to the period prior to Shishak's invasion; Rehoboam may have only began fortification of the cities prior to this campaign, concluding his work after. These fortifications delineate the border of Philistia to the west, and do not include the Negeb or the southern hill region to the south. The description of these fortresses indicates that Rehoboam reduced the lines of defense of his kingdom, intending to hold only its heart. There were, however, no fortifications facing the northern flank; throughout his life, Rehoboam refused to abandon his aspirations of restoring rebellious Israel to the house of David (1 Kings 14:30) and did not want to define the northern boundary of his kingdom by building a chain of fortresses there.

———— Road leading into Judah blocked by fortifications

▪▪▪▪▪ Line of fortifications

░░░░ Road connecting fortresses

2 CHRON. 11: 5–12

119

In the fifth year of King Rehoboam, Shishak king of Egypt came up against Jerusalem...

(1 Kings 14:25)

TYRE

GESHUR

Sea of Chinnereth

Acco

Dor

ISRAEL

Fragment of stele of Shishak found here

Megiddo

Shunem

Aruna

Taanach

Beth-shean

Borim

Rehob

Gath

Yaham

Socoh

Tirzah

Zaphon

Mahanaim

Shechem

Succoth

Penuel

River Jordan

(Tell Qasile)

Aphek

Then Jeroboam built Shechem . . . and he went out from there and built Penuel

(1 Kings 12:25)

Joppa

Adam

PHILISTINES

Zemaraim

Beth-el

Beth-horon

Gezer

Gibeon

Aijalon

Ashdod

Ekron

Rabbah

Kiriath-jearim

Jerusalem

Rehoboam raises tribute for Shishak

Ashkelon

Gath

JUDAH

Dead Sea

Gaza

phia

"Hagarim"

Arad Rabbah

Sharuhen

Beer-sheba

MOAB

Arad of Jerahmeel

Negeb

raelite agricultural ttlement destroyed this period

(Ramat Matred)

JUDAH

Tamar

desh-barnea

EDOM

To Ezion-geber

0   5   10 miles
0 5 10 15 km

120

THE CAMPAIGNS OF SHISHAK
924 B.C.

THE PHARAOHS in Egypt did all they could to weaken Israel in the time of Solomon. Shishak King of Egypt now took the opportunity and in the fifth year of Rehoboam's reign set out on a campaign of conquest and plunder. In addition to the scanty information on Shishak's campaign in the Bible, which mostly concerns the golden shields given to him in tribute, there is an inscription in Egypt listing the places conquered by Shishak. This confirms the biblical narrative that Shishak went up against Jerusalem, but was satisfied with a heavy tribute, and then turned northward toward the kingdom of Israel. Here, he approached Tirzah (and Shechem ?), Penuel and Mahanaim (see 1 Kings 12:25). A fragment of a stele of Shishak has been found in excavations at Megiddo, indicating that the Egyptians held this important fortress for a time.

In the second part of Shishak's list there appear the names of places in the Negeb; some of these were called "hagarim", probably referring to the fortresses surrounded by sloping defences (glacis). Shishak probably proceeded southward to Ezion-geber, whose destruction in this period is inferred from the excavations there. One of the main aims of this campaign undoubtedly was to break up Judean trade with Arabia.

Fortified city
(relief from palace of
Asshurnasirpal II at Calah)

1 KINGS 14: 25–28; 2 CHRON. 12: 2–12;
CITY-LISTS, SHISHAK—KARNAK, EGYPT

THEN ABIJAH stood up on Mount Zemaraim which is in the hill country of Ephraim, and said, "Hear me, O Jeroboam and all Israel!"

(2 Chronicles 13:4)

THE CONQUEST OF ABIJAH
CA. 911 B.C.

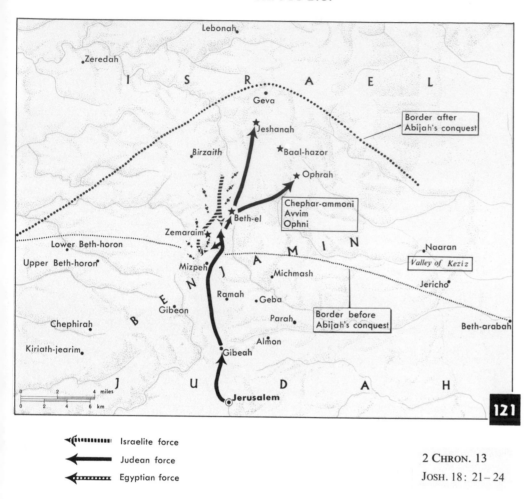

	Israelite force
	Judean force
	Egyptian force

2 CHRON. 13
JOSH. 18: 21–24

THE CAMPAIGN
OF ZERAH THE ETHIOPIAN
CA. 900 B.C.

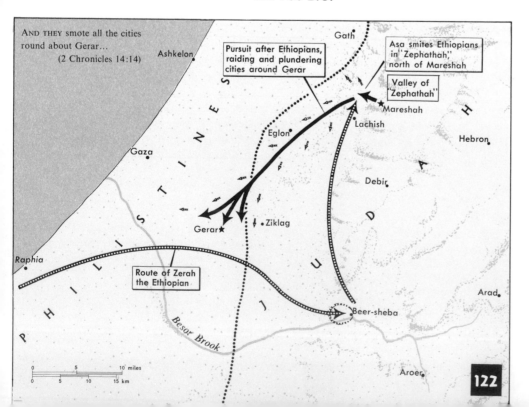

AND THEY smote all the cities round about Gerar...

(2 Chronicles 14:14)

2 CHRON. 14: 8–14; 16: 8

HOSTILITIES between Judah and Israel continued throughout the reigns of Rehoboam, Abijah, and Asa, kings of Judah, and the dynasties of Jeroboam and Baasha in Israel. The war sapped the strength of both kingdoms without either prevailing. The border squabbles were mostly in Benjamin, which Israel claimed. Abijah the son of Rehoboam raised a considerable army and conquered the hills of Beth-el. In the biblical account, the cities of Beth-el, Ephron (Ophrah), and Jeshanah (2 Chron. 13:19) are mentioned, probably referring to the whole of the northern part of the territory of Benjamin. In the days of Asa, however, Israel was stronger, and Baasha was able to recover the conquered territories. He was even able to press on to the cities farther south in Benjamin. To safeguard the new border, Baasha fortified Raman, on the main central highway, some five miles from Jerusalem.

The kingdom of Damascus was allying itself with various Aramean kingdoms and, during the ninth century, became Israel's most serious rival. Their conflict pivoted mainly on control of Transjordan and the northernmost parts of the Holy Land. The kings of Damascus held the title "Ben-hadad"— "the son of (the god) Hadad." Out of dire distress, Asa appealed to the first Ben-hadad king of Aram-damascus, who had taken advantage of the civil strife and invaded eastern Galilee. The excavations at Hazor have revealed that this city, too, was included in the "store-cities" of Naphtali conquered during this campaign (2 Chron. 16:4). The borders of Israel in northern Transjordan were probably reduced, as is indicated by the situation in the time of Ahab.

These blows forced Baasha to retreat from Judah and to return to Tirzah, which had become the capital of Israel, perhaps already at the end of the reign of Rehoboam (1 Kings 14:17). We do not know why the kings of Israel chose it as their capital, but Tirzah was an important center in Mount Ephraim even in Canaanite times. After Baasha had quitted the borders of Judah, Asa hastily fortified Mizpeh and Geba, the cities closest to the northern border of Benjamin. In the excavations at Mizpeh (Tell en-Nasbeh) there came to light the stout wall of the fortress built by Asa. This implies that he de facto accepted the delineation of the border between Israel and Judah in this region. From then on, until the destruction of the kingdom of Israel, there were no significant changes in this border.

During the long reign of Asa in Judah, order was restored and prosperity returned to the kingdom. The fruits were harvested however, by his son, Jehoshaphat. Asa also won a significant military victory in repulsing Zerah the Ethiopian, who had come to Judah with an army of Ethiopians and Lubim (2 Chron. 16:8). Zerah the Ethiopian was perhaps Osorkon 1, the son of Shishak, a pharaoh of the twenty-second, Libyan dynasty. Excavations at Beer-sheba have shown that at that period the city was destroyed for a second time.

AND THEY carried away the stones of Ramah and its timber, with which Baasha had been building; and with them King Asa built Geba of Benjamin and Mizpah.

(1 Kings 15:22)

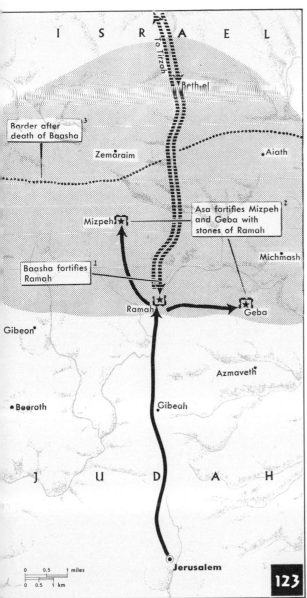

Border after death of Baasha

Asa fortifies Mizpeh and Geba with stones of Ramah

Baasha fortifies Ramah

Israel

Bethel

Zemaraim

Aiath

Mizpeh

Michmash

Ramah

Geba

Gibeon

Azmaveth

Beeroth

Gibeah

JUDAH

Jerusalem

0   0.5   1 miles
0   0.5   1 km

123

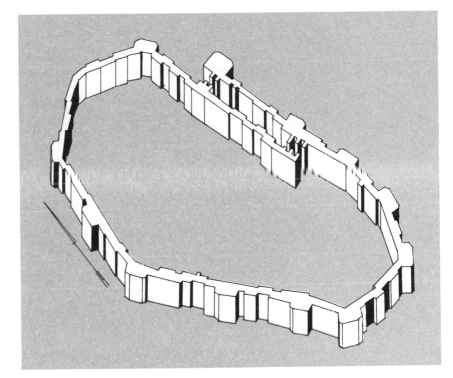

Plan of wall of Mizpeh in the days of Asa

Contested area

City fortifications

AND BEN-HADAD hearkened to King Asa, and sent the commanders of his armies against the cities of Israel, and conquered Ijon, Dan, Abel-beth-maacah, and all Chinneroth, with all the land of Naphtali.

(1 Kings 15:20)

HE WAR OF ASA
ND BAASHA

885 B.C.

1 KINGS 16: 16–22; 2 KINGS 17: 1–6

THE CAMPAIGN
OF BEN-HADAD I

885 B.C.

1 KINGS 15: 18–21; 2 CHRON. 16: 2–5

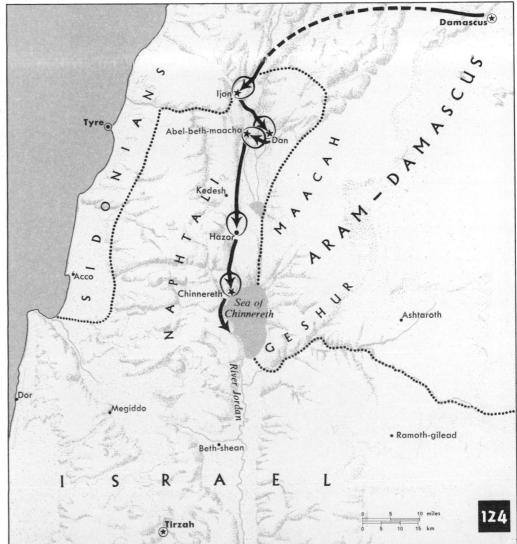

Damascus

Ijon

Tyre

Abel-beth-maacha

Dan

SIDONIANS

Kedesh

NAPHTALI

MAACAH

ARAM-DAMASCUS

Hazor

Acco

Chinnereth

Sea of Chinnereth

GESHUR

Ashtaroth

Dor

River Jordan

Megiddo

Beth-shean

Ramoth-gilead

ISRAEL

Tirzah

0   5   10 miles
0   5   10   15 km

124

ALL ISRAEL made Omri, the commander of the army,
king over Israel that day in the camp.

(1 Kings 16:16)

THE RISE OF OMRI
882 B.C.

FROM THE DAYS of Nadab king of Israel, Gibbethon, a Levitic city, was a sore spot on the border of Philistine Ekron. At the end of the reign of Elah the son of Baasha, news of the revolt of Zimri reached the Israelite forces encamped against Gibbethon; the host then raised their commander Omri as king over them. He hastened to Tirzah, the capital of Israel and the seat of Zimri, laying siege to the town and conquering it. Only after a civil war, however, was Omri able to secure the kingdom for himself.

Omri stabilized the kingdom and strengthened it against Aram. He built Samaria on a strategic location, close to the Via Maris and—like David in Jerusalem—transferred his capital there, and made it the most prominent and powerful Israelite city. The treaty with Tyre was renewed through the marriage of Ahab and Jezebel; relations with Judah were improved and further bonded by the marriage of Athaliah to Jehoram. Judah recognized the dominant status of Israel, and Moab was reconquered, as is related in the Mesha Stele.

1 KINGS 16: 15–28

 Aramean force

Israelite force

BEN-HADAD the king of Syria gathered all his army together; thirty-two kings were with him, and horses and chariots...

(1 Kings 20:1)

THE WARS OF AHAB AGAINST ARAM
855 TO 850 B.C.

AHAB continued the policies of his father Omri. The remains from the period of the reign of Ahab, uncovered at various sites throughout the kingdom of Israel, indicate economic stability and military strength, as is also shown in the Bible, when speaking of the "ivory house" and of all the cities which Ahab built (1 Kings 22:39). The area of the city of Hazor, near the border of Aram, was doubled and the city surrounded by a stout wall. Palaces and royal storehouses were built at Hazor, Megiddo and other places. The "ivory house" at Samaria was completed and Jezreel became the kingdom's winter capital.

In this period Ben-hadad king of Aram-damascus gained control over the other small Aramean kingdoms. He removed their kings by force and replaced them with his governors, thus forming a strong political entity stretching from Israel to Hamath, with great influence in the region.

Then began the struggle between Aram and Israel, echoes of which ring in the accounts of the three wars of Ahab. At first the Arameans laid siege to Samaria itself, but Ahab was able to break the siege and defeat them. In the second conflict, which took place in the Jarmuk Valley, the Arameans were again defeated, fleeing to Aphek. Upon the fall of that city, Ben-hadad was forced to grant Israel rights of commerce at Damascus and to return disputed lands. In the third war, when Aram violated the terms of the Aphek treaty, Ahab and Jehoshaphat set out to war at Ramoth-gilead. Ahab fell in battle, though his courage saved him from utter rout. Ramoth-gilead and the northern part of Transjordan remained in the hands of Aram.

1 KINGS 20: 1–34; 22: 1–40;
2 CHRON. 18: 1–34

Carved ivory from Samaria (time of Ahab)

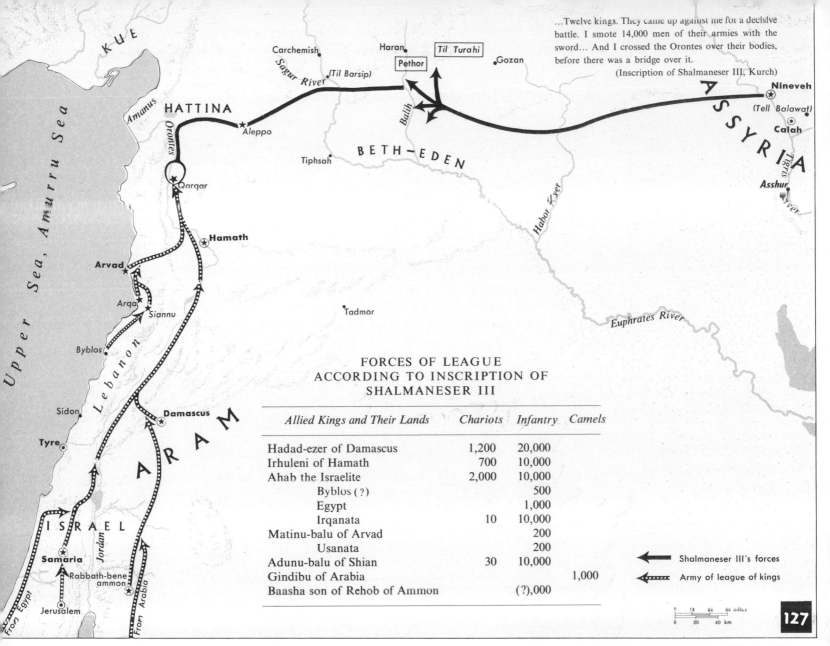

FORCES OF LEAGUE ACCORDING TO INSCRIPTION OF SHALMANESER III

Allied Kings and Their Lands	Chariots	Infantry	Camels
Hadad-ezer of Damascus	1,200	20,000	
Irhuleni of Hamath	700	10,000	
Ahab the Israelite	2,000	10,000	
Byblos (?)		500	
Egypt		1,000	
Irqanata	10	10,000	
Matinu-balu of Arvad		200	
Usanata		200	
Adunu-balu of Shian	30	10,000	
Gindibu of Arabia			1,000
Baasha son of Rehob of Ammon		(?),000	

⬅ Shalmaneser III's forces

⬅ Army of league of kings

127

THE BATTLE OF QARQAR
853 B.C.

1 Kings 22:1; monument, Shalmaneser III—Calah; other inscriptions—Assyria

THE KINGS of the western part of the Ancient East failed to realize the gradual ascendance of Assyria, being deeply involved in their petty wars. Tiglath-pileser I, king of Assyria, had reached the Upper Sea already about 1100 B.C., but under his successors Assyria again reverted to a minor status. At the start of the ninth century Asshurnasirpal II (833–859 B.C.) renewed the expansionist policy of Assyria. His armies reached northern Syria and the coastal cities of Phoenicia—Arvad, Byblos, Tyre, and Sidon—and raised tribute. His son, Shalmaneser III, continued these campaigns and, already in the first year of his reign, reached the Amanus Mountains.

In his sixth year (853 B.C.), Shalmaneser set out from Nineveh to the central region of Syria. He crossed the Euphrates, in flood, near Pethor, going by way of Aleppo. He conquered several cities within the territory of Hamath, including Qarqar. He was, however, facing a league of kings of the west, rulers who had realized the dangerous extent of his conquests. Forsaking their quarrels (1 Kings 22:1), they had united to stop the Assyrian army. The mighty league included armies gathered from throughout Syria and the Land of Israel as far as Egypt. Hadad-ezer king of Damascus (the biblical Ben-hadad

mentioned as an enemy of Ahab), Ahab king of Israel and Irhuleni king of Hamath stood at the head of the league. Ahab had raised 2,000 chariots, comprising more than one-half of all the "mounted" forces of the league; this is an indication of the military strength of Israel in this period. Although Judah is not mentioned specifically, it may be assumed that it too took its place in the league, as an ally of Israel, as it did in the the other Israelite wars of this period.

Shalmaneser's record of the battle of Qarqar lists only eleven countries, in spite of a total of twelve kings. The sum may be "rounded" or there may be a line missing at the bottom, originally reading: Baasha the son of Rehob (from . . .) from Ammon.

The major battle was fought near Qarqar; according to Shalmaneser, Assyria was victorious. It would seem, however, that the kings of the league succeeded in seriously undermining Assyrian power, for four years were to pass before Shalmaneser again set out on another campaign to the west.

With the passing of the danger the league fell apart, and the petty struggles between its members were renewed.

King of Assyria at head of army (bronze relief of Shalmaneser III from Tell Balawat)

THE WANDERINGS OF ELIJAH
MID-9TH CENTURY B.C.

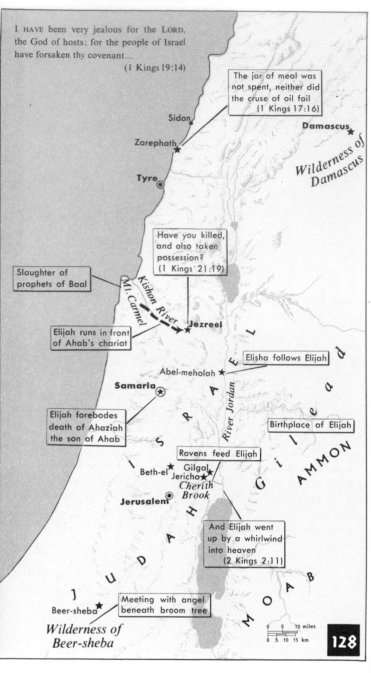

I HAVE been very jealous for the LORD, the God of hosts; for the people of Israel have forsaken thy covenant...
(1 Kings 19:14)

The jar of meal was not spent, neither did the cruse of oil fail
(1 Kings 17:16)

Sidon

Damascus

Zarephath

Wilderness of Damascus

Tyre

Have you killed, and also taken possession?
(1 Kings 21:19)

Slaughter of prophets of Baal

Mt. Carmel

Kishon River

Jezreel

Elijah runs in front of Ahab's chariot

Elisha follows Elijah

I S R A E L

Abel-meholah

River Jordan

G i l e a d

Samaria

Elijah forebodes death of Ahaziah the son of Ahab

AMMON

Birthplace of Elijah

Ravens feed Elijah

J U D A H

Beth-el   Gilgal
Jericho
Cherith Brook

Jerusalem

And Elijah went up by a whirlwind into heaven
(2 Kings 2:11)

M O A B

Beer-sheba

Meeting with angel beneath broom tree

Wilderness of Beer-sheba

0   5   10 miles
0 5 10 15 km

128

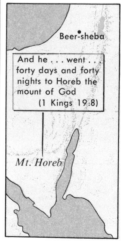

Beer-sheba

And he ... went ... forty days and forty nights to Horeb the mount of God
(1 Kings 19:8)

Mt. Horeb

1 KINGS 19: 16–21; 2 KINGS 2—9; 13

Ivory carving in Phoenician style from Samaria (time of Ahab)

AND JEHU the son of Nimshi you shall anoint to be king over Israel; and Elisha the son of Shaphat of Abel-meholah you shall anoint to be prophet in your place.

(1 Kings 19:16)

THE ACTIVITIES OF ELISHA
LATE 9TH CENTURY B.C.

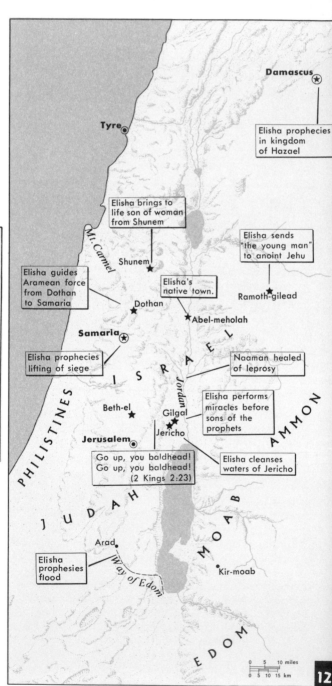

Damascus

Elisha prophecies in kingdom of Hazael

Tyre

Elisha brings to life son of woman from Shunem

Elisha sends "the young man" to anoint Jehu

Mt. Carmel

Shunem

Elisha's native town.

Elisha guides Aramean force from Dothan to Samaria

Dothan

Abel-meholah

Ramoth-gilead

Samaria

Elisha prophecies lifting of siege

Naaman healed of leprosy

I S R A E L

Jordan

Elisha performs miracles before sons of the prophets

Beth-el

Gilgal

P H I L I S T I N E S

Jericho

Jerusalem

AMMON

Go up, you baldhead! Go up, you baldhead!
(2 Kings 2:23)

Elisha cleanses waters of Jericho

J U D A H

M O A B

Arad

Way of Edom

Elisha prophesies flood

Kir-moab

E D O M

0   5   10 miles
0 5 10 15 km

12•

1 KINGS 17—21; 2 KINGS 1: 2—2: 18

THE FIRST of the Major Prophets rose in the kingdom of Israel: Elijah in Gilead and Elisha in the Jordan Valley. Israel was open to foreign influences, and the ties between the house of Omri and Tyre were instrumental in spreading worship of the Phoenician Baal. The spirit behind Israelite law was beyond the grasp of Jezebel the daughter of the king of Tyre, and she decided to instruct Ahab on how to "govern the kingdom of Israel" (1 Kings 21:7). The murder of Naboth the Jezreelite through a perversion of justice, provoked the wrath of Elijah, and his admonition "hast thou killed, and also taken possession?" (1 Kings 21:19), still reverberates in the world today. The activities and missions of Elijah and Elisha extended beyond the borders and included various peoples, for in the view of the Prophets these, too, were to be considered a tool in the hands of the Lord.

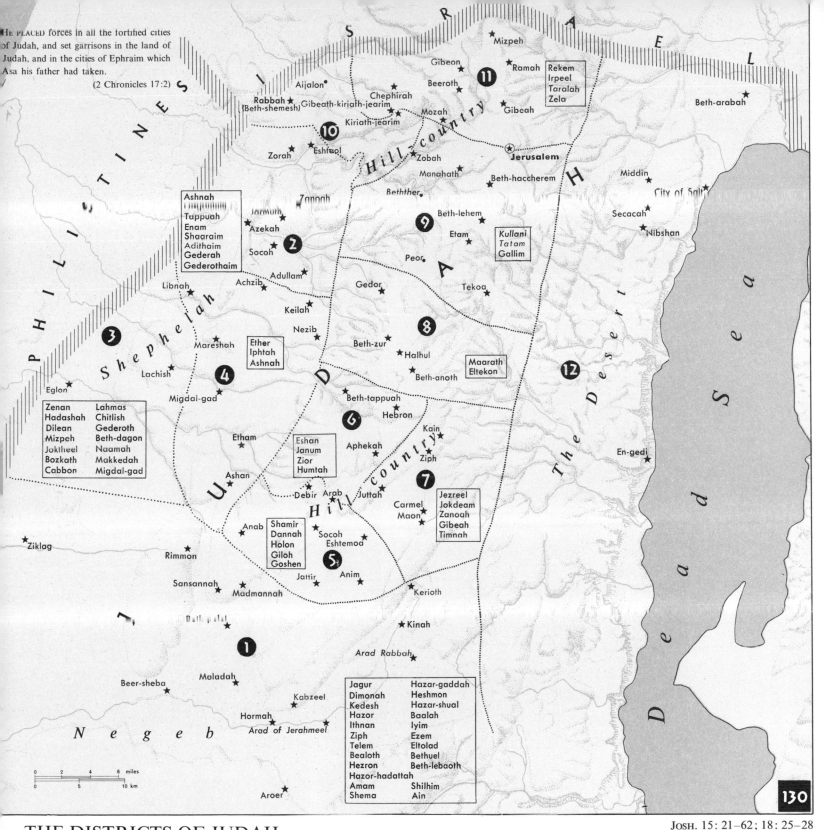

He placed forces in all the fortified cities of Judah, and set garrisons in the land of Judah, and in the cities of Ephraim which Asa his father had taken.

(2 Chronicles 17:2)

ISRAEL

Mizpeh

Gibeon • Ramah
Beeroth ⑪
Aijalon •

Rabbah (Beth-shemesh) Gibeath-kiriath-jearim
Chephirah
Mozah
Kiriath-jearim ⑩
Zorah Eshtaol

Hill country

Gibeah

Rekem
Irpeel
Taralah
Zela

Beth-arabah

Zobah ✦ Jerusalem
Manahath
Beth-haccherem

Middin

City of Salt

Ashnah
(—)
Tappuah
Enam
Shaaraim
Adithaim
Gederah
Gederothaim

Zanoah
Jarmuth
Azekah ②
Socoh
Adullam

Beth-ther

Beth-lehem
Etam

Kullani
Tatam
Gallim

Secacah
Nibshan

Peor

Libnah
Achzib
Keilah
Nezib

③ Shephelah
Mareshah
Lachish
Eglon
Migdal-gad ④

Ether
Iphtah
Ashnah

Gedor
Beth-zur ⑧
Halhul
Beth-anoth

Tekoa

⑨

Maarath
Eltekon

⑫

The Desert

Zenan   Lahmas
Hadashah Chitlish
Dilean   Gederoth
Mizpeh   Beth-dagon
Joktheel Naamah
Bozkath Makkedah
Cabbon   Migdal-gad

Etham

Eshan
Janum
Zior
Humtah

Beth-tappuah
⑥
Hebron
Aphekah
Kain

Ashan

JUDAH

Hill country

Ziph

Jezreel
Jokdeam
Zanoah
Gibeah
Timnah

En-gedi

Debir Arab Juttah
Anab

Shamir
Dannah
Holon
Giloh
Goshen

Socoh
Eshtemoa
⑤

⑦
Carmel
Maon

Ziklag

Rimmon
Jattir Anim

Sansannah
Madmannah

Beth-palet

Kerioth

① Kinah

Sea

Arad Rabbah ✦

Moladah
Beer-sheba

Kabzeel

Hormah
Arad of Jerahmeel

Negeb

Jagur   Hazar-gaddah
Dimonah   Heshmon
Kedesh   Hazar-shual
Hazor   Baalah
Ithnan   Iyim
Ziph   Ezem
Telem   Eltolad
Bealoth   Bethuel
Hezron   Beth-lebaoth
Hazor-hadattah
Amam   Shilhim
Shema   Ain

Aroer

0 2 4 6 miles
0   5   10 km

Dead Sea

130

JOSH. 15: 21–62; 18: 25–28

THE DISTRICTS OF JUDAH IN THE DAYS OF JEHOSHAPHAT

CA. 860 B.C.

JUDAH, which was more isolated than Israel, preserved the patriarchal tradition. Jehoshaphat, the contemporary of Ahab, stood out as a wise and just ruler; under him, and possibly already under Asa his father, Judah renewed its rule over Edom and there were attempts to restore maritime trade at Ezion-geber (1 Kings 22:48–50; 2 Chron. 20:35–37). Jehoshaphat strengthened his kingdom through construction of forts and store cities (2 Chron. 17:12; and compare 2 Chron. 21:3). He also reorganized the royal administration, dividing the kingdom into districts over which he appointed governors (2 Chron. 17:2), similar to the division of Israel under Solomon.

The main lines of this administrative division are probably reflected in the list of Judean cities in Joshua 15:21–62. This list is divided into groups, according to geographical regions of Judah: the Negeb, the Shephelah, the hill region, and the desert. In the Massoretic Text

there are details of ten groups of cities, while in the Septuagint version there is an additional group (after verse 59), which includes the region of Beth-lehem. To arrive at the number of twelve districts, we must add to these eleven the group of cities of that part of southern Benjamin found within the territory of the kingdom of Judah (Joshua 18:25, 28).

Among the districts of Judah, the large Negeb, including about thirty cities, stands out. The number indicates the considerable development of the area, which included the several regions of the Negeb (see map 93). Its capital (Jekabzeel) was at Tel Ira, at the center of the district, where a large Israelite fortress city has been discovered.

In its essentials, this administrative division appears to date from the time of Jehoshaphat, but perhaps the details given in the Bible are later, from the time of Uzziah, or, according to some scholars, Josiah.

Map 131 (left)

ISRAEL

Border after Mesha's conquests

Ahab's forces

Heshbon

Bezer

Nebo

Kiriathaim

And I went at night and fought against it from the break of day till noon
(Moabite Stone, 15)

Medeba

Beth-baal-meon

Beth-diblathaim

Ataroth

Tableland

Jahaz

And the men of Gad always dwelt in the land of Ataroth
(Moabite Stone, 10)

Kerioth

B

Dibon

Aroer

En-gedi

Arnon River

And the king of Israel built Jahaz . . . while fighting me
(Moabite Stone, 18–19)

I built Aroer, and I built the road in Arnon
(Moabite Stone, 26)

A

Madmen

Dead Sea

Ar

City of Moab

O

Kir-hareseth

Descent of Horonaim

M

Chemosh said unto me, Go down and fight Hauronen
(Moabite Stone, 32)

Horonaim

Zoar

Zered Brook

E

D

O

M

Iye-abarim

0   5   10 miles
0   5   10   15 km

131

MOABITE STONE—DIBON, TRANSJORDAN

←—— Israelite force

◁┄┄┄┄ Moabite force

I AM Mesha, son of Chemosh, king of Moab, the Dibonite... I made this high-place for Chemosh... for he delivered me from all the kings and gave me to prevail over all my enemies.

(Moabite stone, lines 1–4)

THE CONQUESTS OF MESHA KING OF MOAB

855 B.C.

THE WARS against Aram gave Moab the opportunity to revolt and to free itself from Israel. This is witnessed by one of the most important epigraphic monuments found in Palestine, the stele of Mesha king of Moab, discovered in 1868 in the ruins of Dibon.

This inscription reveals that Mesha had already revolted under Ahab, most likely during his major wars against Ben-hadad, king of Aram-damascus. Mesha conquered the "plain" all the way to Medeba, Bezer, and Nebo, and slaughtered the Israelite population, as in the case of the "men of Gad" living in Ataroth. The inscription mentions Mesha's war against Ahab in connection with the conquest of Yahaz. Ahab probably attempted a punitive expedition against Moab, at first recovering a part of Mesha's territory, though in the end Mesha prevailed. The inscription also relates of the settling of important cities in the region, of their fortification, and especially of the construction projects carried out by Mesha in Dibon, the twin capital along side Kir-hareseth (Kir-moab), the early capital of Moab. At the end of the inscription, Mesha mentions his war against Horonaim in southern Moab; this is probably the war mentioned in 2 Kings 3.

THEN HE said, "By which way shall we march?" Jehoram answered, "By the way of the wilderness of Edom."
(2 Kings 3:8)

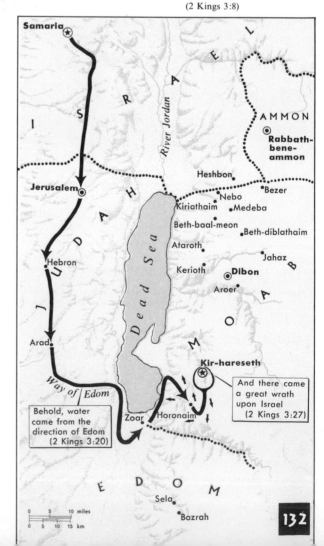

Samaria

Jerusalem

Hebron

Arad

Way of Edom

Behold, water came from the direction of Edom
(2 Kings 3:20)

Zoar

Horonaim

And there came a great wrath upon Israel
(2 Kings 3:27)

Kir-hareseth

River Jordan

AMMON

Rabbath-bene-ammon

Heshbon

Nebo

Bezer

Kiriathaim

Medeba

Beth-baal-meon

Beth-diblathaim

Ataroth

Jahaz

Kerioth

Dibon

Aroer

M O A B

Dead Sea

I S R A E L

J U D A H

EDOM

Sela

Bozrah

0   5   10 miles
0   5   10   15 km

132

THE ISRAELITE CAMPAIGN AGAINST MOAB

850 B.C.

JEHORAM the son of Ahab king of Israel set out on a campaign to Moab, to reconquer and punish the rebel province. This probably took place in the first year of his reign. He was joined by his ally, Jehoshaphat, who was then coregent together with his son Jehoram. They chose to approach along the way of Edom, passing south of the Dead Sea, possibly to avoid the strong defensive works built by Mesha along the northern border of Moab. On the way, they were joined by warriors from Edom. On the desert road, suffering from extreme thirst, they were saved by a sudden flood, a phenomenon not uncommon among the canyons of the Judean Desert. They overpowered the Moabite army and laid siege to Kir-hareseth; not being able to force a surrender, they retreated.

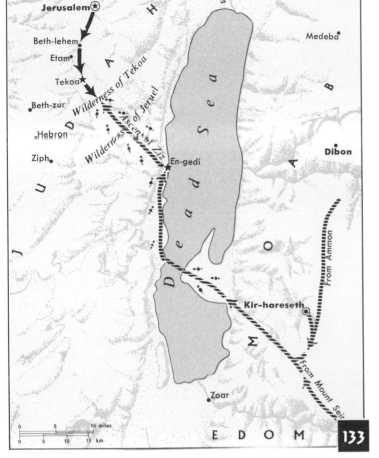

"A GREAT multitude is coming against you from Edom, from beyond the sea; and, behold, they are in Hazazon-tamar" (that is, En-gedi).

(2 Chronicles 20:2)

THE SORTIE OF THE MOABITES AND THEIR ALLIES BY WAY OF EN-GEDI

850 B.C.

AT THE END of the reign of Jehoshaphat, an allied Moabite force invaded Judah by way of En-gedi. This was a daring move in which the invaders had to cross the Dead Sea, probably at the ford opposite Masada, and climb one of the difficult but short ascents directly into the heart of the Judean hills. The invasion was repulsed and, probably in consequence, forts were built on the summits between Masada and En-gedi.

→ Judean force

◄▐▐▐▐▐▐▐▐▐ Moabite and allied force

2 CHRON. 20: 1–28

Mesha stele

"Woman-in-the-window" on ivory plaque (from Calah)

JEZEBEL heard of it; and she painted her eyes, and adorned her head, and looked out of the window. And as Jehu entered the gate, she said, "Is it peace, you Zimri, murderer of your master?"

(2 Kings 9:30–31)

THE REBELLION OF JEHU

842 B.C.

THE WARS between Israel and Aram did not cease after the death of Ahab, and in the days of Jehoram his son, the armies of the two kingdoms again fought at Ramoth-gilead. The fierce revolt of Jehu, supported by the prophets, brought to an end the Omrid dynasty; it also caused the death of Ahaziah king of Judah, who happened to be in Jezreel, the winter capital of the Israelite kings, at that time. With the murder of Jezebel, daughter of the king of Tyre, the close ties between Israel and Tyre also came to an end.

2 KINGS 9–10

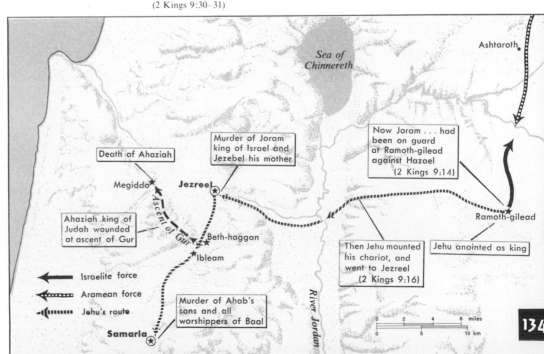

Death of Ahaziah

Murder of Joram king of Israel and Jezebel his mother

Now Joram . . . had been on guard at Ramoth-gilead against Hazael (2 Kings 9:14)

Megiddo

Jezreel

Ashtaroth

Sea of Chinnereth

Ahaziah king of Judah wounded at ascent of Gur

Beth-haggan

Ibleam

Ramoth-gilead

Then Jehu mounted his chariot, and went to Jezreel (2 Kings 9:16)

Jehu anointed as king

→ Israelite force

◄▐▐▐▐▐ Aramean force

◄▐▐▐▐▐▐ Jehu's route

Murder of Ahab's sons and all worshippers of Baal

Samaria

River Jordan

0 2 4 6 miles
0 5 10 km

134

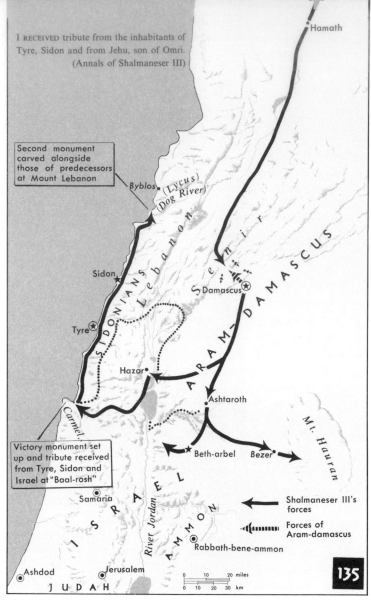

Second monument carved alongside those of predecessors at Mount Lebanon

Victory monument set up and tribute received from Tyre, Sidon and Israel at "Baal-rosh"

Hamath

Byblos (Lycus) (Dog River)

Sidon

Damascus

Tyre

Hazor

Ashtaroth

Carmel

Beth-arbel • Bezer

Mt. Hauran

Samaria

River Jordan

AMMON

Rabbath-bene-ammon

Ashdod • Jerusalem

JUDAH

ISRAEL

SIDONIANS Lebanon Senir ARAM-DAMASCUS

→ Shalmaneser III's forces

◄▥◻▥ Forces of Aram-damascus

0 10 20 miles
0 10 20 30 km

135

INSCRIPTIONS, SHALMANESER III—CALAH; OTHER ASSYRIAN SOURCES

"Jehu the son of Omri" paying tribute to Shalmaneser III (Black Obelisk, from Nimrud)

THE CAMPAIGN OF SHALMANESER III
841 B.C.

SHALMANESER III continued his campaigns in Syria in 849, 848, and 845 B.C., though he did not achieve his aims, for in each of these campaigns he came up against the armies of the league of Syrian kings under the leadership of Hadadezer (the son of Hadad) king of Aram-damascus.

Shortly before Jehu's revolt in Israel, Hazael revolted against Ben-hadad and founded a new dynasty in Damascus. In the year 841 B.C. Shalmaneser again came to Syria, this time successfully defeating Hazael at Mount Senir and subsequently laying siege to Damascus, but the city held out. He continued to the mountains of Hauran, destroying many cities, and proceeded westward, destroying Beth-arbel (Hosea 10:14) and probably Hazor (stratum VIII). Reaching the mountain "Baali-rasi" ("Baal-rosh"), on the coast, he set up his statue. The mountain is probably Mount Carmel, a center of the worship of Baal, known from the accounts of Elijah and other sources. In the Egyptian sources, the Carmel is called "Rosh-kedesh," and the meaning of the name "Baal-rosh" is probably "The Baal of the head (of the Carmel)." In this period, the border between Tyre and Israel passed through Carmel, and thus it was here that Shalmaneser received tribute from Tyre and Israel. The kingdom of Israel was known to the Assyrians as the "Land of the House of Omri"; therefore, Jehu, too, is mentioned in their sources as a "son of Omri." He is thus called on the Black Obelisk of Shalmaneser. Shalmaneser moved northward from the Carmel along the Phoenician coast, having an additional victory monument carved into the cliffside at the month of Nahr el-Kalb (the Dog River, called the Lycus in Hellenistic times) alongside Assyrian and Egyptian monuments left there before him.

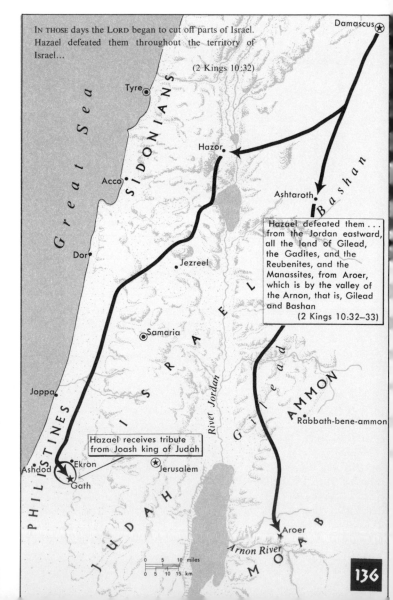

IN THOSE days the LORD began to cut off parts of Israel. Hazael defeated them throughout the territory of Israel...
(2 Kings 10:32)

Damascus

Tyre

Hazor

Acco

Ashtaroth

Bashan

Great Sea

SIDONIANS

Dor

Jezreel

Hazael defeated them . . . from the Jordan eastward, all the land of Gilead, the Gadites, and the Reubenites, and the Manassites, from Aroer, which is by the valley of the Arnon, that is, Gilead and Bashan
(2 Kings 10:32–33)

Samaria

ISRAEL

River Jordan

Gilead

AMMON

Rabbath-bene-ammon

Joppa

Hazael receives tribute from Joash king of Judah

Ashdod • Ekron Gath

Jerusalem

PHILISTINES

JUDAH

Aroer

Arnon River

MOAB

0 5 10 miles
0 5 10 15 km

136

THE CAMPAIGN OF HAZAEL
CA. 815 TO 810 B.C.

IN the following years, however, the Assyrians became entangled in affairs quite distant from the western part of their empire, and thus Damascus was able, for the last time, to spread its rule over most of Syria and Palestine. In the final days of the reign of Jehu, and in the days of Jehoahaz his son, Israel became virtually a vassal of Damascus. Its borders were reduced and its military strength limited to fifty cavalry, ten chariots, and ten thousand foot (2 Kings 13:7). All of Transjordan was conquered by Hazael and echoes of the violent destruction are still heard in the words of Amos (1:3). In approximately 815 B.C. Hazael reached Gath, and even Jehoash king of Judah was compelled to pay a heavy tribute. During these campaigns Hazor was probably destroyed (stratum VII).

2 KINGS 8:12; 10:32–33; 12:18–19; 13:3, 7; AMOS 1:3

MOUNT EPHRAIM IN THE LIGHT OF THE SAMARIA OSTRACA

EARLY 8TH CENTURY B.C.

THE Samaria Ostraca belong to about the same period. These sherds were found in excavations at Samaria. They had been used as receipts for various quantities of wine and oil in the ninth, tenth, fifteenth, and seventeenth years of the reign of one, or possibly two, of the kings of the dynasty of Jehu (most probably Jonah and Jeroboam II). They bear personal names and names of clan holdings in the central Mount Ephraim. The clan names are also known from the genealogical lists of the tribe of Manasseh (Exodus 26:30–33; Joshua 17:2–3; 1 Chron. 7:14–19). They denote the old tribal holdings (see map 65), which continued to serve in the administration of land and taxation. The place names on the Samaria Ostraca are an important addition to our knowledge of the ancient settlements on Mount Ephraim. They indicate the existence of many Israelite settlements not recorded in the Bible.

GENEALOGICAL TABLE OF MACHIR

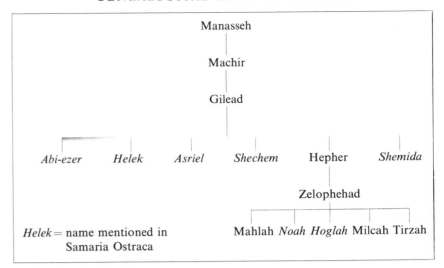

Manasseh

Machir

Gilead

Abi-ezer *Helek* *Asriel* *Shechem* Hepher *Shemida*

Zelophehad

Helek = name mentioned in Samaria Ostraca

Mahlah *Noah Hoglah* Milcah Tirzah

In the ninth year. From Yazith to Ahinoam. A jar of old wine. In the fifteenth year. From Halak to Asa. Ahimelech. Helez. From Hazeroth.

(Samaria Ostraca Nos. 9 and 23)

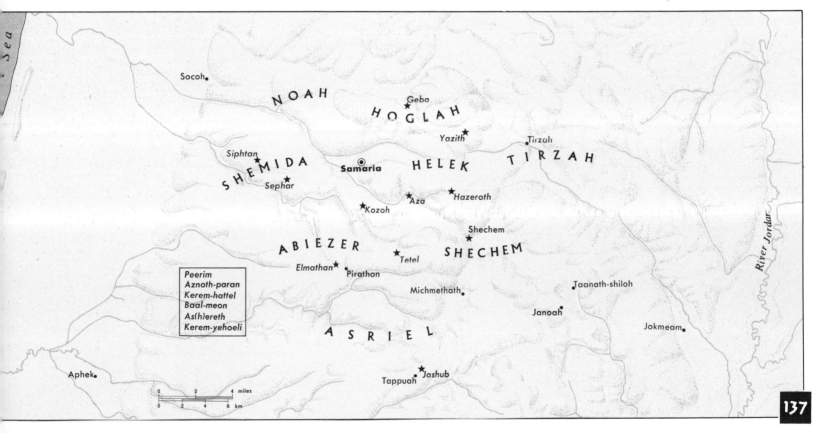

Peerim
Aznoth-paran
Kerem-hattel
Baal-meon
As(h)ereth
Kerem-yehoeli

SAMARIA OSTRACA

Samaria Ostraca

THE CAMPAIGN OF ADAD-NIRARI III TO DAMASCUS
806 B.C.

DELIVERANCE from Aram-damascus came to Israel through Assyria which had renewed its pressure on Syria with the ascension of Adad-nirari III. The Assyrian army reached Damascus in about 806 B.C. The city surrendered and paid a heavy tribute. Adad-nirari also received tribute from Philistia, Israel (the "house of Omri") and Edom, all vassals of Aram-damascus, who with its surrender were also forced to accept Assyrian overlordship.

In the last years of Adad-nirari, however, and in the reign of his successor, all of Assyria's strength was applied to the war against the kingdom of Urartu (Ararat) and it was not able to maintain dominion over Syria and Palestine. This, the last respite from Assyrian pressure in the west, lasted for some fifty years. As Damascus did not resume its former position, following the struggle with Hamath, its neighbor to the north, there began a period of political and economic development in the kingdoms of Judah and Israel.

THE LORD gave Israel a savior, so that they escaped from the hand of the Syrians...

(2 Kings 13:5)

MONUMENTS, ADADNIRARI III—CALAH AND SABAA

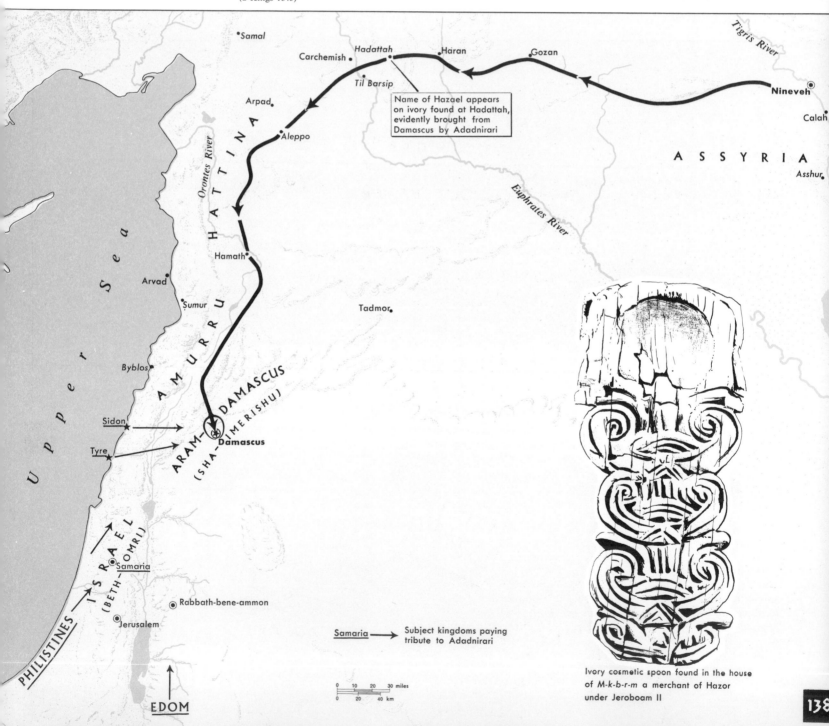

Name of Hazael appears on ivory found at Hadattah, evidently brought from Damascus by Adadnirari

Samara → Subject kingdoms paying tribute to Adadnirari

0 10 20 30 miles
0 20 40 km

Ivory cosmetic spoon found in the house of M-k-b-r-m a merchant of Hazor under Jeroboam II

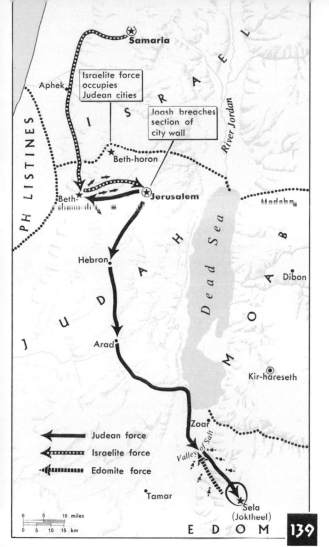

Israelite force
occupies
Judean cities

Joash breaches
section of
city wall

Judean force
Israelite force
Edomite force

139

2 KINGS 14: 7–14; 2 CHRON. 25: 11–24

So JEHOASH king of Israel went up, and he and Amaziah king of Judah faced one another in battle at Beth-shemesh, which belongs to Judah.

(2 Kings 14:11)

THE WARS OF AMAZIAH AND JOASH
CA. 786 B.C.

AMAZIAH king of Judah smote the Edomites in the Valley of Salt and conquered Sela in about 786 B.C. These conquests were connected with the decline of Aram-damascus, which enabled Judah to renew its rule over Edom and the Arabah.

This success brought about a military confrontation between Judah and Israel for prominence in the region, after the decline of Damascus. Amaziah king of Judah was defeated and taken captive, but Joash king of Israel was satisfied with partial destruction of the northern defenses of Jerusalem (see map 114), payment of silver and gold, and taking of hostages. The kings of Israel never aspired to annex Judah to their kingdom and were content with the recognition of their overlordship. At this time, when Israel was again supreme, the league between Israel and Judah, which had disintegrated during the revolt of Jehu, was renewed.

Seal of "Shema servant of
Jeroboam" from Megiddo

THE CONQUESTS
OF JOASH AND JEROBOAM II
CA. 790 TO 770 B.C.

AFTER Amaziah and Joash, Uzziah in Judah and Jeroboam II in Israel came to reign. Both were wise and skilful rulers and the long years of their reigns represent a period of expansion and prosperity.

The borders of the two kingdoms were extended until together they resembled those of David's kingdom at the height of its power. Even though the kingdom of Israel held the more prominent position, Uzziah was able to make Judah a strong and well-developed kingdom.

There is only scanty information on the conquests of Israel and Judah. The decisive battle with Aram-damascus took place during the reign of Joash, in the region of Aphek, as in the days of Ahab (see map 126), and Aram was decisively defeated (2 Kings 13:17). "And Jehoash the son of Jehoahaz took again out of the hand of Ben-hadad the son of Hazael the cities which he had taken out of the hand of Jehoahaz his father ... and recovered the cities of Israel" (2 Kings 13:25). Two other wars were fought near Karnaim and evidently Lo-debar (Amos 6:13), and it is apparent that all of Transjordan now returned to Israelite control. From the summary of the reign of Jeroboam, it becomes evident that he annexed to his kingdom all of Aram-damascus and returned the border of Israel to Lebo-hamath (the "entrance of Hamath") in the Valley of Lebanon. The kingdom of Hamath may also have recognized his overlordship (2 Kings 14:28).

2 KINGS 13: 15–19, 25; 14: 25, 28; AMOS 6: 13

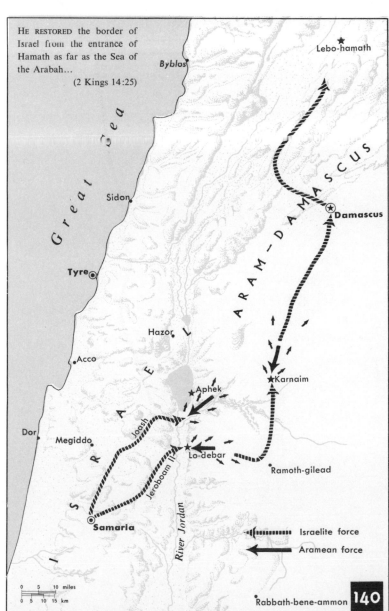

HE RESTORED the border of Israel from the entrance of Hamath as far as the Sea of the Arabah...

(2 Kings 14:25)

Israelite force
Aramean force

140

Map labels

And he built cities in the territory of Ashdod and elsewhere among the Philistines (2 Chron. 26:6)

Moreover Uzziah built towers in Jerusalem (2 Chron. 26:9)

The Ammonites paid tribute to Uzziah (2 Chron. 26:8)

And he built towers in the wilderness (2 Chron. 26:10)

Israelite fortress refurbished

AMMON

Rabbath bene-ammon

River Jordan

Jabneh

Ashdod

Gath

Jerusalem

Gaza

PHILISTINES

J U D A H

Hebron

En-gedi

Dead Sea

Dibon

Arnon River

M O A B

Kir-hareseth

Beer-sheba

Arad Rabbah

Kabzeel

Hormah

Arad of Jerahmeel

Ramat Negeb

Besor Brook

(Rehoboth)

N e g e b

(Rosh Rephed)

Baalath-beer

Zoar

Zered Brook

(Nahal Raviv)

(Avdat)

Tamar

Sela (Joktheel)

E D O M

(Beer Hafir)

Kadesh-barnea

(Mishor Haruah)

(Har Ramon)

Teman

Rekem

M E U N I T E S

(Kuntillat Jiraiya)

(Jotbathah)

Ezion-geber

Elath

Reed Sea

A R A B I A N S

0   5   10 miles
0   5   10 15 km

■ Major Fortress
▪ Fortress

Text column

AND HIS fame spread far, for he was marvelously helped, till he was strong.
(2 Chronicles 26:15)

THE CONQUESTS AND BUILDING PROJECTS OF UZZIAH

MID-8TH CENTURY B.C.

UZZIAH set out on a sweeping campaign against Philistia, reaching Ashdod which had become the capital of Philistia upon the decline of Gath. It is difficult to assume that Uzziah ruled over Ashdod proper after this campaign, though he did reduce its borders, securing his conquests by building cities on lands formerly belonging to Ashdod (2 Chron. 26:6). Thus Uzziah gained an access to the sea, from Jabneh to the mouth of the Jarkon River, renewing the borders of the kingdom of David in this region. He completed the conquest of Edom and proceeded to conquer the southern desert regions in his wars against the Meunim and the Arabians. He developed the economy, founded new settlements, and encouraged agriculture even in the outlying regions and the desert, "for he loved husbandry" (2 Chron. 26:10). Few kings have been given such simple yet exalted praise.

A prior condition for rule over Edom and renewal of the profitable trade at Elath (2 Kings 14:22) was the reconstruction of the Israelite fortresses along the borders and along the roads of the Negeb. Archaeological research has revealed that Israelite settlement in the Negeb and in the Judean desert reached its height in this period. At Ezion-geber, Arad and other sites, strong fortresses from this period have been uncovered, along with finds indicating a prosperous economy. The large fortresses were surrounded with casemate walls and towers, as at Kadesh-barnea and Ramat Negeb near Arad.

2 KINGS 14: 22; 2 CHRON. 26: 2–15

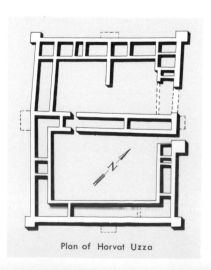

Plan of Horvat Uzza

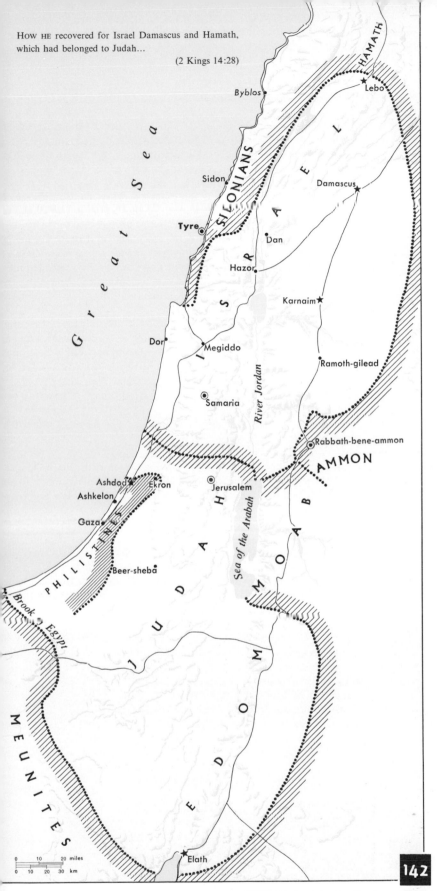

How HE recovered for Israel Damascus and Hamath, which had belonged to Judah...

(2 Kings 14:28)

142

2 KINGS 14: 22; 2 CHRON. 26: 2–15

Seal of Jotham (from Ezion-geber)

ISRAEL AND JUDAH IN THE DAYS OF JEROBOAM II AND UZZIAH
MID-8TH CENTURY B.C.

IN the mid-eighth century B.C., Israel and Judah continued to rule over the important international trade routes, and Samaria and Jerusalem for a time again became political centers of prime importance in the western part of the Fertile Crescent. This period was one more zenith in political and military power and in economic prosperity.

The feeling of peace and tranquility was shattered by the harsh words of the prophet Amos: "Woe to those who are at ease in Zion, and to those who feel secure on the mountain of *Samaria*. . . . Pass over to *Calneh*, and see: and thence go to *Hamath the great; then go down to Gath of the Philistines:* are they better than those kingdoms? Or is their territory greater than your territory? . . . those who lie upon beds of ivory . . . and eat lambs from the flock, and calves from the midst of the stall . . . you have turned justice into poison and the fruit of righteousness into wormwood. . . . For, behold, I will raise up against you a nation, O house of Israel, says the Lord, the God of hosts; and they shall oppress you from *Lebo-hamath to the brook of the Arabah*" (Amos 6:1–4; 12–14).

The momentary prosperity did not blind Amos to the facts of greater historical processes and to the instability of political and economic achievements if they are not connected with righteousness and keeping of moral standards. Only a few of the native cities of the prophets are known; most prominent is the description of Amos's journeying from *Tekoa* in Judah—on the border of the Judean desert—to the centers of the kingdom in Israel. Many of the prophets were from towns near the harsh desert, from which they drew their strength.

THE CITIES OF THE PROPHETS
9TH TO 7TH CENTURIES B.C.

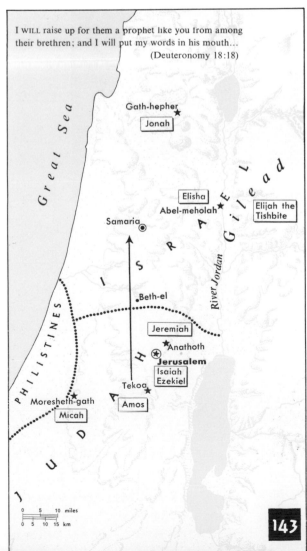

I WILL raise up for them a prophet like you from among their brethren; and I will put my words in his mouth...

(Deuteronomy 18:18)

143

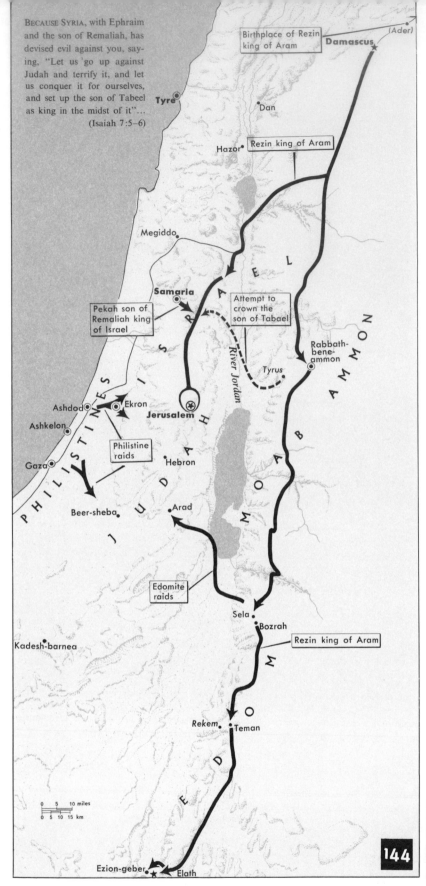

BECAUSE SYRIA, with Ephraim
and the son of Remaliah, has
devised evil against you, saying, "Let us go up against
Judah and terrify it, and let
us conquer it for ourselves,
and set up the son of Tabeel
as king in the midst of it"...

(Isaiah 7:5–6)

THE CAMPAIGN OF REZIN
AND PEKAH AGAINST JUDAH
734 B.C.

2 KINGS 16: 5–9; IS. 7—9; 2 CHRON. 28: 16–21

THE CONQUESTS
OF THE PHILISTINES
IN THE DAYS OF AHAZ
734 B.C.

2 CHRON. 28: 18

THE KINGDOM OF ISRAEL reached its zenith in the mid-
eighth century B.C. and its disintegration followed as quickly as
its sudden rise.

Upon the death of Jeroboam II, and the murder of his son Zachariah
in about 748, the dynasty of Jehu came to an end after ruling in Israel
for about one hundred years. A quick decline of the kingdom now set
in, ending in surrender to Assyria in the days of Tiglath-pileser III.

Tiglath-pileser renewed Assyria's expansionist policy, and is considered to be the founder of the extensive Assyrian Empire which
eventually swallowed up the petty kingdoms of Syria and Palestine.
Unlike his predecessors, Tiglath-pileser was not satisfied with the mere
surrender of the various kings and reception of tribute; rather he
initiated the annexation of conquered territories to the Assyrian
state by reducing them to provinces, governed by Assyrian deputies.
Opposition to permanent Assyrian rule was overcome by exiling the
noble classes of the conquered regions and resettling other populations
in their stead.

The inscriptions of Tiglath-pileser contain the surprising fact that
in the year 738 B.C. he fought in northern Syria against a large league
headed by Azariah of Judah. Apparently, upon Israel's becoming
beset by internal crises, prominence in the region passed to Judah for
the time under the rule of the old king Uzziah (Azariah), though his
son Jotham, and probably also his grandson Ahaz, ruled in all but
title in Jerusalem (2 Kings 15:5).

However, Uzziah's daring attempt failed. The league dissolved in
the face of the Assyrian might, and by 738 B.C. Tiglath-pileser had
already reached the mountains of Lebanon, founding Assyrian
provinces in the former territory of the kingdom of Hamath. The list
of kings paying tribute, includes the kings of Byblos, Tyre, Rezin
king of Aram, Menahem king of Samaria, and even the Queen of
Arabia.

Uzziah died in 735 B.C., the same year that Pekahiah the son of
Menahem was killed by Pekah the son of Remaliah. Pekah then
probably began preparing a new league against Assyria together with
Rezin king of Aram. In reaction to Ahaz's refusal to join this league
the two kings went up against Jerusalem and attempted to set up the
son of Tabeel as king (Is. 7:6). The son of Tabeel was probably one of
the heads of the family of Tobiah, which held an important position
in Transjordan in the days of the Second Temple (see, for instance,
Neh. 2:19). During the campaign of Rezin and Pekah the son of
Remaliah against Ahaz, the Edomites were freed and in turn invaded
Judah (2 Kings 16:6; 2 Chron. 28:17); even the people of Philistia
took the opportunity to overcome the cities of the Negeb and the
Shephelah of Judah (2 Chron. 28:18).

Beset with this plight, Ahaz sent to Assyria for aid—in spite of
the warnings of Isaiah, who clearly foresaw that Assyria was a greater
danger than "these two tails of smoking firebrands" (Is. 7:4).

AND the Philistines had made raids on the cities in
the Shephelah and the Negeb of Judah...

(2 Chronicles 28:18)

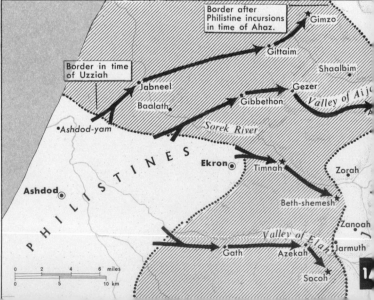

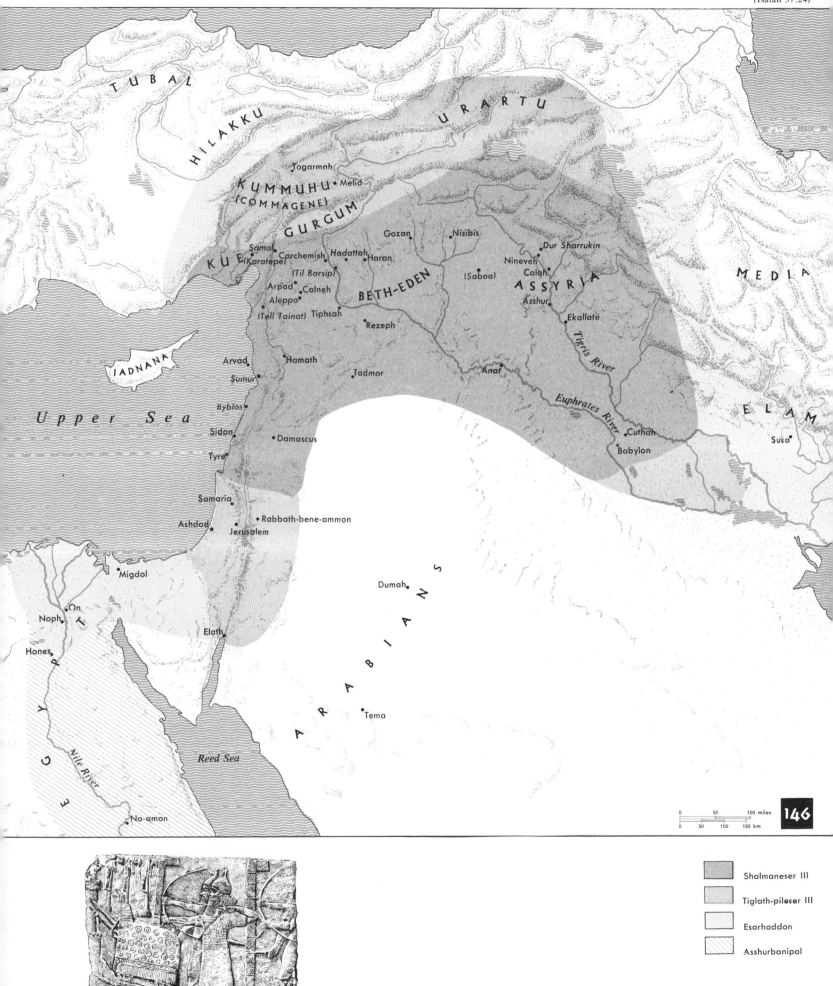

THE RISE OF THE KINGDOM OF ASSYRIA
9TH TO 7TH CENTURIES B.C.

WITH my many chariots I have gone up the heights of
the mountains, to the far recesses of Lebanon...
(Isaiah 37:24)

TUBAL

HILAKKU

URARTU

Togarmah

KUMMUHU
(COMMAGENE)

Melid

GURGUM

KUE

Samal
(Karatepe)

Carchemish

Hadattah

Haran

Gozan

Nisibis

Dur Sharrukin

(Til Barsip)

Arpad

Calneh

Aleppo

(Tell Tainat)

Tiphsah

BETH-EDEN

(Sabaa)

Nineveh

Calah

ASSYRIA

Asshur

MEDIA

Rezeph

Ekallate

Tigris River

IADNANA

Arvad

Hamath

Tadmor

Anat

Sumur

Euphrates River

ELAM

Upper Sea

Byblos

Sidon

Cuthah

Susa

Tyre

Babylon

Damascus

Samaria

Ashdod

Rabbath-bene-ammon

Jerusalem

Migdol

Dumah

On

Noph

A R A B I A N S

Hanes

Elath

E G Y P T

Tema

Reed Sea

Nile River

No-amon

0   50   100 miles
0 50   100 150 km

146

▓	Shalmaneser III
▒	Tiglath-pileser III
☐	Esarhaddon
╱	Asshurbanipal

Assyrian army attacks a city
(relief from palace of Tiglath-pileser III at Calah)

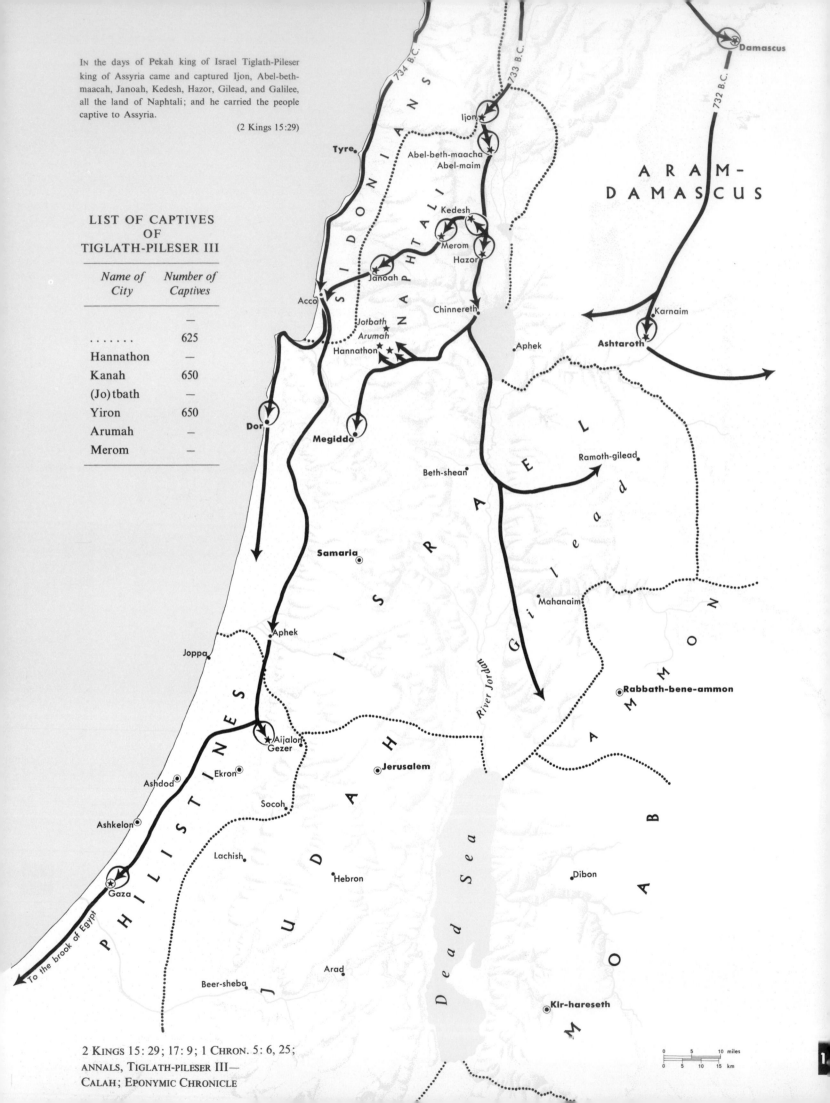

In the days of Pekah king of Israel Tiglath-Pileser
king of Assyria came and captured Ijon, Abel-beth-
maacah, Janoah, Kedesh, Hazor, Gilead, and Galilee,
all the land of Naphtali; and he carried the people
captive to Assyria.

(2 Kings 15:29)

LIST OF CAPTIVES
OF
TIGLATH-PILESER III

Name of City	Number of Captives
	—
. . . . . .	625
Hannathon	—
Kanah	650
(Jo)tbath	—
Yiron	650
Arumah	—
Merom	—

734 B.C.

733 B.C.

732 B.C.

Damascus

Ijon

Tyre

Abel-beth-maacha
Abel-maim

A R A M -
D A M A S C U S

Kedesh

Merom

Hazor

S I D O N I A N S

Janoah

Acco

N A P H T A L I

Chinnereth

Karnaim

Jotbath

Arumah

Aphek

Ashtaroth

Hannathon

Dor

Megiddo

Ramoth-gilead

Beth-shean

I S R A E L

G i l e a d

Samaria

Mahanaim

A M M O N

Aphek

Joppa

River Jordan

Rabbath-bene-ammon

Aijalon
Gezer

P H I L I S T I N E S

Ekron

Ashdod

J U D A H

Jerusalem

Socoh

Ashkelon

Lachish

Dead Sea

Dibon

M O A B

Hebron

Gaza

To the brook of Egypt

Arad

Beer-sheba

Kir-hareseth

2 Kings 15: 29; 17: 9; 1 Chron. 5: 6, 25;
Annals, Tiglath-pileser III—
Calah; Eponymic Chronicle

0	5	10 miles
0	5	10	15 km

THE CAMPAIGN OF TIGLATH-PILESER III
734 TO 732 B.C.

TIGLATH-PILESER'S actions were swift and effective. From Assyrian inscriptions it is known that he set out on a campaign to Philistia in 734 B.C., conquering Gaza. Hanun king of Gaza fled to Egypt, and Tiglath-pileser left permanent forces on the Egyptian border, probably in the region of the brook of Egypt, thus cutting the kings of Palestine off from their southern ally.

In the two following years the decisive campaigns for Israel and Damascus took place. Although there is still some doubt as to which events took place in each of the two campaigns, it is possible to reconstruct their routes in the light of the Bible and on the basis of the Assyrian sources. The campaign in Israel, described in the Bible, probably took place in 733 B.C.: the Assyrian army came from the Valley of Lebanon, conquering the outlying fortresses of Israel in the northern Jordan Valley and then split up into several columns to spread out over the various regions of the Holy Land. The Galilee, Jezreel, Sharon, and Gilead were all conquered; only Mount Ephraim remained untouched. Traces of the fire and destruction were found in excavations at Hazor (stratum V) and Megiddo (stratum IV).

One of Tiglath-pileser's inscriptions preserves a list of numbers of inhabitants taken from several cities in the Upper and Lower Galilee.

Following this defeat, Pekah the son of Remaliah was killed, and Hoshea the son of Elah, the last king of Israel, saved the remnant of his kingdom by raising heavy tribute for payment to Assyria.

A year later (732 B.C.) the Assyrian victory was completed with the conquest of Damascus and the territories under its control. An Assyrian relief from Calah shows the exile of the inhabitants of Ashtaroth, the capital of the Bashan, after its capture by Tiglath-pileser.

Exile of inhabitants of Ashtaroth
(relief from palace of Tiglath-pileser III at Calah)

Is. 9: 1 ; Ez. 47: 16 18; EPONYMIC LISTS,
ADMINSTRATIVE DOCUMENTS—ASSYRIA

THE DISTRICTS OF ASSYRIA IN THE DAYS OF TIGLATH-PILESER III
732 B.C.

THE newly conquered Assyrian provinces were usually named after the city in which the Assyrian governor resided. Aram-damascus was divided into five provinces, all to the south of the provinces of Hamath which had been set up prior to this. The conquered regions of the kingdom of Israel were divided into three provinces, called by the Assyrians Dor, Megiddo, and Gilead; Isaiah (9: 1) refers to them by archaic, poetical names: the way of the sea (Via Maris); Galil-ha-goiim; and Transjordan.

Most of the newly created provinces remained intact without major changes for centuries, later being taken over by the Babylonians and then the Persians. Ezekiel (47:16–18) mentions some of them in his description of the borders of the Land of Canaan (see map 166).

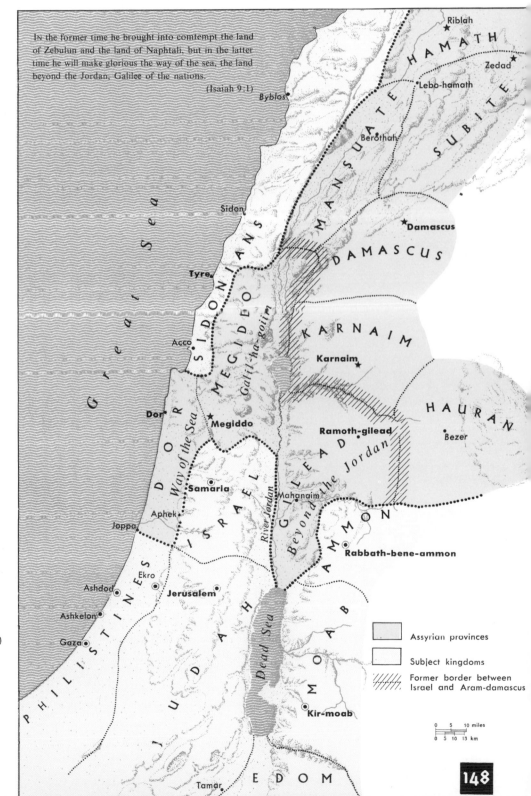

In the former time he brought into contempt the land of Zebulun and the land of Naphtali, but in the latter time he will make glorious the way of the sea, the land beyond the Jordan, Galilee of the nations.

(Isaiah 9:1)

	Assyrian provinces
	Subject kingdoms
	Former border between Israel and Aram-damascus

0 5 10 miles
0 5 10 15 km

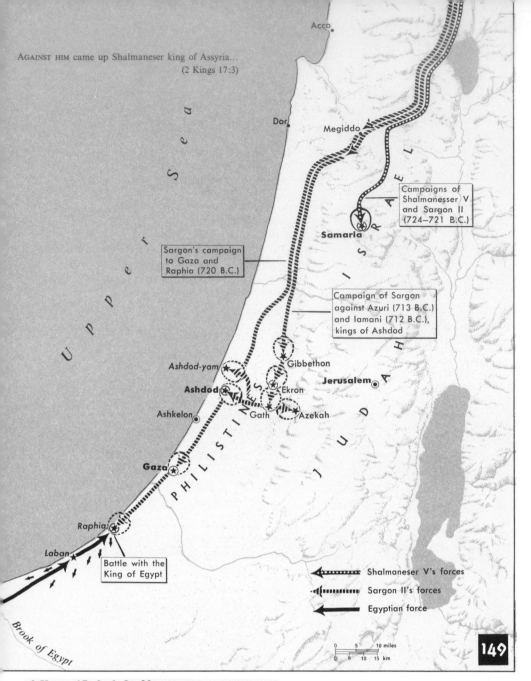

AGAINST HIM came up Shalmaneser king of Assyria...
(2 Kings 17:3)

Campaigns of Shalmanesser V and Sargon II (724–721 B.C.)

Samaria

Sargon's campaign to Gaza and Raphia (720 B.C.)

Campaign of Sargon against Azuri (713 B.C.) and Iamani (712 B.C.), kings of Ashdod

Acco

Dor

Megiddo

Gibbethon

Jerusalem

Ashdod-yam

Ashdod

Ekron

Ashkelon

Gath   Azekah

Gaza

Raphia

Laban

Battle with the King of Egypt

Upper Sea

ISRAEL

JUDAH

PHILISTINES

Brook of Egypt

	Shalmaneser V's forces
	Sargon II's forces
	Egyptian force

0   5   10 miles
0   5   10   15 km

149

THE CAMPAIGNS OF SHALMANESER V AND SARGON II TO PALESTINE
724 TO 712 B.C.

Conquest of Ekron
(relief from palace of Sargon II at Khorsabad)

2 KINGS 17: 3–6; IS. 20; ANNALS,
OTHER LISTS, SARGON II—KHORSABAD ASSHUR

AND the king of Assyria brought people from Babylon,
Cuthah, Avva, Hamath, and Sepharvaim, and placed
them in the cities of Samaria instead of the people of
Israel...
(2 Kings 17:24)

THE EXILE TO AND FROM ISRAEL IN THE DAYS OF TIGLATH-PILESER III
712 B.C.

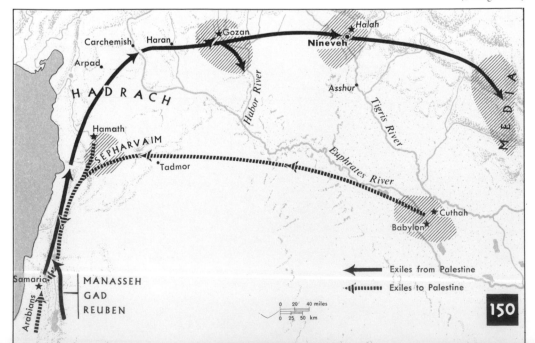

Carchemish   Haran

Arpad

HADRACH

Gozan

Halah

Nineveh

Asshur

Habor River

Tigris River

MEDIA

Hamath

SEPHARVAIM

Tadmor

Euphrates River

Cuthah

Babylon

Samaria

MANASSEH
GAD
REUBEN

Arabians

| | Exiles from Palestine |
| | Exiles to Palestine |

0   20   40 miles
0   25   50 km

150

2 KINGS 17: 6, 24; 30 31; 1 CHRON. 5: 26;
ANNALS, TIGLATH-PILESER III, SARGON II

THE DAYS of the kingdom of Israel were numbered. The Egyptians encouraged revolt against Assyrian rule, and Hoshea was tempted and rebelled after the death of Tiglath-pileser III. In 724 B.C., Shalmaneser V attacked Samaria. Hoshea himself surrendered but the siege continued and Samaria was conquered after three years. Sargon, who in the meantime had succeeded to the throne of Assyria, boasts in his inscriptions that he conquered Samaria, but possibly some of the conquests ascribed to him are actually to be related to his predecessor. In any event, it was he who turned Samaria into an Assyrian province and probably appended to it the small province of Dor.

These activities did not prevent a further rebellion in Palestine and Syria in 720 B.C., also with Egyptian encouragement. Sargon reacted immediately and in a campaign along the coast of the Holy Land conquered Gaza and Raphia. He inflicted defeat upon the Egyptian force sent to aid another rebel, the king of Gaza. In consequence, Sargon received tribute from Egypt, and even from the Arabians. Samaria, too, was involved in this rebellion, and in order to prevent its recurrence, Sargon began extensive shifts of populations within his provinces. Many of the inhabitants of the kingdom of Israel were exiled to distant regions of the Assyrian Empire, to the region of the Habur River, to the region of Nineveh and to the cities of Media, only recently conquered. In their stead, other peoples from Babylonia and Hamath were settled in Samaria, and in 716 B.C. Arabians were also brought there. The new inhabitants brought with them foreign customs and gods, which became part and parcel of the daily life of the local Israelites. The Samaritan community of the period of the Second Temple developed from this conglomeration.

Judah was saved from a similar fate through its submission to Assyria. Unrest in the Holy Land did not cease, however, and in 713–712 B.C. the Assyrians had to put down additional rebellions in Ashdod. The revolt in 712 B.C. was supported by the Ethiopian pharaoh Shabaku, founder of the twenty-fifth dynasty in Egypt (Isaiah 20). According to Sargon's inscriptions, Judah, Edom, and Moab were also involved in the revolt, though they surrendered—evidently quickly, and most of the Assyrian wrath was vent upon Ashdod. In a campaign against Ashdod and its port Asdudimmu (Ashdod-yam), Sargon also conquered Gibbethon, Ekron, and Gath. From the informative description of the capture of Azekah "lying on a mountain ridge like the edge of the sword," it appears that this campaign was directed against Judah as well.

Ashdod, too, became an Assyrian province. The borders of the Assyrian empire now spread to the brook of Egypt. In this period there was little hope for the continued existence of Judah as an independent kingdom.

THE DISTRICTS OF ASSYRIA IN THE DAYS OF SARGON II
733 TO 716 B.C.

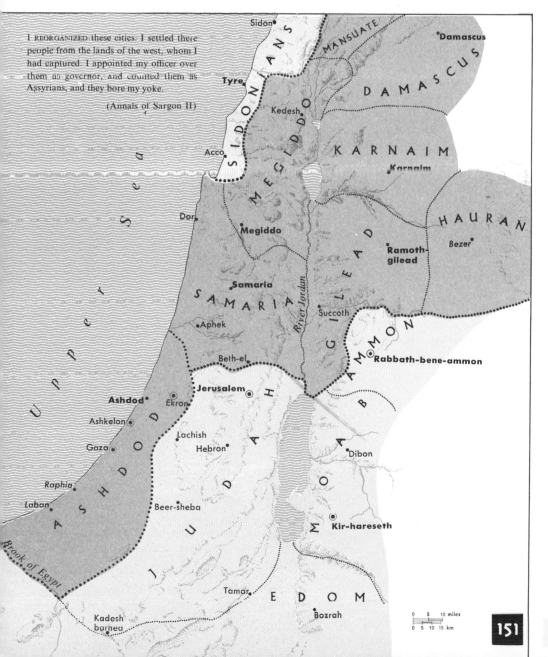

I REORGANIZED these cities. I settled there people from the lands of the west, whom I had captured. I appointed my officer over them as governor, and counted them as Assyrians, and they bore my yoke.

(Annals of Sargon II)

Assyrian provinces

Subject kingdoms

0 5 10 miles
0 5 10 15 km

Sargon II (relief from palace of Sargon II at Khorsabad)

ANNALS, OTHER LISTS,
SARGON II—KHORSABAD, ASSHUR

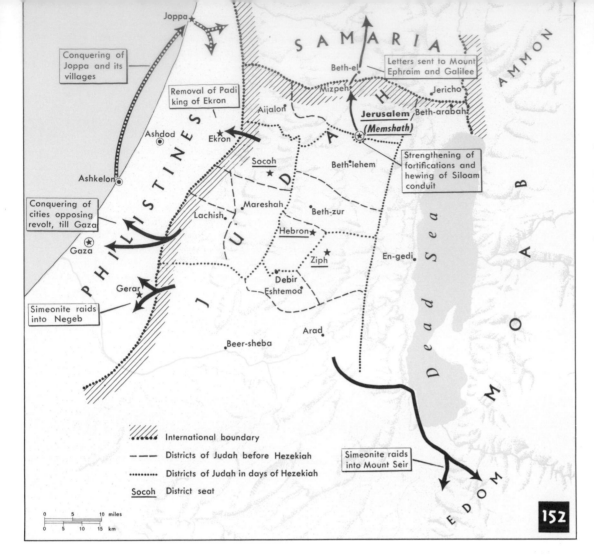

STOREHOUSES also for the yield of grain, wine, and oil... He likewise provided cites for himself... This same Hezekiah closed the upper outlet of the waters of Gihon and directed them down to the west side of the city of David. And Hezekiah prospered in all his works.

(2 Chronicles 32:28–30)

THE PREPARATIONS OF HEZEKIAH FOR REBELLION AGAINST ASSYRIA

705 TO 701 B.C.

2 KINGS 18: 6–8; 20: 12–20;
IS. 22: 8–11; 1 CHRON. 4: 38–43;
2 CHRON. 30; 32: 3–8, 27–31;
ANNALS, SENNACHERIB

Map labels:
- Conquering of Joppa and its villages
- Removal of Padi king of Ekron
- Letters sent to Mount Ephraim and Galilee
- Strengthening of fortifications and hewing of Siloam conduit
- Conquering of cities opposing revolt, till Gaza
- Simeonite raids into Negeb
- Simeonite raids into Mount Seir

Map legend:
- ///// International boundary
- – – – Districts of Judah before Hezekiah
- .... Districts of Judah in days of Hezekiah
- Socoh District seat

0 5 10 miles
0 5 10 15 km

152

Conquest of Lachish by Assyrian army
(relief from palace of Sennacherib at Nineveh)

THE TIME of greatest trial for Judah was soon to come. The death of Sargon was a sign for new uprisings throughout the kingdom and Hezekiah king of Judah stood at the head of the conspirators in Palestine. Among the cities of Philistia, Ashkelon raised the banner of revolt and the people of Ekron joined the conspiracy, after deposing their king, Padi, and sending him in chains to Hezekiah. Messengers from Merodach-baladan king of Babylon also came to Jerusalem in connection with the revolt (2 Kings 20:12–19), which, as usual, was supported by Egypt, (Is. 30:1–5; 31:1–3).

Hezekiah understood the extent of the danger which he incurred and began to prepare extensively for the coming conflict. His most famous work was the hewing of the Siloam water conduit in Jerusalem, which carried water from the spring of Gihon into the city (2 Kings 20:20; 2 Chron. 32:30; see map 114). He also strengthened the fortifications of Jerusalem (Is. 22:8–11) and fortified and provisioned the central cities of Judah (2 Chron. 4:38–41). The borders of the kingdom were expanded at the expense of the kingdoms which had refused to join the conspiracy, mainly in the direction of Gaza and Edom (2 Kings 18:8, 1 Chron. 4: 42–43). Letters were sent to the Israelite population in the provinces of Samaria and Megiddo in order to bring them closer to Judah. Thus Hezekiah renewed the aspirations of the House of David to reunite the entire country.

It was in this period that the use of special seals on the handles of storage jars is first noted; these were probably intended for purposes of taxation. The impressions contain the royal symbol accompanied by the inscription "(belonging) to the king" and the name of one of four cities: Hebron, Socoh, Ziph, and Memshe(le)th (=government, referring to Jerusalem). It appears that these were the four new administrative centers, assigned in place of the twelve older districts (see map 130), to simplify the administration of the kingdom and raise its efficiency.

THE CAMPAIGN OF SENNACHERIB
IN THE LAND OF SIDON
701 B.C.

SENNACHERIB attacked Palestine in 701 B.C., after quelling various rebellions in Mesopotamia and the east of his kingdom. Details of his campaign are
given in Assyrian sources and in the Bible; the order of events given in the latter
seems to be the more accurate. He advanced along the Phoenician coast, dethron-
ing the king of Tyre ("the king of the Sidonians"), and after the surrender of
Ashkelon and Ekron turned toward Judah.

He made his headquarters at Lachish; reliefs found at Nineveh show the
breaching of the double walls and the fortifications of the gate by siege rams.
Traces of the intense destruction have been found in the excavations on the site
(stratum III) and also at Tell Beit Mirsim (Ashan) and Beer-sheba. The inscriptions of Sennacherib mention the capture of forty-six cities in Judah, some of
which are probably referred to by Isaiah (10:28–32) and Micah (1:10–16). The
heavy tribute now sent to Sennacherib by Hezekiah did not suffice him, and he
demanded the complete surrender of Jerusalem.

Isaiah, who from the first opposed the rebellion, revived the spirit of the
besieged; and now a miracle took place. When Rabshakeh returned from Jerusalem he did not find Sennacherib at Lachish. Sennacherib had gone to besiege
Libnah, and from there set out for the Valley of Eltekeh to meet the Egyptian
Army which had come to the aid of Judah. Then the Assyrians retreated; we
know nothing of the circumstances of this sudden turn of events.

Judah was able, in consequence, to endure for more than a century longer.
Its miraculous salvation left an indelible impression upon the people.

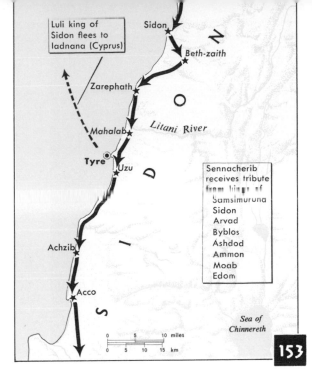

THE CAMPAIGN OF SENNACHERIB
IN PHILISTIA AND JUDAH
701 B.C.

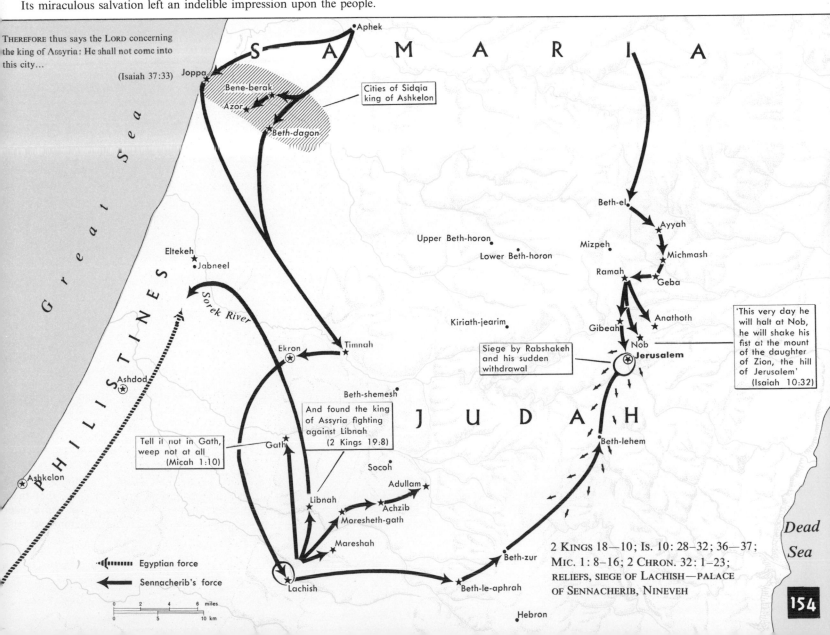

THEREFORE thus says the LORD concerning
the king of Assyria: He shall not come into
this city...

(Isaiah 37:33)

Cities of Sidqia king of Ashkelon

'This very day he
will halt at Nob,
he will shake his
fist at the mount
of the daughter
of Zion, the hill
of Jerusalem'
(Isaiah 10:32)

Siege by Rabshakeh
and his sudden
withdrawal

And found the king
of Assyria fighting
against Libnah
(2 Kings 19:8)

Tell it not in Gath,
weep not at all
(Micah 1:10)

2 KINGS 18—10; IS. 10: 28–32; 36—37;
MIC. 1: 8–16; 2 CHRON. 32: 1–23;
RELIEFS, SIEGE OF LACHISH—PALACE
OF SENNACHERIB, NINEVEH

Egyptian force

Sennacherib's force

153

154

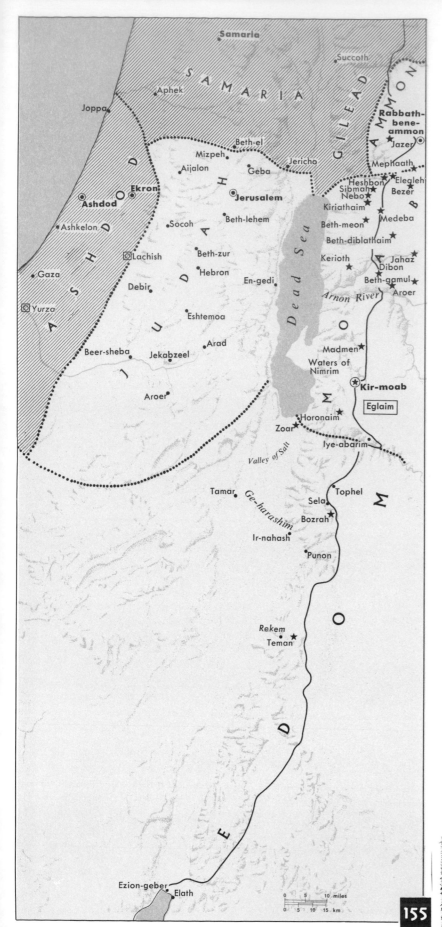

Samaria
SAMARIA
Aphek
Joppa
Succoth
Beth-el
Mizpeh
Jericho
Aijalon
Geba
Ekron
Jerusalem
Ashdod
ASHDOD
Ashkelon
Socoh
Beth-lehem
•Gaza
Lachish
Beth-zur
Yurza
Hebron
En-gedi
Debir
JUDAH
Eshtemoa
Beer-sheba
Jekabzeel
Arad
Aroer
Tamar
Ge-harashim
GILEAD
AMMON
AMMON
Rabbath-bene-ammon
Jazer
Mephaath
Heshbon
Elealeh
Sibmah
Bezer
Nebo
Kiriathaim
Medeba
Beth-meon
Beth-diblathaim
Kerioth
Jahaz
Dibon
Beth-gamul
Arnon River
Aroer
Madmen
Waters of Nimrim
Kir-moab
Eglaim
Horonaim
Zoar
Valley of Salt
Iye-abarim
Tophel
Sela
Bozrah
Ir-nahash
Punon
Rekem
Teman
Ezion-geber
Elath
Dead Sea

0 5 10 miles
0 5 10 15 km

155

JER. 48—49: 22

Province under direct Assyrian administration

Assyrian palace

JUDAH AND HER NEIGHBORS IN THE DAYS OF MANASSEH
EARLY 7TH CENTURY B.C.

WE HAVE no definite information on the reign of Manasseh son of Hezekiah, who reigned for fifty-five years over the much reduced Judah under the shadow of Assyria. This was a period of quiet prosperity and healing of deep wounds left by the campaign of Sennacherib. On the north, Judah was bordered by the provinces directly ruled by Assyria, on the east and west there remained the kingdom of Philistia and the three small kingdoms of Transjordan: Ammon, Moab, and Edom. Between the years 639 and 637 B.C., Asshurbanipal carried out a punitive campaign against the Arabians who had revolted against Assyria, and who evidently took advantage of every opportunity to raid Transjordan. It was probably during this period that the drastic decline in population began. Abundant material on its cities in the eighth and seventh centuries B.C. is found in the prophecies of Isaiah (15–16) and Jeremiah (48–49). There is a great similarity between the city names mentioned in these prophecies and the cities mentioned on the Mesha Stele, which precedes the former by 100–200 years (see map 131). It is natural that they mention the central Moabite settlements, especially on the plains which in the past had been an area of contention between Israel and Moab. It is possible, however, that the prophecies refer to the very words of boasting on the Moabite victory stele, and express joy at the misfortune of the Moabite cities.

Conquest of Egyptian town by Assyrian army
(relief from palace of Asshurbanipal at Nineveh)

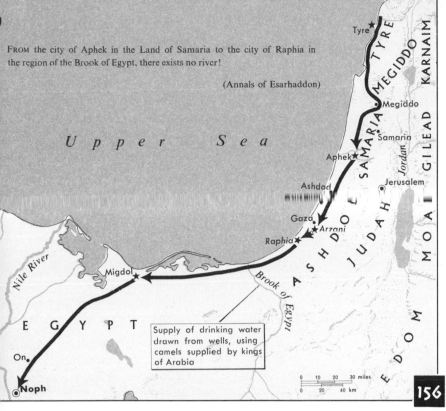

FROM the city of Aphek in the Land of Samaria to the city of Raphia in the region of the Brook of Egypt, there exists no river!

(Annals of Esarhaddon)

Supply of drinking water drawn from wells, using camels supplied by kings of Arabia

156

THE CONQUEST OF EGYPT BY ESARHADDON

669 B.C.

THE EXPANSION of the kingdom of Assyria reached its height in the first half of the seventh century. In 669 B.C. Esarhaddon conquered Lower Egypt, and his entrance into the city of Noph realized a very old Assyrian dream. Two years later, however, Esarhaddon was forced to set out on another campaign to Egypt to meet the resistance of Tirkhaka; on the way he became ill and died. His son, Asshurbanipal put down the insurrection and in 663 B.C. put Assyrian government in control over Upper Egypt. He conquered No-amon and put an end to the twenty-fifth dynasty in Egypt. The Assyrian sphere of control now extended over the entire Fertile Crescent, from Upper Egypt to the Persian Gulf and Elam (see map 146). The minor vassal kingdoms left on the edge of the desert were entirely dependent upon the Assyrian giant, and, among the kingdoms which loyally paid tribute mention is made of Manasseh king of Judah.

ANNALS ESARHADDON; OTHER ASSYRIAN DOCUMENTS; BABYLONIAN CHRONICLE, DAYS OF ESARHADDON

LIST OF TRIBUTARIES OF THE KING OF ASSYRIA

Balu king of Tyre	Ikansu king of Ekron
Manasseh king of Judah	Milkiashapa king of Byblos
Qaushgabri king of Edom	Matanbaal king of Arvad
Musuri king of Moab	Abi-baal king of Shamsimuruna
Sil-bel king of Gaza	Puduil king of Beth-ammon
Metinti king of Ashkelon	Ahimilki king of Ashdod

ASSYRIA'S DECLINE and fall came with surprising rapidity. Already under Asshurbanipal Egypt freed itself from Assyrian rule. The successors of Asshurbanipal found themselves between two emerging rivals, Babylon and the Medes, both of whom abetted the process of internal disintegration within the extensive empire. In 626 B.C., Babylon rose and defeated the Assyrians at the gates of Babylonia. Then a surprising event occurred: Egypt, the avowed foe of Assyria, came to its aid against the rising Babylon, probably out of consideration that Assyria had passed its peak, and to renew Egyptian rule in Palestine and Syria. Even this, however, did not hold the tide for long. In 614 B.C. the army of the Medes conquered the city of Asshur; two years later Nineveh fell before a combined attack by Babylon and the Medes and, in 610, Haran was also captured. This was the last stronghold left to Asshuruballit, the last king of Assyria; with its fall the kingdom of Assyria ceased to exist.

THE DESTRUCTION OF THE KINGDOM OF ASSYRIA

END OF 7TH CENTURY B.C.

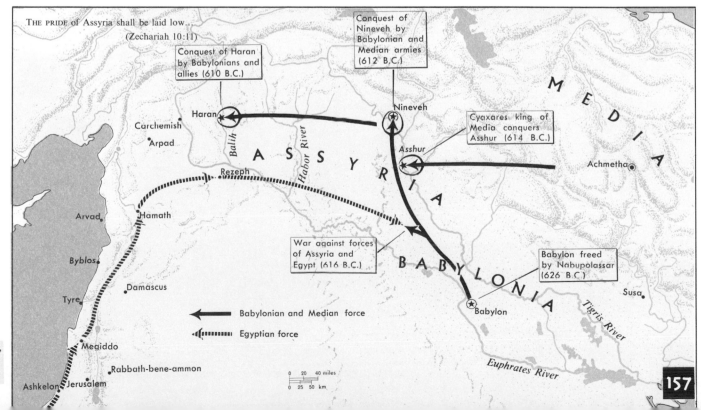

THE PRIDE of Assyria shall be laid low...
(Zechariah 10:11)

Conquest of Haran by Babylonians and allies (610 B.C.)

Conquest of Nineveh by Babylonian and Median armies (612 B.C.)

Cyaxares king of Media conquers Asshur (614 B.C.)

War against forces of Assyria and Egypt (616 B.C.)

Babylon freed by Nabupolassar (626 B.C.)

← Babylonian and Median force

◄ Egyptian force

YLONIAN CHRONICLE, S OF NABUPOLASSAR G OF BABYLON

157

THE KINGDOM OF JOSIAH
628 TO 609 B.C.

THE LAST PERIOD of greatness in the history of Judah was the reign of Josiah. He took advantage of Assyria's decline and aspired to renew the kingdom of the House of David in all of Palestine. The political and national revival in his day was intertwined with extensive religious reformations. The high places and altars in the rural areas were destroyed and defiled; and the purified Israelite worship was concentrated from this time on entirely on the temple in Jerusalem.

The information preserved in the Bible on Josiah mostly concerns his religious reformations and only in passing do we learn of his daring political and military activities. The purification of worship was carried out not only in Jerusalem and Judah, but also "in the cities of Manasseh and Ephraim and Simeon, even unto Naphtali . . . throughout the land of Israel" (2 Chron. 34:6–7). Thus, we may assume that Josiah again ruled in all these areas and annexed the Assyrian provinces which had been founded in the territory of the kingdom of Israel: Samaria, Megiddo, and possibly also Gilead. This is confirmed by the fact that he fought at Megiddo. A Hebrew letter written in his time has been found at "Meṣad Ḥashavyahu," a fortress built on the coast between Jabneh and Ashdod. According to the letter, an Israelite governor resided at the fort; thus, Josiah ruled also over this area, expanding his kingdom at the expense of the Philistine cities.

BEHOLD a son shall be born to the house of David,
Josiah by name...

(1 Kings 13:2)

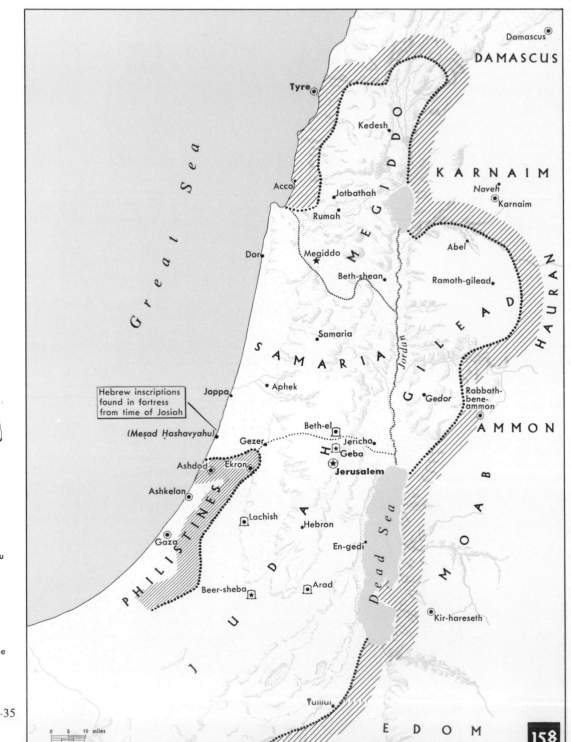

Hebrew Letter from Meṣad Ḥashavyahu

⌂ Large temple before the time of Josiah

2 KINGS 22:1—23:30; 2 CHRON. 34—35

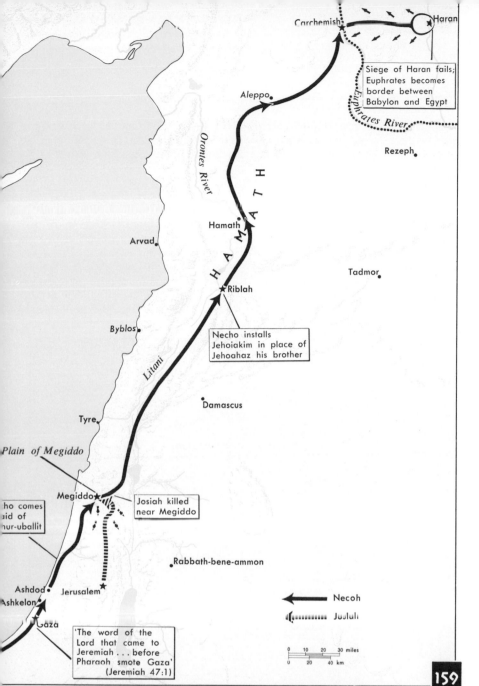

In his days Pharaoh Neco king of Egypt went up to the king of Assyria to the river Euphrates. King Josiah went to meet him; and Pharaoh Neco slew him at Megiddo...

(2 Kings 23:29)

THE FIRST CAMPAIGN OF NECOH

609 B.C.

Concerning the army of Pharaoh Neco, king of Egypt, which was by the river Euphrates at Carchemish and which Nebuchadrezzar king of Babylon defeated in the fourth year of Jehoiakim the son of Josiah, king of Judah...

(Jeremiah 46:2)

THE FIRST CAMPAIGN OF NEBUCHADNEZZAR

605 TO 604 B.C.

Map labels (page 159):
- Carchemish
- Haran
- Siege of Haran fails; Euphrates becomes border between Babylon and Egypt
- Aleppo
- Rezeph
- Orontes River
- Euphrates River
- HAMATH
- Hamath
- Arvad
- Tadmor
- Riblah
- Necho installs Jehoiakim in place of Jehoahaz his brother
- Byblos
- Litani
- Damascus
- Tyre
- Plain of Megiddo
- Megiddo
- Josiah killed near Megiddo
- ...ho comes ...id of ...hur-uballit
- Rabbath-bene-ammon
- Ashdod
- Jerusalem
- Ashkelon
- Gaza
- 'The word of the Lord that came to Jeremiah ... before Pharaoh smote Gaza' (Jeremiah 47:1)
- ← Necoh
- Judah

0 10 20 30 miles
0 20 40 km

159

KINGS 23: 29–30; JER. 47; 2 CHRON. 35: 20–24; BABYLONIAN CHRONICLE, ...AYS OF NEBOPILESSER AND NEBUCHADNEZZAR, KINGS OF BABYLON

THE KINGDOM of Josiah disintegrated upon his tragic death near Megiddo, described briefly in the Bible and additional details on the events leading up to this battle are found in Babylonian sources. "Pharaoh-necoh" went up to Carchemish on the Euphrates in 609 B.C. to the aid of Asshuruballit, the last king of Assyria, in his attempt to reconquer Haran. Josiah met his death trying to stop Necoh's advance near Megiddo, probably in order to prevent the reinstitution of Egyptian control in Palestine.

Although the Assyrian-Egyptian attempt failed, Necoh controlled Palestine and Syria for several years. Upon Necoh's return from the war, Jehoahaz the son of Josiah hastened to him at Riblah in the Land of Hamath, but Jehoiakim his brother was enthroned in his stead (2 Kings 23:33–35; Jer. 22:10–12; 2 Chron. 36:1–4).

In the fourth year of Jehoiakim (605 B.C.), Nebuchadnezzar king of Babylon defeated an Egyptian army at Carchemish (Jer. 46:2) and again at Hamath. A year later he marched through the Holy Land, conquered Ashkelon, and reached the brook of Egypt (2 Kings 24:7). Again Judah became a small vassal kingdom of Babylon, soon to be ground down by the perennial wars between Babylon and Egypt.

JER. 46: 2; BABYLONIAN CHRONICLE,
DAYS OF NEBUCHADNEZZAR, KING OF BABYLON

◄□□□□□ Babylonian force
← Egyptian force

Map labels (page 160):
- Carchemish
- Haran
- 609 B.C.
- Aleppo
- 605 B.C.
- Euphrates River
- Rezeph
- Hamath
- Arvad
- Tadmor
- Byblos
- Damascus
- Tyre
- Conquest of Ashkelon by Nebuchadnezzar in 604 B.C.
- Samaria
- Rabbath-bene-ammon
- Ashkelon
- Jerusalem
- Nile River
- Brook of Egypt
- Noph

0 20 40 miles
0 25 50 km

160

THE KINGDOM OF BABYLON
EARLY 6TH CENTURY B.C.

THE KINGDOM of Babylon inherited most of the Assyrian Empire, and reached its zenith under Nebuchadnezzar. In the east and the north, it bordered on the kingdom of the Medes, and in the south stood Egypt, its rival. A petty kingdom like Judah needed in this period a king like Manasseh, who submitted to the yoke of the mighty power, sufficing in the minor role given him. The sons of Josiah were more ambitious. Even Jeremiah, the great prophet who rose in Judah in this period, could not curb their rash adventures with his harsh warnings.

Jehoiakim the son of Josiah remained on the throne after the Holy Land had come under Babylonian control and continued to aspire toward freedom from the Babylonian yoke with the aid of Egypt. Further proof of his daring ambitions can be seen in the remains of the magnificent palace uncovered at Ramat Rahel (probably the biblical Beth-haccherem). This was intended for the garrisoning of large military forces close to the capital. For this construction, he did not refrain from using much forced labor, earning the hatred of the people of Jerusalem (2 Kings 24:4; Jer. 22:13–19). Three years after his surrender to Nebuchadnezzar, he felt ready to revolt against Babylonian rule. The reaction was swift: at first the Babylonians directed the unrest of Judah's neighbors toward her, mainly in the east, and the Chaldean army came up against Jerusalem in 598 B.C. Jehoiakim died at the start of the siege; he may have been murdered (Jer. 22:18–19; 36:30). His son Jehoiachin surrendered and was exiled to Babylon together with many of his family and the notables of the kingdom, " . . . all the princes, and all the mighty men of valor, even ten thousand captives, and all the craftsmen and the smiths; none remained, save the poorest sort of the people of the land" (2 Kings 24:14).

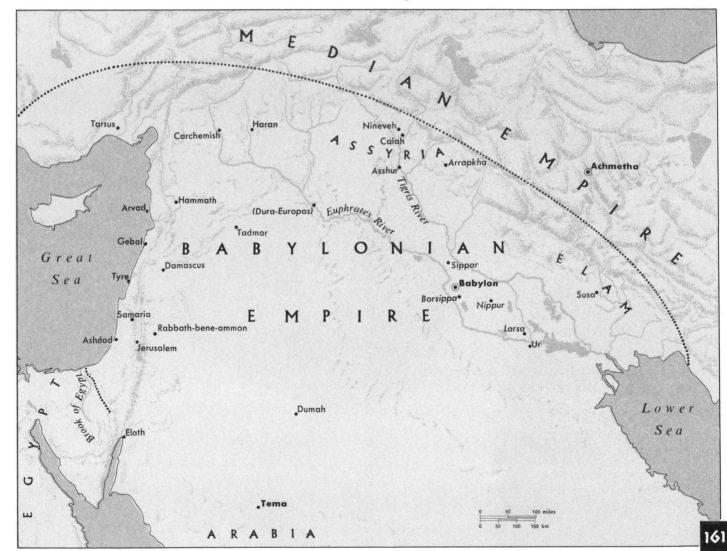

161

Stone window railing
(from palace of Jehoiakim at Ramat Rahel)

‍N the army of the king of Babylon
fighting against Jerusalem and against
he cities of Judah that were left, Lachish
Azekah; for these were the only fortified
s of Judah that remained.

(Jeremiah 34:7)

Map 162 labels:
- Tyre
- Kedesh
- Acco
- Dor
- Megiddo
- Samaria
- Capture of Judean cities and siege of Jerusalem
- Aphek
- Joppa
- Jordan River
- Jericho
- Zedekiah caught
- ‍ening of ‍ian hold ‍nd Jerusalem approach ‍gyptians
- Ashdod
- Beth-shemesh
- Jerusalem
- Beth-haccherem
- Azekah
- Renewal of siege after Egyptian defeat; capture of Jerusalem
- Gaza
- Lachish
- Hebron
- Raphia
- Beer-sheba
- Arad
- Ramat Negeb
- Edomites raid into Judah
- MEGIDDO
- SAMARIA
- GILEAD
- PHILISTINES
- JUDAH
- MOAB
- KARNAIM
- EDOM
- 10 miles / 10 15 km

162

2 KINGS 25: 1–21; JER. 37: 5; 52: 4–27;
2 CHRON. 36: 17–21; LACHISH OSTRACA

THE CAMPAIGN OF NEBUCHADNEZZAR AGAINST JUDAH
587 B.C.

THIS is the number of the people whom Nebuchadnezzar carried away captive: in the seventh year, three thousand and twenty-three Jews; in the eighteenth year of Nebuchadrezzar he carried away captive from Jerusalem eight hundred and thirty-two persons; in the twenty-third year of Nebuchadrezzar, Nebuzaradan the captain of the guard carried away captive of the Jews seven hundred and forty-five persons; all the persons were four thousand and six hundred.

(Jeremiah 52: 28–30)

THE EXILE FROM JUDAH
597 TO 582 B.C.

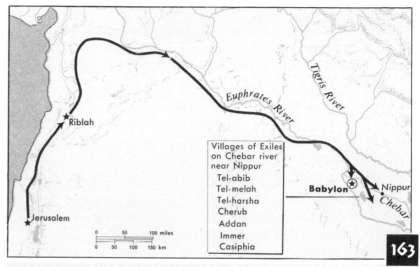

Map 163 labels:
- Tigris River
- Euphrates River
- Riblah
- Jerusalem
- Villages of Exiles on Chebar river near Nippur
  - Tel-abib
  - Tel-melah
  - Tel-harsha
  - Cherub
  - Addan
  - Immer
  - Casiphia
- Babylon
- Nippur
- Chebar
- 0 50 100 miles / 0 50 100 150 km

163

2 KINGS 24: 11–16; 25: 11; JER. 52: 28–30; EZEK. 3: 15; EZRA 2: 59; 8: 17

NEBUCHADNEZZAR enthroned Zedekiah the son of Josiah. In 589 B.C. he was drawn into a new rebellion against Babylon. Upon the approach of Nebuchadnezzar's punitive campaign Judah was, in effect, abandoned to face the mighty Chaldean army alone. The Edomites again took advantage of the circumstances and invaded Judah (Obad. 1:10–14; Ps. 137:7; Lam. 4:21–22). In this connection, a letter has been found at Arad in which the local commanders ordered urgent reinforcements to be sent to Ramat Negeb to meet an Edomite attack.

This time the Babylonian reprisal was hard and without pity. The cities of Judah were destroyed one after the other. In various excavations, such as at Ramat Rahel, Beth-zur, Beth-shemesh, Lachish, Arad, and En-gedi, absolute destruction is apparent. The last of the fortified cities of Judah to fall were Lachish and Azekah (Jer. 34:7). The sentence: "We are watching for the signals of Lachish, according to all the indications which my lord hath given, for we cannot see Azekah," in one of the Lachish Letters (no. 4), was obviously written after the fall of Azekah. Finally, Jerusalem was besieged; the siege, however, was lifted for a short period following a rumor of the approach of the Egyptian army (Jer. 37:5), though unlike in the days of Sennacherib it was immediately reimposed. In the summer of 587 B.C. the walls of the city were breached and Jerusalem was captured. A month later the Babylonians burned the entire city, including the temple, and again many people were exiled to Babylonia.

More people were exiled in 582 possibly as a result of another rebellion; most of the exiles were settled in various villages on the Chebar River near Nippur and Babylon. The number of exiles is given in the Book of Jeremiah (52:28–30), though this includes probably only the important families.

THE FLIGHT TO EGYPT
CA. 586 B.C.

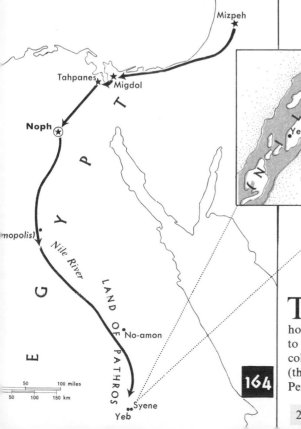

Map 164 labels:
- Mizpeh
- Tahpanes
- Migdol
- Noph
- Yeb
- Syene
- ‍mopolis)
- Nile River
- No-amon
- Syene
- Yeb
- EGYPT
- LAND OF PATHROS
- NILE VALLEY
- 50 100 miles / 50 100 150 km

164

THE BABYLONIANS left the internal rule of Judah in the hands of Gedaliah the son of Ahikam, who ruled from Mizpeh; he was, however, murdered by hotheads. Out of fear of Babylonian reprisal for his murder, many families fled to Egypt (2 Kings 25:22–26; Jer. 40–44). Here they founded Jewish military colonies, the most famous of which, at Yeb (Elephantine) in southern Egypt (the Land of Pathros), is well known through the archive from the period of Persian rule found there.

2 KINGS 25: 25–26; JER. 42—45

Figure of king painted on jar fragment
(from palace of Jehoiakim at Ramat Rahel)

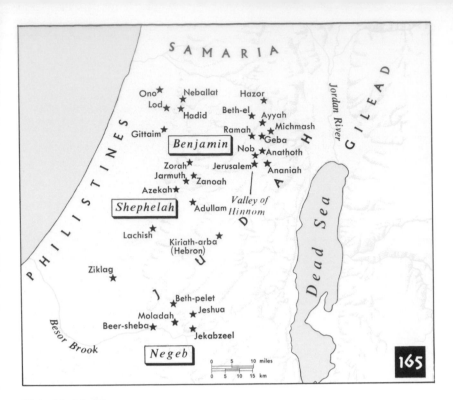

THE INHABITANTS of these waste places in the land of Israel...

(Ezekiel 33:24)

JUDAH UNDER BABYLONIAN RULE
EARLY 6TH CENTURY B.C.

THE DESTRUCTION was harsh and cruel and overlooked none of the important cities of Judah. Some of the lands and destroyed settlements were quickly occupied by the "residue of the people" (Jer. 40:10), causing much resentment among the captive exiles (Ez. 33:21–27).

The central highlands of Judah, however, were denuded of their populations, and the Babylonians did not bring new settlers here to fill the void. These areas were gradually seized by the Edomites—who were crowded by the pressure of Arabian tribes—and the southern Judean hills to the region of Beth-zur now became "Idumea" (see map 171).

Judean settlements remained mainly in the outlying regions, some of which probably became detached from Judah already in 597 B.C. These were included in the list of the "residue of Israel" preserved in Nehemiah 11:20–36, which records mostly sites in Benjamin, the Negeb, and the Shephelah on the border of Philistia.

NEH. 11: 20–36

EZEK. 47: 13—48:29

PALESTINE IN THE VISION OF EZEKIEL

MOST of the exiles in Babylon who were settled in scattered agricultural communities preserved their spiritual and religious heritage and cultivated the vision of "Return to the Promised Land." This found expression in the visions of Ezekiel, who was exiled to Babylon together with Jehoiachin. In chapters 47–48, appears his utopian redistribution of the Holy Land among the twelve tribes, settled one alongside the other in adjacent inheritances. The borders of the land are in accordance with the ancient borders of the Land of Canaan (compare map 50); Ezekiel "modernized" them by working into his description contemporary geographical names, including several of the Babylonian provinces of his day.

So YOU shall divide this land among you according to the tribes of Israel.

(Ezekiel 47:21)

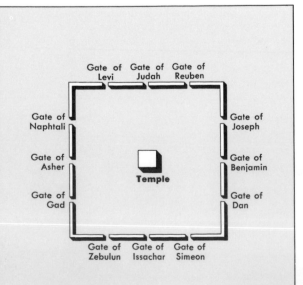

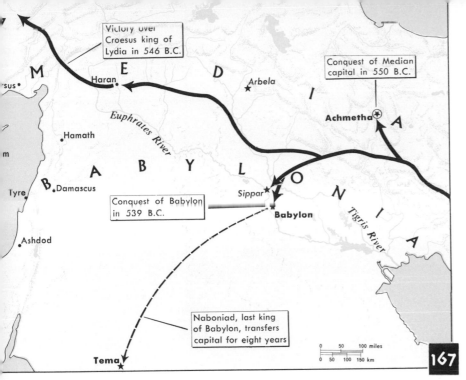

Victory over Croesus king of Lydia in 546 B.C.

Conquest of Median capital in 550 B.C.

Achmetha

Haran

Arbela

Euphrates River

Hamath

Damascus

Tyre

Conquest of Babylon in 539 B.C.

Sippar

Babylon

Tigris River

Ashdod

Naboniad, last king of Babylon, transfers capital for eight years

Tema

0 50 100 miles
0 50 100 150 km

167

CLAY BARREL, CYRUS

THE FALL OF BABYLON
539 B.C.

THE HOPES of the exiles rose with the disintegration of the shortlived kingdom of Babylon. After the death of Nebuchadnezzar in 562 B.C., three successors followed over a period of seven years. The first was Evil-Merodach who freed Jehoiachin from prison (2 Kings 25:27–30). Nabonidus of Haran seized the throne of Babylon in 556 B.C. He aspired to weaken the power of the priests of Marduk and busied himself with archaeological excavations more than with affairs of state. Nabonidus moved his capital to the oasis of Tema on the border of Arabia when the danger—in the form of Cyrus the Persian—became apparent, remaining there until about 545 B.C., and leaving the administration at Babylon in the hands of his son Belsharuzur, the Belshazar of the Bible (Dan. 8:1).

The end of the kingdom came quickly. In 550 B.C., Cyrus king of Anshan conquered Achmetha and inherited the vast kingdom of the Medes, the rivals of Babylonia. Four years later he defeated Croesus king of Lydia and captured his capital at Sardis. In 539 B.C. he entered Babylon without even a fight, as the restorer of the ancient worship of Marduk.

Darius enthroned (relief from Persepolis)

THE PERSIAN EMPIRE
538 TO 332 B.C.

CYRUS founded the largest empire the Ancient East had ever seen. His son Cambyses conquered Egypt, and his successor, Darius I, reached India. The immense empire was divided into provinces (satrapies) ruled by "satraps and the governors and the princes of the provinces from India to Ethiopia, a hundred twenty and seven provinces" (Esther 8:9). The fifth satrapy was Abar Nahara, that is, beyond the river Euphrates, and one of its lands was "Yehud"—Judah.

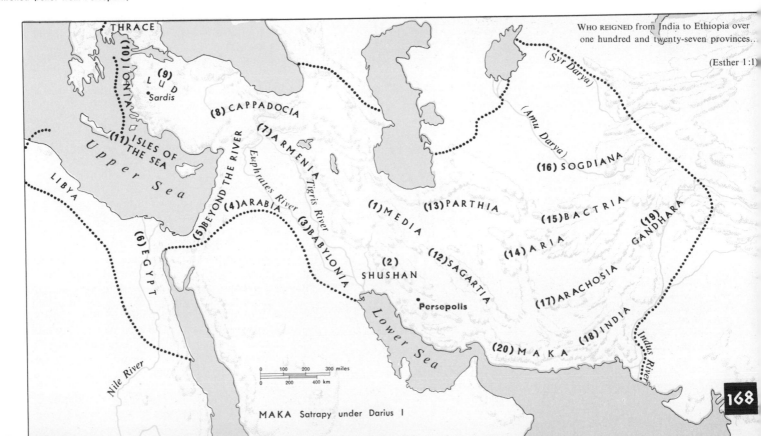

WHO REIGNED from India to Ethiopia over one hundred and twenty-seven provinces..

(Esther 1:1)

THRACE

(10) IONIA

(9) LUD
Sardis

(8) CAPPADOCIA

(11) ISLES OF THE SEA

(7) ARMENIA

Upper Sea

LIBYA

BEYOND THE RIVER

Euphrates River

Tigris River

(4) ARABIA

(5)

(3) BABYLONIA

(6) EGYPT

(1) MEDIA

(13) PARTHIA

(16) SOGDIANA

(15) BACTRIA

(14) ARIA

(19) GANDHARA

(12) SAGARTIA

(2) SHUSHAN

(17) ARACHOSIA

Persepolis

(18) INDIA

Lower Sea

(20) MAKA

Indus River

Nile River

(Syr Darya)

(Amu Darya)

0 100 200 300 miles
0 200 400 km

MAKA Satrapy under Darius I

168

The map shows geographic locations and routes:

Carchemish, Haran, Arbela, Arpad, Aleppo, Rezeph, Asshur, Achmetha, Hamath, Sumur, Tadmor, Euphrates River, Byblos, Sidon, Tyre, Damascus, Samaria, Ashdod, Rabbath-bene-ammon, Jerusalem, Sippar, Tigris River, Babylon, Susa, Nippur, Nehemiah

BEYOND THE RIVER

Return of Exiles in days of Sheshbazzar and Zerubbabel (537–515 B.C.)

Ezra uses dangerous route without military escort

Return under Ezra and Nehemiah (457–428 B.C.)

Judean Exiles concentrated in area around Nippur

THE RETURN TO ZION
538 TO 445 B.C.

EZRA 1—2; NEH. 1—3

0   50   100 miles
0   50   100   150 km

169

CYRUS desired to win over the peoples of his vast kingdom through tolerance of religious and national feelings; he allowed the renewal of worship in religions which had been suppressed by the Babylonians. In the first year of his reign he published a royal decree concerning the renewal of worship of Jehovah in Jerusalem and the return of the exiles to Judah. In 537 B.C., the first of these returned to Judah under the leadership of the prince Sheshbazzar (Ezra 1:8; 5:14), probably Shenassar the son of Jehoiachin king of Judah (1 Chron. 3:18). The spiritual uplift of the returning exiles and the hope of redemption found expression in the magnificent prophecies of Isaiah (40 ff.).

These high aspirations were, however, quickly dashed in the reality of the "day of small things" (Zech. 4:10). Judah lay wasted, surrounded by hostile provinces on every side, and the returning exiles came up against the inhabitants that had remained, the "remnant" who had seized their lands. Only in 515 B.C. was the Second Temple finished, but to those who remembered the First, disappointment was greater than joy (Ezra 3:12–13).

THEN I arose in the night, I and a few men with me; and I told no one what my God had put into my heart to do for Jerusalem.

(Nehemiah 2:12)

JERUSALEM IN THE DAYS OF THE RETURN
CA. 440 B.C.

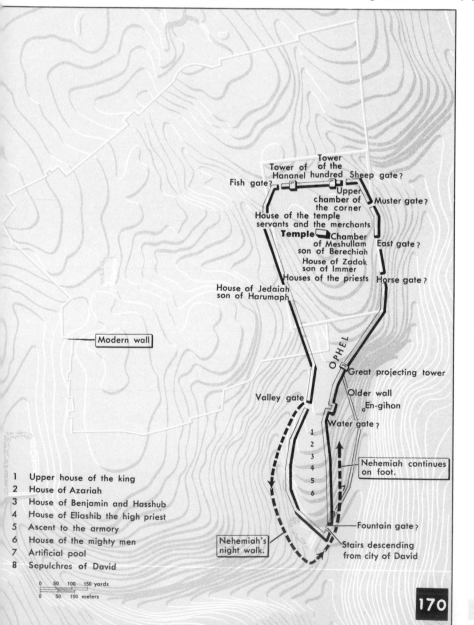

Tower of the hundred
Tower of Hananel
Sheep gate?
Fish gate?
Upper chamber of the corner
Muster gate?
House of the temple servants and the merchants
Temple
Chamber of Meshullam son of Berechiah
East gate?
House of Zadok son of Immer
Houses of the priests
Horse gate?
House of Jedaiah son of Harumaph
Modern wall
OPHEL
Great projecting tower
Older wall
En-gihon
Valley gate
Water gate?
1
2
3
4
5
6
7
8
Nehemiah continues on foot.
Nehemiah's night walk.
Fountain gate?
Stairs descending from city of David

1 Upper house of the king
2 House of Azariah
3 House of Benjamin and Hasshub
4 House of Eliashib the high priest
5 Ascent to the armory
6 House of the mighty men
7 Artificial pool
8 Sepulchres of David

0   50   100   150 yards
0   50   100 meters

170

WE HAVE no information on the history of Judah during the following 60–70 years, until the return of Ezra and Nehemiah, at about the middle of the fifth century B.C. It was the enthusiastic work of these two leaders, who led waves of additional exiles, that laid the foundations for the renewed kingdom of Judah in the period of the Second Temple. Ezra, priest and scribe, worked mainly in the spiritual-religious sphere; Nehemiah, the governor, confined himself to political-military matters. Nehemiah refurbished the fortifications of Jerusalem, in spite of the extreme opposition of the governors of the neighboring provinces; the description of his night walk along the ruined walls (Neh. 2:12–15) and the listing of the builders of the walls (Neh. 3:1–32) includes much information on the gates, towers, and many buildings next to the wall. The plan of the city of Jerusalem can largely be reconstructed from Nehemiah's description; only the general outlines, especially of several of the gates and the southern sections of the wall, are known from archaeological research. This has revealed that the area of the city was reduced in the southeast, in comparison with the older city, as a result of raising the line of the wall from the side of the slope to its summit. Especially in this section, many houses are mentioned by Nehemiah as being along the newly built wall.

NEH. 2:12–15; 3:1–32

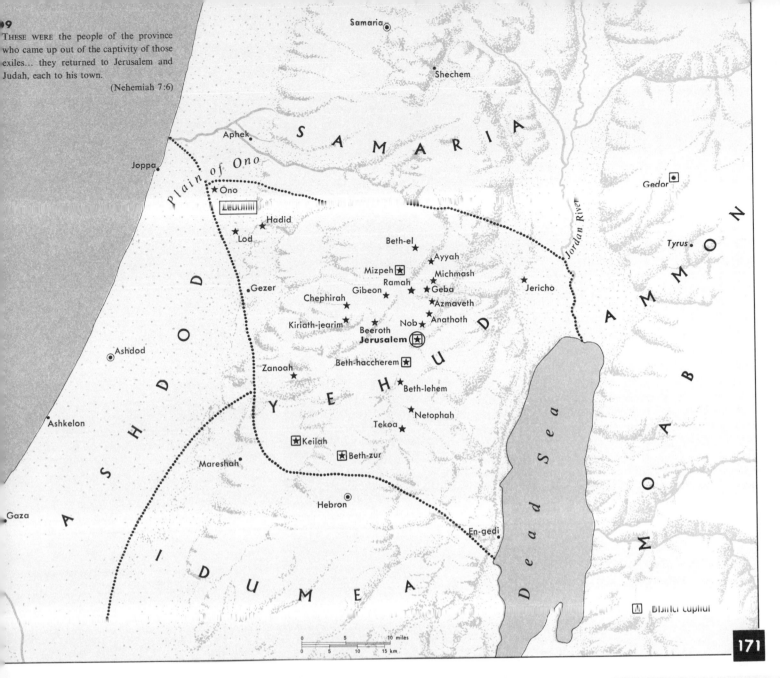

THESE WERE the people of the province who came up out of the captivity of those exiles... they returned to Jerusalem and Judah, each to his town.

(Nehemiah 7:6)

Samaria

Shechem

S A M A R I A

Aphek

Joppa

Plain of Ono

Ono

LEUUIIII

Hadid

Lod

Gezer

Beth-el

Ayyah

Mizpeh

Michmash

Ramah

Chephirah

Gibeon

Geba

Azmaveth

Kiriath-jearim

Nob

Anathoth

Beeroth

Jerusalem

Beth-haccherem

Zanoah

Beth-lehem

Netophah

Tekoa

Keilah

Beth-zur

Mareshah

Hebron

En-gedi

Gaza

Ashkelon

Ashdod

A S H D O D

I D U M E A

Y E H U D

Gedor

Tyrus

Jordan River

A M M O N

M O A B

Dead Sea

District capital

0   5   10 miles
0 5   10   15 km

171

THE LAND OF JUDAH IN THE DAYS
OF THE RETURN
CA. 440 B.C.

EZRA 2: 1–34; NEH. 3: 1–32; 7: 6–38

Inscription "Yehud" in seal-impression

Inscription "Yehud" on coins (Persian period)

IN THE LISTS of the returning exiles (Ezra 2:1–34; Neh. 7:6–38) there also appear the names of the major settlements of Yehud-Judah; the list of the builders of the wall gives details of the district governors. Additional evidence of the extent of Judah are the seal-impressions on storage jars—similar to the "(belonging) to the king" seal-impressions of the days of the First Temple—on which appear the name "Yehud" in various forms, often accompanied by a symbol or the name of a priest or governor. The distribution of these sealings reaches from Mizpeh and Jericho in the north to Beth-zur and En-gedi in the south, and Gezer in the west. These were the borders of the reduced Judah of the beginning of the period of the Second Temple, the nucleus around which grew the kingdom of the Hasmoneans.

The Persian Monarchy came into conflict with the Greek nation, settled on the shores of the Aegean Sea, in the fifth century B.C. After two unsuccessful Persian invasions (490 and 480 B.C.), the Greeks took the offensive and restricted Persian power in the Eastern Mediterranean. Internal discord and wars between the two leading Greek cities, Athens and Sparta, again strengthened the hand of the "Great King" of Persia. However, when in the middle of the fourth century B.C. Philip of Macedonia united Greece under his hegemony, he prepared the ground for the great expedition against Persia, which was launched by his son, Alexander the Great.

The last centuries of Persian rule conclude the period for which the Old Testament is our principal authority; from this point on the thread of the story is taken up by the Books of the Maccabees and other apocryphal books, by Josephus Flavius, and then by the New Testament and the Fathers of the Christian Church.

ARRIAN: ANABASIS; PLUTARCH:
LIFE OF ALEXANDER; DIODORUS 17;
CURTIUS RUFUS; JUSTIN 11:12.

THE CAMPAIGN OF ALEXANDER DOWN TO THE SIEGE OF TYRE
334 TO 332 B.C.

IN 334 B.C. Alexander, son of King Philip II of Macedonia, set out against Persia at the head of an army of 35,000 men. He took the same route as had Xerxes in 480 B.C., but in the reverse direction. Alexander crossed the Dardanelles at Eleus and fought his first battle against the Persian satraps who governed Asia Minor, routing their armies on the banks of the river Granicus. After this victory, Alexander ordered his general, Parmenio, to secure the royal treasury at Dascylium; he himself proceeded south and captured Sardis and then the coastal cities of Ionia, after besieging Miletus and Halicarnassus. The strong Persian navy attacked the coastal towns, but did not succeed in halting Alexander's advance into Caria and Lycia. From Side in Pamphylia Alexander turned inland toward the centers of opposition, Aspendus and Sagalassus. He took the latter by storm. After this he reached Gordium, the ancient capital of Phrygia, and continued on his way to Ancyra.

Meanwhile, it had come to Alexander's knowledge that Darius III, king of Persia, was amassing an army in Assyria. At Gordium Alexander joined forces with Parmenio, who had arrived from Sardis. The combined armies moved south, passing unopposed through the narrow Cilician Gates in the Taurus Mountains, and reached Tarsus, capital of Cilicia. From there, the king set out on a punitive expedition in the Cilician mountains until he reached Soli. After breaking all resistance there, Alexander marched eastward through the Syrian Gates, a pass in the Amanus Mountains, and came to Myriandrus. Here he learned that Darius and his army had arrived at Issus, at his rear. He hastened back and, by a daring cavalry attack

(333 B.C.), defeated nis foe; Darius escaped with his life, but lost his family and treasury to the victor.

Alexander did not pursue the fleeing king, but headed south, to capture the Phoenician cities. As long as their fleets remained loyal to Persia, they might cut him off from Macedonia and even incite the Greek cities to revolt. Aradus, Sidon, and Byblos surrendered without resistance. Alexander proceeded along the coast to Tyre, while Parmenio marched on Damascus to seize the royal treasury. Tyre was Phoenicia's major city and Greece's most serious competitor in Mediterranean trade. The Tyrians refused to surrender their city, relying on its location on an island off the coast and on the help of their colony Carthage. Alexander's army labored and fought for seven months, until they had completed a mole joining the island to the coast. The Tyrian fleet was defeated and the city fell in July, 332 B.C.

The amazing success of Alexander stemmed from the tactical superiority of his forces, mainly the Macedonian cavalry, and his own strategic brilliance; he well knew how to inspire his soldiers and urge them on to ever greater exertions. In contrast, Persia, mighty in the days of Darius I, now suffered from feeble leadership; ironically only the Greek mercenaries in the Persian army showed courage and military ability.

In the course of his early conquests, Alexander retained the Persian forms of administration, merely substituting Macedonians for the Persian satraps. In some instances, he even appointed native Persians to high office.

AFTER the surrender of Tyre, Alexander proceeded along the coast toward Egypt. While still besieging the city, Syrian and Palestinian delegations arrived, offering peaceful submission.

According to a tradition Sanballat, satrap of Samaria, and his army of 8,000 men, joined Alexander; the king, however, placed little trust in reinforcements of this kind. There was, however, some resistance, and Alexander sent cavalry units into the mountains of Lebanon to suppress rebellious tribes. Acco, the royal fortress in northern Palestine, surrendered without a fight and the army advanced south, most probably along the coast, to Strato's Tower. Here it was undoubtedly forced to swerve east, for the coastal area was at that time still covered by swamps and sand dunes. From Lod the Macedonian army probably turned again to the coast, there to accept the surrender of Azotus and Ascalon. At Gaza the eunuch Batis, commander of the fortress, aided by Arab mercenaries, refused to surrender and Alexander once more started a siege. The fierce resistance of Gaza can be explained by the apprehension of its citizens and their Nabatean allies, who feared the domination of their Greek competitors in this important port city, their outlet to the Mediterranean. Alexander captured Gaza in September, 332 B.C., after a siege of two months, by means of earth works and siege machinery brought from Tyre. Most male captives were killed on the spot; the women and children were sold into slavery. The city was repopulated with people from the neighboring areas. While the siege was still in progress, Greek cavalry proceeded against the Nabateans. It is possible that troops were also sent to Lachish, the capital of the province of Idumea.

With Gaza fell the last obstacle on Alexander's way to Egypt, where he wintered in 332–331 B.C. He crossed Palestine once more on his return to Tyre. Two traditions are connected with this journey: Samaritan allegiance to the Greeks was, according to some sources, short lived, and they rose against their governor Andromachus and burned him alive. In revenge, Alexander destroyed Samaria and, on its lands, settled Macedonian veterans. According to another version, it was not Alexander but the regent Perdiccas who founded this colony. However that may be, archaeological evidence proves that the city was destroyed at about that time. The Macedonians seem to have penetrated as far inland as Jericho, and it can be presumed that some troops, and maybe the king himself, forayed into the interior. These units then rejoined the main force, which must have marched along the coastal road, probably at Acco.

Of a more legendary nature is the story of Alexander's visit to Jerusalem and his meeting with the high priest Jaddua. Josephus ascribes this to the time of the siege of Gaza (Ant. 11:325–339). Talmudic sources repeat this tradition, but refer it to the high priest Simon the Just.

Dium and Gerasa, two cities beyond the Jordan, were thought to have been founded by Alexander, but this story also lacks foundation.

AND [he] made many wars, and won many strongholds.
(1 Maccabees 1:2)

ALEXANDER IN PALESTINE
332 TO 331 B.C.

Alexander the Great (from a mosaic found at Pompeii)

→ Campaign to Egypt—332 B.C.
←-- Secondary movements
←▭▭ Campaign to the north—331 B.C.
◁▭▭ Secondary movements

ARRIAN: ANABASIS; PLUTARCH: LIFE OF ALEXANDER; DIODORUS 17; CURTIUS RUFUS; JUSTIN 11: 12.

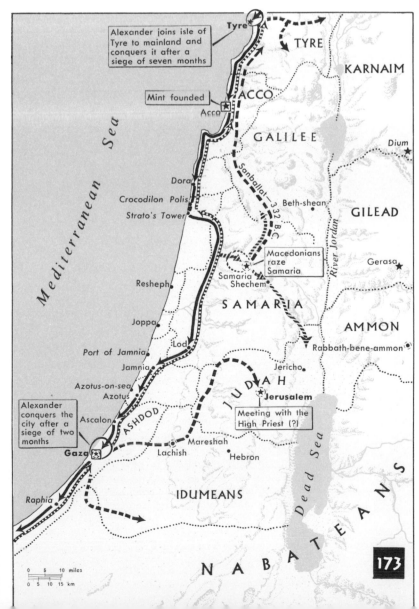

Alexander joins isle of Tyre to mainland and conquers it after a siege of seven months

Mint founded

Macedonians raze Samaria

Meeting with the High Priest (?)

Alexander conquers the city after a siege of two months

TYRE
KARNAIM
ACCO
Acco
GALILEE
Dium
Dora
Crocodilon Polis
Strato's Tower
Beth-shean
GILEAD
Gerasa
Sanballat 332 B.C.
River Jordan
Resheph
Samaria Shechem
SAMARIA
Joppa
AMMON
Lod
Rabbath-bene-ammon
Port of Jamnia
Jamnia
Jericho
Azotus-on-sea
Azotus
JUDAH
Jerusalem
Ascalon
ASHDOD
Mareshah
Lachish
Hebron
Gaza
Dead Sea
Raphia
IDUMEANS
NABATEANS
Mediterranean Sea

0   5   10 miles
0 5 10 15 km

173

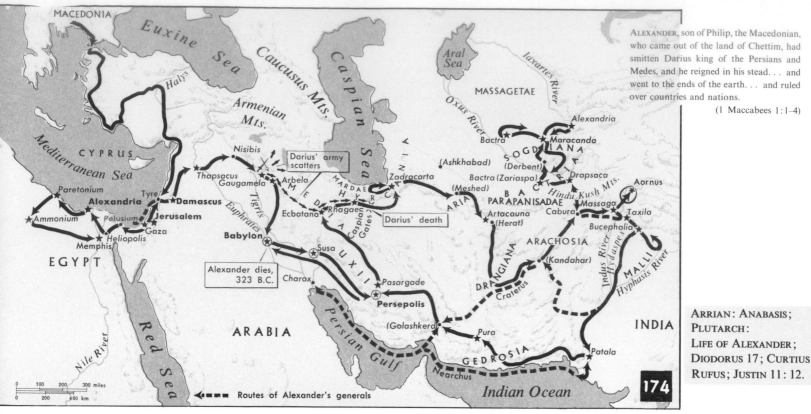

ALEXANDER, son of Philip, the Macedonian, who came out of the land of Chettim, had smitten Darius king of the Persians and Medes, and he reigned in his stead... and went to the ends of the earth... and ruled over countries and nations.

(1 Maccabees 1:1–4)

ARRIAN: ANABASIS; PLUTARCH: LIFE OF ALEXANDER; DIODORUS 17; CURTIUS RUFUS; JUSTIN 11: 12.

174

◄---- Routes of Alexander's generals

THE LATER CAMPAIGNS OF ALEXANDER
331 TO 323 B.C.

FROM Tyre and Damascus, Alexander advanced to Thapsacus, crossing the Euphrates there. On his way along the foot of the Armenian mountains, he passed the Tigris and reached Gaugamela. Between this village and the town of Arbela waited the last of Darius' armies, and here in 331 B.C. came the decisive battle. Darius was defeated and fled to Media and then to the Caspian Sea, where he was put to death by his own followers, a few hours before Alexander reached the Persian camp. The Macedonian had by then already captured the administrative centers of Persia: Babylon, Susa, and Persepolis. After Darius' death, Alexander continued his campaign through eastern Persia. He advanced into the steppes of Central Asia and crossed the Hindu Kush mountains into the valley of the Indus. In India, on his way to the Ganges valley—close to the end of the earth as Alexander conceived it—his army mutinied and refused to go any farther. Alexander turned south to the mouth of the Indus River and returned to Babylon after much suffering, mainly in the desert of Gedrosia. The Macedonians returned in three corps: the force of Craterus; the naval forces under Nearchus; and the king's army. In the month of June, 323 B.C., Alexander died in Babylon at the age of thirty-two.

Coin of Ptolemy I, king of Egypt

THE great horn was broken, and instead of it there came up four conspicuous horns. . .

(Daniel 8:8)

PTOLEMY I IN PALESTINE
320 B.C.

ALEXANDER'S HEIRS were Philip, his half-witted brother, and his unborn child, who later became Alexander IV. Real power devolved upon his generals, who soon set aside the dynastic heirs and began to fight among themselves. The main struggle was between those wishing to keep the empire intact (such as the regent Perdiccas or Antigonus Monophtalmus) and those provincial governors who wished to divide it. Ptolemy, the son of Lagos, who had obtained the satrapy of Egypt, was among the principal leaders of this second group. Firmly established in Egypt, he defeated an attempt by Perdiccas to unseat him; then, to safeguard his Egyptian realm, he coveted Palestine, which he proceeded to occupy with his land forces, led by Nicanor, while he himself advanced by sea.

DIODORUS 18: 43; 19: 58–59, 79–80, 90–92, 100–105, 20: 73–76; APPIANUS: SYRIACA 52; ANT. 12: 1–9

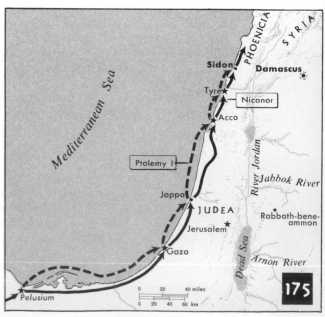

175

Now PTOLEMY, after taking many captives both from the hill country of Judea and the district round Jerusalem and from Samaria. . .

(Antiquities 12:7)

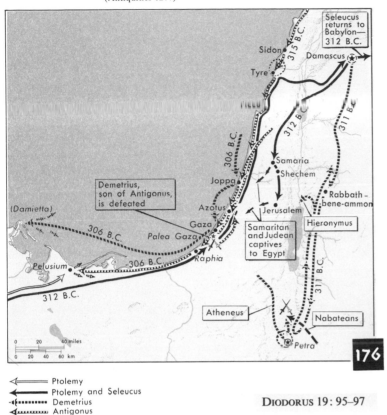

DIODORUS 19: 95–97

Ptolemy
Ptolemy and Seleucus
Demetrius
Antigonus

176

THE STRUGGLE OF THE DIADOCHI IN PALESTINE

315 TO 306 B.C.

AFTER the death of Perdiccas, the central power of Alexander's empire rested with Antigonus Monophthalmus ("One-Eyed"), who was ably assisted by his son Demetrius Poliorcetes ("taker of towns"). Antigonus first suppressed the last supporters of Alexander's dynasty (in particular, Eumenes of Cardia) and then, assuming the title of king, he turned against his fellow generals. Seleucus, governor of Babylonia, fled to Ptolemy, ruler of Egypt, who was the main support of the divisive tendency. In the years 315–306 B.C., the forces of Antigonus and Ptolemy played seesaw with the eastern approaches to Egypt. Antigonus and Demetrius thrice advanced to the borders of the Nile valley. The first time, in 315, Ptolemy retreated without a fight; the second (312 B.C.), he defeated Demetrius, but retreated before the superior forces of Antigonus, dismantling the fortresses of Palestine and taking with him many prisoners from Jerusalem, Judea, and Samaria, whom he settled in Egypt. In the same year, Seleucus returned to Babylon to stir the East against Antigonus. In 311 B.C. Atheneus, the general of the Antigonids, and then Demetrius himself twice attempted to seize Petra, the Nabatean stronghold, with its riches, and also to obtain control of the Dead Sea and its valuable asphalt resources; but they failed both times. A combined sea and land assault by Antigonus and Demetrius in 306 B.C. failed before Pelusium and the Damietta branch of the Nile. Finally, in 301 B.C., Ptolemy joined forces with Seleucus and a third general, Lysimachus. With the help of Seleucus' Indian elephants (for which he had traded the province of India), these allies triumphed over Antigonus and his son at Ipsus in Asia Minor. With this battle, the dream of a united Hellenistic Empire came to an end.

THE TRAVELS OF ZENON IN PALESTINE

259 TO 258 B.C.

AFTER the defeat of Antigonus, the Ptolemies were in the ascent, and Palestine was integrated into the complex administration of their empire. The forms of administrative division and institutions established at this time continued to exist until the Roman period, and many of them lasted until the destruction of the Second Temple. The Ptolemaic Empire was distinguished by its economic activity. Agents of the royal monopolies traveled to the far corners of the Land, in search of goods required by Egypt, mainly olive oil (Egyptian oil was inferior), wine, timber, and slaves. One such agent was Zenon, son of Agreophon from Caria, a subordinate of Apollonius, minister of finance under Ptolemy II.

Zenon's archives were discovered at Philadelphia in the Fayum, where he had settled after his retirement from government service. These archives contain documents that are an important source for the Ptolemaic administration in Palestine. Zenon traveled there in 259–258 B.C. He landed at Strato's Tower (Herodian Caesarea, see map 220) and proceeded to Jerusalem, most likely by way of Pegae. He then went to Jericho, where large-scale irrigation works were started in the Hellenistic period, and to Abila, city of vineyards, beyond the Jordan. He visited Tyrus, the capital and military colony of the Tobiads, founders of an ancient Jewish principality. Zenon then reached Lacasa (Kisweh, near Damascus); it is doubtful whether Damascus itself was at that time under Ptolemaic rule; he returned to Eeitha (Hit), and then continued to Beth-anath where there was the wine producing estate of a Greek officer. From Beth-anath he went to Cadasa and embarked at Ptolemais (Acco). Apart from this journey, the archives contain evidence of the many contacts Zenon had with agents and officials at various administrative centers, mainly in the south, e.g., Marisa and Joppa.

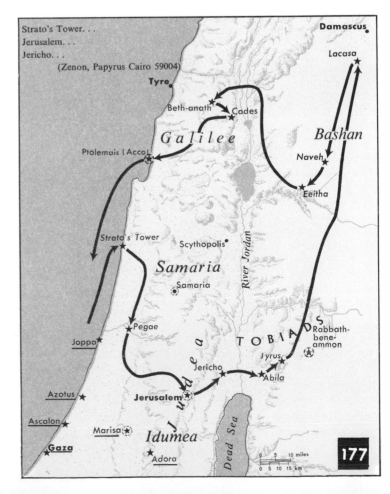

Strato's Tower. . .
Jerusalem. . .
Jericho. . .

(Zenon, Papyrus Cairo 59004)

177

ARCHIVE OF ZENON

Azotus City with agent of Zenon

DIODORUS 19; PLUTARCH: DEMETRIUS;
JUSTIN-TROGUS 13–15

⬚⬚⬚ Under Ptolemaic control

IN the year 223–222 B.C., two young rulers ascended the thrones of Syria and Egypt, almost simultaneously; Antiochus III began to reign at Antioch and Ptolemy IV at Alexandria. The Seleucid was the stronger of the two and almost at once set out to realize an ambition of his predecessors—to wrest Palestine from the rival dynasty. Invading the valley of Lebanon in 221 B.C., he was brought to a stop between Brocchoi and Gerrha at the strong line of fortifications erected by Theodotus, Ptolemy's general. In 219 B.C. Antiochus had better luck: he captured Seleucia, and Theodotus and his second in command, Panetolus, went over to Antiochus in 218 B.C. With their help he defeated the new Egyptian commander Nicolaus at the river Damuras, south of Beirut. Sidon, Tyre, and Ptolemais surrendered. While Nicolaus was blockaded in Dora, the king himself proceeded from Tyre inland. The first cities to surrender were Philoteria, an administrative center on the shores of the Sea of Galilee, and Scythopolis; he captured Itabyrium (Mount Tabor) by a ruse (a feigned retreat), and took Pella, Gephrus, and Camus. He then advanced to Abila and Gadara, which opened their gates without resistance. At the same time the Nabateans, allies of Antiochus III, attacked Philadelphia (Rabbath-bene-ammon). He rushed to their aid and, after penetrating by way of the city's water system, he captured it. From Philadelphia, Antiochus returned to Ptolemais and wintered there during 218–217 B.C. Hippolochus and Cereas, two commanders who had earlier deserted Ptolemy, were ordered into Samaria with five thousand horse.

Meanwhile, the Egyptians mobilized all their forces and, for the first time in Ptolemaic history, even recruited local auxiliaries. Ptolemy IV set out at the head of an army numbering seventy thousand soldiers, five thousand horsemen, and 73 war elephants, crossed the desert and, in the spring of 217 B.C., reached Raphia. Waiting for him there was Antiochus III with sixty-two thousand foot-soldiers, six thousand horse, and 102 elephants. The Egyptians prevailed and Antiochus retreated from Palestine. Ptolemy III then embarked on a triumphal march throughout the country; he visited Marisa, Jerusalem, Ptolemais, and Tyre, and proceeded to the borders of his empire. It seemed as if Egyptian rule in Palestine had once more been stabilized.

⬩⬩⬩⬩ Antiochus III
⟵ Ptolemy IV
⬚⬚ Under Ptolemaic control—219 B.C.

POLYBIUS 5: 54–86

AND the daughter of the king of the south shall come to the king of the north to make peace... a branch from her roots shall arise in his place; he shall come against the army and enter the fortress of the king of the north...

(Daniel 11:6–7)

THE THIRD SYRIAN WAR
246 TO 240 B.C.

AFTER the battle of Ipsus, Ptolemy III kept Palestine and Phoenicia for himself, contrary to an agreement made with Seleucus Nicator prior to the battle. When Seleucus became king of Asia, he refrained from fighting Ptolemy, his old comrade-in-arms. Seleucus' successors were less hesitant, and the result was a series of conflicts—the Syrian Wars. In the First and Second of these, the Ptolemies were on the offensive. Temporary peace was restored in 255 B.C., when Antiochus II wed Berenice, sister of Ptolemy III, and repudiated his previous consort, Laodice.

The deposition of Berenice, after the death of Antiochus II, and her subsequent death at the hand of Laodice, caused the renewal of war between Syria and Egypt.

The king of Egypt attacked Antioch and Seleucia in a combined land and sea operation; both cities surrendered. He then invaded Babylonia but decided to turn back on hearing rumors of a revolt in Egypt. The Syrians, who at first had welcomed Egyptian rule, soon turned their backs on the Ptolemies. Seleucus II, the son of Laodice, returned to his capital in 242 B.C. and reconquered Mesopotamia, where he founded the town of Callinicum on the banks of the Euphrates. He also relieved the besieged garrisons of Orthosia and Damascus. Peace was made in 240 B.C. Of all his conquests, Ptolemy III held on only to Seleucia, the port of Antioch, which remained in Egyptian hands until 219 B.C.

THE FIRST CAMPAIGN OF ANTIOCHUS III
219 TO 217 B.C.

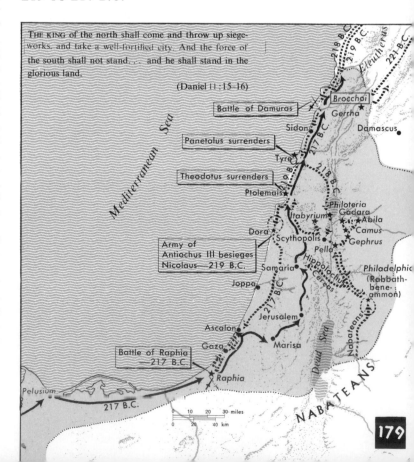

THE KING of the north shall come and throw up siege-works, and take a well-fortified city. And the force of the south shall not stand... and he shall stand in the glorious land.

(Daniel 11:15–16)

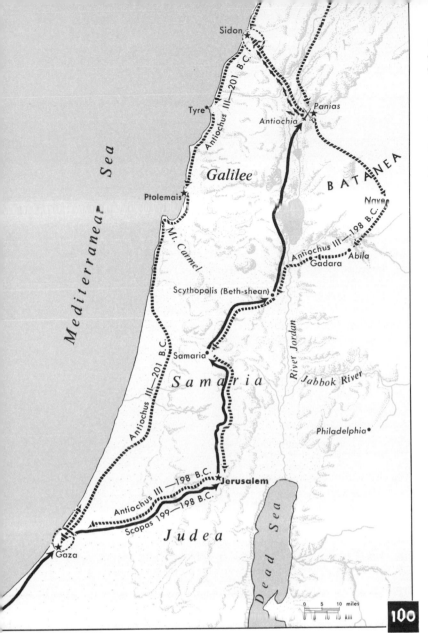

POLYBIUS 15: 13, 25; 16: 18–19, 22, 39; ANT 12: 133–146

Antiochus III, king of Syria

THE FINAL CONQUEST
OF PALESTINE BY ANTIOCHUS III
201 TO 198 B.C.

ANTIOCHUS returned to his capital after having quelled a major
rebellion in Asia Minor, and after a prolonged campaign in the
interior of Asia, he again invaded Palestine. In 201 B.C. his army penetrated as far as Gaza, which remained loyal to Ptolemy and held
out bravely. In the end Antiochus III captured the town, but he retreated in the face of the advancing Egyptian army led by Scopas.
Scopas headed for the interior, reached the gates of Jerusalem (the
Jews there may have favored Antiochus III), and occupied the city.
He then proceeded to Panias (Banyas near Dan); there Antiochus
lay in wait for him. The armies of Ptolemy IV were defeated in a decisive battle; their remnants and Scopas himself fled to Sidon, where
they were besieged.

Antiochus and his army then passed through Batanea, Abila, and
Gadara to Jerusalem. The Jews received him willingly, supplied the
needs of his army, and fought alongside him when he attacked the
garrison left by Scopas at the Acra of Jerusalem. Antiochus in turn
granted them many favors: he provided ritually clean cattle, as well
as wine, oil and frankincense, wheat, flour, and salt for sacrifices,
and timber for the maintenance of the Temple. He allowed the Jews
to live according to their ancestral laws, exempted the Gerousia
(Council of Elders), the priests, and the scribes of the Temple from
paying head and salt taxes; the other citizens of Jerusalem enjoyed the
same privilege for three years and were also remitted one-third of
their bond-service. He ordered prisoners released and forbade import
into the city of ritually unclean meat. For thirty-one years Judea
remained tranquil under Seleucid rule.

While the Hellenistic kingdoms were frittering away their strength
in internecine fighting, a new power arose in the West: Rome had
first united Italy, and then, in the Second Punic War (218–201 B.C.)
defeated Carthage. Mistress of the Western Mediterranean, she struck
down the Macedonian monarchy in 197 B.C.; then she turned upon
the Seleucids.

Antiochus III tried to forestall the danger threatening his kingdom.
His victories over Egypt had rendered his southern border safe; he
therefore turned northward, occupying large parts of Asia Minor.
In 196 B.C. he crossed the Hellespont and occupied Thrace. The
Romans declared war upon him in 192 B.C., whereupon Antiochus
landed in Greece, accompanied by Hannibal, the inveterate foe of
the Romans. However, the Syrian army was not equal to the Roman
legions; Antiochus was defeated at the Thermopylae in 191 B.C. and
had to evacuate Greece. His final defeat came in 190 B.C. at Magnesia
in Asia Minor. In the peace signed at Apamea, Antiochus gave up all
Asia Minor, disarmed most of his army, and paid a huge indemnity.

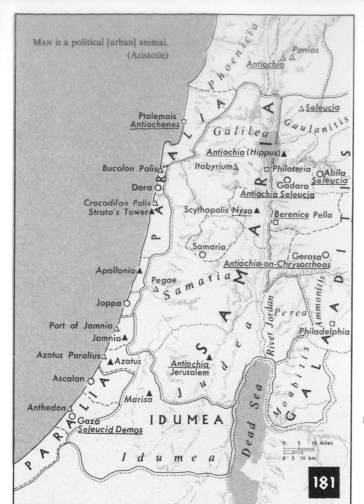

THE GREEK CITIES IN PALESTINE
312 TO 167 B.C.

TO the Greeks, the city (polis) was the only form of political organization fit for a civilized people. The founding of new cities was, therefore, the best way to spread Hellenic culture. Nevertheless, the Ptolemies were circumspect in the granting of municipal rights to the settlements within their boundaries because these involved a large measure of autonomy. They honored existing privileges, but gave dynastic names to only two cities: Philadelphia and Ptolemais. Similar in status were Pella, for a time called Berenice after a Ptolemaic queen, another Berenice—Elath—on the shores of the Red Sea, and Philoteria, named after the sister of Philadelphus. The Seleucids, in contrast, relied heavily on the cities for support of their rule. Antiochus III and his heirs were therefore very generous to the cities under their control. They gave them dynastic names and the freedom to organize in the Greek manner, with archons, a boulé (council), and a demos (all citizens, but not all the population).

─────	Border of Seleucid eparchy
- - - - -	Border of Ptolemaic city
··········	Border of Ptolemaic hyparchy
PARALIA	Seleucid eparchy
Judea	Ptolemaic hyparchy
<u>Seleucia</u>	City given Seleucid dynastic name
□	City given Ptolemaic dynastic name
○	City with municipal rights under Ptolemaic rule
△	Town given Greek name
▲	City given Greek name

THE JEWISH DIASPORA IN THE PTOLEMAIC KINGDOM
3RD TO 1ST CENTURIES B.C.

Epitaph mentioning the "all-highest god" found at Rhenea near Delos

THE small land of Judea could not feed its entire population. Already in the Hellenistic period we find, side-by-side with the ancient forms of population movement (exile and military colonies), the emigration of individual families attracted by the material prosperity of the surrounding world. Thus there appear in Egypt, in addition to the military colonies of Pelusium-Migdol, Daphne, Elephantine, Cyrene, many Jews who earned their bread by farming or government service. They were concentrated in Alexandria the capital and in the Arsinoite District (Fayum), which had been resettled through the initiative of the Ptolemies. Many others lived in Thebes (Diospolis Magna), in upper Egypt and its vicinity. Evidence exists of Jewish settlements throughout Egypt. Of special interest is the temple built by Onias, the deposed high priest, at Leontopolis in the Delta in the second century B.C., known in Talmudic literature as the "House of Onias." It stood until after the destruction of the Second Temple, but it too was destroyed soon after.

▨	Ptolemaic realm
•	Settlement with Jewish population
▨	Area of dense Jewish population
··········	Borders—240 B.C.

Schedia	Siron Come
Samaria	Migdola
Tricomias	Alexandrou
Hephaestium	-nesus
Pseniris	Ibium Argeu
Heracla	

THE JEWISH DIASPORA
IN BABYLONIA, ASIA MINOR AND GREECE
3RD TO 1ST CENTURIES B.C.

FOR I believe that they [the Jews] will guard our well-wishers
from the wrath [in their hearts].
(Letter of Antiochus III to the governor of Phrygia)

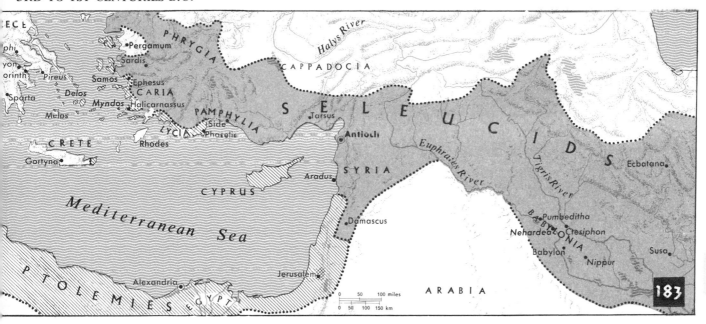

INSCRIPTIONS;
ANT. 12: 148–153;
1 MACC. 15: 22–23

WHILE the relative abundance of papyri found in Egypt enables us to reconstruct the map of Jewish settlement there with reasonable detail, there are few sources for the Jews in other parts of the Hellenistic world. The Diaspora there falls into three groups: the early Babylonian exiles, agricultural-military settlements established by the Seleucids in Asia Minor—mainly in Caria, Pamphylia and Phrygia—and isolated communities in the commercial centers of Greece and Asia Minor. These are known mainly from 1 Macc. 15:22–23.

WHEN the kingdom was established before Antiochus, he thought to
reign over Egypt, that he might have the dominion of two kingdoms.
(1 Maccabees 1:16)

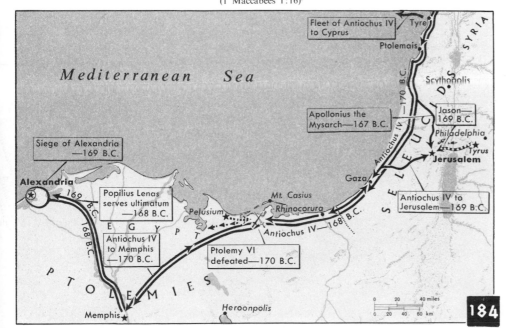

Ptolemaic realm	
Seleucid realm	
•	City with Jewish population
▨	Area of dense Jewish population
··········	Borders—240 B.C.

THE EGYPTIAN CAMPAIGNS
OF ANTIOCHUS IV EPIPHANES
170 TO 167 B.C.

1 MACC. 1: 17 24; POLYBIUS 28: 18; DIODORUS

THE defeat of Antiochus III at Magnesia (190 B.C.) shook the Seleucid Empire to its very foundations. Antiochus III and his sons, Seleucus IV and Antiochus IV, saw the necessity of preparing their country for the coming struggle with Rome. Antiochus IV, a man of vision, desired to strengthen his kingdom through religious unity, integrating all its gods with Olympian Zeus at their head. In this context, Antiochus Epiphanes violated the promise of his father Antiochus III to the Jews, to respect their religious autonomy, and supported Menelaus, a Hellenized high priest.

Antiochus IV also thought the time ripe to conquer Egypt, then at its lowest ebb, under the rule of Ptolemy VI Philometer. Invading Egypt in 170 B.C., he defeated its army between Mount Cassius and Pelusium, and reached Memphis, where he proclaimed himself king of Egypt. Antiochus then proceeded to Alexandria and besieged the city (169 B.C.); however, he turned back to Asia before its fall. While beleaguering Alexandria, Antiochus learned that Jason, a former high priest dismissed by the king, had tried to capture Jerusalem with the aid of the Tobiads, thus endangering the lines of communication of his army in Egypt. Antiochus proceeded against Jerusalem and appropriated the Temple treasure. In 168 B.C. Antiochus set out once more against Egypt, while he sent his fleet to Cyprus. Again he advanced to within four miles of Alexandria, but was now met by the Roman Popilius Laenas ("the commander" in Dan. 11:18) who ordered him to withdraw from Egypt. When the king requested time for consideration, the Roman drew a circle on the ground around him and forced him to "decide before leaving this circle"; Antiochus submitted. On his return, he sent Apollonius, commander of the Mysian mercenaries, with twenty thousand of his men to Jerusalem; this is probably what is intended by the "forces from him" in Dan. 11:31.

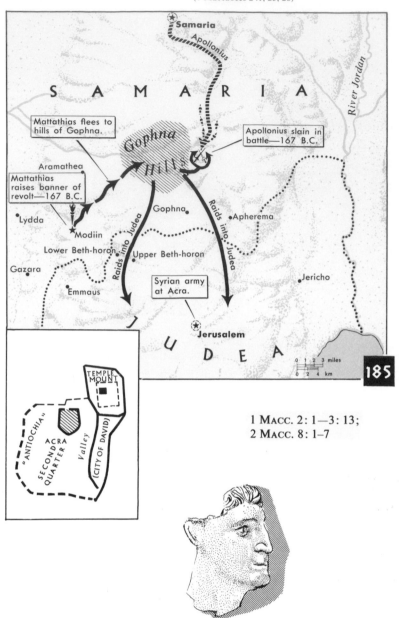

THE BEGINNINGS OF THE MACCABEAN REVOLT
167 B.C.

ANTIOCHUS and his advisers, heeding the more extreme of the Hellenized Jews, believed that the majority of the Jewish nation was ready to accept Greek culture. Antiochus decided to turn the House of God into a Greek temple of Zeus or Dionysius, whom he equated with the God of Israel. The strong resistance of the people led to the first known instance of religious persecution in history: worship of God was forbidden and the Jews were forced to sacrifice to other gods. The Hellenists built a fortress, the "Acra," to secure their position in Jerusalem, and next to it, on the western hill, a new city, in the Greek style (see map 204).

The persecution led to a revolt that broke out not in Judea proper, but in the Jewish townlet of Modiin, in the district of Lydda that was administratively outside Judea. Mattathias, priest of the Hasmonean family, and his sons refused to obey the royal order to sacrifice to Zeus. Mattathias killed a Jew who was about to do as bid, as well as the king's representative, and destroyed the altar there. Modiin itself was close to Lydda, the district capital, and thus exposed to reprisals. Mattathias and his sons fled, probably to the mountains of Gophna. There they were joined by the "Hasidim," pious Jews who rallied to the defense of the Law. From their refuge Mattathias and his men went forth, overturned the altars of the foreign gods, and roused the Jewish villages against the Hellenizers living in Jerusalem under the protection of the Seleucid army. Apollonius, commander of the troops at Samaria and governor of the region that included Gophna, went out to crush the rebellion. Judas Maccabeus, who had assumed command on the death of his father Mattathias, attacked the royal troops, probably at the ascent of Lebonah, and destroyed them. Apollonius was killed in the fighting and Judas took his sword "and fought with it thereafter" (1 Macc. 3:12).

1 MACC. 2: 1—3: 13;
2 MACC. 8: 1–7

Antiochus IV (from bronze statue)

THE BATTLE OF BETH-HORON
166 B.C.

NEWS of Apollonius' crushing defeat, and the increasing distress of the Hellenizers isolated in Jerusalem, moved Seron, a Seleucid commander, to suppress the growing rebellion. To relieve Jerusalem he chose the traditional route from Lydda by way of the ascent of Beth-horon. While Seron's men labored up the steep ascent, Judas Maccabeus unexpectedly attacked and Seron and his men were swept before him. The remnants of the defeated army fled back to the coastal plain and retreated to "Philistia." The second attempt to break the blockade of Jerusalem had also ended in failure.

1 MACC. 3: 13–24

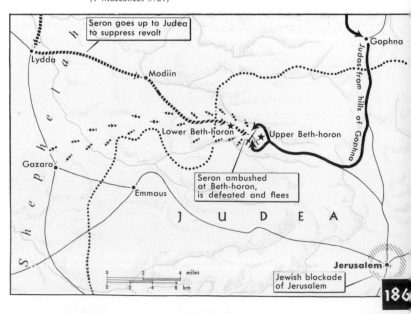

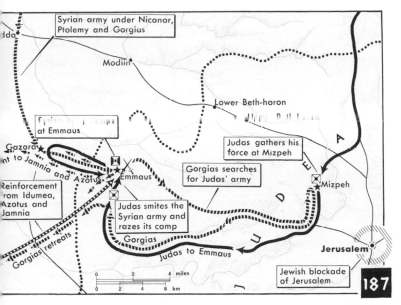

1 MACC. 3:38—4:25; 2 MACC. 8:8–29

Hellenistic tomb-painting at Marisa

THE BATTLE OF EMMAUS
165 B.C.

ANTIOCHUS IV, at this time warring against Persia and Media, had entrusted the administration of the empire west of the Euphrates to Lysias, the superior of Seron. Upon Seron's defeat, Lysias raised a strong army and put it under the command of Ptolemy, Dorimenes, Nicanor, and Gorgias. The army camped at Emmaus, as the commanders feared entanglement in the mountain passes leading to Jerusalem. They were reinforced by troops from Idumea and the district of Jamnia and Azotus ("Philistia").

Judas Maccabeus rallied his men at Mizpeh. Here he was strategically placed in relation to both Jerusalem and the coast. In the end the Seleucid generals decided to seek out the rebels; Gorgias with five thousand soldiers and one thousand horsemen went out under cover of night and, guided by men from the Acra, proceeded toward the rebel camp. Judas Maccabeus, on hearing of the division of the enemy forces, left Mizpeh and bivouacked probably south of Emmaus. At dawn, Judas and his men (three thousand in all) advanced toward the Syrian camp. The Seleucid army formed for battle but was defeated and pursued to Gazara, the strong royal fortress at the approaches to Jerusalem. Judas restrained his men from an ill-considered chase, and while the enemy was still fleeing in the direction of Jamnia and Azotus, he returned to Emmaus to face Gorgias.

At the end of his night march, Gorgias found Judas' camp abandoned; he had worn his men out in vain. Returning to Emmaus, he saw from a hilltop that his camp was aflame. He retreated to the coast without having made contact with the rebels, and thus failed in the third attempt to free the Hellenizers encircled in Jerusalem.

THE BATTLE OF BETH-ZUR AND THE REDEDICATION OF THE TEMPLE

165 B.C.

LYSIAS made one last attempt against the Jews. He chose the route along the water divide in Idumea, rather than endangering his forces in the narrow passes and on the steep ascents, which thrice had been the undoing of the Seleucid army. The new campaign passed along the coast to Marisa, inhabited at the time by Hellenized Sidonians and Idumeans—enemies of the Jews. From Marisa they marched with ease and arrived opposite Beth-zur, the border fortress of Judea.

The Maccabean, who surely used his interior lines of communication to follow the movements of the enemy, went forth from Beth-zur to face the invader and succeeded in repulsing the attack. Lysias retreated and Judas and his men, rejoicing, went up to Jerusalem. The fortress of Acra was still in the hands of their enemies, but the Temple Mount was regained by the Jews. Judas and his men now cleansed the Temple and repaired it after the long period of neglect. Service of God was restored after having been interrupted for three and one-half years, and they lit the lamps of the menora to light up the temple.

Thus, the feast of Hanukkah was observed for the first time on the twenty fifth of Kislev, 165 B.C. Judas fortified Mount Zion (the "Mount of the Temple") and Beth-zur, "that the people might have a fortress against Idumea."

BEHOLD, our enemies are discomfited: let us go up to cleanse and dedicate the sanctuary.

(1 Maccabees 4:36)

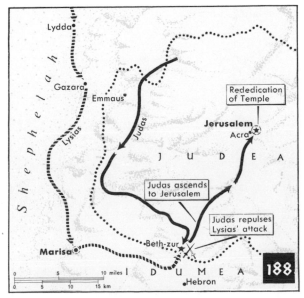

1 MACC. 4:28–61

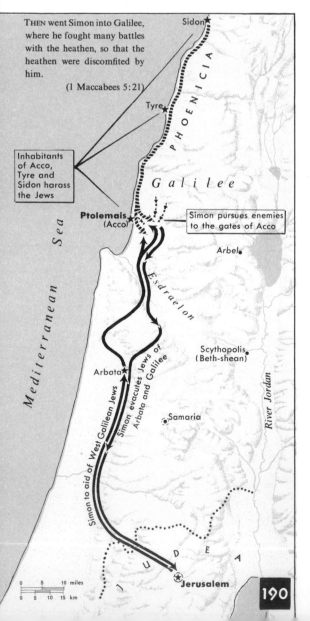

1 MACC. 5: 3–13, 24–55; 2 MACC. 10: 24–37, 12: 10–11

THEY [the heathen] thought to destroy the generation of Jacob that was among them. . .

(1 Maccabees 5:2)

JUDAS MACCABEUS' EARLY CAMPAIGNS

JUDAS' SUCCESSES aroused the ire of the neighboring peoples and he undertook several defensive campaigns. He first attacked the Idumeans in Acrabetene who were oppressing the Jews living among them; he mounted a similar operation against the tribe of the Beonites beyond the Jordan.

His most difficult military feat, however, was the relief of the Jewish population of Gilead. Disturbing news from there told about the persecution of the Jews, in Bostra, Bosora, Alema, Caspein, Macer, and Carnaim, all fortified cities, and in the land of Tob. Many of the Jews fled to the fortress of Dathema and were besieged there. Judas, with his brother Jonathan and eight thousand men, set out to relieve them. Instead of going straight to Gilead, they utilized their good relations with the Nabateans east of Gilead, cut across the desert in a three-day march, and appeared, quite unexpectedly, at the gates of Bostra.

After capturing Bostra, Judas and his men marched all night, arriving at Dathema in the morning, at the very moment the enemy was about to storm the city. Judas launched a three-pronged attack on the army of Timotheus, commander of Gilead; the enemy fled on recognizing their attacker. Judas continued on to Alema, Caspein, Macer, and Bosora, everywhere relieving the beleaguered Jewish populations. Soon thereafter, Dositheus and Sosipater, commanders under Judas, overcame Charax in the Land of Tob.

Timotheus had meanwhile reorganized his army and reinforced it with auxiliary Arab troops (probably Itureans, for the Nabateans sympathized with the Jews); he confronted Judas near Raphon. In this battle too the enemy was vanquished, Judas took Carnaim and burned down the temple of Atargatis. From Carnaim Judas and the Jewish evacuees began their long march, passing through Ephron (which refused them entrance, but was taken by storm) and Scythopolis (Beth-shean), whose inhabitants received Judas cordially. The caravan finally ascended Zion with song and dance. There was one more confrontation with Timotheus, at Jazer; here too the Jews were victorious. Timotheus fell on the battlefield, and Jazer was captured.

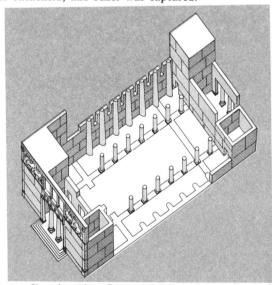

Plan of temple at Tyrus, capital of the Tobiads, Transjorda

SIMON'S EXPEDITION TO WESTERN GALILEE

WHILE JUDAS campaigned in Gilead, his brother Simon at the head of three thousand men proceeded to Galilee, where the Jews had been attacked from Ptolemais, Tyre, and Sidon. Simon scattered the enemy and pursued them to the gates of Ptolemais. He took with him the Jews of Galilee and Arbata (Narbata?) near Strato's Tower and brought them safely to Jerusalem. It must be noted that even after this campaign Jews remained settled in the Esdraelon valley and Eastern Galilee.

1 MACC. 5: 14–15, 20–23

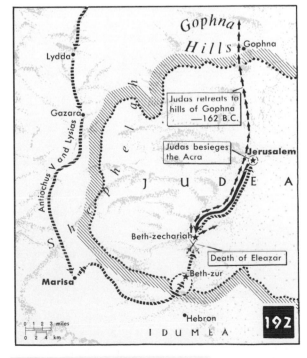

1 MACC. 5:1–2, 37–55, 65–68; 2 MACC. 12: 1–15, 20–31

JUDAS IN THE COASTAL PLAIN AND IDUMEA
163 B.C.

WHILE JUDAS and Simon were occupied in Gilead and Galilee, Joseph (the son of Zacharias) and Azarias, two commanders who had remained in Judea, tried their luck against Jamnia. Here camped Gorgias (of the battle of Emmaus), who had probably remained behind as governor of Idumea. This action failed utterly. After Judas' return from Gilead, he himself went against Idumea. He attacked Hebron and Marisa, and even reached the gates of Azotus, and there destroyed a pagan temple.

In another campaign Judas avenged the Jews of Joppa, after their fellow townsmen had drowned them, in an act of atrocious deceit. He destroyed the port of Joppa and burned the ships. He repeated this deed at the port of Jamnia upon learning that the inhabitants of this city intended to imitate Joppa. In yet another campaign near Marisa, Gorgias was almost taken prisoner, but in the end Judas disengaged his forces and retired to Odollam in the Judean mountains.

NOTWITHSTANDING all the victories of Judas in remote places, Jerusalem remained divided between Mount Zion (the Temple Mount), which was in the hands of the rebels, and the Acra, which was held by the Hellenizers (see map 204). On his return from campaigning, Judas beleaguered the Acra, whose inhabitants appealed to young king Antiochus V (Antiochus IV had died in Persia in 163 B.C.). In response to their call, Lysias arrived from Syria with a vast army. Having learned from experience, the Syrians took the longer but easier route through Idumea and attacked Beth-zur. Judas left Jerusalem and encamped at Beth-zechariah, north of Beth-zur. The royal army advanced toward Judas and a great battle ensued.

Eleazar (also called Avaran), the youngest of Judas' brothers, fell in this battle; in the belief that a war elephant, richly caparisoned with the king's arms, carried the king in person, he slew the animal but was thus crushed to death—the first to die of the five sons of Mattathias. This act of valor had no influence on the outcome of the battle. The Jews "turned away from them" (1 Macc. 6:47). Beth-zur surrendered for lack of food (it was a Sabbatical year, when fields were left fallow), and Judas was forced to retreat to his original refuge in the mountains of Gophna. Antiochus and Lysias arrived at the Temple Mount and breached its fortifications. However, remembering the fierce Jewish reaction in the days of Antiochus IV, they did not interfere with the religion as such or with the Temple services.

THE BATTLE OF BETH-ZECHARIAH
162 B.C.

Seleucid war elephant

1 MACC. 6: 28–63; 2 MACC. 13: 1–23

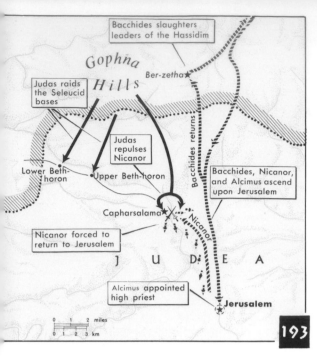

Maps and labels:

Gophna Hills

Bacchides slaughters leaders of the Hassidim

Ber-zetha★

Judas raids the Seleucid bases

Judas repulses Nicanor

Bacchides returns

Bacchides, Nicanor, and Alcimus ascend upon Jerusalem

Lower Beth-horon

Upper Beth-horon

Capharsalama★

Nicanor forced to return to Jerusalem

Nicanor

Alcimus appointed high priest

J U D E A

★ Jerusalem

0 1 2 miles
0 1 2 3 km

193

1 MACC. 7: 19–31;
2 MACC. 14: 15–18

WHEN Alcimus saw that Judas and his company had gotten the upper hand, and knew that he was not able to abide their force...

(1 Maccabees 7:25)

THE BATTLE OF CAPHARSALAMA
162 B.C.

IN 162 B.C. Demetrius I, the son of Seleucus IV, landed at Tripolis on the Syrian coast, thus starting a chain of fraternal wars within the House of Seleucus, ending in the destruction of their rule. Antiochus V was taken prisoner and put to death. The new king sent to Judea his general, Bacchides (who was in charge of the countries west of the Euphrates), with one Alcimus (Eliakim), whom he made high priest. The pious majority ("Hasidim") acknowledged in Alcimus a descendant of the high priest Aaron; they believed his promises of peace and abandoned the Maccabees, who alone persisted in their struggle for freedom.

In Jerusalem, Bacchides enthroned Alcimus, who began by slaying several leaders of the Hasidim. Bacchides, too, on his way back to Antioch, killed many of them at Beth-zetha (Ber-zetha). Judas Maccabeus continued the struggle with reduced forces, and Alcimus once more had to ask for help. King Demetrius I sent Nicanor, one of the commanders in the battle of Emmaus. In one of his first actions, Nicanor tried to open the road of Beth-horon connecting Jerusalem with the Seleucid bases in the coastal plain. This attempt failed at Capharsalama (near Gibeon), and Nicanor, shamefaced, returned to Jerusalem.

THE BATTLE OF ADASA
161 B.C.

INFURIATED, Nicanor at once renewed the struggle. This time he succeeded in reaching Beth-horon, where he was joined by Syrian auxiliaries from the coast. On his way back, however, he was attacked near Adasa, south of the main highway; Nicanor, apparently, was expecting an attack from the north. On the thirteenth of Adar (the "Day of Nicanor" of Jewish tradition) the enemy was vanquished. Nicanor himself fell in battle; his army, cut off from Jerusalem, fled in the direction of the royal fortress at Gazara, being pursued to its very gates by Judas, and by the villagers who were stirred into action by the sounding of trumpets.

ON the thirteenth [day] of Adar, the day of Nicanor.
(Scroll of Fasting)

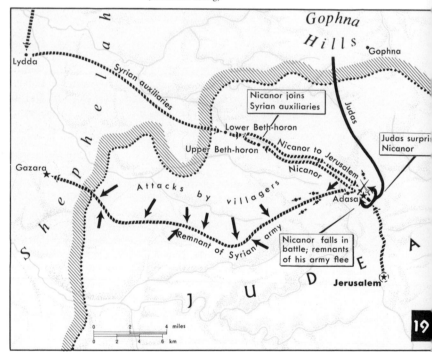

Maps and labels:

Gophna Hills

•Gophna

Lydda

Shephelah

Syrian auxiliaries

Nicanor joins Syrian auxiliaries

Judas

Lower Beth-horon

Upper Beth-horon

Nicanor to Jerusalem

Judas surprises Nicanor

Gazara★

Attacks by villagers

Nicanor

Adasa

Remnant of Syrian army

Nicanor falls in battle; remnants of his army flee

J U D E A

★ Jerusalem

0 2 4 miles
0 2 4 6 km

19

1 MACC. 7: 39–49; 2 MACC. 15: 25–28

HE sent Bacchides and Alcimus into the land of Judea the second time...

(1 Maccabees 9:1)

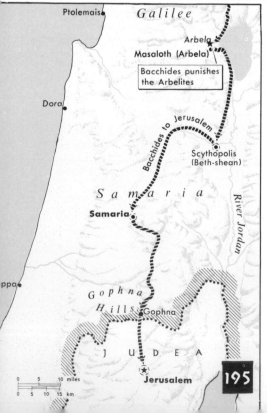

Maps and labels:

Ptolemais•

Galilee

Arbela
Masaloth (Arbela)

Bacchides punishes the Arbelites

Dora•

Bacchides to Jerusalem

Scythopolis (Beth-shean)

S a m a r i a

River Jordan

Samaria•

ppa•

Gophna Hills

•Gophna

J U D E A

★ Jerusalem

0 5 10 miles
0 5 10 15 km

195

THE CAMPAIGN OF BACCHIDES
161 B.C.

TIDINGS of Nicanor's defeat impelled Demetrius I again to dispatch Bacchides, with a first-class army—the so-called right wing—to Judea. The suppression of the revolt had now become urgent to the Seleucid king, for Judas in the meantime had entered into an alliance with the Romans, who were ready to support all enemies of the Seleucids. On his march from Damascus, Bacchides passed through Galilee, taking vengeance on the Jewish citizens of Arbela, near the Sea of Galilee. Then he proceeded through Samaria and Judea to Jerusalem. Judas dared not attack the powerful enemy forces.

1 MACC. 9: 1–4; ANT. 12: 420–422

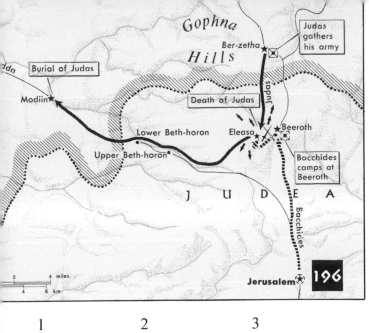

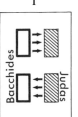 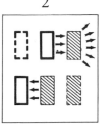 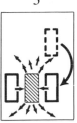

1   2   3

1 MACC. 9: 5–19; ANT. 12: 426–434

THEN JUDAS said, God forbid that I should do this thing, and flee away from them: if our time be come, let us die manfully.

(1 Maccabees 9:10)

THE BATTLE OF ELEASA AND THE DEATH OF JUDAS
161 B.C.

BACCHIDES set out from Jerusalem in order to destroy the rebel stronghold in the mountains of Gophna. He encamped at Beeroth, while Judas arraigned his forces at Ber-zetha.

When Bacchides moved his camp, apparently to secure the Beth-horon road, Judas tried to separate him from his base and attacked from the east. The battle developed near Eleasa, where Bacchides was with his right (northern) wing. Judas forced the Syrian to retreat in the direction of the ascent of Beth-horon. The Seleucid left wing, which had meanwhile overcome and defeated the weaker right wing of the Judeans, now turned to surround Judas' remaining forces, for the Syrians of the northern wing had reformed and rejoined the battle.

Judas lost his life on the battlefield and his army scattered. Simon and Jonathan were, however, able to carry away his body and bury it in the family tomb at Modiin.

Seleucid coin with Apollo on reverse

JONATHAN IN THE WILDERNESS OF JUDEA
160 TO 155 B.C.

AFTER the defeat at Eleasa, the Maccabeans could no longer maintain their stronghold in the mountains of Gophna. They elected Jonathan as their leader and promptly repaired to the wilderness of Tekoa, in the Judean desert, encamping near the well of Asphar.

The wilderness of Judea has served as a refuge for the oppressed and as a hideaway for insurgents since time immemorial (see map 92); it was here that Jonathan rallied his supporters.

To secure control of Judea, Bacchides surrounded Jerusalem with a chain of fortresses: Bethel to the north, Beth-horon to the northwest, Emmaus to the west, Thamna and Tekoa to the southwest and southeast, respectively, Jericho to the east, and Pharathon to the northeast. These and the royal fortresses at the Acra, Gazara, and Beth-zur formed a system of defense considered adequate to safeguard rule in rebellious Judea.

JONATHAN took the governance upon him at that time, and he rose up instead of his brother Judas.

(1 Maccabees 9:31)

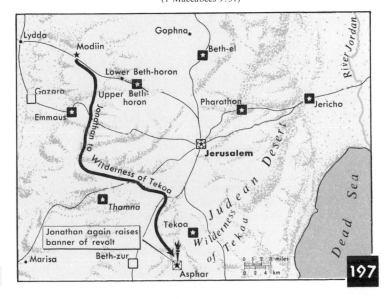

☐ Fortress strengthened by Bacchides
✠ Fortress built by Bacchides

1 MACC. 9: 28–33, 50; ANT. 13: 5–8, 15

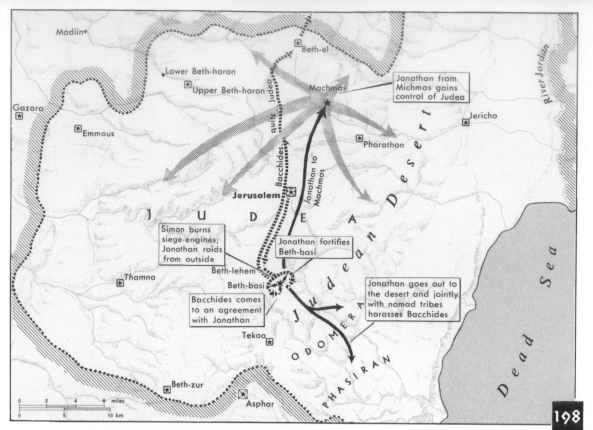

THEN went he and laid siege against Beth-basi; and they fought against it a long season, and made engines of war.

(1 Maccabees 9:64)

1 MACC. 9: 62–73; ANT. 13: 26–34

THE SIEGE OF BETH-BASI,
JONATHAN AT MACHMAS
156 TO 152 B.C.

ALCIMUS the high priest died in 159 B.C., after he had offended the Hasidim by opening the lattice surrounding the Temple in the outer court, the limit beyond which Gentiles were not allowed to enter. Bacchides returned to Antioch, and the country remained at peace for two years. Bacchides then returned with his army, but his attempt to capture Jonathan and his men, who apparently lived in peace in Modiin, came to nothing. The Maccabeans occupied Beth-basi, an abandoned fortress southeast of Bethlehem. This was a daring move because it occurred in a settled region, even if on the outskirts of the desert. Jonathan and his men thus gained a foothold in populated Judea, not far from the road which passes along the water divide.

Thus challenged, Bacchides assaulted Beth-basi with heavy siege machinery. Jonathan, however, was too experienced a fighter to let the enemy entrap him. He charged his brother Simon with the defense of Beth-basi and went forth to harrass Bacchides. Traveling through the desert, Jonathan came across two wandering tribes; called Odomera and Phasiran in 1 Maccabees, they are not known from any other source. Odomera resembles the name of a Bedouin tribe, the Beni Ta'amre, who live in the area of Khirbet Beth-basi to this day. Jonathan's forcefulness persuaded the tribesmen to join his attack on Bacchides. At the same time, Simon sallied forth from the city and burned the siege works. This induced Bacchides to negotiate.

The internal situation in the Seleucid kingdom had become unsettled and many plots against Demetrius I were contrived by rivals. Jonathan received permission in the agreement made, probably in 155 B.C., to settle in Machmas, while the Hellenizers continued to hold Jerusalem. However, after Bacchides' army had left Judea, Jonathan extended his rule over the whole country, except for the capital and the fortress of Beth-zur: "And (Jonathan) began to govern the people; and he destroyed the ungodly men out of Israel" (1 Macc. 9:73).

Hellenistic cavalryman (painted tombstone from Sidon)

AND sent him a buckle of gold, as the use is to be given to such as are of the king's blood: he gave him also Accaron with the borders thereof in possession.

(1 Maccabees 10:89)

THE EXPANSION OF JUDEA IN THE DAYS OF JONATHAN
152 TO 142 B.C.

JONATHAN exploited the decline of Seleucid rule to raise the prestige of Judea. When Demetrius I learned that Alexander Balas, who claimed to be the son of Antiochus IV, had invaded Ptolemais, he felt endangered and granted Jonathan the privileges of a royally appointed commander. He permitted the Hasmonean to recruit an army and to forge weapons. He also returned the Jewish hostages held in the Acra. These concessions enabled Jonathan to establish himself in Jerusalem and repair the fortifications of the Temple Mount. Except for the Acra and Beth-zur, Jonathan was the de facto ruler of Judea.

Alexander Balas, who also wanted Jonathan's support, appointed him high priest. Jonathan wore the finery of this office for the first time during the feast of Tabernacles in the year 152 B.C. Demetrius in turn tempted Jonathan by offering him the three districts with Jewish populations, still under the administration of Samaria. Jonathan, however, supported Alexander, the weaker of the two rivals; and Alexander defeated Demetrius I in 150 B.C.

At a meeting in Ptolemais between Alexander and Ptolemy VI in the same year, Jonathan was also present and the Syrian king granted him the title "Strategus and Meridarches" (commander and governor) of Judea. After Jonathan had overcome the forces of Demetrius II in the battle of Jamnia (see map 200), Alexander gave him the district of Accaron as an estate (147 B.C.). Demetrius II then also realized that it was preferable to have Jonathan as a friend rather than an enemy and approved the transfer of three districts (Lydda, Aramathea, and Apherema) from Samaria to Judea. When Tryphon, regent for Antiochus VI, rose against Demetrius II, he too wished to remain in the good graces of Jonathan and, in 144 B.C., endorsed his annexation of the "four districts." From the phrasing of the endorsement we can infer that Jonathan had meantime added the Perea—Jewish "Transjordan"—a legacy from the Tobiads, to his dominions (see map 177).

And cast darts at the people, from morning till evening. But the people stood still, as Jonathan had commanded them and so the enemies' horses were tired.

(1 Maccabees 10:80-81)

199

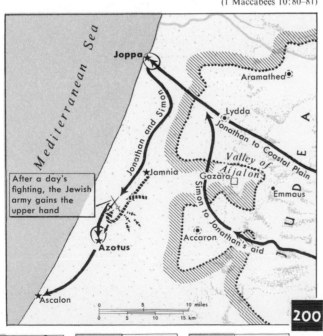

200

□ Seleucid fortress
••••• Judean border—152 B.C.
▨ Judean border after Jonathan's conquests
········ District border

1 MACC. 11: 33, 57–74; ANT. 13: 102, 128

Coin of Demetrius I

THE FIRST CONQUEST OF JOPPA AND THE BATTLE OF JAMNIA
147 B.C.

IN 147 B.C., when Demetrius II had triumphed over his rival Alexander Balas, he appointed one Apollonius as commander of Coele-Syria and instructed him to take strong measures against Judea, which had supported Alexander Balas. Apollonius, encamped at Jamnia, challenged Jonathan to a contest "in the valley, where there is no stone, no rock, no place to flee to." He believed that the Jewish army could win only by irregular warfare in the mountains. But the Maccabean army had grown stronger and Jonathan, at the head of ten thousand men, went to war in the plain, joined by Simon and a further battalion. As a start to their campaign, the Maccabeans forced Joppa to open its gates to them.

Apollonius had meanwhile prepared an ambush between Jamnia and Azotus. He concealed a regiment of horsemen along the road between the two towns and feigned a retreat. Jonathan followed him and when the two armies clashed, the Jewish forces were attacked from the rear. In the ensuing battle the Jewish army proved its prowess; "the people" stood fast for a whole day until the enemies' horses wearied. At eventide Simon attacked the cavalry, who fled toward the coast. The remainder of Apollonius' army retreated to Azotus, with Jonathan pursuing them. Azotus was captured, and the Jewish force proceeded to Ascalon, which received Jonathan cordially.

The Maccabean army emerged from the battle as the strongest military power in the whole Land of Israel.

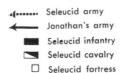

◄······· Seleucid army
◄── Jonathan's army
▬ Seleucid infantry
◩ Seleucid cavalry
□ Seleucid fortress

1 MACC. 10: 69–87; ANT. 13: 88–101

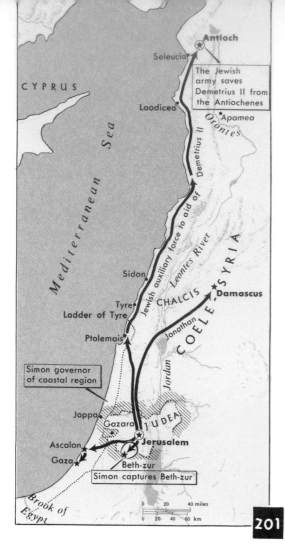

THE CAMPAIGN OF JONATHAN IN COELE-SYRIA

150 B.C.

THE position of Demetrius II was further weakened when he dismissed his Cretan mercenaries. The king was forced to seek the aid of Jonathan in suppressing Tryphon's rebellion. Jonathan sent three thousand men to defend Demetrius from the Antiochian mob besieging him in his palace. The Jews gained the upper hand and—for a time—saved the throne of Demetrius II. The latter, as soon as he felt himself secure, forgot his promises to Jonathan.

Meanwhile, the power of Tryphon and Antiochus VI increased steadily. To win Jonathan's support, Tryphon appointed Simon royal governor of the coastal plain, from the Ladder of Tyre to the brook of Egypt. Jonathan and his army passed through the whole region of Coele-Syria at their pleasure, arrived once more at Ascalon, and there were received with great pomp. The residents of Gaza, however, kept their gates shut. Jonathan devastated the outskirts of the city and forced the citizens to conclude a treaty with him. Again Jonathan crossed the country to Damascus. At the same time, Simon captured Beth-zur. In all Judea, only the Acra of Jerusalem remained in alien hands.

1 MACC. 10: 57–65; ANT. 13: 103–105, 133–142, 146, 148–153

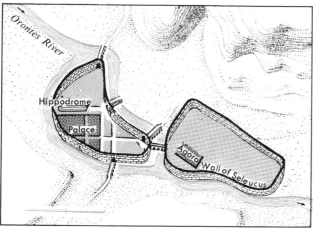

Plan of Antioch in the Hellenistic period

THE BATTLE OF HAZOR

144 B.C.

THE daring exploits of Jonathan in Coele-Syria made Demetrius' commanders suspicious for, in theory at least, Jonathan was acting for his rival, Antiochus VI. To curb his activities, Demetrius' troops advanced beyond Damascus and camped at Cadasa on the boundary of Galilee. Jonathan left Gennesaret and went up to the plain of Hazor. Demetrius' generals again tried the ruse used by Apollonius at Jamnia (see map 200). They hid part of their army in the hills of Cadasa and attacked Jonathan from the rear after he had joined battle with the main force. A large part of the Maccabean army panicked; only Jonathan and his generals, Mattathias son of Absalom and Judas son of Hilphai, stood fast and finally defeated the enemy, chasing them to Cadasa and capturing their camp.

AFTERWARD turning again to battle, he put them to fight, and so they ran away.

(1 Maccabees 11:72)

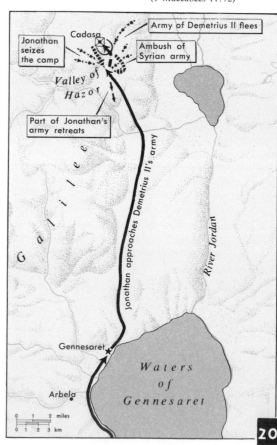

1 MACC. 11: 63–74; ANT. 13: 158–162

THE HAMATH CAMPAIGN
143 B.C.

JONATHAN felt the tide turning in his favor and sent delegations to Rome and Sparta to renew old alliances. Again the armies of Demetrius started out against him, but for once the fight did not take place in the Land of Israel, for Jonathan "gave them no opportunity to come into the land" (1 Macc. 12:25). The armies deployed in the district of Hamath in the valley of Lebanon. When Demetrius' armies saw no chance to defeat Jonathan, they secretly retired across the river Eleutherus, which marked the boundary of Coele-Syria. Jonathan turned towards Beth-zabdai, in the land of Chalcis (where the remnants of the Jewish population were being persecuted), freed his brethren and took booty from the enemy. From there he proceeded to Damascus and crossed the breadth of Coele-Syria. Simon had meanwhile captured Joppa for the second time, and fortified Adida, overlooking the Via Maris near Lydda.

MACC. 12: 24–32, 38; ANT. 13: 174–180

JERUSALEM OF THE MACCABEES
164 TO 141 B.C.

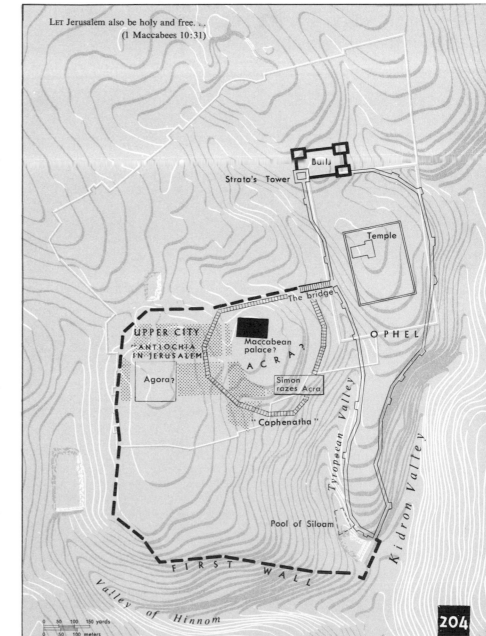

LET Jerusalem also be holy and free...
(1 Maccabees 10:31)

AT the beginning of Hellenization, the more "progressive" citizens felt that the old city on the eastern hill, surrounded by ancient walls (restored by Nehemiah, and again in the days of Antiochus III), was hardly fit to be the new "Antiochia." They probably decided to build a city in the Hippodamic tradition: straight streets intersecting at right angles. They started to construct this city on the western hill between the valley of Hinnom and the Tyropoeon valley. A hillock at the eastern end of this new Hellenistic city, protected by a small valley to the west, served as its fortress. In the Maccabean period it was called Acra—not to be confused with the other Acra, the citadel (Baris) of the days of Nehemiah, which was situated north of the Temple Mount.

With the capture by Judas Maccabeus of the Temple Mount (see map 188) and the renewal of worship in the Temple, in 164 B.C., the city was divided into two parts, a division which lasted till 141 B.C. The Maccabeans held Mount Zion in the days of Judas, and again in the days of Jonathan and Simon—always in opposition to the Hellenizers' fortress. By raising a siege wall, the "Caphenatha," and rebuilding a quarter named after it, Jonathan and Simon tried to cut off the garrison of the Acra from the market place (the Hellenistic "agora") and to force its surrender through starvation.

After the final conquest of the Acra in 141 B.C., the Jews razed the part of the fortress commanding the Temple (Ant. 13:217). The Maccabeans, now lords of the entire city, built a wall round the western hill, constructed a bridge across the Tyropoeon valley, between the Temple Mount and the western hill, and built a palace for themselves on the ruins of the Acra. They also strengthened the "Citadel" by adding towers, one of which was called Strato's Tower in the days of Aristobulus I.

MACC. 4: 37–60, 6 61–62,
10: 10–12, 12: 36–37, 13: 49–53

Older construction
Maccabean construction
Siege wall
Area of "Antiochia"

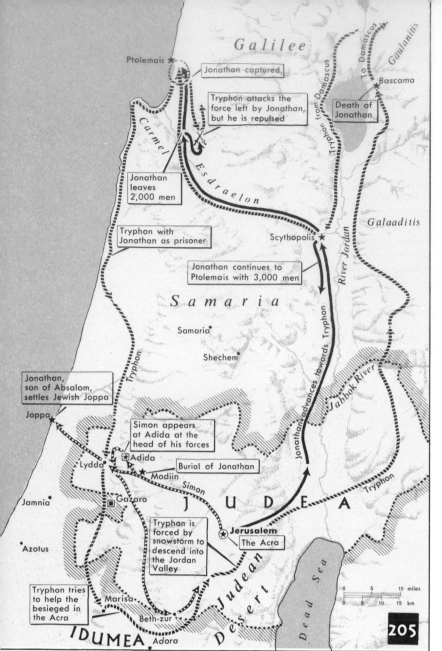

Map labels:

Galilee

Ptolemais ★

Jonathan captured.

Tryphon attacks the force left by Jonathan, but he is repulsed

To Damascus

Bascama

Death of Jonathan

Tryphon from Damascus

Gaulanitis

Carmel

Jonathan leaves 2,000 men

Esdraelon

Tryphon with Jonathan as prisoner

Scythopolis ★

River Jordan

Galaaditis

Jonathan continues to Ptolemais with 3,000 men

Samaria

Samaria•

Shechem•

Tryphon

Jonathan advances towards Tryphon

Jabbok River

Jonathan, son of Absalom, settles Jewish Joppa

Joppa

Simon appears at Adida at the head of his forces

Lydda

⊞ Adida

Burial of Jonathan

Modiin

Simon

Jamnia•

Gazara

J U D E A

Tryphon

Tryphon is forced by snowstorm to descend into the Jordan Valley

⊛ Jerusalem

The Acra

•Azotus

Judean Desert

Dead Sea

Tryphon tries to help the besieged in the Acra

Marisa•

Beth-zur•

IDUMEA

Adora•

0 5 10 miles
0 5 10 15 km

205

1 MACC. 12: 39–54, 13: 1–30; ANT. 13: 187–212

AND they answered with a loud voice, saying, Thou shalt be our leader instead of Judas and Jonathan thy brother.
(1 Maccabees 13:8)

TRYPHON'S CAMPAIGN AGAINST JONATHAN
143 TO 142 B.C.

Cavalry and infantry battle (on sarcophagus from Sidon)

//////// Judean border at succession of Simon

WHEN TRYPHON had the upper hand (while his rival Demetrius II was occupied with the preparation of his campaign against the Parthians) he decided to cut Jonathan down to size, the ruler of Judea seemingly having become too independent. Tryphon and his army set out for Judea, but Jonathan met him at Beth-shean with so strong a force that it was obvious to the Seleucid regent that he could not overcome the Jews in battle. Tryphon therefore decided to ensnare Jonathan by leading him on with promises of turning over Ptolemais, the royal fortress. He persuaded Jonathan to send home most of his forces, which he did but for a guard of three thousand. Both men marched toward the coast. Near Ptolemais, Jonathan was induced to leave an additional two thousand men in western Galilee and Esdraelon (where Jewish settlement had apparently been renewed). Thus, only one thousand men accompanied him to within Ptolemais. The inhabitants, who had conspired with Tryphon, closed the gates of the city and slaughtered the Jewish troops; thus Jonathan was taken captive by his enemies.

Tryphon wished to exploit the confusion now reigning among the Jews, in order to subdue them, but his attack on Jonathan's troops remaining in Galilee was repelled, and Simon assumed command and encouraged the dejected people. Tryphon then went up against Judea, with Jonathan a prisoner in his camp. Simon ordered his general, Jonathan son of Absalom, to capture Joppa and resettle it with Jews. He then positioned his army near the new fortress of Adida. Tryphon dared not meet the Jewish army face to face, but tried Lysias' old ruse: he passed through Idumea near Adora to the road along the water divide. The Hellenizers beleaguered in the Acra, in their despair, called for his help and Tryphon tried to reach Jerusalem in a forced march through the Judean desert. Caught by a snowstorm, however, he was forced to retreat to the warmth of the Jordan valley.

After this failure, Tryphon returned by way of Gilead, putting Jonathan to death at Bascama (Beth-shikma). Jonathan was buried with great pomp in the family tomb in Modiin. Simon was elected to lead the people in his brother's stead.

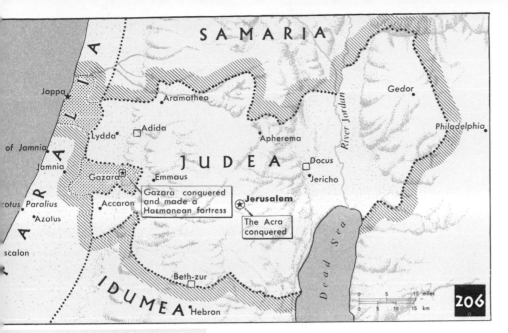

THEN did they till their ground in peace...
(1 Maccabees 14:8)

THE CONQUESTS OF SIMON
142 TO 135 B.C.

☐ Maccabean fortress

░░░ Areas conquered by Simon

(Map 206 labels: SAMARIA, Joppa, Aramathea, Adida, Lydda, of Jamnia, Jamnia, Gazara, Emmaus, Accaron, otus Paralius, Azotus, scalon, JUDEA, Apherema, Docus, Jericho, Jerusalem, Gedor, Philadelphia, River Jordan, Dead Sea, Beth-zur, IDUMEA, Hebron, "Gazara conquered and made a Hasmonean fortress", "The Acra conquered")

MACC. 13: 42–48, 14: 5; ANT. 13: 215

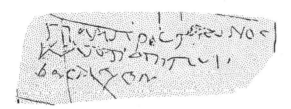

Inscription from Gezer (Gazara) cursing the "House of Simon."

TRYPHON'S TREACHERY drove Simon to side with Demetrius II, who granted independence to Judea in 142 B.C. Now "the yoke of the foreigners was removed from Israel, and the people began to write: 'In the first year of Simon the high priest. . .'"

But Simon was not satisfied with Judean independence within its existing boundaries. Already in the days of Tryphon he had added Joppa (see map 205): "He took Joppa for a harbor and made it an entrance to the islands of the sea." He also took Gazara (Gezer) with the aid of a siege machine (helepolis), and then built there a fortress and a palace, and turned the city into a Jewish military center second only to Jerusalem. And finally, he forced the people of the Acra to surrender, and "a great enemy was annihilated in Israel."

IN 137 B.C., Antiochus VII succeeded in evicting the pretender Tryphon from Dora. He now found himself in Judea with a strong army and tried to wrest from Simon the districts that, in his opinion, the Jews held unlawfully—in particular, Joppa and Gazara. The Seleucid king appointed his general, Cendebeus, as commander of the "Paralia" district and put at his disposal both mounted and foot soldiers. Cendebeus was ordered to build a fortress at Kidron (near modern Gedera) on the Judean border. He then transferred his headquarters to Jamnia, from whence he proceeded to harrass the population of Judea.

To counter this new danger, John Hyrcanus, the son of Simon, moved to Gazara, facing Kidron. From there John and Judas, his brother, went forth with twenty thousand soldiers to surprise the Seleucid forces (passing a night in Modiin). At dawn they advanced to Kidron until only the river in the lower part of the valley of Sorek separated the opposing forces. The Seleucids were deployed in their usual manner—infantry in the center and horse flanking. However, John—with little cavalry—scattered his horses among his foot soldiery. In spite of the difficult terrain, which required crossing the river, the Maccabeans prevailed; the Syrians fled, first to Kidron and later to forts in the territory of Azotus. Judas was wounded at Kidron, but John doggedly pursued his enemy to Azotus and destroyed the forts there.

Simon was not for long to enjoy the victory of his sons; Ptolemy son of Abubus, his own son-in-law, whom he had appointed as governor of Jericho, treacherously killed him together with his sons Judas and Mattathias, during a banquet at Docus (135 B.C.). But the murderer's scheme, to hand Judea over to Antiochus VII, failed. John Hyrcanus, who at the time was at the fortress of Gazara, escaped the assassin. Thus perished Simon, the last surviving of Mattathias's five sons—none of whom died a natural death.

This brings to a close the history of the Hasmoneans in the first book of Maccabees. It is written there (16:23–24): "As concerning the rest of the acts of John, and his wars . . . behold, these are written in the chronicles of his priesthood. . ."; but this latter book has not come down to us. From here on we rely upon Josephus's *Antiquities* as the main source of Jewish history.

THE BATTLE OF KIDRON
137 B.C.

HE himself advanced with his force in another direction... came through without losing a single engagement.
(Antiquities 13:227)

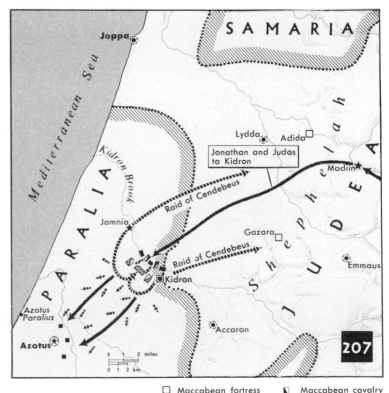

(Map 207 labels: SAMARIA, Joppa, Mediterranean Sea, Kidron Brook, PARALIA, Jamnia, Lydda, Adida, Modiin, Raid of Cendebeus, Raid of Cendebeus, Gazara, Emmaus, Kidron, Shephelah, JUDEA, Azotus Paralius, Accaron, Azotus, "Jonathan and Judas to Kidron")

☐ Maccabean fortress ◣ Maccabean cavalry
■ Seleucid fortress ▨ Seleucid infantry
▪ Forts of Azotus ◪ Seleucid cavalry
▬ Maccabean infantry

1 MACC. 15: 38—16: 10; ANT. 13: 223–235

AND he captured Medeba... next he captured Samaga...
(Antiquities 13:255)

THE CONQUESTS OF HYRCANUS BEYOND THE JORDAN

128 B.C.

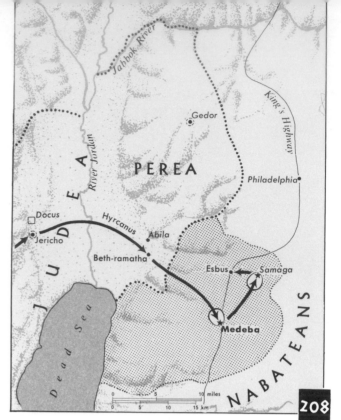

208

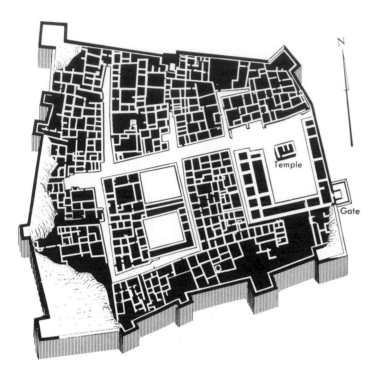

Plan of Hellenistic Marisa

ANT. 13: 255; WAR 1: 63

IN 129 B.C. Antiochus VII was killed warring against the Parthians. With his death, the power of the once mighty Seleucid dynasty came virtually to an end. Hyrcanus was now completely free from the interference of Syria. His army was the most powerful in the region, and he began to reacquire what he considered to be the patrimony of the Israelites from the days of David. His first conquests were beyond the Jordan near Perea, where the Jews had had a foothold since the days of Jonathan and the Tobiads (see map 199). Hyrcanus attacked Medeba and captured it after a prolonged siege; he then took Samaga, a town in the region of Esbus. With this, the Maccabeans acquired a strong position straddling the "King's highway," the important international route from Aila on the Red Sea to Damascus following the edge of the desert. This, together with possession of a section of the Via Maris between Lydda and Pegae, gave Hyrcanus control of the two major commercial routes crossing the Land of Israel.

☐ Maccabean fortress
······ Judean border at succession of Hyrcanus
▒▒ Hyrcanus' conquests

HE further took numerous cities in Idumea, including Adora and Marisa.
(War 1:63)

THE CONQUESTS OF HYRCANUS IN IDUMEA

125 B.C.

HYRCANUS next turned against two small peoples isolated between emerging Judea and the Greek cities: the Samaritans (see map 210) and the Idumeans. The latter had previously lived in southern Transjordan, but were drawn to the fertile parts of southern Judea following the depopulation brought about by the exile under Nebuchadnezzar (see map 163). These Idumeans had lost contact with their Arab neighbors and offered little resistance. Their conquest gained Hyrcanus Hebron, Adora, and En-gedi in eastern Idumea. Even in semi-Hellenized Marisa, Hyrcanus' conquest hardly caused a ripple in everyday life. Consistent with Maccabean policy, which was intended to ensure the loyalty of occupied areas, the Idumeans were forced to accept the Jewish religion, and within a few generation they were integrated into the Jewish nation, as witnessed by their great bravery in the war against the Romans. The conquest of Idumea extended the borders of Judea to Beersheba and Orda.

ANT. 13: 257–258;
WAR 1: 63

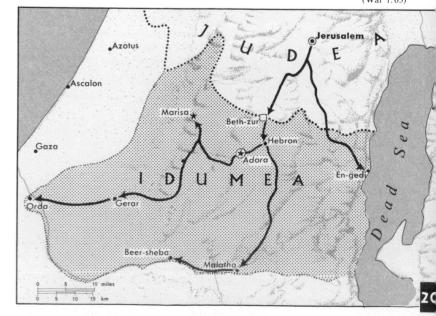

2O

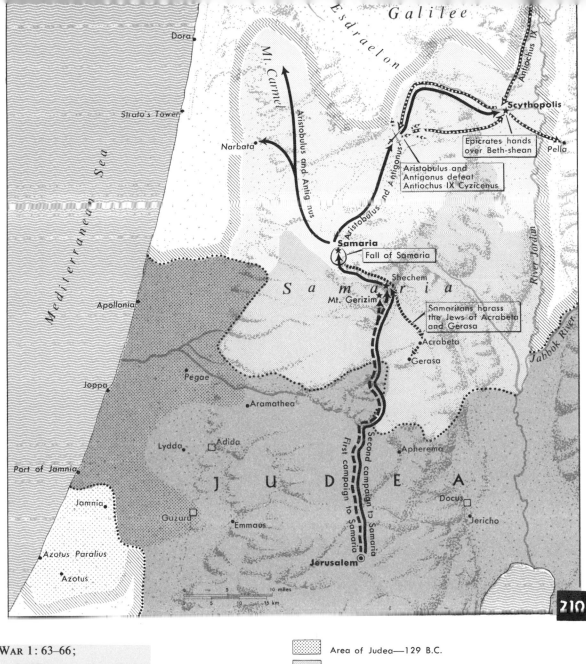

the twenty-fifth (day of Heshwan) the wall of
...ria was taken.

(Scroll of Fasting)

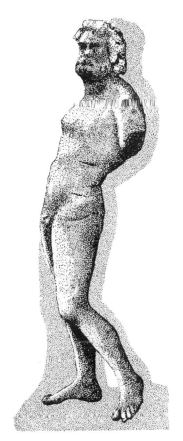

Statue of Hercules found at Samaria

ANT. 13: 255–256, 275–283; WAR 1: 63–66;
SCROLL OF FASTING, 21 KISLEV, 25 HESHVAN, 15–16 SIVAN

Area of Judea—129 B.C.

Area conquered during first campaign to Samaria

Area conquered during second campaign to Samaria

Hyrcanus' conquests in Coastal Plain

THE CONQUESTS OF HYRCANUS
IN SAMARIA AND THE COASTAL PLAIN
126 TO 104 B.C.

BEFORE setting out against the Idumeans (see map 209). Hyrcanus
embarked on a campaign against the Samaritans. This people
lived isolated in the mountains of Ephraim. Hyrcanus captured
Shechem and also the temple on Mount Gerizim. The Samaritans,
however, did not accept Judaism but continued (to this day) to preserve their unique identity. Only the district of Acrabeta, where there
were many Jews, was annexed to Judea proper. Hyrcanus extended
his domain in the coastal plain, too. Shortly after the death of
Antiochus VII, he recaptured the districts temporarily lost in 132 B.C.:
Joppa, Gazara, Pegae, and "the harbors" (Apollonia and the port of
Jamnia); before he died, he also held Jamnia and Azotus with its harbor.

After the annexation of Idumea and Samaria, Hyrcanus set out
for his primary objective: the string of Greek cities, which prevented
Judea's expansion to the north and its union with Galilee. These were
Strato's Tower, Samaria, and Scythopolis—forming a line from the
sea to the river Jordan. In 108–107 B.C., Hyrcanus began to beleaguer

Samaria, whose inhabitants had provoked him and were further
harassing the Jews of Gerasa in the district of Acrabeta (Antiquities
13:275, reading "Gerasa" instead of "Marisa").

The siege of Samaria was protracted and difficult, the Greeks defend-
ing themselves valiantly. They appealed to Antiochus IX Cyzicenus
for aid; he came to Scythopolis, but while proceeding to Samaria, a
heavy defeat was inflicted upon him by Aristobulus I and Antigonus,
the sons of Hyrcanus. The latter pursued him and captured Scythopolis (according to Josephus' Antiquities). In Josephus' War, however,
they are reported to have purchased the city from the local commander,
Epicrates. At the same time the brothers had also invaded the Carmel
area and possibly conquered the region of Narbata. Samaria was
finally captured and destroyed by Hyrcanus (as evidenced in archaeological excavations) and its citizens exiled. The site, however, was
resettled soon thereafter under Janneus. Thus, the way to Galilee
was opened to the Jews.

THE BOUNDARIES OF JUDEA ACCORDING TO THE BOOK OF JUDITH
108 TO 107 B.C.

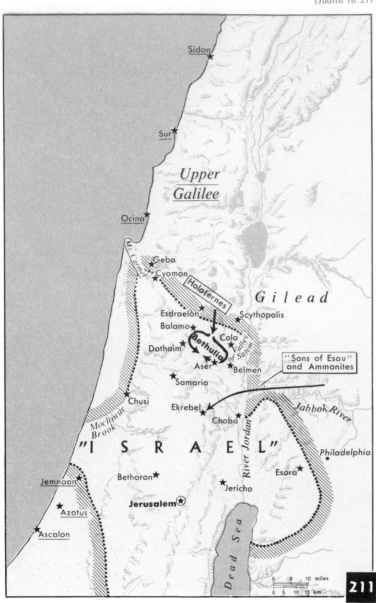

Azotus City or region invaded by Holofernes

JUDITH 1: 8–9, 2: 28, 3: 1–6, 10, 4: 4, 6, 7: 4

A STORY that is not historical in content often reflects the historical reality at the time of its writing. The Book of Judith seems to have been composed in the days of the siege of Samaria (its Hebrew original is lost and only a Greek translation has survived). This dating is based not only on the national-religious spirit permeating the book, but mainly on the boundaries of an imaginary "Israel" outlined by its author.

The Book of Judith, as a story, takes place in the days of "Nebuchadnezzar, king of Assyria" and relates of a town, "Bethulia," (similar to Beth-el, the "House of God," a synonym for Judea), besieged by Holophernes, commander of the Assyrian army. Holophernes (a name appearing in the list of Persian satraps) was killed by the heroic Jewess Judith, after which his army dispersed in confusion. Both from what is included and from what is omitted in the story, we learn of the extent of Jewish rule within the historic reality of the period of the author. Thus, Nebuchadnezzar turns to the "nations of Carmel, Gilead and Upper Galilee" (Judith 1:8), and also to Sidon, Sur (Tyre), Ocina (Ptolemais), and Jemnaan (Jamnia), Azotus and Ascalon (2:28), indicating that these cities were not under Judean rule. Also, Holophernes encamped "against Esdraelon, near unto Dothaim. And he pitched between Geba and Scythopolis" (3:9-10), and from "Belmen [Abel-maim]. . . unto Cyamon [Jokneam]". He sent troops of the "Sons of Esau" (Edomites) and Ammonites to Ekrebel (Acrabeta) which is near Chusi (Kuzi) on the brook Mochmur (Wadi Makhmur, one of the tributaries of the Jarkon river) (7:18). To counter this danger, the "children of Israel that dwelt in Judea" sent messages to "the coasts of Samaria", Cola (Qa'un), "Bethoron [Beth-horon] and Belmen [Abel-maim] and Jericho and to Choba and Esora [Jazer] and to the valley of Salem" (4:4). This serves to define a boundary of Judea, from Samaria to Jokneam and the valley of Salem, south of Scythopolis, but excluding the latter itself, Geba, the Carmel, Jamnia, Azotus and Ascalon. The whole Jordan valley and Transjordan up to Jazer were included. Ptolemais, Tyre, Sidon, Philadelphia, and Ascalon were independent cities.

Those boundaries, as described in the story, existed in only one historical period, to wit, 108–107 B.C., during the siege of Samaria and prior to the capture of Scythopolis.

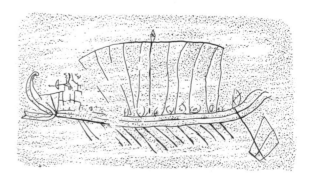

Warship (depicted in Jason's Tomb, Jerusalem)

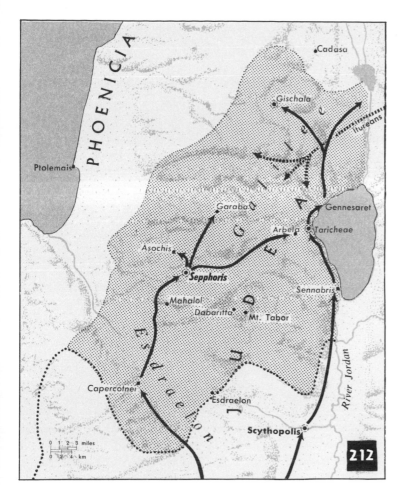

THIS man was a kindly person and very serviceable to the Jews. . .
(Strabo, quoted by Josephus, Antiquities 13:319)

ARISTOBULUS CONQUERS GALILEE
104 TO 103 B.C.

JOHN HYRCANUS lived to a ripe old age; when he died, he left a prosperous kingdom, in spite of the split between the rival Sadducees and Pharisees, a dissension that forebode evil days for Judea. His successor, Judas Aristobulus I, reigned for only one year, but in this short period he succeeded in conquering Galilee. This region, inhabited by many Jews even before its annexation to Judea, was in constant danger of occupation by the Itureans, an Arab tribe which had exploited the weakness of the Seleucids to expand toward Lebanon and the sea. Aristobulus anticipated them and converted Galilee into a Jewish land. Within a year or two of his conquest, Sepphoris and Asochis were purely Jewish cities. With the acquisition of Galilee, the entire mountain region west of the Jordan was under Maccabean rule.

◁·······	Itureans
◀──	Aristobulus' army
·······	Judean border at succession of Aristobulus
░░░░	Area conquered by Aristobulus

ANT. 13: 319; WAR 1: 76

Coin of Alexander Janneus

THE KINGDOM OF ALEXANDER JANNEUS
103 TO 76 B.C.

ARISTOBULUS' SUCCESSOR, his brother Alexander Janneus (103–76 B.C.), completed the conquest of almost the whole of the Land of Israel. Although generally unlucky in the field, he succeeded through his perseverance in a series of campaigns, and added to the Maccabean domains Dora and Strato's Tower, together with the Carmel cape; Gaza and her satellite towns down to Rhinocorura on the brook of Egypt; the lands surrounding the Dead Sea; and most of the lands east of the Jordan from Panias at the source of the river southward—only Philadelphia remained unconquered. Alexander also succeeded in staving off various enemies—Ptolemy Lathyrus, king of Cyprus; the Seleucids Demetrius III and Antiochus XII; and the Nabatean kings. He was less successful in the interior; dissension between the ruling dynasty and its Sadducee followers, and the Pharisees (who first rose under Hyrcanus) waxed under Janneus into a rebellion, subsequently suppressed with great cruelty. Under Janneus, the Maccabean state reached its apogee.

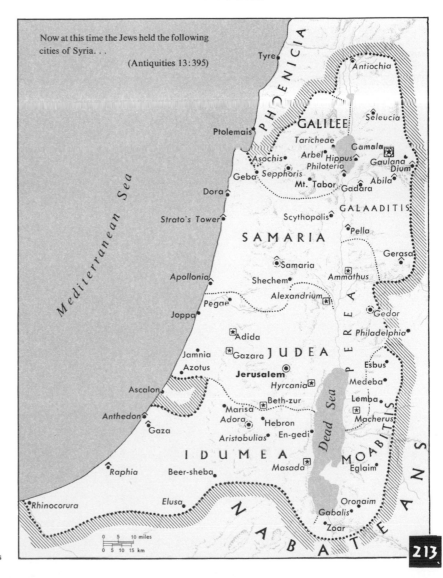

Now at this time the Jews held the following cities of Syria. . .
(Antiquities 13:395)

·········	District border
☒	Fortress
⌂	Greek city held by Janneus

ANT. 13: 395–404; WAR 1: 106

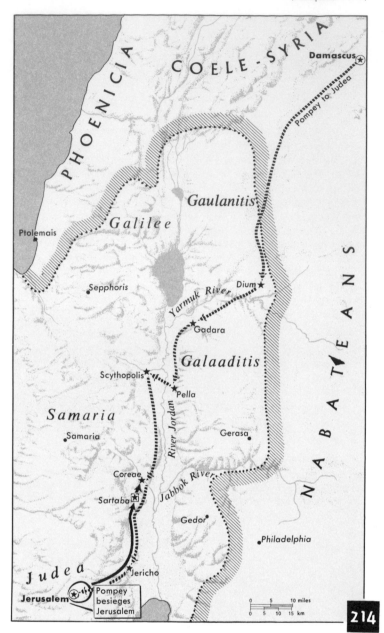

POMPEY... took the army..., and the auxiliaries...
as well as the Roman legions already at his disposal,
and marched against Aristobulus.

(Antiquities 14:48)

ANT. 14: 48–55; WAR 1: 133–139

←———— Aristobulus' army
-◁············· Pompey's army

POMPEY'S CAMPAIGN IN PALESTINE

63 B.C.

Pompey (from a coin)

AFTER Janneus' death (76 B.C.), his widow Alexandra reigned till 67 B.C. Upon her death, civil war broke out between her sons, Hyrcanus II and Aristobulus II. The former was weaker and, prompted by Antipater the Idumean (the evil genius of the Hasmonean dynasty), called Aretas, the Nabatean king, to his aid. The invaders besieged Jerusalem, but the Romans finally intervened.

Rome had gradually annexed the entire Hellenistic East after defeating the Seleucids. From 88 to 64 B.C., she fought Mithradates king of Pontus, her most dangerous enemy in the East. In 64 B.C. Pompey, who finally defeated Mithradates, came to Damascus, annexed the Seleucid kingdom (which then became the province of Syria) and turned his attention toward Judea.

At first he sent Scaurus, one of his commanders, to Judea and ordered a truce. Aretas and Hyrcanus retreated (on their way back they were soundly defeated by Aristobulus at Papyron near the Jordan). Pompey next ordered the two rivals to appear before him; seeing that Hyrcanus was the weaker personality of the two, he chose him to rule over the Jews. Aristobulus retired to the fastness of Alexandrium, overlooking the Jordan valley. Pompey followed him with his army, passing Dium (and probably also Gadara), Pella, and Scythopolis. At Coreae the Roman army entered Judea proper. Aristobulus negotiated from weakness and finally surrendered. Pompey then advanced to Jericho, where he learned that Aristobulus' adherents refused to surrender the capital; thereupon the Roman army—now in high spirits, for at Jericho news had arrived of the death of Mithradates of Pontus, Pompey's old foe—marched upon the Holy City.

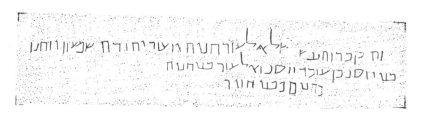

Inscription on tomb of the sons of Hezir, Jerusalem

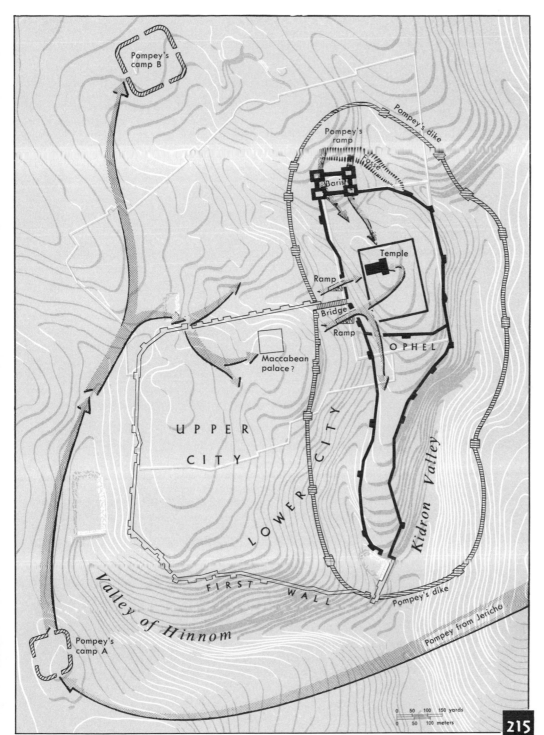

FOR we lost our freedom and became subject to the Romans, and the territory which we had gained by our arms... we were compelled to give back...

(Antiquities 14:77)

POMPEY'S SIEGE OF JERUSALEM

63 B.C.

Pompey's camp B

Pompey's dike

Pompey's ramp

Baris

Temple

Ramp

Bridge

Ramp

OPHEL

Maccabean palace?

UPPER CITY

LOWER CITY

Kidron Valley

FIRST WALL

Valley of Hinnom

Pompey's dike

Pompey from Jericho

Pompey's camp A

0 50 100 150 yards
0 50 100 meters

215

Pompey's army

Section of wall held by Aristobulus' supporters

ANT. 14: 57–71; WAR 1: 141–151

WHEN the Roman army approached the gates of Jerusalem, it encamped to the south of the city. The Upper City and the King's palace were in the hands of Hyrcanus' partisans, who opened the gates to Pompey. Aristobulus' supporters demolished the bridge connecting the Upper City with the Temple and prepared their resistance from the Temple Mount and the nearby Baris. The Romans put a dike around the Temple fortifications and built a camp to the north. They prepared a two-pronged assault: across the fosse next to the "towers" of the Baris in the north and at the ruined bridge in the west.

They built a ramp and positioned their siege engines and catapults. Work was facilitated by taking advantage of the Jews' reluctance to fight on the Sabbath: on this day, the Jews hesitated to interfere with the building of the ramps, unless physically attacked. The assault finally came on the Sabbath, of course. The towers and the wall gave way, and the Romans invaded the Temple, but the priests continued the service as if nothing had happened. According to Josephus, twelve thousand people died on this one day. Pompey entered the Holy of Holies, but did not touch the Temple or its treasures.

He also set up five councils and divided the
nation into as many districts.
(Antiquities 14:91)

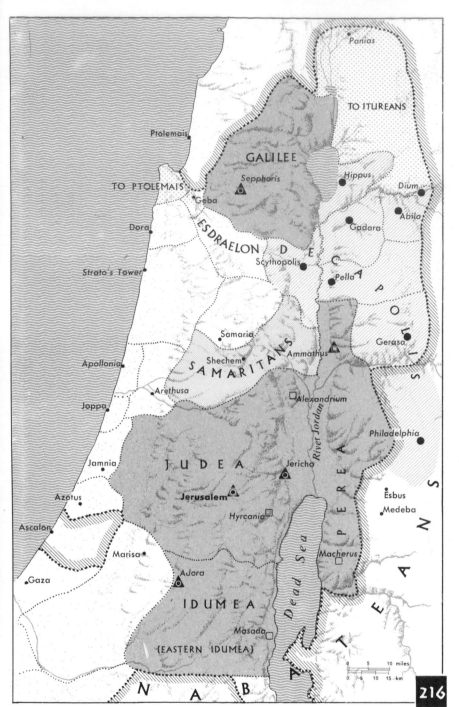

ANT. 14: 74–76, 88; WAR 1: 156–166, 169–170

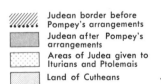

Key	
Judean border before Pompey's arrangements	Independent city under proconsul of Syria
Judean after Pompey's arrangements	City of Decapolis
Areas of Judea given to Iturians and Ptolemais	Gabinius' synedria
Land of Cutheans	Municipal boundary

Coin of Mattathias Antigonus

POMPEY'S TERRITORIAL ARRANGEMENTS
63 TO 55 B.C.

THE arrangements of Pompey after the conquest, completed by Gabinius (proconsul of Syria in 57–55 B.C.) were relatively easy on the Nabateans, harder on the Itureans, and very harsh on the Jewish state. Pompey "liberated" the Greek and Hellenized cities occupied by the Jews since the days of Hyrcanus and subjugated their rural populations to these Greek cities. Thus, there again rose autonomous units (under the supervision of the Roman proconsul in Syria) such as: Gaza, Azotus, Jamnia, Joppa, Apollonia, Arethusa (Aphek), Strato's Tower, and Dora on the coast; in the interior: Marisa, Sebaste, and Scythopolis. Beyond the Jordan, Gadara, Hippus, Abila, Dium, Pella, and Gerasa were reestablished. The Jews kept Judea proper, the eastern part of Idumea, Perea, and Galilee. The Samaritans became independent, and the plain of Esdraelon was detached from Galilee. Esbus was returned to the Nabateans who, except for being removed from Damascus, hardly suffered any diminution of the area under their control. The area of Lake Semechonitis, Panias, and Gaulanitis were given to the Itureans, but they lost their possessions on the Mediterreanean coast.

Pompey joined the majority of the cities beyond the Jordan into a "League of Ten Cities"—the Decapolis, including also Scythopolis west of the Jordan, to minimize the danger of their being isolated. The Carmel was returned to Ptolemais. The Jews held on to those areas that were densely populated by them, except Joppa and its neighborhood and the plain of Esdraelon.

In all the Greek cities reestablished by Pompey and Gabinius, the populations exiled by the Maccabeans were returned. Hyrcanus II became again high priest in Jerusalem, but administration was entrusted to Antipater. Aristobulus II and his family were exiled to Rome.

During the rule of Gabinius, an attempt was made to split the Jewish State into five synedria (districts), a tactic applied by the Romans in Macedonia. The seats of the synedria were in Sepphoris (Galilee), Ammathus (Perea), Jericho, Jerusalem, and Adora (Eastern Idumea). But the unity of the people could not be destroyed by such means, and the synedria were dissolved after a short time.

Judea profited from the civil war between Pompey and Julius Caesar. When Caesar emerged victorious, he pursued Pompey to Egypt and there became entangled in fighting at Alexandria.

In the ensuing events, Antipater was of great assistance to the relieving army of Mithradates of Pergamum and was duly regarded by Caesar.

Hyrcanus II was appointed as Ethnarch by Caesar, and Antipater as the effective administrator of the State. In appreciation of the help he had received from the Jews, Julius Caesar returned to them Joppa and the plain of Esdraelon. From then on Antipater was the actual ruler of the land. He appointed Phasael, his firstborn, as governor over Jerusalem, and his younger son Herod, who was yet a boy, as governor of Galilee.

JULIUS CAESAR AND JUDEA
47 B.C.

Julius Caesar

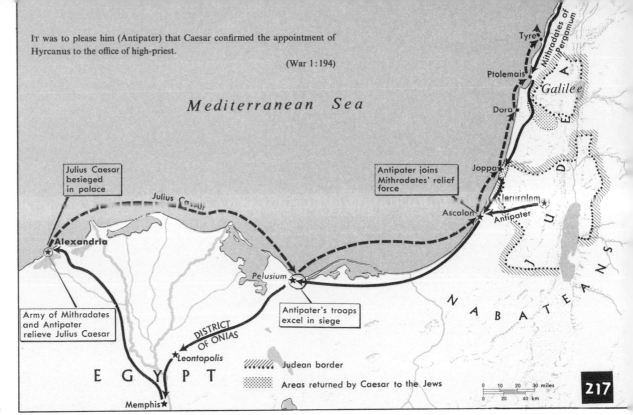

It was to please him (Antipater) that Caesar confirmed the appointment of Hyrcanus to the office of high-priest.

(War 1:194)

Julius Caesar besieged in palace

Army of Mithradates and Antipater relieve Julius Caesar

Antipater's troops excel in siege

Antipater joins Mithradates' relief force

Mediterranean Sea

DISTRICT OF ONIAS

E G Y P T

Leontopolis

Memphis

Alexandria

Pelusium

Ascalon

Jerusalem

Antipater

J U D E A

N A B A T E A N S

Tyre

Ptolemais

Dora

Joppa

Galilee

Mithradates of Pergamum

////// Judean border

▓▓▓▓ Areas returned by Caesar to the Jews

0 10 20 30 miles
0 20 40 km

217

ANT. 14: 127–143, 205, 207

...TTATHIAS the high priest and the community of the ...s.

(Coin of Antigonus)

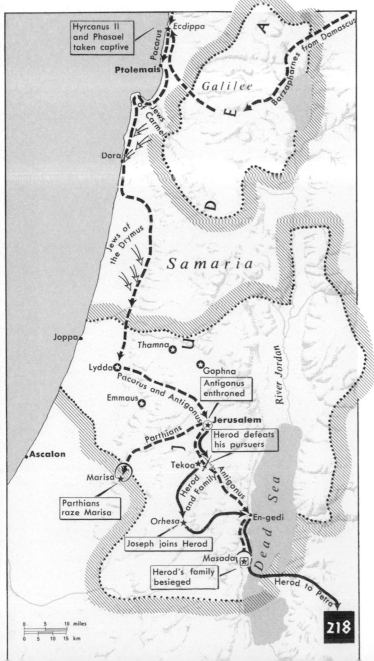

Hyrcanus II and Phasael taken captive

Parthians raze Marisa

Joseph joins Herod

Herod's family besieged

Ecdippa

Ptolemais

Galilee

Dora

Jews of Carmel

Jews of the Drymus

Samaria

Joppa

Lydda

Emmaus

Ascalon

Marisa

Orhesa

Masada

Thamna

Gophna

Jerusalem

Tekoa

En-gedi

Antigonus enthroned

Herod defeats his pursuers

River Jordan

Dead Sea

Pacorus

Barzapharnes from Damascus

Pacorus and Antigonus

Parthians

Herod and Family

Antigonus

Herod to Petra

0 5 10 miles
0 5 10 15 km

218

THE PARTHIAN INVASION AND THE ESCAPE OF HEROD
40 B.C.

THE assassination of Julius Caesar in Rome (44 B.C.) caused the renewal of the civil war, but Antipater and his sons succeeded in keeping the reins of government by submitting to the various Roman rulers. One of these was Cassius, proconsul of Syria, who tyrannized the population of Judea. He sold into slavery the inhabitants of Lydda, Thamna, Gophna, and Emmaus, and razed their towns, when they were late in paying taxes. In 43 B.C., Antipater was murdered by one of his opponents, but Herod avenged his father, and suppressed the unrest; and he, together with his brother Phasael, was appointed ruler over all Judea (42 B.C.).

When the Parthians invaded Syria two years later, they were joined by Antigonus (Mattathias), the son of Aristobulus II. He accompanied Pacorus, son of Ordes king of the Parthians, along the coast; simultaneously the satrap Barzapharnes invaded Galilee from Damascus. When Pacorus came up to Jerusalem, he was joined by the Jews of Carmel and of the Drymus (the great forest in the Sharon plain). In Jerusalem, the people revolted against Phasael and Herod, who were forced to open the gates to the Parthians. Phasael submitted to Barzapharnes, but was imprisoned near Ecdippa, together with Hyrcanus II; he committed suicide in captivity, and Hyrcanus was maimed to make him unfit for the priesthood. Mattathias Antigonus was thereupon crowned in Jerusalem.

Herod and his family (including his betrothed, Mariamme the Hasmonean, daughter of Alexander and granddaughter of Aristobulus) fled south. At Tekoa, where the fortress Herodium was later to rise, he overcame his pursuers and continued on his way to Idumea. He was joined by his brother Joseph at Orhesa, and together they proceeded to Masada, where Herod's family was later besieged by Antigonus. Herod himself crossed the Dead Sea and went to the Nabateans. When Malchus II, king of the Arabs, refused to come to his aid, Herod continued to Alexandria in Egypt and thence to Rome. The siege of Masada was meanwhile carried on in a most lethargic manner; at one time the defenders were saved from thirst only by a sudden cloud-burst. The Parthians, allies of Antigonus, returned beyond the Euphrates after invading Judea.

✪ City oppressed by Cassius

◀━━━ Herod

◀- - - Parthians and Antigonus

ANT. 14: 330–362; WAR 1: 248–268

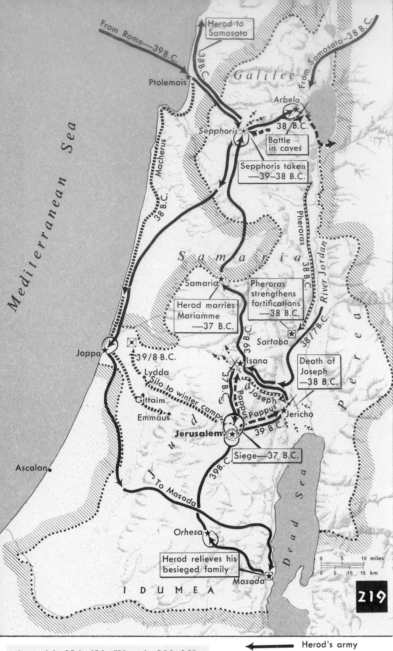

ANT. 14: 394–491; WAR 1: 290–353

→ Herod's army
◄┄┄┄ Herod's brothers
◄┄┄┄ Roman army
◄━━━► Antigonus' army
39 A.D. Year of campaign

THE GROWTH OF HEROD'S KINGDOM
40 TO 4 B.C.

HEROD maintained his position under Cleopatra, and when the battle of Actium (31 B.C.) made Octavian—now the emperor Augustus—undisputed master of the Roman world, Herod quickly gained the favor of his new overlord. He was confirmed in his kingdom, to which Augustus in 30 B.C. added Gaza and the coastal cities (except Ascalon and Dora) as well as Gadara and Hippus. In 23 B.C., Herod received the task of pacifying the unruly Batanea, Trachonitis, and Auranitis, and in 20 B.C., Panias and Gaulanitis were placed under his rule. By then Herod's kingdom had reached its greatest extent.

Apart from the conquest of his own kingdom (see map 219) Herod made only one conquest by arms: having in 32 B.C. defeated the Nabateans in the field, he annexed Esbus and settled veterans there.

ANT. 15: 217, 343, 344, 360;
WAR 1: 396, 398, 400;
APPIAN: CIVIL WARS 5: 75

▓ Additions—40 B.C.
░ Additions—30 B.C.
⬜ Additions—23 B.C.
▨ Additions—20 B.C.
▦ Conquests from Nabateans

BUT they [the Hasmoneans] lost their royal power through internal strife, and it passed to Herod, son of Antipater...

(Antiquities 14:end)

THE RISE OF HEROD
40 TO 37 B.C.

HEROD was received in Rome with great honors. Octavian (Caesar's nephew and successor) and Mark Antony persuaded the Senate to appoint him king of the Jews. They also added Western Idumea and the lands of the Samaritans to his kingdom. The new king, however, had to fight for every inch of the land, for not only was the country destined for him in the hands of Antigonus, his rival, but the people hated the "Idumean slave"; even his Roman allies deserted him at times. But Herod overcame all these difficulties.

He landed at Ptolemais, for Joppa the port of Jerusalem was in hostile hands. In the winter of 39 B.C. he sent out to establish his rule in Galilee, and from there proceeded to capture Joppa, then continuing on to Masada. He freed his family, returned to Idumea, where he took Orhesa and went up against Jerusalem. Together with the Roman commander, Silo, he attacked the city, but the Romans broke off the siege having been bribed by Antigonus, and departed for their winter camp on the coast. Herod returned to Galilee, took Sepphoris during a snowstorm (winter, 39–38 B.C.), pursued his opponents to the river Jordan, and stormed their fortified caves at Arbela, where the Jews put up a stout resistance.

In the summer of 38 B.C. Macherus, a Roman leader, was sent to Herod's aid; he attacked Emmaus while Pheroras, Herod's youngest brother, advanced through the Jordan valley and rebuilt the fortifications of Alexandrium. Herod himself went to meet Mark Antony who, at the time, was besieging Samosata on the Euphrates. On Herod's return he learned of his brother Joseph's defeat and death at the hands of Pappus, general of Antigonus. Herod left Jericho for the Judean mountains, routing Pappus near Isana. He and his allies again turned toward Jerusalem in the winter of 38–37 B.C. While the siege was in progress, Herod married Mariamme in Samaria. Jerusalem fell in the summer of 37 B.C. and many of the citizens were slaughtered. Antigonus, too, was executed, by order of Mark Antony. Herod was now undisputed ruler of Judea.

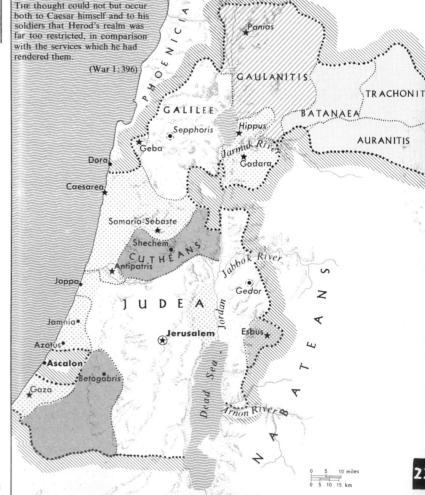

THE thought could not but occur both to Caesar himself and to his soldiers that Herod's realm was far too restricted, in comparison with the services which he had rendered them.

(War 1:396)

Reconstruction of Herod's Temple

HEROD'S BUILDING
IN JERUSALEM

Coin of Herod the Great

WHOEVER has not seen Herod's Temple has never seen a beautiful building.

(Baba Bathra 4a)

HEROD'S love of pomp, his wish to immortalize his name, to secure his rule, and to appease the hostile population and provide it with work—these were the main motives for fortifying and embellishing Jerusalem. His revenues derived from trade and from taxes allowed him to build a magnificent palace in the northwestern corner of the Upper City; it was guarded on the north by three strong towers that he named Phasael (after his brother), Mariamme (in honor of his wife), and Hippicus (after his friend). He also built a theater in the part of the city inhabited by wealthy Hellenizers, raised an inner wall to protect the Upper City, and strengthened the North Gate in the Second Wall. South of the Temple Mount he built a stadium, probably in the Tyropoean valley.

Herod was even more active on the Temple Mount: doubling the area of the Temple esplanade, he girdled it with walls and porticoes. Its most prominent feature was the "royal portico" (basilica) in the south of the square, which Herod connected with the Upper City by a second bridge, now known after its discoverer as "Robinson's arch." The king also rebuilt the Temple proper and to secure control over the Temple rebuilt the old Baris, at the northwestern corner of the Temple Mount, into a huge fortress, which he called "Antonia" in honor of Mark Antony.

Herod was also active as a builder outside his capital: he founded the harbor city of Caesarea in place of Strato's Tower and rebuilt Samaria, calling the new city "Sebaste" in honor of the emperor Augustus. He built fortresses at Herodium and near Jericho, and entirely reconstructed Macherus and Masada on the two opposing shores of the Dead Sea.

Herodian construction

ANT. 15: 318, 380–425;
WAR 1: 401, 5: 108, 161, 238, 246, 507, 7: 172–177

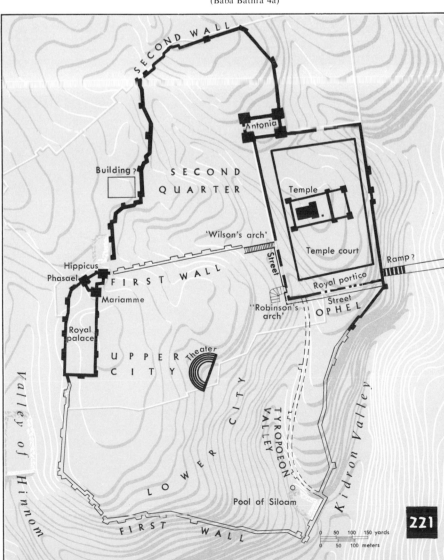

SECOND WALL

Antonia

Building?

SECOND QUARTER

Temple

'Wilson's arch'

Temple court

Hippicus
Phasael

FIRST WALL

Street

Ramp?

Mariamme

Royal portico

'Robinson's arch'

Street

OPHEL

Royal palace

UPPER CITY

Theater

Valley of Hinnom

LOWER CITY

TYROPOEON VALLEY

Kidron Valley

Pool of Siloam

FIRST WALL

0   50   100   150 yards
0   50   100 meters

... Caesar... appointed Archelaus not king indeed but ethnarch of half the teritory... Antipas received... Perea and Galilee... Batanea, Trachonitis, Auranitis...
(Antiquities 17: 317–318)

THE DIVISION OF HEROD'S KINGDOM
4 B.C. TO 6 A.D.

A FTER much hesitation, the emperor Augustus decided in 4 B.C. to divide Herod's kingdom among his three surviving sons, as recommended by the dead king. Archelaus, the son of Malthace the Samaritan, was appointed ethnarch ("ruler of the nation") over Judea, Idumea, and Samaria. The cities of Caesarea and Sebaste were included in his domain, which included Jews and non-Jews in about equal proportions. Herod Antipas, the second son, received two purely Jewish, but widely separated, areas: Galilee and Perea (Jewish Transjordan). The third son, Herod Philip, was endowed with the newly settled lands of the Gaulanitis, Batanea, Trachonitis and Auranitis, as well as Caesarea Panias. Most of his subjects were probably non-Jews, but as the Jews in his lands had been settled by Herod the Great, they were loyal to the dynasty. Salome, Herod's sister, was given Jamnia and Azotus, and Phasaelis in the Jordan valley. The cities of Gaza, Gadara, and Hippus, which had borne Herod's rule with much dissatisfaction, were attached to the province of Syria.

All of Herod's sons tried to emulate their father in building cities; Archelaus even called a new settlement in his own name: Archelais. Antipas built Tiberias (named in honor of the emperor Tiberius) and Livias (in honor of the emperor's mother). Philip added to Caesarea Panias, which was from this time called Caesarea Philippi, and built Julias (also in honor of Livia) near Bethsaida.

Archelaus had a short and turbulent reign and was banished in 6 A.D., his lands being handed over to a Roman procurator. Herod Antipas remained till 39 A.D. (see map 249). Only Philip died in possession of his tetrarchy, in 34 A.D.

ANT. 17: 317–321; WAR 2: 93–98

~~	Border of Herod's realm
	To Archelaus
	To Herod Antipas
	To Philip
	To Province of Syria
	Salome's portion
★ *Julias*	City founded by Herod's sons

THE ECONOMY OF JUDEA
4TH CENTURY B.C. TO 1ST CENTURY A.D.

T HANKS to its agricultural wealth, Judea was prosperous in the days of the Second Temple, a prosperity that began with the Hellenistic period. The areas suitable for wheat-growing were indeed few, and their extent limited: the Esdraelon valley, parts of the coastal plain and some of the larger mountain valleys. In the south, barley took the place of wheat. Olives and vineyards thrived in the mountains. Dates were grown mainly in the hot Jordan valley and balsam on the royal estate near Jericho. Flax from Galilee and wool from the mountains of Judea served to clothe the population. The western slopes of the mountains, on both sides of the Jordan, were still covered with extensive forests, and a good part of Sharon was wooded with oaks. These regions also served as pasture lands for sheep and cattle.

Various industries connected with the Temple and life in the metropolis in general existed in Jerusalem. Pottery, tied as it was to sources of raw material, was probably the country's one major industry; the others (mainly spinning and weaving) were home industries. Fishing boats plied the Sea of Galilee and the Mediterranean, and murex shells yielding purple were collected and processed at Azotus, Dora, and farther north. The name Taricheae, "place of salted fish," is evidence of a fish-preserving industry, which probably exported its produce. Copper from the Arabah, iron from the mountains of Gilead, and bitumen from the Dead Sea were the main natural resources; to these must be added the hot springs at Callirrhoe and Baaras as well as those near Pella, Gadara, and Tiberias.

Coin of Herod Antipas, struck at Tiberias

THE DEAD SEA SECT
AND ITS "TREASURES"

WELL, ours is not a maritime country; neither commerce nor. . . We devote
ourselves to the cultivation of the productive country with which we are blessed.

(Against Apion 1:60)

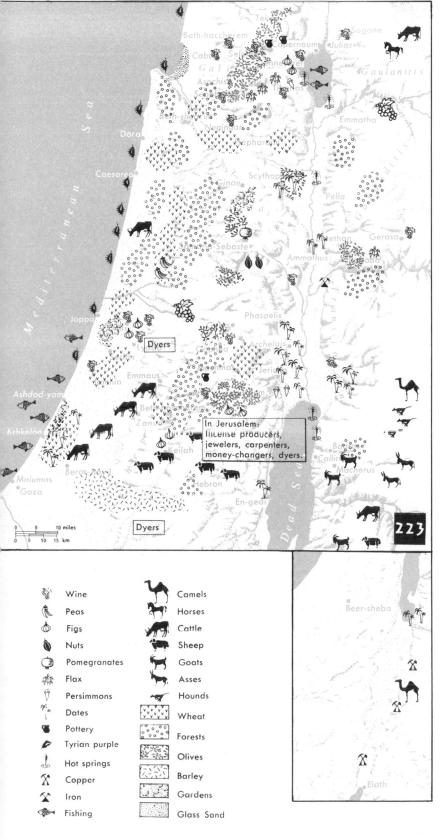

Dyers

In Jerusalem:
incense producers,
jewelers, carpenters,
money-changers, dyers.

Dyers

223

Wine		Camels	
Peas		Horses	
Figs		Cattle	
Nuts		Sheep	
Pomegranates		Goats	
Flax		Asses	
Persimmons		Hounds	
Dates		Wheat	
Pottery		Forests	
Tyrian purple		Olives	
Hot springs		Barley	
Copper		Gardens	
Iron		Glass Sand	
Fishing			

AND all who come into the
order of the community shall
pass over into the covenant
before God. . .
(Manual of Discipline 1:16)

★ Beth-shean

Samaria

Mt. Gerizim ★

Valley of Achor

Docus ★
★ Beth-hakkoz
Beth-tamar ★ Chozba ★ ★ Jericho
Nahal Hakipah
★ Beth-haccherem (Amud Cave)
Jerusalem ★ Haazelah
Valley of Secacah ★ **Meṣad Ḥasidim** ✠ ★ Nebo
★ Kobaa (Khirbet Qumran)

Beth-marah ★

Capharbarucha ★

Judean Desert

Dead Sea

0 5 10 miles Masada ★
0 5 10 15 km

224

★ Alleged treasure caches
of the Dead Sea Sect

COPPER SCROLL; MANUAL OF DISCIPLINE;
THANKSGIVING HYMNS; THE DAMASCUS COVENANT

TOWARD the end of the days of the Second Temple, a sect known
to us only from scrolls found at Khirbat Qumran, south of
Jericho (probably then called Meṣad Ḥasidim, the "Stronghold of
the Pious"), made its appearance as one of the outgrowths of the
cultural and religious ferment prevailing at the time. The sect was
probably founded in the days of Janneus by a prophet called the
"Teacher of Righteousness." One of its tenets disqualified the Hasmonean dynasty for the office of high priest; because of this, and
because of their adherence to the priestly house of Zadok, Janneus
had the Teacher of Righteousness executed. The sect organized its
secluded life in the desert in the vicinity of the Dead Sea, and according to its "Manual of Discipline" (the code of the sect), all property
was vested in the community. The sect held a belief in predestination;
fate had, for better or worse, been decreed by God and no human
act could change it. Naturally the members of the sect believed themselves to be among the elect, destined for divine grace. Their calendar
feasts and holidays were at variance with those of the mainstream of
Jews and they rejected worship in the Temple in Jerusalem. In Herod's
days, the sect lived in Jerusalem, but later in the days of Archelaus,
it returned to the desert where it existed until 68 A.D. (see map 256).

Among the documents found in the caves near Qumran were two
copper scrolls. Only recently opened and deciphered, they were found
to contain lists of hidden treasure, silver, gold, incense, spices, and
precious woods. The value of these treasures was immense, and
scholars are still divided on whether they were real or imaginary.
Twenty-six of the sixty-eight secret caches were in Jerusalem or its
vicinity.

Many scholars have identified the sect with the Essenes, or a branch
of them. The Essenes are known from ancient sources, and there is a
great resemblance between the sect as it appears through its writings
and the description of the Essenes given by Josephus and Pliny.

AND she gave birth to her first-born son... and laid him in a manger, because there was no place for them in the inn.

(Luke 2:7)

THE BIRTH OF JESUS AND THE FLIGHT INTO EGYPT

THE STORY of Jesus is set out in the four gospels of Matthew, Mark, Luke, and John. The first three are called the "synoptic" gospels, because they are studied together owing to their similarity; the fourth gospel, that of John, contains many details not found in the others and is different in many other ways also. According to Christian tradition, Jesus was born at Bethlehem in the days of King Herod (who died in the spring of 4 B.C.); Jesus' birth probably occurred in December, 5 B.C. According to Luke (2:22–24), the child was presented at the Temple. Menaced by Herod, Joseph and Mary decided to flee to Egypt by night. The shortest way to leave Herod's domain was seemingly by way of Ascalon, which lay on the main route to Egypt; the safer way of the desert would have been too arduous for a woman and a new born babe. The family arrived unharmed in the land of the Nile, where they found shelter and sustenance among the many Jews then inhabiting Egypt (see map 238).

225

MT. 1: 18—2: 15; LK. 2: 4–38

AFTER THE death of Herod, Joseph had a vision in which he was told to return to the Land of Israel. Fearing Archelaus, the ethnarch of Judea, Joseph decided to return to his native Nazareth, then under the milder rule of Herod Antipas (see map 222). Nazareth was a small Jewish village about seven miles southeast of Sepphoris, the capital of Western Galilee. There Jesus grew into manhood. The only story of these "hidden years" in the gospels is that related by Luke (2:41–51), according to which Jesus went with his parents to Jerusalem when he was twelve years old. Jesus stayed behind in Jerusalem when his parents went a day's journey on their way back to Nazareth (presumably down to Jericho, so as to return by way of Jewish Perea rather than through Samaria). Missing the boy, they returned to the Holy City and there found him debating with the teachers in the Temple. They then returned with him to Nazareth.

The name "Jesus," as written in Hebrew on an ossuary

THE RETURN FROM EGYPT; THE BOY JESUS IN THE TEMPLE

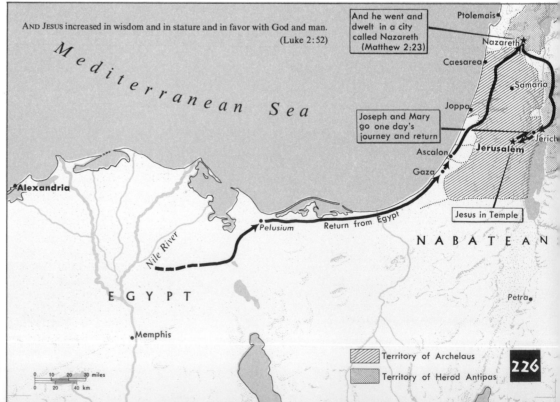

AND JESUS increased in wisdom and in stature and in favor with God and man.

(Luke 2:52)

And he went and dwelt in a city called Nazareth (Matthew 2:23)

Joseph and Mary go one day's journey and return

Jesus in Temple

Return from Egypt

Territory of Archelaus

Territory of Herod Antipas

226

MT. 2: 19–23; LK. 2: 41–52

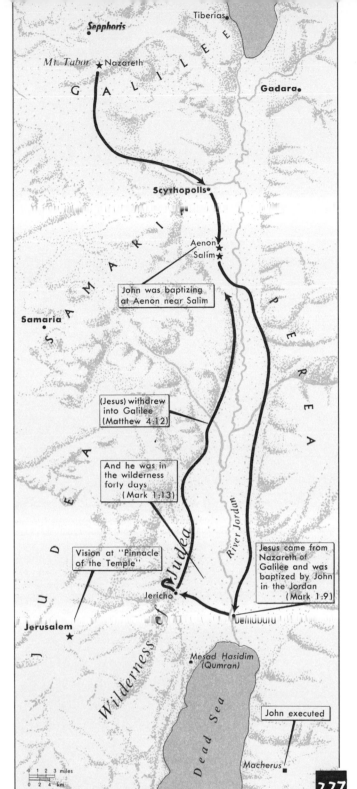

Inscription honoring Philip, son of Herod

In the fifteenth year of the reign of Tiberius Caesar... the word of God came to John the son of Zechariah in the wilderness.

(Luke 3:1-2)

THE BAPTISM OF JESUS AND THE SOJOURN IN THE DESERT

THE BEGINNING of Jesus' public activity, the "fifteenth year of the reign of Tiberius Caesar" (that is, A.D. 27–28), was also when John the Baptist began to preach "a baptism of repentance for the forgiveness of sins" (Luke 3:1–3). Combining the Gospel story with other historical sources of the period (in particular Josephus and the Qumran documents), we see the activity of John as part of a deep spiritual ferment pervading the whole of Judea at that time. John's activity was concentrated in the Jordan valley, either at Beth-abara at the fords of the Jordan near Jericho, or higher up the river at Aenon near Salim, south of Scythopolis (Beth-shean). Among the multitudes who flocked to be baptized was Jesus, who came from Nazareth in Galilee. This was the beginning of his ministry. According to the Gospels his baptism was followed by forty days of seclusion in the wilderness, most probably the wilderness of Judea above Jericho. This has from time immemorial been a refuge for those who have wished to isolate themselves from the world. The sequence of baptism and seclusion in the wilderness was common at the time, especially among the Dead Sea Sect, whose headquarters were at Meṣad Ḥasidim (Khirbet Qumran) not far away; no positive evidence has, however, been found to connect John or Jesus with the sect. Gospel tradition has it that Jesus was tempted by Satan in the desert and carried by the evil spirit to the "pinnacle of the Temple" in Jerusalem—presumably the southeastern corner of the Temple Mount—which had a sheer drop of 130 feet. Having overcome temptation, Jesus returned to Galilee. John continued to preach and baptize and was ultimately arrested by order of Herod Antipas, kept in prison for some time (traditionally at Macherus in southern Perea), and executed when Herod succumbed to the wiles of his wife, Herodias, who hated the prophet because he denounced her evil ways (Mark 6:14–29; Matthew 14:1–12; Luke 3:19–20). These events occurred during Jesus' ministry, but they cannot be chronologically fixed on the evidence available.

Mt. 3—4: 12, 14: 1–2;
Mk. 1: 4–14; 6: 14–29;
Lk. 3: 1–22, 6: 18–30, 9: 7–9;
Jn. 1: 6–8, 15–42, 3: 22–24

Tiberius Caesar

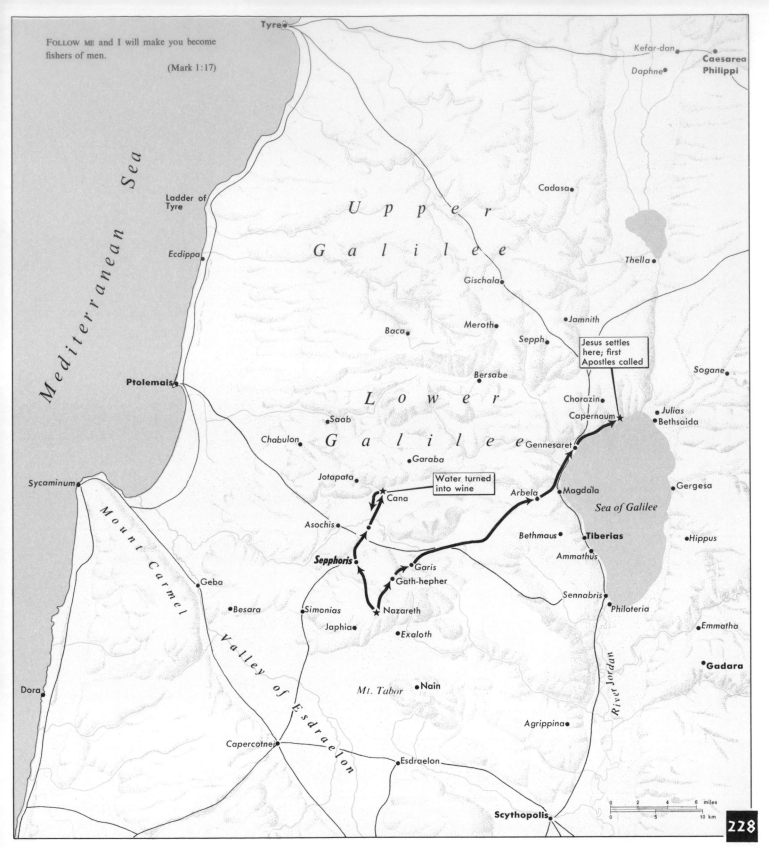

FOLLOW ME and I will make you become fishers of men.

(Mark 1:17)

Mediterranean Sea

Tyre

Upper Galilee

Kefar-dan

Daphne

Caesarea Philippi

Ladder of Tyre

Cadasa

Ecdippa

Thella

Gischala

Ptolemais

Meroth

Jamnith

Baca

Sepph

Sogane

Lower Galilee

Jesus settles here; first Apostles called

Saab

Bersabe

Chorazin

Julias

Chabulon

Capernaum

Bethsaida

Garaba

Gennesaret

Jotapata

Water turned into wine

Cana

Arbela

Magdala

Gergesa

Sycaminum

Asochis

Sea of Galilee

Bethmaus

Tiberias

Hippus

Sepphoris

Garis

Ammathus

Gath-hepher

Mount Carmel

Geba

Sennabris

Philoteria

Besara

Simonias

Nazareth

Japhia

Emmatha

Exaloth

Gadara

Dora

Valley of Esdraelon

Mt. Tabor

Nain

River Jordan

Agrippina

Capercotnei

Esdraelon

Scythopolis

0 2 4 6 miles
0 5 10 km

228

FROM NAZARETH TO CANA AND CAPERNAUM

MT. 4: 12–22, 8: 5–17, 9: 9–10, 18–20; MK. 1: 16–34, 2: 1–1
5: 22–43; LK. 4:31–41, 5:27–32, 7: 1–10, 8: 40–56; JN. 2: 1–

ACCORDING to Luke 3:23, Jesus was about thirty years old when he began his ministry. It appears that his first preaching at Nazareth was unsuccessful, and he left the town to settle at Capernaum on the shores of the Lake Gennesaret. Capernaum (in the original Hebrew, Kefar-nahum, "Village of Nahum") was a prosperous townlet whose inhabitants engaged mainly in fishing (a great haul of fish is recorded in Luke 5:6). Being a frontier town between the domains of Antipas and Philip, it had a custom post (the Apostle Matthew may have been called from his duty there as a tax-collector; Matthew 9:9; Mark 2:13–14; Luke 5:27). A centurion commanding the local garrison, though a Gentile, had built the local synagogue (Luke 7:5), where Jesus often preached. It was at Capernaum that Jesus called his first disciples, the fishermen Simon, Peter, and Andrew,

men of nearby Bethsaida east of the Jordan (John 1:44), as well as James and John, the sons of Zebedee; and here he invested the Twelve Apostles (Mark 3:13–19; Matthew 10:1–4). It was here also that he performed many of the miraculous deeds reported in the Gospels. From then on Capernaum was called "his own city" (Matthew 9:1). As Capernaum had a more varied population and was nearer the borders of the Decapolis than landlocked Nazareth, it is likely to have been more receptive to the new teachings. Yet Jesus did not entirely sever his ties with the town of his youth. John 2:11 continues, after the story of his baptism, with a miracle performed by Jesus at Cana in the presence of Mary and the disciples. Therefore, if we follow John's Gospel, the visit to Cana occurred at the beginning of Jesus' ministry.

. . . A great multitude, hearing all that he did, came to him.

(Mark 3:8)

THE HOLY LAND AND COELE-SYRIA IN THE TIME OF JESUS

THE GOSPELS tell that the teachings of Jesus drew crowds from Galilee, Judea, Jerusalem, Idumea, the lands beyond the Jordan, Tyre, and Sidon (Mark 3 : 7–8; Matthew 4 : 25 [adding "the Decapolis]" and Luke 6:17). The list of countries and towns reflects the area of Jewish settlement in the Holy Land at the time. In Judea, Jerusalem is singled out as the only "city" proper in the land; Idumea had been a separate administrative unit since the days of Alexander Janneus, although its inhabitants were merging more and more with the rest of the Jews. The lands "beyond the Jordan," or Perea, were Jewish from the days of Tobiad dynasty on (see map 213). There were Jewish communities in the cities of the Decapolis which were, however, predominantly Gentile. Finally, the territories of Tyre and Sidon, although predominantly Phoenician (see map 229), had considerable Jewish populations. Though politically split up between various territories and rulers (all of which were subject to Roman suzerainty), the Jews of the Holy Land were one spiritually and any wave of religious feeling rising in one community could sweep them all. It is significant that Samaria and the coastal cities are absent from the list, though later (see map 258) Christianity made much progress there.

MT. 4: 25; MK. 3: 7–8; LK. 6: 17

□ Territory of Herod Antipas

□ Territory of Herod Philip

▨ Territory of the Procurator of Judaea

□ The Decapolis

▨ Kingdom of the Nabateans

▨ Cities under the Proconsul of Syria

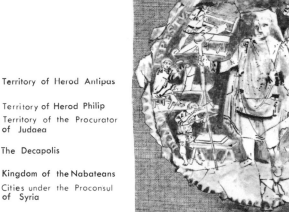

Gold glass from Rome depicting carpenters at work

CANA AND NAZARETH REVISITED

MARK (6 : 1–6) inserts, within the story of Jesus' teaching around the Sea of Galilee, an episode of a visit to Nazareth. Jesus preached in the synagogue there, but was rejected by the worshipers who refused to believe that "the carpenter" was an inspired prophet. In Matthew 13:53–58 the episode is placed in the same context, though Jesus is here called "the carpenter's son." Luke, on the other hand, (4:16–30) places the incident at the very beginning of Jesus' ministry. It is in connection with this visit to Nazareth that we may perhaps place Jesus' second visit to Cana, during which (according to John 4:46) he healed the son of an "official" (the original Greek has "basilikos," "the king's man"). Cana was situated at the border of the plain of Asochis, where there were royal estates and the "king's man" was probably the royal steward administering this domain.

During another of Jesus' visits in the neighborhood, he healed the widow's son at Nain (Luke 7:11–17). Although called "a city," Nain was a mere village five miles southeast of Nazareth; situated on a hilly slope, it had a gate and wall. In later times Nain was the capital of a separate district. Remains of the cemetery of this ancient village are still visible in the rocky area by the side of the road leading from Nain to the Via Maris.

MT. 13: 53–58;
MK. 6: 1–6; LK. 4: 16–30, 7: 11–17; JN. 4: 46–54

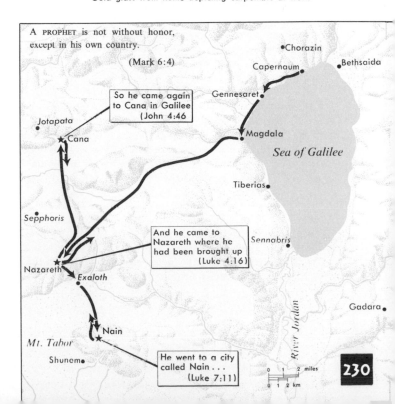

A PROPHET is not without honor, except in his own country.

(Mark 6:4)

So he came again to Cana in Galilee (John 4:46

And he came to Nazareth where he had been brought up (Luke 4:16)

He went to a city called Nain . . . (Luke 7:11)

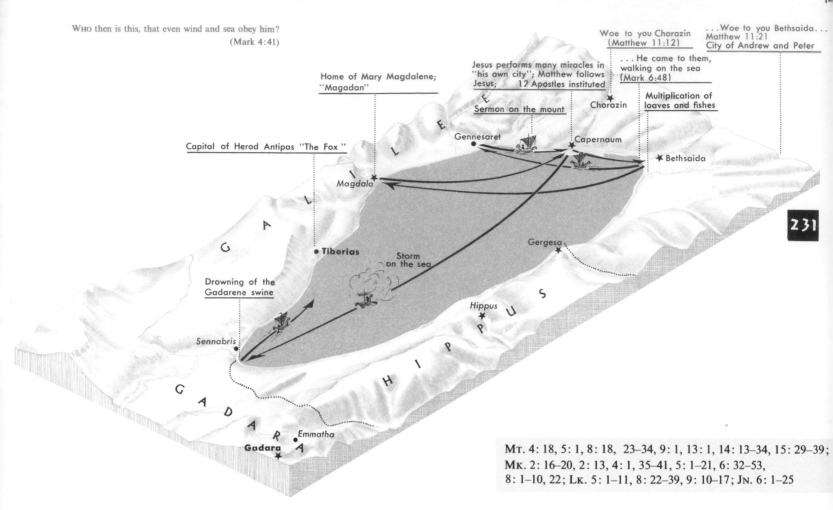

WHO then is this, that even wind and sea obey him?
(Mark 4:41)

Woe to you Chorazin
(Matthew 11:12)

...Woe to you Bethsaida...
Matthew 11:21
City of Andrew and Peter

Jesus performs many miracles in
"his own city"; Matthew follows
Jesus; 12 Apostles instituted

...He came to them,
walking on the sea
(Mark 6:48)

Home of Mary Magdalene;
"Magadan"

Sermon on the mount

Chorazin

Multiplication of
loaves and fishes

Gennesaret

Capernaum

Bethsaida

Capital of Herod Antipas "The Fox"

Magdala

231

Tiberias

Storm
on the sea

Gergesa

Drowning of the
Gadarene swine

Hippus

G A L I L E E

H I P P U S

Sennabris

G A D A R A

Emmatha

Gadara

MT. 4: 18, 5: 1, 8: 18, 23–34, 9: 1, 13: 1, 14: 13–34, 15: 29–39;
MK. 2: 16–20, 2: 13, 4: 1, 35–41, 5: 1–21, 6: 32–53,
8: 1–10, 22; LK. 5: 1–11, 8: 22–39, 9: 10–17; JN. 6: 1–25

AROUND THE SEA OF GALILEE

APART FROM several journeys, Jesus' entire activity before his final departure for Jerusalem was concentrated around the Sea of Galilee (Matthew 15:29; Mark 1:16; 6:31), also called Lake Gennesaret (Luke 5:1) and Lake Tiberias (John 6:1; 21:1), and usually just "the sea" in the Gospels. Gennesaret seems to be an earlier name, for it replaces the biblical "Sea of Chinnereth" (Numbers 34:11), because the city of Gennesaret was located on the site of Chinnereth (Tell Ureime). "Sea of Tiberias" is clearly posterior to the foundation of that city in A.D. 18/19 (see map 222). The first Apostles were fishermen; sometimes Jesus taught standing in boats, with the crowds listening on the shore. The Sermon on the Mount was delivered according to tradition near Capernaum (Matthew 8:1 and 5), the site is said to be located on the height just behind Capernaum. Only occasionally did Jesus upbraid the cities that refused to repent ("Woe to you Chorazin , woe to you Bethsaida. Capernaum shall be brought down to Hades"—Matthew 11:21–23; Luke 10:13–15).

On the Sea of Galilee there are frequent storms. During one such storm, Jesus slept while sailing across to the Gadarenes (Mark 5:35–41; Matthew 8:23–27; Luke 8:22–24) and upon his awakening the sea was suddenly becalmed. The location of the incident of the "Gadarene swine" has been much disputed (the usual version "Gerasene" is

quite impossible, for there was no territory of Gerasa on the lake shore); the two possibilities are "Gergasene"—pointing to Gergasa (Kursi) on the eastern shore of the lake in the territory of Hippus —and "Gadarene"; Gadara might have possessed a stretch of the shore, situated between the river Jordan and Kefar-semaḥ. The shore there is steep; thus the plunging of the herd of swine into the waters of the lake is plausible. The inhabitants of Gadara, being Gentiles, did not share Jewish scruples regarding the raising of swine.

Other events recorded in the Gospels pertaining to the Sea of Galilee and its surrounding are the Multiplication of Loaves and Fishes at a lonely spot near the town of Bethsaida; the story of Jesus' walking on the water; and Peter's attempt to follow his example (Mark 6:45–51; Matthew 15:22–23; and John 6:15–21). Other journeys of Jesus include a visit to "Magadan" ("Dalmanutha," in Mark 8:10); in both cases we should read Magdala, the most important town on the sea shore after Tiberias, and famous for its fish-curing industry. This locality was the home of Mary Magdalene, who followed Jesus to Jerusalem; she was one of a group of women "who had been healed of evil spirits and infirmities...who provided for him out of their means" (Luke 8:2–3).

A Phoenician woman (on a sarcophagus from Sidon)

AND from there he arose and went away to the region of Tyre and Sidon.

(Mark 7:24)

THE VISIT TO TYRE, SIDON, AND CAESAREA PHILIPPI

THE ONLY time Jesus left the traditional boundaries of the Holy Land proper was during his journey to Tyre and Sidon. Mark (7:24) and Matthew (15:21) define this journey as one to the "region" or "district" of these two cities; we are not told whether he entered the cities themselves. Both had extensive territories; that of Sidon had a common border with the city of Damascus, far inland. The region of Tyre reached Cadasa in the mountains overlooking the Huleh valley (Ulatha). During this journey Jesus healed the daughter of a "Greek" or "Syrophoenician" woman; that is to say, a Phoenician woman who had adopted the Hellenistic culture then common in the Roman East. According to Mark (7:31) Jesus passed through the region of the Decapolis on his return to the Sea of Galilee—possibly detouring inland through Gaulanitis to the territories of Abila, Dium, Hippus, and Gadara.

Another, shorter, journey took Jesus and his disciples to the district of Caesarea Philippi, Hellenistic Panias, rebuilt by Herod and his son Philip. The outstanding feature of the region were the high cliffs near the city with a cave dedicated to the god Pan and many rock-cut niches holding dedicatory statues of the Nymphs. The sight of this great rock-cliff may have inspired the naming of Peter, "The Rock," on which the church was to be built.

Mt. 15: 21–29, 16: 13–20; Mk. 7: 24–31, 8: 27–30

THE TRANSFIGURATION

AFTER the return to the Sea of Galilee, the Gospels relate the visit of Jesus, together with the Apostles Peter, James, and John, to "a high mountain"—where the Transfiguration is said to have taken place. This mountain is not named in the sources, but tradition connects the event with Mount Tabor, a prominent landmark that had served in biblical times as a boundary point between the territories of three tribes; later it was a Hellenistic and Jewish fortress. Owing to its shape and isolated position, it is visible from practically the whole of Lower Galilee and the valley of Esdraelon.

After the Transfiguration Matthew tells of a significant incident at Capernaum: Jesus had Peter pay the half-shekel tax to the Temple for both of them, so as "not to give offense" (Matthew 17:24–27).

Mt. 17: 1–8; Mk. 9: 2–8; Lk. 9: 28–36

AND after six days Jesus took with him Peter and James and John, and led them up a high mountain. . .

(Mark 9:2)

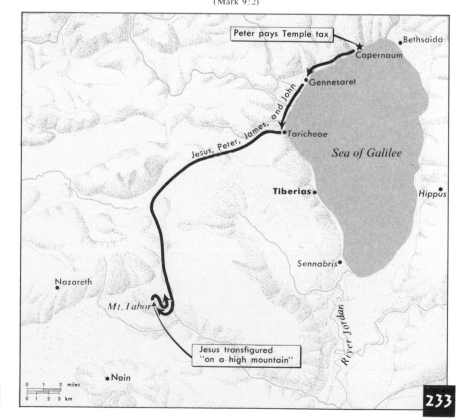

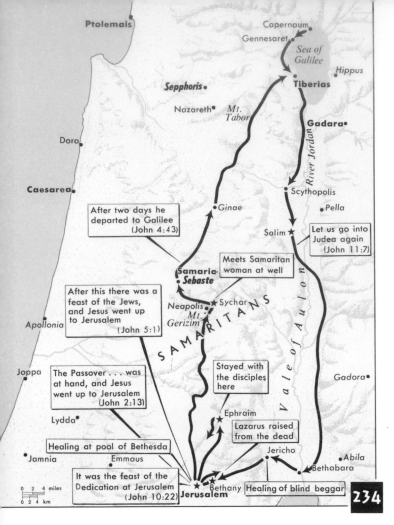

THE PASSOVER of the Jews was at hand, and Jesus went up to Jerusalem.

(John 2:13)

JESUS' VISITS TO JERUSALEM

THE GOSPEL according to John records several more journeys of Jesus to Jerusalem, about which the other Gospels are silent. Thus, in John (2:13–3:21) there is the story of a visit to Jerusalem at Passover, during which Jesus cleansed the Temple of money-changers and sellers of animals, an event placed by the other Gospels in his last days in Jerusalem (Mark 11:15–17; Matthew 21:12–13; Luke 19:45–46). During this stay Jesus was baptizing in Judea while John was doing the same in the well-watered plain of Aenon, near Salim (John 3:22–24). It was on his return from this ministry in Judea that Jesus passed through Samaria and met the Samaritan woman at the well of Sychar, staying two days with the Samaritans, many of whom believed in him.

One more journey to Jerusalem, during which a paralytic was healed at the pool of Bethesda in the Holy City, is recorded in John 5.

John (chapter 7) gives a slightly different version of Jesus' last journey than that found in the three other gospels. According to John, he went secretly to Jerusalem at the Feast of Tabernacles (in the autumn); and was still there at the Feast of Dedication (in early winter, John 10:22), after which he returned beyond the Jordan, probably to Bethabara (John 10:40). He then came back to Bethany, raised Lazarus from the dead (John 11:1–46), and retired once again into the wilderness of Ephraim, northeast of Jerusalem (John 10:54).

JN. 2: 13—2: 22, 3: 22, 4: 1–42,
5: 1–18, 7: 1–10, 10: 40, 11: 1–44, 54

WHEN the days drew near for him to be received up, he set his face to go to Jerusalem.

(Luke 9:51)

JESUS' LAST JOURNEY TO JERUSALEM

"WHEN THE days drew near for him to be received up" (Luke 9:51), at the end of his stay in Galilee, Jesus began to foretell of his fate in Jerusalem to his disciples, "and they were greatly distressed" (Matthew 17:23).

We may possibly insert into the story of Jesus' last journey to Jerusalem the incident mentioned in Luke 9:52–56. Perhaps Jesus intended to take the shorter route to Jerusalem by way of Samaria but, as the people would not receive him, he turned eastward and went through Perea, the "Judea beyond the Jordan." From there, he and his disciples crossed the Jordan and continued by way of Jericho, where he stayed at the house of Zacchaeus, a chief tax-collector (probably of the imperial estates in the Jordan valley, inherited by the emperor from the Herodian dynasty). Two blind beggars were healed outside the town. Then Jesus continued along the pilgrim road, which went up to the Mount of Olives and so to Bethphage on the mount and to Bethany, where he stayed at the house of Martha and Mary, the sisters of Lazarus.

MT. 16: 21, 17: 22–27, 19: 1–2, 20: 17, 29–34;
MK. 8:31, 10:1, 32, 46 52, 11: 1–2;
LK. 9: 51–56, 10: 38–42, 13: 22,
18: 31–42, 19: 1–10, 28–35; JN. 12: 1–8

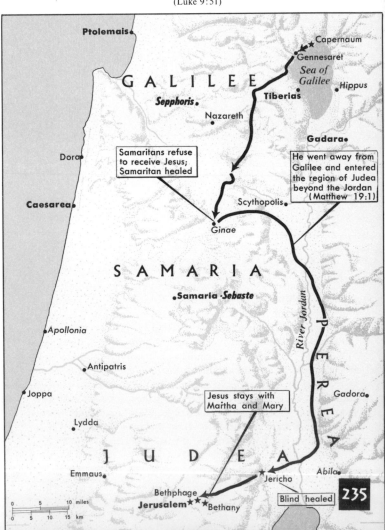

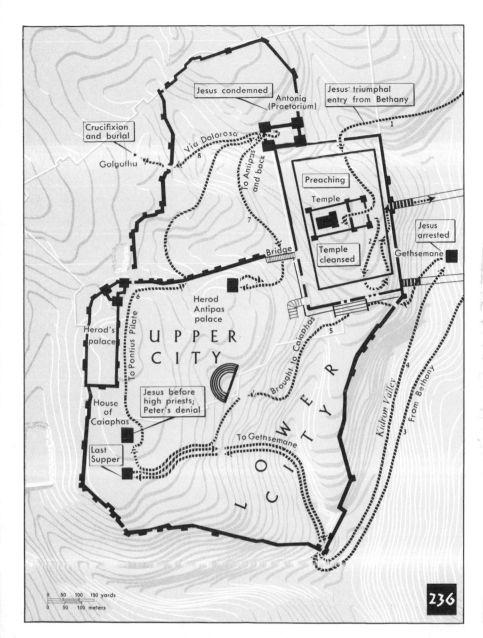

JESUS' TRIAL, JUDGMENT AND CRUCIFIXION

Inscription of Pontius Pilate, found at Caesarea

Mt. 21–27; Mk.11–15;
Lk. 19: 28–23; Jn. 12—19

JESUS BEGAN his stay in Jerusalem with what is invariably referred to as the triumphal entry, riding on the colt of a she-ass found at a village opposite Bethphage. He was received by the people with cries of "Hosanna" ("Save now!"); they spread their garments on the road and waved palm branches in blessing. After teaching in the Temple he returned to Bethany. The synoptic Gospels place the cleansing of the Temple courts during this second visit (see also map 234). Next day he and his disciples held the Last Supper at a house, the large upper room of which was "furnished and ready" (Mark 14:15 and Luke 22:12); we may assume that it took place in the rich Upper City of Jerusalem, at the home of one of Jesus' followers. This supper has been held to correspond with the Pascal meal and certainly is colored by Passover motifs. After the Supper, Jesus and the disciples descended to the Kidron valley, to Gethsemane (the "Oil Press") at the foot of the Mount of Olives. There he was arrested by a crowd armed with swords and clubs, led by Judas Iscariot, one of the Twelve, who had betrayed his master. According to the Gospels Jesus was led to the house of the high priest Caiaphas, there to be interrogated first by the former high priest Annas and then by an informal tribunal presided over by the high priest himself. It was during these events that Peter, who was waiting outside in the court-yard of the palace, thrice denied Jesus.

Jesus was interrogated as to his beliefs; but though his inquisitors regarded his utterances as blasphemous, in the judgment of most scholars they were not empowered to inflict the death penalty. They decided therefore to accuse Jesus before the governor, Pontius Pilate, of a political offense—rebellion against the emperor, implied in Jesus' claim to be "King of the Jews." According to Luke (23 : 6–12) Pilate sent Jesus to Herod Antipas (as "he belonged to Herod's jurisdiction") who sent him back to Pilate. Antipas most probably resided in the old Hasmonean palace, which was the residence of the Herodians on their visits to Jerusalem. Pilate, as governor, would have resided either at the palace of Herod on the western side of the city, or at the fortress of Antonia north of the Temple. As his main reason for staying in Jerusalem was to supervise the Temple during the mass pilgrimage at Passover, we can accept the tradition that the judgment on Jesus was passed at the praetorium set up in Antonia. From there, Jesus was led by Roman soldiers to Golgotha, traditionally a place outside the Second Wall of Jerusalem; here he was executed according to Roman practice, by being affixed to a cross. According to the same tradition he was buried nearby, in a tomb belonging to Joseph of Arimathaea.

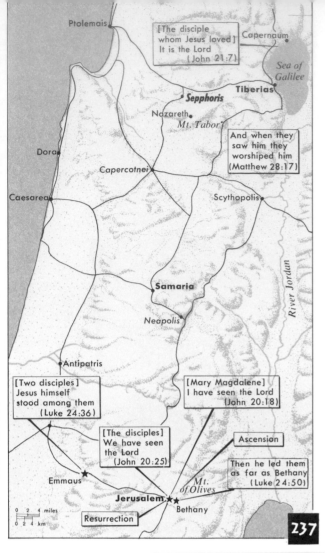

[The disciple whom Jesus loved]
It is the Lord
(John 21:7)

And when they saw him they worshiped him
(Matthew 28:17)

[Two disciples] Jesus himself stood among them
(Luke 24:36)

[Mary Magdalene] I have seen the Lord
(John 20:18)

[The disciples] We have seen the Lord
(John 20:25)

Ascension

Then he led them as far as Bethany
(Luke 24:50)

Resurrection

237

MT. 28; MK. 16; LK. 24; JN. 20–21; ACTS 1: 1–8; 1 COR. 15: 7

ACTS 2: 8–11; 1 MACC. 15: 23; ANT. 14: 213–264;
PAPYRI; INSCRIPTIONS

AND they found the stone rolled away from the tomb, but when they went in they did not find the body.
(Luke 24:2–3)

The rolling stone in Herod's family tomb, Jerusalem

THE RESURRECTION AND ASCENSION

THE GOSPELS are unanimous in continuing the story of Jesus after the Crucifixion. According to Christian belief, Jesus rose from the dead on the third day after crucifixion. The Gospels record appearances of the risen Christ in Galilee (Matthew and Mark) and in Judea, at Emmaus, Bethany, Jerusalem (John, Luke and Matthew by inference). Finally, we are told (Acts 1:2–12), he ascended to heaven from the Mount of Olives.

THE JEWISH DIASPORA IN THE TIME OF JESUS

AT THE beginning of the Christian era, the Jewish communities were mainly concentrated in the Eastern, Greek-speaking half of the Roman Empire. Two outlying areas were central Italy, where Jews had been brought as slaves after Pompey's campaign and where conditions became favorable under Julius Caesar, and Babylonia, where the communities grew strong under Parthian rule. But the bulk of the Jewish diaspora was still confined to the Greek world. There the Jewish communities were centered around the synagogue, with full internal autonomy, their own archons and elders, communicating with each other and with Jerusalem. This state of affairs goes far to explain the context of Paul's missionary activity (see maps 242–247). The communities were on the whole prosperous, but dependent on Gentile authorities and anxious to preserve good relations with them.

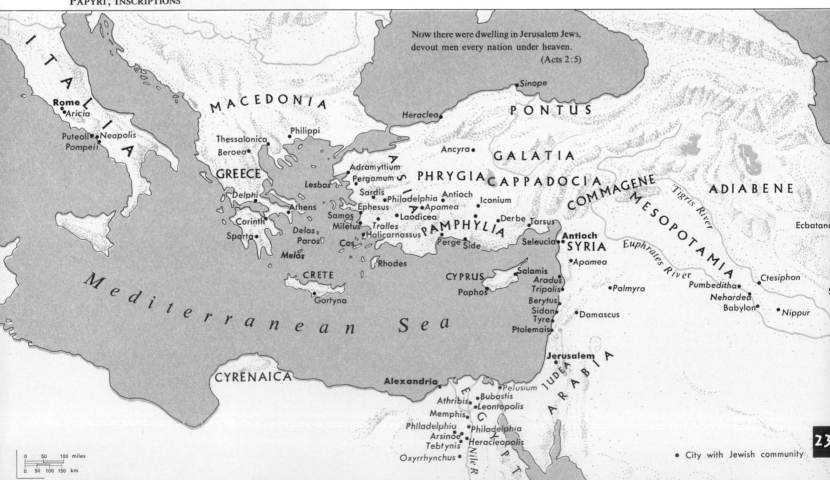

Now there were dwelling in Jerusalem Jews, devout men every nation under heaven.
(Acts 2:5)

• City with Jewish community

23

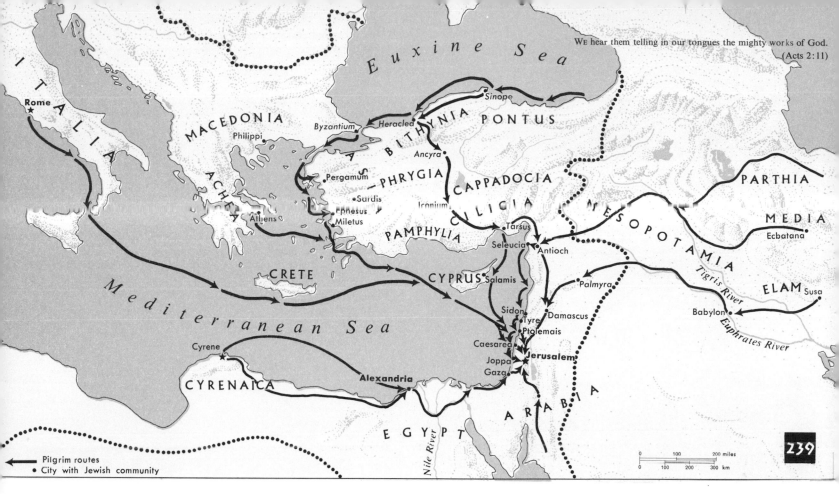

WE hear them telling in our tongues the mighty works of God.
(Acts 2:11)

239

THE PENTECOST

ACTS 2: 9–11

THE JEWISH diaspora was linked to Jerusalem by strong religious bonds; as long as the Temple stood, thousands of pilgrims came every year from outlying communities to fulfill the duty of "going up to the mountain of the Lord" on one of the three main festivals. At these times Jerusalem assumed a strangely cosmopolitan air, people from West and East jostling one another, speaking a rich variety of languages. According to the story as told in Acts, many of the pilgrims came to hear the Apostles and were astounded to be addressed in their own languages. On this occasion, the author of Acts gives (Acts 2:9–10) an extensive survey of the diaspora of his time which possibly looks back symbolically to the tower of Babel and the giving of the Law), beginning with the East, which was beyond the boundaries of the Roman Empire: Parthia, Media, Elam, and Mesopotamia. He then gives Judea and, going north, lists Cappadocia and Pontus; from the shores of the Black Sea he turns westward to the province of Asia, then inland to Phrygia and Pamphylia. From there his thought crosses the sea to Egypt and its neighbor, Cyrene. Rome, with its Jews and proselytes, represents the western diaspora; Crete and Arabia (the "Nabatene") rounds off his survey.

GOD has shown me that I should not call any man common or unclean.
(Acts 10:28)

PETER AND PHILIP TO SAMARIA AND THE COASTAL PLAIN

THE SUCCESS of the Apostles' preaching at Jerusalem provoked a reaction. Some of the Apostles were arrested and then freed on the sage advice of the Pharisee Gamaliel; but when the men of the synagogue of the freedmen (former slaves) accused Stephen, a deacon of the Christian community, he was tried for "blasphemy" and stoned to death or lynched. The Apostles now turned further afield: Philip preached in Samaria, and even converted a certain Simon Magus, who joined the Church from impure motives and was confounded by Peter and John, who also preached in the villages of Samaria. Peter then went to Lydda and healed Aeneas, and continued to Joppa where he healed Tabitha and stayed with Simon the tanner. It was at Joppa that he had a vision which led him to accept the invitation of Cornelius, the centurion (a Gentile), to come to Caesarea. Thus Peter, who in general represented a conservative attitude, accepted the extension of the teachings of the church beyond Jewry.

ACTS 8: 4–25, 9: 32—11: 2

240

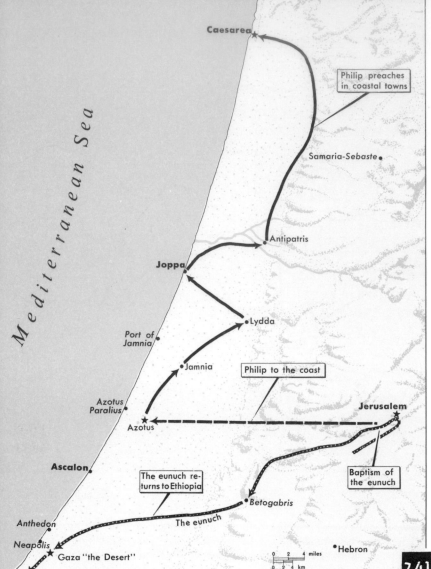

Philip preaches
in coastal towns

Philip to the coast

Baptism of
the eunuch

The eunuch re-
turns to Ethiopia

The eunuch

Mediterranean Sea

Caesarea

Samaria-Sebaste

Antipatris

Joppa

Lydda

Port of
Jamnia

Jamnia

Azotus
Paralius

Azotus

Jerusalem

Ascalon

Betogabris

Anthedon

Neapolis

Gaza "the Desert"

Hebron

0 2 4 miles
0 2 4 km

241

(Acts 8:40)

AND passing on he preached the gospel to all the towns till he came to Caesarea.

THE JOURNEY OF PHILIP
36 A.D.

THE APOSTLE Philip was called to go to Gaza, "the Desert." This was the city that had once been destroyed by Alexander Janneus, but after having lain desolate for many years, was rebuilt—in contrast to "Old Gaza" (Beth-eglaim) and "New Gaza" (Neapolis) on the coast. The Apostle set out in the direction of Betogabris (Beth-govrin) but, before having gone far, he met a eunuch, a proselyte in the service of the Ethiopian queen Candace. Philip converted him and baptized him in a spring by the roadside. The Ethiopian continued his way home (probably by way of Gaza) whereas Philip went on to preach the gospel along the coast from Azotus to Caesarea.

A Roman carriage for interurban travel of the type probably used by the Ethiopian eunuch

ACTS 8: 26–40

HE is a chosen instrument of mine to carry my name before the Gentiles.

(Acts 9:15)

PAUL'S JOURNEY TO DAMASCUS
36 TO 38 A.D.

ONE INVOLVED in the martyrdom of Stephen, the deacon (see map 240), was Saul, a Pharisee of Tarsus. He asked to be sent to Damascus to seek out Christians, and was dispatched by the high priest. On approaching Damascus, Saul had a vision of Jesus and was converted. Temporarily blinded, he arrived in the city and was received by a certain Judas. A disciple called Ananias was sent to meet Saul, who recovered his sight and was baptized. His zealous preaching in the synagogues of Damascus enraged some of the Jews; to save his life he was smuggled out of the city. He came to Jerusalem, where the local community accepted him only after some hesitation. When his life again became endangered at the hands of the Hellenists, Paul went down to Caesarea and departed thence to his native Tarsus.

ACTS 9: 1–30

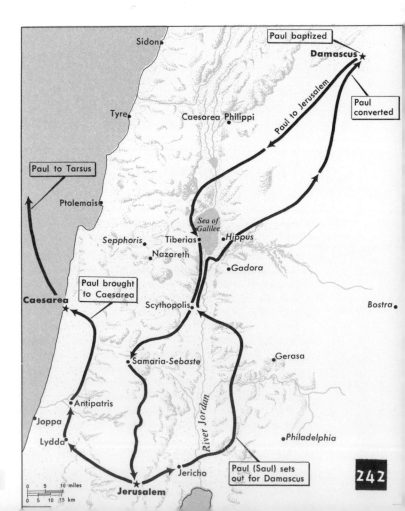

Paul baptized

Damascus

Sidon

Paul to Jerusalem

Paul
converted

Tyre

Caesarea Philippi

Paul to Tarsus

Ptolemais

Sea of
Galilee

Sepphoris

Tiberias

Hippus

Nazareth

Gadora

Bostra

Paul brought
to Caesarea

Caesarea

Scythopolis

Samaria-Sebaste

Gerasa

Antipatris

River Jordan

Joppa

Philadelphia

Lydda

Jericho

Paul (Saul) sets
out for Damascus

Jerusalem

0 5 10 miles
0 5 10 15 km

242

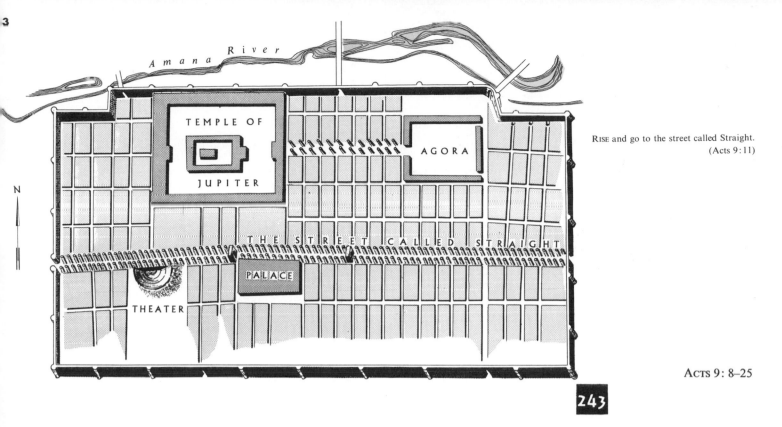

RISE and go to the street called Straight.
(Acts 9:11)

ACTS 9: 8–25

243

DAMASCUS IN THE TIME OF PAUL

THE ANCIENT city of Damascus, situated in an oasis irrigated by the rivers Amana and Parphar, was entirely replanned in Hellenistic times, when it was one of the main towns of the Seleucid empire. Today's city still bears traces of the Hippodamic town of classical times, sourrounded by a wall with gates. (It is recalled that Paul was lowered over the wall in a basket, as the gates were guarded.) Rectangular in shape, the city had two parallel main streets running the length. One of these is "the street called Straight" of Acts 9:11, running past the theater and the former royal palace, in Paul's day the residence of the city's Nabatean governor (2 Corinthians 11:32). The second parallel street connected the agora (market place) with the temple of Jupiter, once the sanctuary of Haddad and later the Church of St. John (now the Ummayyad mosque).

THE disciples were for the first time called Christians.
(Acts 11:26)

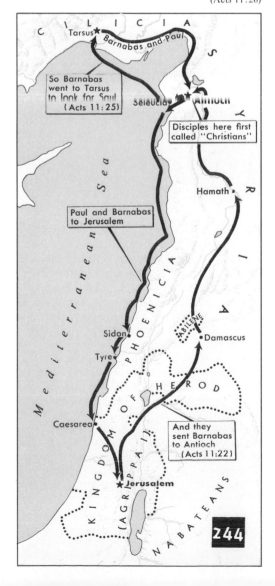

PAUL'S JOURNEY TO ANTIOCH AND HIS RETURN TO JERUSALEM
40 TO 46 A.D.

ANTIOCH, the capital of Syria and the third largest city of the Roman empire, had an old established Jewish community that we may conjecture became a base for Christian preaching. The first Apostle to be sent there was Barnabas. It was at Antioch that the disciples were first called "Christians," that is, followers of Christos, "the anointed one," or the Messiah. The community there was able to succor the Church of Jerusalem at a time of famine in the days of emperor Claudius (Acts 11:27-30). With the Christian community at Antioch safely established, Barnabas went to Tarsus, and returned with Paul of Antioch, where they labored for a year, setting the Church on a firm basis.

It is related in Acts that at that time "Herod the king" (Agrippa I) took strong measures against the Christian community. Sometime after Agrippa's death (A.D. 44) Barnabas and Paul returned to Jerusalem, bringing with them John, "whose other name was Mark" (Acts 12:12).

ACTS 11: 22–30

244

ACTS 13—14

By my mouth the Gentiles should hear the word of the gospel and believe.

(Acts 15:7)

THE FIRST MISSIONARY JOURNEY OF PAUL

46 TO 48 A.D.

FROM JERUSALEM Paul returned to Antioch. From there he, Barnabas and Mark, set out upon the missionary journeys which are divided into three stages in the Acts of the Apostles. From Seleucia, the harbor of Antioch, they sailed to Cyprus, preaching first at Salamis and then at Paphos, the capital. There they confounded a Jewish magician called Elymas, greatly impressing the proconsul Sergius Paulus. From Paphos they continued to Perge in Pamphylia (where Mark left them, much to Paul's displeasure—Acts 15:38). Barnabas and Paul continued on to Antioch in Pisidia, preaching on the Sabbath in the synagogue of that locality and causing great dissension in the community. Those of the Jews who clung to the religion of their forefathers appealed to the rulers of the city and forced the Apostles to leave; the same occurred at Iconium. Paul and Barnabas continued to Derbe and Lystra; in the latter town they healed a cripple and narrowly escaped being worshiped as gods. They returned to Pamphylia and took ship from Attalia to Antioch in Syria.

MEN of Athens, I perceive that in every way you are very religious.

(Acts 17:22)

THE SECOND MISSIONARY JOURNEY OF PAUL

49 TO 52 A.D.

ON HIS second journey Paul took Silas as his companion (they were joined by Timothy at Iconium), while Barnabas and Mark went to Cyprus. Paul returned by land to the cities previously visited in Pisidia and traversed Phrygia until he reached Alexandria Troas on the Aegean Sea. There he was called in a vision to go to Macedonia. Arriving at Philippi, he converted many Gentiles, including Lydia of Thyatira, "a seller of purple goods who was a worshiper of God" (a semiproselyte) (Acts 16:14). Paul and Silas were arrested there, but were released with apologies when the authorities realized that Paul was a Roman citizen. They continued to Thessalonica where Jason, Paul's host, was attacked, and then continued by ship to Athens. In this capital of the Hellenic spirit, Paul is reported to have made his famous speech to the philosophers at the hill of Areopagus, beginning with a reference to the altar of "an unknown god." From Athens Paul went to Corinth, the capital of the province of Achaia, where he was arrested and brought before the proconsul Gallio (who, however, refused to interfere in matters of religion). From Corinth Paul sailed to Ephesus and then to Caesarea in Palestine. After he had "greeted the church" at Jerusalem, he returned to Antioch.

ACTS 15: 39—18: 22

THE THIRD MISSIONARY JOURNEY OF PAUL

53 TO 57 A.D.

ACTS 18: 22—21: 16

AND argued daily in the hall of Tyrannus
(Acts 19:9)

DEPARTING from Antioch, Paul went by way of the provinces of Galatia and Phrygia (a region divided between the provinces of Galatia and Asia) to Ephesus, the metropolis of Asia, a land he had not previously been allowed to visit. He settled there for two years, teaching in the "hall of Tyrannus" and laying the foundations for the churches of Asia. From Ephesus he dispatched Timothy and Erastus to Macedonia. His success in the end enraged the worshipers of Artemis "of the Ephesians," who rioted in the city and theater, till calmed down by the magistrates. Paul then left for Macedonia and Greece. Finally, he departed from Philippi, passing Troas where he miraculously saved a young man called Eutychus), and sailed by way of Assos Mitylene, Chios, Samos, and Miletus to Cos Rhodes, and Patara. From there he took a ship to Phoenicia, passing south of Cyprus, and landed at Tyre. The Apostles returned to Jerusalem via Ptolemais and Caesarea.

Ancient merchant ship represented on a sarcophagus from Sidon

UPON HIS return to Jerusalem, Paul was recognized by a "Jew from Asia" and was accused of profaning the Temple. He escaped with difficulty and was taken into protective custody by the Romans. From the fortress of Antonia he was sent to Caesarea under military guard, to be judged by the procurator, Felix. After a spirited defense, the governor decided to keep Paul in open confinement; and thus the Apostle remained for two years. Brought again before the new governor, Festus, Paul appealed to the emperor as a Roman citizen, and the governor, bound by law, sent him to Rome. The first part of the voyage was via Sidon to Myra in Lycia. There, the party embarked on a wheat ship sailing from Alexandria to Rome. Though late in the season, the captain decided to brave the weather. After passing Crete, the ship was caught by a tempest near the Adriatic Sea and was shipwrecked at Malta. Paul and his companions spent the winter there, continuing the voyage in the spring. After touching at Syracuse and Rhegium, they landed at Puteoli and proceeded to Rome, where Paul continued his missionary activity.

You have appealed to Caesar; to Caesar you shall go.
(Acts 25:12)

PAUL'S VOYAGE TO ROME

59 TO 62 A.D.

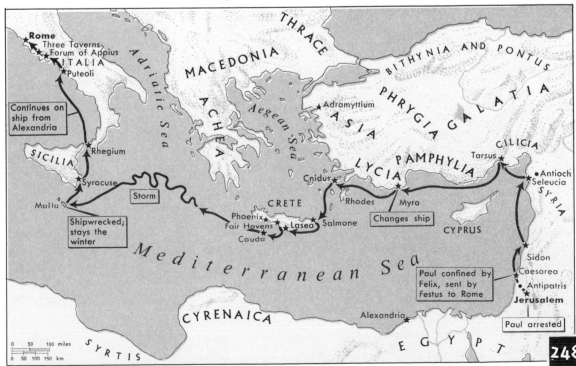

ACTS 27—28: 16

THE KINGDOM OF AGRIPPA I
37 TO 44 A.D

AGRIPPA was the grandson of king Herod and the son of Aristobulus, whose mother was Mariamme, the last of the Hasmoneans. After an adventurous youth, passed mostly at Rome, he became the favorite of Caius Caesar (Caligula), the successor of Tiberius as emperor. In 37 A.D. Caligula endowed him with Philip's tetrarchy, and in 39 A.D. when Antipas had fallen out of the emperor's favor, with that of his other uncle. Caligula was assassinated at Rome in 41 A.D. Agrippa, who was then on a visit to the imperial capital, rendered such services to the emperor Claudius, on his accession, that the grateful ruler gave him the lands of Archelaus. Thus Agrippa united under his hand almost the whole of his grandfather's kingdom. Once established in Jerusalem, Agrippa became the favorite of the people by his strict observance of Jewish Laws: his reign was regarded as the last peak in the Second Temple period, before disaster overcame the nation. As part of his orthodox policy, Agrippa was severe with the Christians in his domain (see map 244). Agrippa I died suddenly at Caesarea during a performance in the theater, and his death was regarded as a punishment from heaven for having allowed himself to be acclaimed as divine.

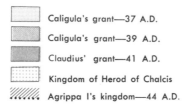

- Caligula's grant—37 A.D.
- Caligula's grant—39 A.D.
- Claudius' grant—41 A.D.
- Kingdom of Herod of Chalcis
- Agrippa I's kingdom—44 A.D.

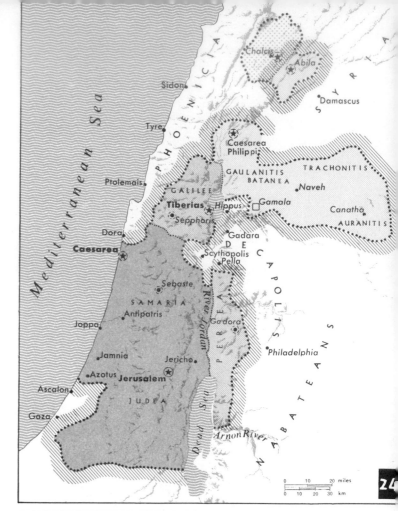

ANT. 18: 237, 252, 19: 274–275; WAR 2: 181, 183, 215

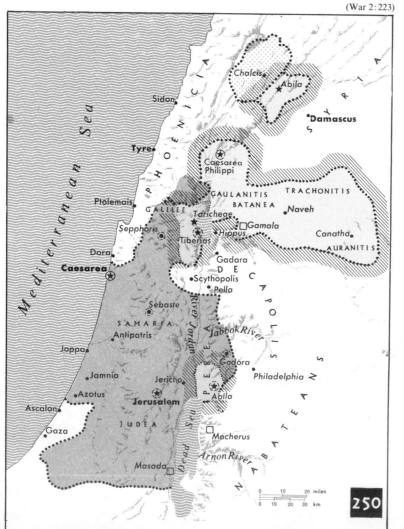

250

THE KINGDOM OF AGRIPPA II
44 TO 66 A.D.

ON HIS death Agrippa I left only an adolescent son; the emperor Claudius therefore decided to return Judea to the rule of Roman procurators. Four years later, however, he granted Agrippa II the land of Chalcis in Lebanon, and in 53 A.D. exchanged this area for Abila (near Damascus) and the tetrarchy of Philip (Gaulanitis, Batanea, Trachonitis, Auranitis, and Caesarea Philippi). Under Nero, Agrippa II also received Tiberias and Taricheae, as well as Abila in Perea, with its surrounding villages. The revolt against the Romans prevented Agrippa II from enlarging his kingdom, as did his father before him, but he remained in power until his death (about 95 A.D.).

Among the procurators ruling Judea after 44 A.D. were Tiberius Alexander (scion of a patrician Jewish family from Egypt, a nephew of Philo, who had forsaken his religion, and joined the Romans) and Felix, a slave freed by Claudius. Felix, and after him Albinus (62–64 A.D.) and Gessius Florus (64–66 A.D.), were corrupt and cruel, and by their acts helped spark the revolt.

- Area held by Agrippa II—48–53 A.D.
- Area transferred to Agrippa II—53 A.D.
- Area transferred to Agrippa II—61 A.D.
- Area of Roman procuratorial rule in Judea
- Agrippa II's kingdom—61 A.D.

ANT. 20: 104, 138, 159; WAR 2: 223, 247, 252

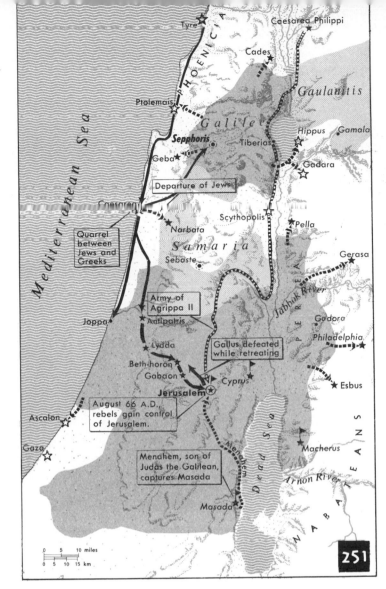

This action laid the foundation of the war with the
Romans; for the sacrifices
offered on behalf of that nation and the emperor were in
consequence rejected.

(War 2:409)

THE OUTBREAK OF THE FIRST REVOLT AGAINST ROME

FEARING the recurrence of Caligula's attempt to desecrate the Temple by putting up his statue there and inspired by messianic hopes, the majority of Pharisees joined the Zealots, who had been fighting Rome relentlessly since the days of Herod; thus the revolt of the people against Rome became general. After a clash at Caesarea between Jews and Greeks, the Jews were forced to leave Caesarea for Narbata. When news of this reached Jerusalem, riots broke out there too; the appearance of the hated procurator, Gessius Florus, together with his soldiers, only served to fan the flames. Agrippa II tried to calm the people but his efforts came to nought.

Menahem, son of Judas the Galilean, arrived in Jerusalem with his men, after he had secured Masada with its stores of arms. Eleazar, son of Ananias, the Temple captain, ordered the sacrifice for the emperor to cease, thereby giving the signal for open revolt. One by one, the strongholds of Jerusalem were captured and in the month of August the entire city was in the hands of the Jews. Though Menahem was put to death by his aristocratic rivals among the Jews, the revolt continued. The Jews captured the fortresses of Cyprus and Macherus, and the rebellion spread throughout the entire country. Jews attacked the Greek cities in the vicinity of Judea, these in turn revenging themselves on the Jews living in their midst. Most cruel were the inhabitants of Scythopolis, who repulsed the Zealot attack with the help of their Jewish fellow-citizens, whom they later treacherously slaughtered in cold blood. Only the people of Gerasa, among all the cities, protected the lives of its Jewish citizens.

Hearing of the outbreak at Jerusalem, the governor of Syria, Cestius Gallus, who was in general charge of the affairs of Judea, decided to intervene (for the local procurator had no legionary troops at his disposal). Taking with him the Twelfth Legion Fulminata ("the Thundering One"), he marched along the coast until he reached Antipatris. Several forays were made by the Romans to intimidate the rebels of Galilee and Joppa. Advancing by way of Lydda, Beth-horon, and Gabaon, Gallus arrived in Jerusalem. He even penetrated into the city, but faltered before the walls of the Temple and began to retreat. During the descent the Romans were attacked in the pass of Beth-horon and suffered disastrous losses. The Twelfth Legion lost its eagle, and all its siege equipment, which afterward did good service to Jerusalem. The Romans finally disengaged themselves, but their defeat turned the revolt into a full-scale rebellion. Freed from the imminent menace of Roman intervention, the rebels set up a government in Jerusalem, struck silver coins, and divided the country into seven military districts, each with its own commander. The most exposed post, the command of Galilee, was given to a young priest, Joseph, the son of Mattathias (the future historian, Josephus Flavius), who lacked all military experience.

WAR 2: 278–486

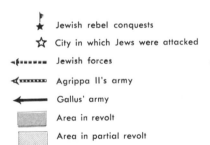

Jewish rebel conquests
City in which Jews were attacked
Jewish forces
Agrippa II's army
Gallus' army
Area in revolt
Area in partial revolt

Roman legionary eagle

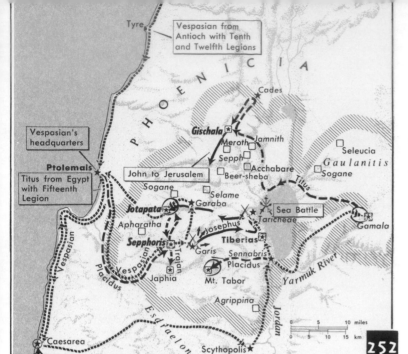

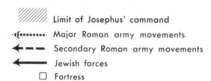

GALILEE was thus now wholly subdued, after affording the Romans a strenuous training for the impending Jerusalem campaign.

(War 4:120)

VESPASIAN'S CAMPAIGN IN GALILEE

ONCE in his new command, Josephus wasted most of his time in suppressing various opposing factions. He did indeed make some preparations for the coming Roman attack, trying to raise and drill troops in the Roman manner, and fortifying a chain of posts around Galilee. His efforts were negated, however, by the fact that the city of Sepphoris refused to abandon the Romans. In the meantime, the emperor Nero, apprised of the seriousness of the situation, sent his best general, Titus Flavius Vespasianus, with three legions to Judea. Vespasian set up his headquarters at Ptolemais, and from there easily penetrated Josephus' defenses and reached Sepphoris. The Galilean army dispersed almost without fighting and Josephus took refuge in the fortress of Jotapata. There he was besieged and forced to surrender after forty-seven days; he himself saved his life by a trick and was kept prisoner by the Romans. After a short rest, Vespasian again led his army into Galilee in order to complete the conquest. He came from the south by way of the Jordan valley. Tiberias surrendered, and the remaining rebels were routed by land and sea at Taricheae. Then Vespasian turned against Gamala and took this fortress after a difficult siege, thus cutting the insurgents' life-line to Babylonia. Some minor fortresses, Japhia and Mount Tabor, had also been captured. Before returning to Caesarea, Vespasian sent his son Titus against John of Gischala; the wily Zealot outwitted the Roman and arrived safely at Jerusalem. All Galilee, however, was now in the hands of the Romans.

WAR 3: 29–34, 59–69, 110–115, 127–134, 289, 409–413, 443–505, 522–542, 4: 1–120

▨▨▨ Limit of Josephus' command
◁••••••• Major Roman army movements.
◀◄‒ ‒ Secondary Roman army movements
◀‒‒‒ Jewish forces
☐ Fortress

WHY was the Second Temple destroyed?
Because of blind hatred.

(Yoma 9b)

VESPASIAN'S CAMPAIGN IN JUDEA

WHILE the fighting was going on in Galilee, Vespasian sent Cerealis to Samaria to disperse the Samaritans gathered in the region of Mount Gerizim. With the completion of the conquest of Galilee, troops were dispatched to Joppa by land and sea. The city was captured and the Jewish ships there, which had been used to interfere with Roman sea transport, were destroyed in a surprise attack. The Romans also captured Jamnia and Azotus and thereby insured their free movement along the coastal road. Meanwhile the Jews, occupied with their own internecine strife—between the aristocracy and the Zealots, the latter supported by the Idumeans—did nothing to interfere with the Roman advance. The raid of the extreme Zealots from their stronghold at Masada against the village of En-gedi (on Passover eve, of all nights) illustrates the extreme bitterness of the factional fighting among the Jews.

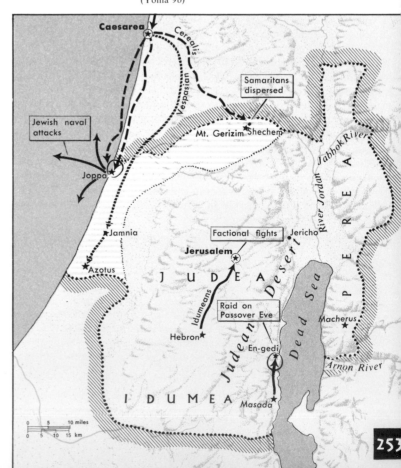

▨▨▨ Area lost by Jews by end of 67 A.D.
◁••••••• Main body of Roman army
◀◄‒ ‒ Secondary Roman forces
◀‒‒‒ Jewish forces

WAR 3: 307–315, 414–427, 4: 130, 233–305, 399–405

VESPASIAN, with a view of investing Jerusalem on all
sides, now established camps at Jericho and at Adida.
(War 4:486)

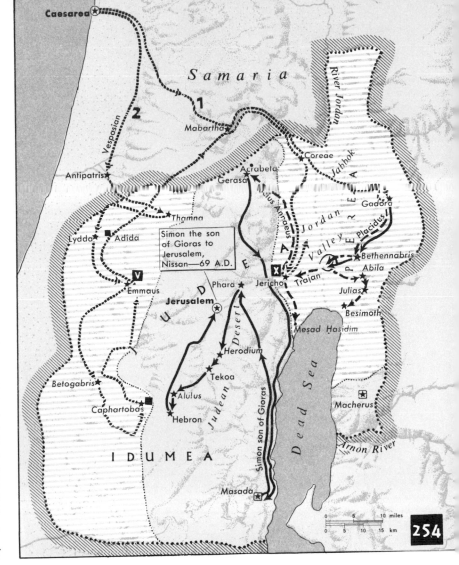

THE CAMPAIGN OF 68 A.D.

WITH the renewal of fighting in the spring of 68 A.D., Vespasian systematically dismembered Judea, subduing district after district. In the spring he embarked on the conquest of Jewish Perea. Gadora surrendered, and the main part of the Roman army returned to Caesarea. The Zealots among the people of Gadora retreated to the Jordan, pursued by troops of the Roman tribune Placidus. The Romans first captured Bethennabris and slaughtered the refugees on the bank of the Jordan. After this they conquered Abila, Julias, and Besimoth; of all Perea, only Macherus and its environs remained in Jewish hands.

Later in the year Vespasian set out on a second campaign. Marching from Caesarea to Antipatris, he subdued the districts of Thamna and Lydda, and proceeded to Emmaus, where he stationed the Fifth Legion. From Emmaus, Vespasian turned south and captured Betogabris and Caphartobas, where troops were left with orders to harass Eastern Idumea. Vespasian himself turned north and passing through Emmaus, left a detachment at Adida. The Romans marched through Samaria to Mabartha, a village between Mount Gerizim and Mount Ebal (which later became the city Neapolis). Vespasian then entered the Jordan valley by way of Coreae, captured Jericho and advanced to the shores of the Dead Sea. It appears that at this time occured the final destruction of Meṣad Ḥasidim (Khirbet Qumran), the center of the Dead Sea sect. Trajan (father of the emperor of the same name) joined the main body of the Roman army at Jericho and his legion, the Tenth, was stationed there.

Vespasian then sent a cavalry regiment under the command of Lucius Annaeus to destroy Gerasa, in the district of Acrabeta, the birthplace of Simon the son of Gioras. The mission seems to have been aimed at the growing influence of this Zealot leader. Simon had been forced to leave his district, because of the pressure of his Jewish opponents. He went to Masada and was there accepted after some hesitation. Simon, however, did not remain in the desert, but transferred his headquarters to Phara near Jerusalem, from whence he began to extend his influence to Idumea. He captured Herodium, fought his rivals near Tekoa and came to terms with them at Alulus. Having taken Hebron, he went on to Jerusalem where he became one of the Zealot commanders in chief contending all the time with the existing leadership and with John of Gischala his main rival.

WAR 4: 410–439, 443–450, 486–490, 503–544

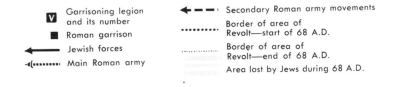

V Garrisoning legion and its number	← - - Secondary Roman army movements	
■ Roman garrison	····· Border of area of Revolt—start of 68 A.D.	
← Jewish forces	············· Border of area of Revolt—end of 68 A.D.	
◄······ Main Roman army	Area lost by Jews during 68 A.D.	

Dedicatory inscription on the Arch of Titus, Rome

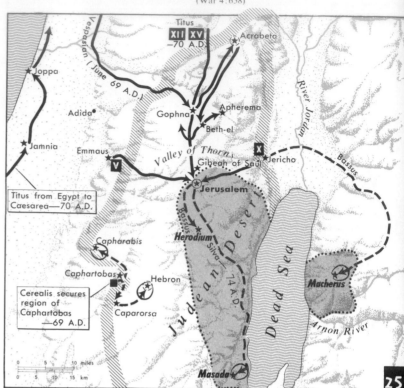

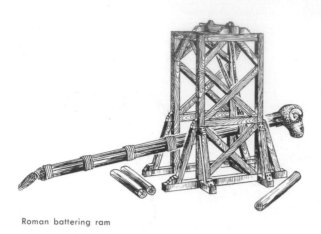

Roman battering ram

THE CAMPAIGNS OF 69 TO 74 A.D.

IN 68 A.D., a revolt broke out against Nero in Gaul and Spain, and the emperor committed suicide, seeing his cause was lost. During the ensuing uncertainty as to the imperial succession, Vespasian prudently suspended his operations in Judea. Three emperors—Galba. Otho, and Vitellius—succeeded one another within a year. Even before the suspension of fighting, Vespasian had succeeded in completely isolating Jerusalem, capital of the revolt. In the spring of 69 A.D., he took the districts of Acrabeta and Gophna, and his general, Cerealis, captured Capharabis and Hebron. In the summer of 69 A.D. the Jews held only the triangle of Jerusalem—Herodium—Masada, as well as Macherus on the opposite shore of the Dead Sea. In July, 69 A.D., the troops at Alexandria and Caesarea proclaimed Vespasian emperor; the Pannonian army joined him and defeated his rival, Vitellius. In the spring of 70 A.D., Vespasian ascended the throne in Rome. He sent Titus, his eldest son, from Alexandria to continue the campaign in Judea. Titus assembled two legions at Caesarea and approached Jerusalem from the north; before the gates of the city he was joined by the Tenth Legion, which had arrived from Jericho, and by the Fifth Legion from Emmaus. (For the siege itself, see map 256.) After the fall of Jerusalem, Lucilius Bassus, the Roman legate, captured Herodium and Macherus and his successor, Silva, accomplished the difficult feat of conquering Masada (see map 257) where the last of the rebels met their death in 74 A.D.

WAR 4: 550–555, 566–584, 658–663; 5: 39–53, 67–69, 7: 17–20, 23–40, 163–177, 190–215

V	Roman Legion	◄- - -	Secondary Roman force
■	Roman garrison	/////////	Area of Revolt at start of 69 A.D.
◄━━━	Major Roman force	....	Area of Revolt at end of 69 A.D.

Triumphal parade with Temple vessels—Arch of Titus, Rome

THE SIEGE OF JERUSALEM IN THE YEAR 70 A.D.

WITH the approach of the Romans, conflicts among the Zealots finally ceased; their commanders, Simon the son of Gioras and John of Gischala, divided between them responsibility for the defense of the city. Simon was to guard the section running from the northeastern corner of the wall to the Pool of Siloam, while John was assigned the eastern wall. At a later stage, Simon defended the Upper City and John the Temple itself. Their combined armies did not exceed 25,000 men; against them were drawn up four legions (the Fifth, Tenth, Twelfth and Fourteenth), and a great number of auxiliaries, about 80,000 men in all.

After preliminary skirmishes in the orchards just outside the Gate of Women (No. 1 in the map), the Romans set up their main camp in the west and a secondary one (that of the Tenth Legion) on the Mount of Olives (2). They breached the third wall about May 25th (3) and,

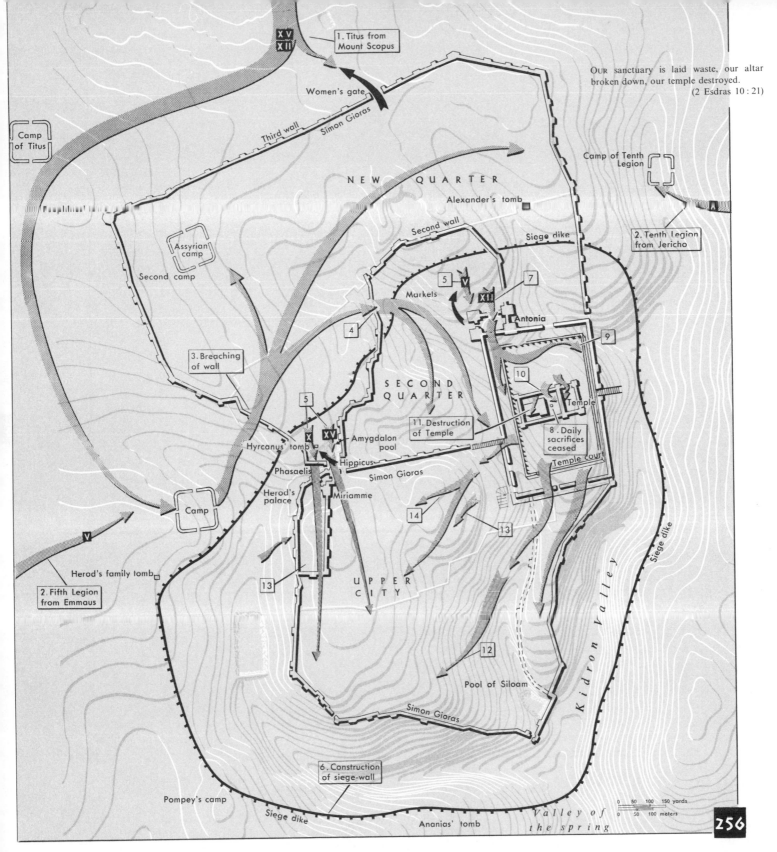

1. Titus from Mount Scopus

XV XII

Women's gate

Simon Gioras

Third wall

Camp of Titus

Our sanctuary is laid waste, our altar broken down, our temple destroyed.
(2 Esdras 10:21)

NEW QUARTER

Alexander's tomb

Camp of Tenth Legion

Second wall

Siege dike

2. Tenth Legion from Jericho

Assyrian camp

Second camp

5 V XII

Markets

7

Antonia

4

3. Breaching of wall

9

SECOND QUARTER

10

Temple

5

11. Destruction of Temple

8. Daily sacrifices ceased

Temple court

X XV

Hyrcanus' tomb

Amygdalon pool

Hippicus

Phasaelis

Simon Gioras

Herod's palace

Miriamme

14

13

V

Herod's family tomb

2. Fifth Legion from Emmaus

13

UPPER CITY

Camp

12

Pool of Siloam

Kidron Valley

Siege dike

Simon Gioras

6. Construction of siege-wall

Pompey's camp

Siege dike

Ananias' tomb

Valley of the spring

0 50 100 150 yards
0 50 100 meters

256

about May 30th, the second wall (4); the main camp was then transferred inside the city. About June 16th, the Romans launched an all-out attack on the towers north of Herod's palace and on the fortress of Antonia (5). Great damage was inflicted by the defenders on the siege machinery and dikes, and the assault was fended off.

Titus ordered a siege-wall to be thrown around the city (early in July) to starve out the defenders (6); the results were soon apparent, for much food had gone up in flames during the internecine strife among the Zealot factions. The Romans renewed their onslaught on July 20th–22nd (7). Simon the son of Gioras held fast, but the fortress of Antonia, under the command of John of Gischala, was taken and razed. On August 6th, the perpetual sacrifice ceased in the Temple (8),

and the porticoes were burned on August 15th–17th (9). After a ramp had been raised against the inner wall, the Temple itself was entered (10) and burned on the ninth of Ab (about August 28th) (11).

On August 30th, the Romans captured the Lower City (12). Even then, the defenders of the Upper City did not surrender. But after another month of effort the Romans succeeded in capturing the Upper City and Herod's palace (13–14), and only then did resistance cease. By decree of Titus, all the people of Jerusalem were taken captive and its buildings were leveled to the ground. The three towers around which the Tenth Legion had camped were alone left standing, and the ruins of Jerusalem and its region were placed under the surveillance of this legion.

WAR 5: 1–38, 52–66, 71–135, 248–361, 420–572, 6: 1–95, 112–287, 316–317, 353–434

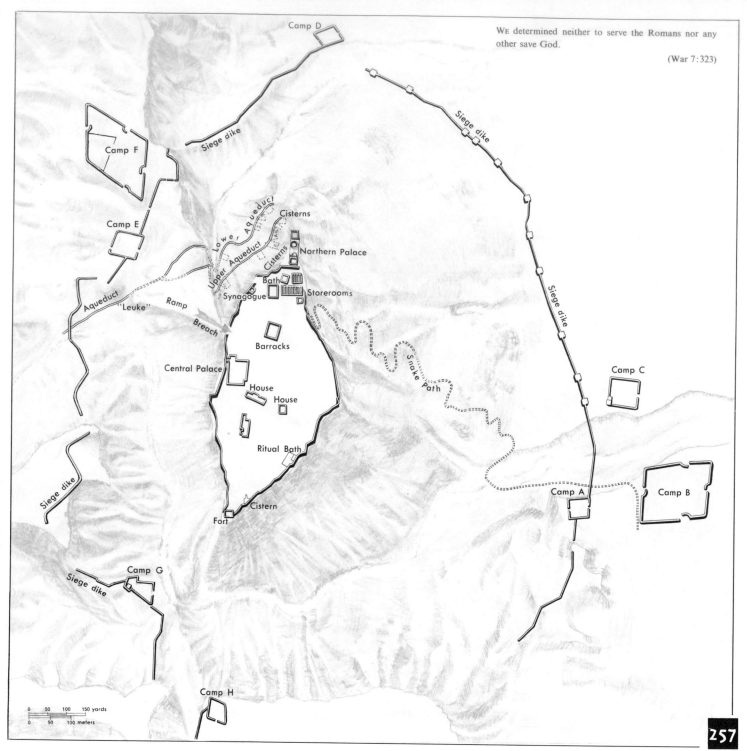

Camp D

WE determined neither to serve the Romans nor any
other save God.

(War 7:323)

Siege dike

Camp F

Siege dike

Camp E

Lower Aqueduct

Cisterns

Cisterns

Northern Palace

Upper Aqueduct

Aqueduct

"Leuke"

Ramp

Breach

Bath

Synagogue

Storerooms

Barracks

Siege dike

Central Palace

House

House

Snake Path

Camp C

Ritual Bath

Camp A

Camp B

Cistern

Siege dike

Fort

Camp G

Siege dike

0   50   100   150 yards
0   50   100 meters

Camp H

257

THE FALL OF MASADA
73 A.D.

WAR 7: 252–259, 275–406

MASADA was built atop a rock, its sheer cliffs rising out of the
deep ravines surrounding it. The Roman siege-force was divided between the lower camp (B) and the upper camp (F, which also
contained the headquarters). The problem facing the Romans was
how to get their siege-towers up to the walls of the fortress, at the top
of the cliffs. They first built a siege-wall around the whole of the rock,
except for the impassable areas. The wall, which was equipped with
catapults, completely isolated the defenders, yet there was little pros-
pect of vanquishing them quickly through thirst and hunger, for there
were abundant stores of food and water inside.

Silva chose a site to the west of Masada, where there is a low saddle
between the two surrounding ravines, and began a ramp from the
so-called White Rock (Leuke) up to the defenders' wall, a height of

300 cubits, (according to Josephus; in actuality, it is only 260 feet).
At 200 cubits the Romans raised a platform of wood and iron, 50
cubits tall; on this he placed a siege-tower reaching another 60 cubits,
its top thus standing about 20 feet above the walls of Masada. The
wall was breached with the aid of an iron battering-ram on the first
of May, 73 A.D. The defenders hastily put up a barricade of wood and
the Romans tried to burn this; at first they had the wind against them,
but later in the day it changed and the barricade caught fire and burned.

With victory assured, the Romans put off their final assault until the
next day, but the 960 defenders of Masada—men, women, and children—the last vestige of open defiance of Rome in the first Jewish
war, committed suicide during the night.

It is not you that support the root but the root that supports you.

(Romans 11:18)

CHRISTIANS AND JEWS IN PALESTINE AFTER THE FIRST REVOLT

73 TO 131 A.D.

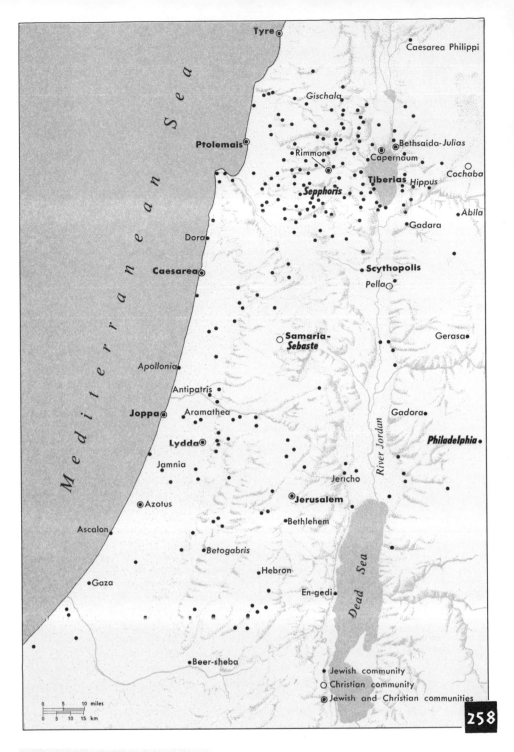

ACTS; JOSEPHUS; TALMUDIC SOURCES

The Tabernacle as represented in the synagogue at Capernaum

ALTHOUGH the war of 66–70 A.D. was fierce both in Galilee and in Judea—and especially in Jerusalem and a few other areas where the fighting was most severe—the Jewish population in general remained intact; many lands did, however, pass from Jewish to imperial possession. The evidence of the revolt of Bar-Kokhba (see maps 259–262) is itself enough to show that Judea was still settled with Jews at the beginning of the second century; the continuation of Judaism in Galilee in later centuries points in the same direction. After the destruction of the Temple and the uprooting of the leading classes, some Jews did remain in Jerusalem. The reconstituted Sanhedrin at Jamnia (Jabneh) extended its authority over the nation.

The disasters of the Jewish War seem to have caused an estrange-ment between the Jews and the Judeo-Christians. The Jerusalem community of Christians had left the Holy City on the eve of the siege, taking refuge at Pella beyond the Jordan. Some of its members later returned to continue in Jerusalem; others stayed behind. The communities founded by the Apostles in the coastal plain survived, as did a few Judeo-Christian groups at Capernaum, Rimmon in Galilee and Cochaba in the Gaulan, but there is little evidence of the thousands of converts mentioned in early sources. The breach with Judaism was not yet formal, though the traditional constancy of most of the Jews, along with other factors, turned the efforts of the Christian missionaries more and more toward the Gentiles in the Holy Land and abroad.

Tenth Legion and Roman citizens evacuate Jerusalem and leave for Caesarea

To Caesarea

Neapolis
Mt. Gerizim

Joppa
Bene-berak
Tur-shimon

Lydda
Caphar-harub
Modiin
Outbreak of Revolt
Sacrifices resumed
Emmaus
Jericho

Jamnia

Jerusalem

Beththter
Meṣad

Beth-lehem
Kiriath-arabiya
Herodium
Tekoa

Ir-nahash
Betogabris

Hebron
Adora
En-gedi

Judean Desert

Dead Sea

Rebel ships

Twenty-second "Deioterian" Legion from Egypt

Mehoz-zoar

259

0   5   10 miles
0   5   10   15 km

RABBI AKIBA, when he saw the son of Kosiba, was wont to say: This is the Anointed King.

(Palestinian Talmud, Taanit 84, 68d)

THE BEGINNINGS OF THE BAR KOKHBA REVOLT
131 TO 132 A.D.

Bar Kokhba Letter from the Judean Desert

→ Jewish forces
◁┄┄┄ Major Roman forces
⌇ Jewish fortification
✳ City held by Romans
▨ Extent of Revolt

Coin of Bar Kokhba

TALMUDIC SOURCES, SCROLL OF SCROLL OF FASTING; DIO CASSIUS; EUSEBIUS; COINS, JUDEAN DESERT DOCUMENTS

NEWS of Hadrian's plan to found a Roman colony in the city of Jerusalem, including the usual pagan temples—bringing to an end all hope of reconstructing the Temple—stirred anew the spirit of the struggle against Rome. The Jews had learned a lesson in the First Revolt, in which proper preparations and unity were lacking. This time they chose the most suitable moment, at a time that the emperor was far from Judea. They prepared fortified positions in the countryside, so as not to be trapped in fortresses. They made ready quantities of arms and mobilized the people as a whole. A unified command was set up and this remained in control from the beginning of the Revolt to the end. Rabbi Akiba, spiritual leader of the Revolt, traveled abroad prior to the outbreak in order to gather support in the Jewish Diaspora—going as far as Gaul and Africa in the west, as well as to Babylonia and Media, beyond the confines of the Roman Empire.

The Bar Kokhba Revolt lacks a chronicler such as Josephus was for the First Revolt, and we are forced to glean our information from various Talmudic and other sources, and from documents and other archaeological finds made in the caves in the Judean Desert. The documents reveal that Bar Kokhba (Bar Kosiba) was the same man as "Simeon Prince of Israel" mentioned on Jewish coins of the Revolt, and that his full title was "Simeon son of Kosiba Prince of Israel." It may be assumed that this Simeon, who was regarded as the "Messiah," was descended from the Davidic line.

The Revolt broke out in the fall of 131 A.D., evidently at Caphar-harub, near Modiin. The careful preparations bore fruit: the people of Judea rallied around Jerusalem, where the Tenth Legion was stationed. The extent of the Revolt included all of Judea down to the Coastal Plain. There is some evidence that part of the Samaritans joined the Bar Kokhba rebels, and there are also indications that Gentiles, mainly from among the oppressed classes of the local inhabitants, also found their way to the rebel camp and joined the "brotherhood" of warriors. The new leader, who was supported by the Sanhedrin, saw in his government the only legal rule in the Holy Land, and those who opposed his orders—such as the Christians of

Jewish extraction, who obviously could not regard Bar Kokhba as the "Messiah"—were persecuted by the rebel authorities.

The suddenness of the outbreak and the defensive preparations of the rebels were such that the Roman governor, Tinius Rufus, had no alternative but to order the evacuation of Jerusalem. The Tenth Legion and the non-Jewish inhabitants left for Caesarea, and the Jews once again controlled their ancient capital. An orderly administration was set up and a new reckoning of the calendar was instituted. The first year of the Revolt (131/32 A.D.) was declared "The Year One of the Redemption of Israel," and the following years "Year... of the Freedom of Israel." Documents found in the Judean Desert Caves reveal the efficiency of the new land registry and the leasing of former imperial lands. District commanders were appointed and the new government issued silver and bronze coinage, struck over imperial Roman and provincial city coins.

Upon the success of his uprising in Judea, Bar Kokhba attempted to extend the Revolt to the Galilee. There is evidence of battles in the region of Scythopolis and of damage to Sepphoris, and the uprooting of olive groves in the area. However, it is clear that most of the Jews of Galilee did not join the rebel effort. On the other hand, the Romans made every effort to suppress the Revolt, which they regarded as highly dangerous. The proconsul Julius Severus was called from Britain, and the emperor himself joined him in Palestine. Besides the two legions already stationed in Judea (the Sixth and the Tenth), forces were brought from Syria, Arabia, Mysia on the Danube, and Egypt, in addition to smaller cavalry and infantry units from Panonia, Rhetia and other lands. Pressure was put on Bar Kokhba and his followers from every quarter.

Julius Severus decided to advance slowly, to conquer position after position and village after village, in order to keep up and ensure continued pressure on the rebels. The reason behind this course is evident from the fate of the Twenty-second Legion, which had dared rashly to advance into the interior and was completely wiped out; from this time onward its name disappears from the Roman army list.

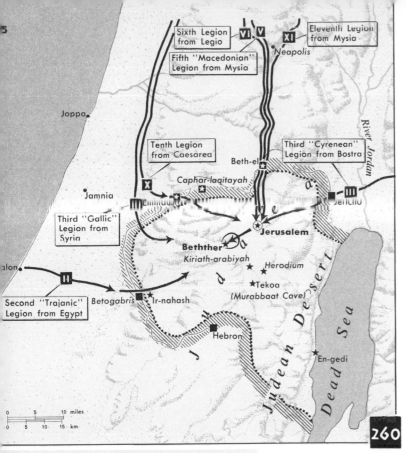

Sixth Legion from Legio

Fifth "Macedonian" Legion from Mysia

Eleventh Legion from Mysia

Neapolis

Joppa

Tenth Legion from Caesarea

Beth-el

Third "Cyrenean" Legion from Bostra

Caphar-laqitayah

Jamnia

Jericho

Third "Gallic" Legion from Syria

Jerusalem

Bethther

Kiriath-arabiyah

Herodium

Tekoa (Murabbaat Cave)

Second "Trajanic" Legion from Egypt

Betogabris ★ Ir-nahash

Hebron

En-gedi

Judean Desert

Dead Sea

River Jordan

0   5   10 miles
0   5   10   15 km

260

● CASSIUS; EUSEBIUS; JUDEAN DESERT DOCUMENTS

THE WRETCHED Hadrian stationed three guard forces: one at Emmaus; one at Caphar-laqitiyah; and one at Beth-el.
(Lamentations Rabbah 81)

THE THIRD AND FOURTH YEARS OF THE BAR KOKHBA REVOLT
133 TO 134 A.D.

IN the end Roman perseverence overcame Bar Kokhba and the rebels were forced to abandon Jerusalem in the third year of the Revolt. The Romans surrounded them on every side and set up forti fied positions at check points along the roads in order to prevent their flight from the enclosed area. The fighting was very heavy: the historian Dio Cassius tells us that during the Bar Kokhba Revolt the Romans captured fifty fortresses, destroyed 985 villages, and slaughtered more than a million persons. However, the Roman army also suffered great losses, so much so that at the end of the war Hadrian was obliged, in his address to the Senate, to refrain from using the normal formula "The Emperor and the Army are well."

In spite of heavy losses, Bar Kokhba and his followers kept up their high spirit. From documents dated to the "Year Three" of the Revolt, and even of the "Year Four," it is apparent that civilian and economic life went on as usual. In Bar Kokhba's letters to his commanders, we can still feel, along with the tension, the care of his staff concerning the fulfilling of religious commandments: along with orders for the confiscation of foodstuffs, for the transport of supplies from the port of En-gedi, and for the suppression of opposition elements, we read instructions for the gathering of lulabs and ethrogim for the Feast of Tabernacles.

THE SIEGE OF BETHTHER
135 A.D.

IN the fourth year of the Revolt (spring 135 A.D.), Bar Kokhba and his army were driven into the fortress of Bethther (southwest of Jerusalem), to which Severus and his legions promptly laid siege. (Hadrian had in the meanwhile left Judea, upon the restoration of Roman control in Jerusalem.) The fortress is situated on a hill overlooking a deep canyon and was protected by a fosse on the south. The position was quite strong, though it lacked a sure water supply. The Romans surrounded it with a siege-wall and, later in the siege, crossed the fosse by means of a siege dam. At the end of summer, 135 A.D., the Romans had breached the wall and slaughtered the surviving defenders, including Bar Kokhba himself.

THE BAR KOKHBA FIGHTERS IN THE JUDEAN DESERT CAVES
135 A.D.

ONCE SIXTY men descended the rampart of Beth-ther, and not one returned (again).
(Tosephta Yebamoth)

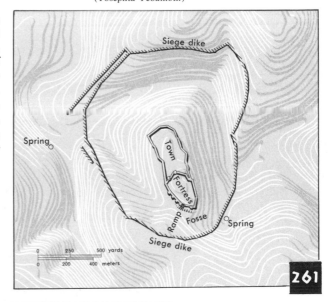

Siege dike

Spring

Town

Fortress

Ramp   Fosse

Spring

Siege dike

0   250   500 yards
0   200   400 meters

261

TALMUDIC SOURCES; EUSEBIUS

(Cave of the Pool)

★ En-gedi

Camp

Camp

(Cave of Letters)

Camp

(Cave of Horror)

Nahal Hever

Cave

Caves

Judean Desert

Dead Sea

Masada

0   1   2 miles
0   1   2   3 km

262

AND THEY were sitting in the cave, and they heard a noise above the cave.
(Babylonian Talmud, Shabbath 60a)

WHEN it became evident to Bar Kokhba's supporters in En-gedi that the Romans had finally gained the upper hand, they fled to caves located in the cliffs of the canyons descending to the Dead Sea. The fates of the several groups were not the same: in the "Cave of the Pool" east of En-gedi, advance preparations had been made to provide a water supply and the refugees there evidently survived. In Nahal Hever, two caves were used as refuge, on opposite sides of the canyon. As the Romans could not directly assault the caves, they built camps above them and waited for hunger and thirst to do their work. The fate of the refugees in the "Cave of Letters" (including Babatha of the family of Johanan son of Bayan, one of the rebel commanders at En-gedi, and possibly also the latter himself) is not clear. On the other hand it is established that the refugees in the "Cave of Horror" (forty men and one woman) declined to surrender and when it was evident that they had no further hope they burned all their belongings and perished within the cave.

JUDEAN DESERT DOCUMENTS

THE CHURCH IN THE FIRST CENTURY A.D.

Nero Caesar

THE GEOGRAPHICAL distribution of the Christian communities in the Roman Empire in this century reflects the missionary activities of Paul and his fellow-apostles, based on the network of synagogues in the Jewish diaspora. As born Jews, they were freely admitted to the synagogues, where their teachings often provoked dissension, splitting the local community; but almost always there remained, after the expulsion or departure of the Apostles themselves, a small group of Christians to perpetuate the existence of the church. These scattered communities were assiduously nursed by Paul and his representatives, as is evident from the Apostle's letters. Gradually the missionary teachings attracted a growing number of Gentiles, among whom the Judeo-Christians were gradually absorbed. Apart from Edessa beyond the Euphrates, the Church of the first century A.D. was restricted to the Roman empire. Most of the early Christians were possibly concentrated in Asia Minor, where the Jewish communities were long established and had created around them a circle of half proselytized "God fearing" Gentiles. It was in these latter circles that the Christian message based upon a reinterpretation of the venerated Old Testament took root. In the West, only Rome and its vicinity, and possibly also Spain, had Christian communities at that early stage. The first persecution (under Nero) was short and did not hinder the growth of the Church.

ACTS; EPISTLES; TACITUS: ANNALS 15: 44; SUETONIUS: NERO 16

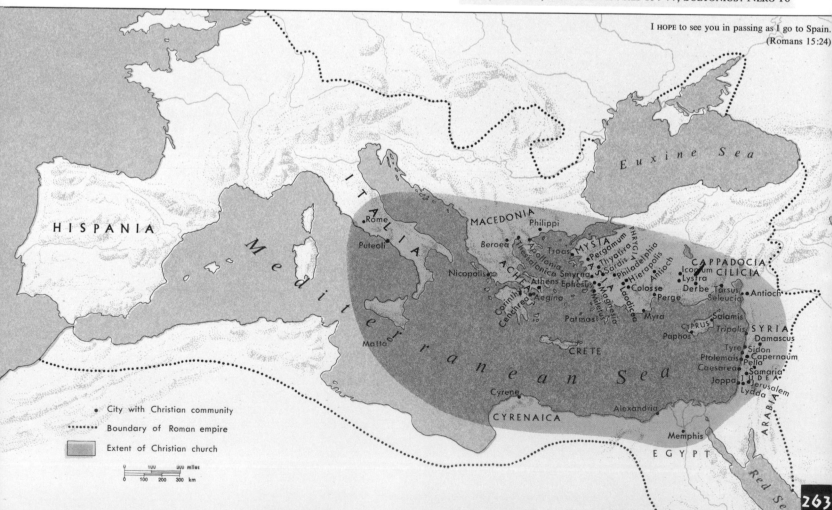

I HOPE to see you in passing as I go to Spain.
(Romans 15:24)

- • City with Christian community
- ••••• Boundary of Roman empire
- Extent of Christian church

263

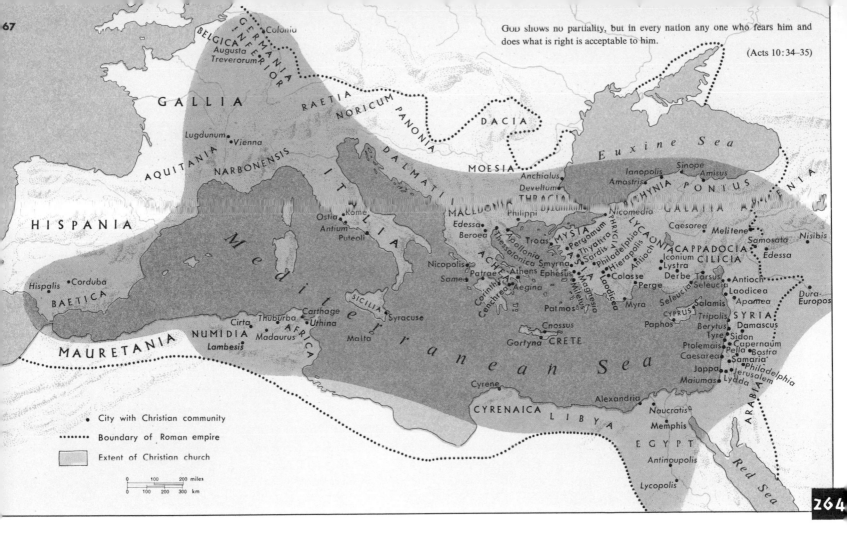

God shows no partiality, but in every nation any one who fears him and does what is right is acceptable to him.

(Acts 10:34–35)

City with Christian community
····· **Boundary of Roman empire**
▨ **Extent of Christian church**

```
0    100      200 miles
0  100  200  300 km
```

CHURCH FATHERS; EUSEBIUS
HISTORY; PLINY: LETTER TO TRAJAN; PAPYRI

THE CHURCH IN THE SECOND CENTURY A.D.

THE SECOND century, and in particular the period of the Bar Kokhba revolt (see maps 259–262), saw the decisive split of the Church with Judaism. The destruction of Jerusalem and the exile of the Jews from Judea after the war of Bar Kokhba (and the transfer of the Jerusalem bishopric to a Gentile) intensified the breach. Most of the Christians were by then of Gentile origin. The national Jewish catastrophe hindered Jewish missionary work among the Gentiles, the Church profiting greatly from this state of affairs. The Christian communities spread to the west and north, into Gaul and Germany in the second century A.D. Many groups were founded in Africa, laying the basis for the strong African church of the third century A.D. In Egypt, too, Christianity began to extend beyond Alexandria into the countryside. In Mesopotamia, more communities were founded; in Asia Minor the church reached the northern and eastern parts of the peninsula. Under the Antonine emperors, the Christians were left in peace and were no longer molested by the authorities, a state of affairs which greatly helped the growth of Christianity throughout the Empire.

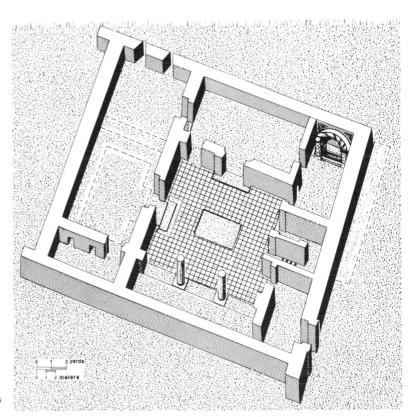

Plan of a church at Dura-Europos

KEY TO MAPS ACCORDING TO BOOKS OF THE BIBLE

CHRONOLOGICAL TABLE – GENERAL

East

B.C.	*	Mesopotamia	Anatolia-Aram-Tyre	Palestine	Egypt	West
2800	EARLY BRONZE AGE — II	FIRST DYNASTY OF UR / KINGDOM OF ACCAD / SUMERIAN PERIOD				EARLY KINGDOM
2700					1st–2nd Dynasties	
2600						
2500	III			Beth Yerah Culture	3rd–5th Dynasties (Pyramid Builders)	
2400						
2300		Sargon I / Naram-Sin			6th Dynasty — Pepi I	
2200	IV				Pepi II	MIDDLE MINOAN PERIOD
2150				Rise in Population		
2100					First Intermediate Period	
2000	MIDDLE BRONZE AGE — I	3rd Dynasty of Ur / Gudea of Lagash	EARLY HITTITE KINGDOM	Amorite Wave	12TH DYNASTY — Amenemhet I / Senusert I	MIDDLE KINGDOM
1950		Independent Assyria			Amenemhet II / Senusert II	
1900					Senusert III	
1800	IIa				Amenemhet III / Amenemhet IV	
1750		Mari Period			Second Intermediate Period (13th Dynasty)	
1700	IIb	Hammurabi				
1600		1st (Amorite) Dynasty in Babylon			Hyksos Rule 16th–17th Dynasty	
1550						
1500	LATE BRONZE AGE — I	Cassite Dynasty in Babylon	Aramean Invasion / KINGDOM OF MITANNI	Strengthening of Egyptian Control	18th Dynasty	NEW KINGDOM
1400	IIa	MINOR KINGDOMS	NEW HITTITE KINGDOM	El-Amarna Period / Strengthening of Egyptian Control		Downfall of Crete / Height of Mycenean Culture
1300					19th Dynasty	
1200	IIb			Israelite Wave of Conquest / Philistine Penetration	Syrian Interregnum	Achean Invasion of Greece / Trojan War
1100	IRON AGE — I				20th Dynasty	
1000			Aramean Kingdoms / Hiram of Tyre	Institution of Kingship in Israel	21st Dynasty	Dorian Invasion of Greece
900				Divided Monarchy		
800	II	Kingdom of Assyria			22nd Dynasty	Etruscan Invasion of Italy / Homer
700			Assyrian Rule	Destruction of Samaria and Exile of Israel	23rd–25th Dynasties	First Olympic Games
600		Kingdom of Babylonia	Babylonian Rule		Assyrian Conquest	Height of Etruscan Culture
587	PERSIAN PERIOD			Destruction of Jerusalem and Exile of Judea	26th Dynasty	
500		Persian Empire		Return to Zion	Persian Conquest	Roman Republic Established / Persian Wars
400			Persian Rule		28th–30th Dynasties	Herodotus / Decline of Athens
300	HELLENISTIC PERIOD	Conquest of Alexander the Great / Seleucid Rule		Conquest of Alexander the Great	PERSIAN RULE	
200			Seleucid Rule	Ptolemaic Rule	Ptolemaic Rule	Punic Wars / Hannibal
100		Parthian Empire		Seleucid Rule / Maccabeans		Roman Rule in Greece / Caesar
B.C. 0 / A.D.	ROMAN PERIOD		Roman Rule	King Herod / Birth of Christ	Roman Rule	Roman Empire
100		Parthian Wars		Destruction of Second Temple / Bar Kokhba revolt		

* Archaeological period in Palestine

PERIOD OF ISRAELITE SETTLEMENT

Left Table

Year	*	Meso-potamia	Anatolia and Syria	Palestine	Egypt
1640	MIDDLE BRONZE AGE	1ST AMORITE DYNASTY IN BABYLON	KINGDOM OF MITANNI / EARLY HITTITE KINGDOM	Hyksos Period	
1630					
1620					
1610					
1600					
1590		IIb			
1580					
1570					1570
1560					
1550		CASSITE DYNASTY IN BABYLON			Aahmes
1540	LATE BRONZE AGE			EGYPTIAN RULE	1545
1530					Amenhotep I
1520					1525
1510					Thutmes I
1500					1508
1490					Thutmes II
1480					1486
1470					Hatshepsut
1468					1468
1460				Strengthening of Egyptian Rule	
1450					Thutmes III
1440					
1436					1436
1430					
1420					Amenhotep II
1410					1410
1402					Thutmes IV / 1402
1400					
1390					Amenhotep III
1380					
1375			1375		
1364					1364
1360	IIa		Shupiliuma		
1350			NEW HITTITE KINGDOM	Weakening of Egyptian Rule (El-Amarna Period) 1346	Amenhotep IV (Ikhnaton)
1340					Tutankhamon
1335			1335		1333
1320			Mursil II	Strengthening of Egyptian Rule	Horemheb
1310					
1306			1306		1303
1300					19TH DYNASTY
1290			Muwatillis		Seti I / 1290
1286			1286 Battle of Kedesh		
1282			1282 Urhi-Teshub		
1280					
1275		IIb	1275		
1270					
1260			Hatusil III		Ramses II
1250			1250	Period of Israelite Conquest	
1240				PERIOD OF ISRAELITE SETTLEMENT	
1230			Tudhaliya IV		1223
1220			1220		Merneptah
1210					
1200				Deborah's War	

Right Table

Year	*	Mesopotamia	Aram-Tyre	Judea	Israel	Egypt
1190						Syrian Interregnum
1180	Ia	MINOR KINGDOMS	ARAMEAN CONTROL	PERIOD OF ISRAELITE SETTLEMENT / PERIOD OF THE JUDGES		
1175				Philistine Penetration		1175
1170						
1160						Ramses III
1150						
1144						1144
1140						
1130						Ramses IV to Ramses IX
1120						1120
1116		1116				
1110		Tiglath-pileser I	KINGDOM OF ASSYRIA			
1100						
1090						1090
1078	Ib	1078				21ST DYNASTY
1070						
1060						
1050				Battle of Aphek		
1040				Samuel		
1030			Hadadezer King of Zobah			
1025				1025		
1020				Saul		
1010						
1006				1006		
1000						
990				David		
980						
976			976			
974						974
968				968		Siamun
960	IIa		Hiram I King of Tyre			
957						957
950				Solomon		
945			943			945
940						
930				Division of Monarchy		Shishak I
928				928	928	
924						924
920				Rehoboam	Jeroboam Son of Nabat	
911				Abiah 911		
910						
908				908	907 Nadab / 906	Osorkon
900						
890			Ethbaal King of Tyre	Asa	Baasha	
884		884	880		883 Elah / 882	884
880			Ben-hadad I King of Aram-Damascus			
871		Ashur-nasirpal II			Omri 871	
867					867	
860		860	Ben-hadad II King of Aram-Damascus	Jehoshaphat	Ahab	
859		859				
851			Mattan King of Tyre	Jehoram	851 Ahaziah / 850	
850	ISRAELITE PERIOD					
843	IIb			Ahaziah 843 / 842 Athaliah	Joram 842	
842		Shalmaneser III	842			
836					836	
830			Hazael King of Aram-Damascus		Jehu	
824		824				
820		Shamshi-adad				
814					814	
811		811		Jehoash		
806			806			
800					Jehoahaz	
799				Amaziah 799	800	
790		Adadnirari				
786			Ben-hadad III		786 785 Joash	
783		783				
780		Shalmaneser IV				
773		773		Uzziah	Jeroboam II	
760		Asshur-dan III				
758					758	
755		755				
750		Asshurninari		Jotham		

Marginal labels (left table, *): MIDDLE BRONZE AGE; IIb; LATE BRONZE AGE; IIa; IIb

Marginal labels (right, Aram-Tyre column): Elijah; Elisha; Jonah; Amos; Hosea; KINGDOM OF ASSYRIA

71

Left Chart

(★) Years	Mesopotamia·Persia	Aram	Palestine — Judah / Israel	Egypt	West
740	—745— Tiglath-pileser III	—740— Rezin	Isaiah / Micah — Jotham — 742 / —749 Zachariah —748 Shallum — Menachem —737 Pekahiah —735 Pekah —731		—753 Rome Founded?
730		—732—	Ahaz —726 / —737 —735 —731 / Hosea		Height of Etruscan Power
720	—727— Shalmaneser —722— V		—722 Fall of Samaria	(23TH DYNASTY)	Phoenician and Greek Colonization in West
710	Sargon II		Hezekiah	—710—	
705	—705—			Shabaka	
690	Sennacherib				
681	—681—				—683 Kingship Abolished in Athens
670	Esarhaddon —669		Manasseh	—685— Tirhaqa Assyrian Conquest 671 —663	
650	Asshurbanipal			26TH DYNASTY	
640			Amon —642 —640 Zephaniah		
630	—633— Nabopileser —625—		—628 Josiah		—621 Draconic Law
610	—612 Fall of Nineveh —605—	—609 Egyptian Rule —604	Habakkuk / Jeremiah —609 Jehoahaz —608 / —609 Egyptian Rule —604	—609 Necho II	
600			Jehoiakim —597 Jehoiachin Zedekiah Destruction 587 of Temple		
590	Nebuchadnezzar	BABYLONIAN PROVINCE	Ezekiel / Obadiah BABYLONIAN PROVINCE	—593 Psammtik II —588	—594 Solon's Reforms
570	—562—		Deutero-Isaiah		
560	—550—			—560—	
550	Nabunaid —539 Fall of Babylon Cyrus	—539	Haggai / Zechariah —538 Return to Zion		
530	—530 Cambyses —522			Psammtik —526 —525 Persian Conquest —527	Pesistratos Rules in Athens
510	Darius I				Roman Republic
500			Malachi		—499
490	—486—	PERSIAN SATRAPIES	PERSIAN SATRAPIES		—490 Battle of Marathon
480	Xerxes I				—480 Battles of Thermopylae and Salamis —479
470	—464—				
460			—457 Ezra —445		—461 Age of Pericles
450	Artaxerxes I			PERSIAN RULE	
440			Nehemiah —425		—431 —429 Peloponnesian War
420	—423— Darius II				
410	—404—				
404				—404	—404
390	Artaxerxes II			28TH–30TH DYNASTIES / Egyptian Revolt against Persia	—390 Sack of Rome by Gauls
360	—358—				
350	Artaxerxes III		Revolt against Artaxerxes III ?	—341	Philip II —336
340	—335— Darius III		—332 Conquered by Alexander —331 Conquered by Alexander —323		Macedonian Rule in Greece
323	—323 Death of Alexander				
312	—312 Seleucus at Babylon Battle —301 of Ipsus		—315 Overrun by Antigonus —312 Overrun by Ptolemy I / Conquered by —301 Ptolemy I	Ptolemy I	—316 Antigonus Defeats Eumenes

Left margin period labels: ISRAELITE PERIOD, KINGDOM OF BABYLON, PERSIAN PERIOD, HELLENISTIC PERIOD
Egypt margin: ASSYRIAN PROVINCE, BABYLONIAN PROVINCE, WARS OF DIODACHI
West margin: Persian Wars, ANTIGONIDS

Right Chart

(★) Years	East	Palestine	Egypt	West
290	Seleucus I	Simon son of Onias High Priest	Ptolemy I	
280	—281—	Eleazar brother of Simon High Priest	—283—	
276	—276 First Syrian War —272			
270	Antiochus I		Ptolemy II	
260	—261 —259 Second Syrian War —255	—259/8 Zenon's visit		—264 First Punic War
250	Antiochus II		—246	—241
246	—246 —240 Third Syrian War			
240	Seleucus II	Onias II son of Simon High Priest	Ptolemy III	
226	—226 —223 Seleucus III		—221—	—218
218	Antiochus III	—218 Antiochus III in Palestine —217 Battle of Raphia	Ptolemy IV	Second Punic War
200		Simon the Just High Priest —198 Battle of Panias Conquest of Antiochus III	—203—	—201 —197 Battle of Cynoscephalae
189	—189 Battle of Magnesia —187		Ptolemy V	
180	Seleucus IV	Onias III High Priest	—181—	
175	—175 Antiochus IV (Epiphanes)	—174 Jason High Priest —171 Menelaus High Priest —167 Maccabean Revolt	Ptolemy VI	—169 Battle of Pydna Conquest of Macedonia
164	—164 Antiochus V —162	—164 Rededication of Temple —161 Death of Judas Maccabeus	—170 Antiochus' Campaign to Egypt	
160	Demetrius I		Ptolemy VII	
150	—150 Alexander Balas —145	—152		—146 Destruction of Carthage and Corinth Conquest of Greece
142	—142 Antiochus VI —139 Tryphon —138	—143 Jonathan High Priest	—145	
135	Antiochus VII —135	Simon High Priest		—133
129	—129		Ptolemy VIII	Revolt of Gracchi —121
120		John High Priest	—117—	
110			Ptolemy IX	
104	—104 —103	Judas High Priest	—107—	
94	—94	Civil War	Ptolemy X	—90 Revolt of Roman —88 Allies —87/6 Marius
88	—88 Mithradates' War —84 against Rome	—88 Janneus High Priest and King	—88 Ptolemy XI —80	—84 —79 Sulla Dictator
76		—76 Alexandra Hyrcanus II High Priest		
66	—66 Pompey's Campaign —64	—67 —64 War between Aristobulus II and Hyrcanus II / Siege of Pompey	Ptolemy XII	—58 Julius Caesar Conquers Gaul
57	—57 Gabinius Proconsul —55 in Syria —53 Defeat of Crassus at Carrhae	—57 Unsuccessful Revolts against —55 Gabinius	—51	First Triumvirate —49 Civil War Battle of Pharsalus —44 Caesar Murdered
47		Julius Caesar in Judea		Second Triumvirate
40	—40	Parthian Invasion Mattathias Antigonus Crowning of Herod at Rome —37	Cleopatra VII	—36
36	—36 Antony's Parthian —33 War		—30 Conquest of Egypt by Rome	—31 Battle of Actium
20		Reign of Herod		Augustus Caesar
B.C. / A.D.	—5 —4	Birth of Jesus Archelaus		
6	—6			—14
18/19		—18/19 Founding of Tiberias		
29	—29 —30 Jesus' Ministry			Tiberius
34	—34 Parthian Wars —36	—34 —37 Agrippa I Enthroned —39		—37 Caligula —41
41	—41 —44	—44 Agrippa I King of Judea		Claudius
54	—54 Corbulo's Campaign —63 against Parthia	—53 Ministry of Apostles		—54 Nero —61 Paul to Rome —64 Persecution of Christians
66		—66 First Jewish Revolt —70 Destruction of Jerusalem —73 Fall of Masada		—68 Revolt against Nero —69 Galba, Otho, Vitelius
79		Jewish Center at Jamnia		Vespasian —79 —81 Titus
90				Domitian
96				—96 Nerva —98
106	—106 Conquest of Nabateans			—101 Conquest of Dacia —106 Trajan
114	—114 Trajan's Wars in —117 Mesopotamia		—115/116 Jewish Revolt in Cyrenaica, Egypt and Cyprus	—117
130	—130 Hadrian in Palestine —131 Founding of Alia Capitolina —135 Bar Kokhba Revolt / Fall of Beththter / Hadrian's Persecution	Re-establishment of Sanhedrin		Hadrian —138 Antoninus Pius

Right margin labels: HELLENISTIC PERIOD, PTOLEMAIC RULE, SELEUCID RULE, MACCABEAN RULE, INTER DYNASTIC WARS, ROMAN RULE, ROMAN PERIOD, Philip Antipas First Procurators in Judea, Later Procurators, Agrippa II

INDEX

The index contains all geographical names appearing in the maps.
Only the important occurences of each name are given.
Biblical names which have not been identified as to location have not been given in
the maps or in the index, except where the sources indicate their general location.

IDENTIFICATIONS: T. Rekhesh   =   Hebrew name   BEFORE NAME: No sign =   Bible (including Apocrypha)
               T. el-Mukharkhash   =   Arabic name   * =   Ancient external source
                                                                            ° =   Modern source

ABBREVIATIONS: T. =   Tel (Hebrew), Tell (Arabic)—"mound"
                        Ḥ =   Ḥorvat (Hebrew)—"ruin"   AFTER NAME: No sign =   Identification definite
                       Kh. =   Khirbet (Arabic)—"ruin"   ? =   Identification not definite
                                                                             ?? =   Identification doubtful

PRONUNCIATION: Ḥ as in Scottish Lo*ch*; Ṣ as in hi*ts*   (—) =   Not identified

A

ABARIM MTS.:   8
* ABDERA: 172
ABDON: T. *'Avdon, Kh. 'Abdeh*   108
* ABEL:
— (in Galilee) *'Ain Ibl*   34
— (near Damascus) *Suq Wadi Barada*   34, ABILA 249, 250
— (in Gilead) T. *Abil*   158, ABILA 179, 180, 181, 213, 216, 229, 232, 258, ABILA SELEUCIA 181
— (near Dead Sea) *Kh. el-Kafrein,* ABILA   177, 199, 250, 254
ABEL-BETH-MAACAH: see Abel-beth-maacha
ABEL-BETH-MAACHA: T. Avel Bet Ma'akha, *Abil el-Qamḥ*   34, 111, 124, 147, ABEL-MAIM 147
ABEL-KERAMIM: *?Na'ur*   78
ABEL-MAIM: see Abel-beth-maacha
ABEL-MEHOLAH: *?Kh. T. el-Ḥilu*   76, 113, 128, 129, 143
ABEL-SHITTIM: *T. el-Ḥammam*   52
ABIEZER: 65, 137
* ABILA: see Abel
ABRONAH: *?Elat, Umm Rashrash*   48
° ABYDOS: 20, 182
ACCAD: (country)   4, 20, 25
* ACCAD: (city)   9, 15
ACCARON: see Ekron
ACCHABARE: *'Akhbere, 'Akbara*   252
ACCO:
— (city) T. *'Akko, T. el-Fukhkhar*   21, 23, 34, 38, 40, 41, 45, 68, 69, 153, 173, 175, 176, OCINA 211, PTOLEMAIS: *'Akko,*   177, 178, 179, 180, 184, 190, 201, 205, 216, 217, 218, 219, 238, 239, 247, 249, 250, 251, 252, 258, 263, 264, ANTIO-CHENES (in Ptolemais) 181
— (district)   173, PTOLEMAIS 232

ACHEA: 239, 246, 247, 263, 264
ACHMETHA: 9, 11, 157, 161, 167, 169, ECBATANA 174, 183, 238, 239
ACHOR, VALLEY OF: 73, 224
ACHSHAPH: *?T. Regev, Kh. el-Harbaj*   23, 34, 38, 40, 45, 59, 62, 63, TEL REGEV 17, 18
ACHZIB:
— (in Asher) T. Akhziv, *ez-Zib*   18, 19, 68, 69, 153, ECDIPPA 218
— (in Judah) ?Ḥ. Lavnin, *Kh. T. el-Beida*   130, 154
ACRA: (in Jerusalem)   188, 199, 204
ACRABETA: *'Aqrabba, 'Aqrabba*   189, 199, 210, 254, 255, EKREBEL 211
ADAM: *T. ed-Damiyeh*   54, 76, 120
ADAMAH: *?Qarne Ḥittim, Qarn Ḥattin*   72, 113, SHEMESH-EDOM 34, 35, 36
* ADAMIM: see Adami-nekeb
ADAMI-NEKEB: T. Adami. *Kh. et-Tell*   72, ADA-MIM 34, 35
ADASA: *Kh. 'Addasa*   194
ADDAN: (—)   163
° ADER: 17
* ADIABENE: 264
* ADIDA: T. Ḥadid, *el-Ḥaditha*   203, 205, 206, 207, 210, 213, 254
ADITHAIM: (—)   130
ADMAH: (—)   24
* ADORA: see Adoraim
ADORAIM: *Dura*   119, ADORA 177, 209, 213, 216, 259
ADRAMYTTIUM: 238, 249
ADULLAM: Ḥ. 'Adullam, *esh-Sheikh Madhkur*   57, 63, 92, 119, 130, 154, 165, ODOLLAM 191
ADUMMIM, ASCENT OF: *Tal'at ed-Damm*   73
* ADURU: *ed-Dura*   45
* AEGAE: 172
AEGEAN SEA: 172, 246, 247, 248

* AEGINA: 263, 264
AENON: 227
* AFRICA: 264
° AFULA: see Ophrah (in Jezreel)
* AGRIPPINA: see Jarmuth (in Issachar)
AHLAB: *Kh. el-Maḥalib*   68, MAHALAB 153
AI: *Kh. et-Tell*   17, 18, 21, 26, 54, 63
AIATH: *?Kh. Ḥaiyan*   154, 'AYYAH 165, 171
AIJALON: Ḥ. Ayyalon, *Yalo*   38, 39, 56, 64, 68, 107, 108, 113, 119, 120, 145, 200
AIJALON, VALLEY OF: 56, 145
AIN:
— (on border of Canaan) *?Kh. 'Ayyun*   50
— (in Simeon) (—)   108, 130
* AKHETATON: 37, EL-AMARNA 37
* ALALAKH: 25, 28, 30
ALEMA: *'Alma*   189
* ALEPPO: 9, 25, 28, 30, 43, 127, 138, 146, 159, BEROEA 178, 238, 246, 263, 264
ALEXENDRIA: (in Egypt)   174, 178, 182, 183, 184, 217, 238, 239, 248, 263, 264
* ALEXANDRIA: (on Iaxartes)   174
* ALEXANDRIUM: see Sartaba
* ALEXANDRU-NESUS: (—)   182
ALLAMMELECH: (—)   92
ALMON: *Kh. 'Almit*   108
ALMON-DIBLATHAIM: *?Kh. Deleilat esh-Sher-qiyeh* 52, BETH-DIBLATHAIM 131, 155
* ALULOS: see Halhul
AMAAD: (—)   72
AMALEK: 90
AMALEKITES: 24
AMAM: (—)   130
AMANA:
— (mountain) *Jebel Zebedani*   8
— (river) *Nahr Barada*   8
* AMANUS MTS.:   3, 20, 127, 172

B

D

E

N

O

T